Toxic Schools

FIELDWORK ENCOUNTERS AND DISCOVERIES
A Series Edited by Robert Emerson and Jack Katz

Toxic Schools

High-Poverty Education in New York
and Amsterdam

BOWEN PAULLE

The University of Chicago Press
Chicago and London

Bowen Paulle teaches at the University of Amsterdam. A native New Yorker, he lives in the Netherlands.

The University of Chicago Press, Chicago 60637
The University of Chicago Press, Ltd., London
© 2013 by The University of Chicago
All rights reserved. Published 2013.
Printed in the United States of America

22 21 20 19 18 17 16 15 14 13   1 2 3 4 5

ISBN-13: 978-0-226-06638-7 (cloth)
ISBN-13: 978-0-226-06641-7 (paper)
ISBN-13: 978-0-226-06655-4 (e-book)
DOI: 10.7208/chicago/9780226066554.001.0001

Paulle, Bowen, author.
    Toxic schools : high-poverty education in New York and Amsterdam / Bowen Paulle.
        pages ; cm. — (Fieldwork encounters and discoveries)
    ISBN 978-0-226-06638-7 (cloth : alk. paper) — ISBN 978-0-226-06641-7 (pbk. : alk. paper) — ISBN 978-0-226-06655-4 (e-book) 1. Urban schools—New York (State)—New York 2. Urban schools—Netherlands—Amsterdam. 3. Low-income high school students—New York (State)—New York. 4. Low-income high school students—Netherlands—Amsterdam. 5. Education, Urban—Social aspects. 6. School violence.   I. Title.
    LC5133.N4P386 2013
    370.9173'209747—dc23
                                                          2013007998

♾ This paper meets the requirements of ANSI/NISO Z39.48–1992 (Permanence of Paper).

CONTENTS

Whatcha gonna do when real niggaz roll up on ya?[1]

I come hard, yeah, that's what they say.[2]

In 1996, after two years of graduate study in sociology, I started teaching at a public high school in the South Bronx. Fancying myself more worthy of "street cred" than the average teacher, I imagined standing tall and delivering in uncharacteristically productive classrooms. After all, I thought, I had been the only "white"[3] boy on the basketball team in a Catholic high school that was also located in the South Bronx. Six foot three, two-forty, and still reasonably athletic at twenty-six years of age, I was sure to be one of the best basketball players in the school. Something of an aficionado of hip-hop culture, I was still tight with several of the "ballers" from the "projects" with whom I had grown up. And after having written a thesis on educational reforms, I was committed to make "progressive" pedagogic principles work in practice. Brimming with largely (if not fully) unconscious assumptions but with no firm theoretical commitments or hypotheses to test, the scholar in me sensed it would be a good idea to spend an academic year investigating the inner city from a unique vantage point before returning as a doctoral student to the New School for Social Research to take on big historical questions about "durable inequalities" (Tilly 1996).

The reality stick walloped me the moment I actually started trying to teach. Like the majority of my colleagues old and young, certified and uncertified, white and minority, I failed as a teacher in the school I will call Johnson High School for the purposes of this book. The entire ordeal was discouraging, disorienting, and extremely stressful. At the same time, being inside the interactional processes generating the statistics on "outcomes"—being part of how inequality actually worked in real time—was more vivid than anything I had learned as a graduate student. Something visceral was at work, something hard to put into words yet potent enough to draw me back and alter the course of my life.

Initially as a social studies teacher trying to cope rather than as an intellectual who cared a great deal about scholarly debates, I returned to the research literature about failing urban schools. I found some masterful studies that helped me rethink what I was observing and doing. I also found myself opening up further to the possibility that research based on sustained, full-bodied immersion inside "my" nonselective secondary school could lead to deeper, clearer, and more certain knowledge about sorts of educational worlds that are still poorly understood. I had come in touch with what students and teachers actually go through in one of the worst of New York's worst schools, and I had no choice but to critique the relevant research literature from the inside.

A temporarily professional challenge became a lasting sociological obsession; my besieged workplace became my field. I canceled my other plans and became a long-term teacher-ethnographer. All told, from 1996 to 1999, I spent three years working full time in Johnson High.

Ethnographic rigor required sustained immersion for a number of reasons. Establishing and maintaining unguarded ethnographic relationships with students and staff took time. Eventually, some insiders made it clear that they were eager to share their stories. Seeming to enjoy being the focus of my attention, several of them welcomed me into their families, homes, and peer-group mediated scenes inside as well as outside school. This was time consuming in part because it required that I be observed (dys)functioning as an everyday participant, not as an occasional observer. Meaningful relationships demanded, one might say, that my students and colleagues have time to ethnographize (and gossip about) me. Their repeated observations of me averting my gaze (if not shriveling up) in "wild" hallways, confidently pulling up for a three-pointer on the star of the basketball team, and depressed about "my" failure in classrooms gradually generated levels of access (i.e., trust, friendship, interest, feeling safe about showing weakness) in my second and third years that I did not enjoy in the first. More broadly, in and around my neighborhood school, I was observed going through countless experiences that allowed me to build myriad relationships with students, their family members, teachers, nonteaching staff, and various types of local figures (from police to shopkeepers to coaches) that helped me understand what it was like to spend a large percentage of one's waking hours, year after year, in a school for the truly disadvantaged.

Relatedly, it took time to soak up the relevant lessons allowing me to operate as a reasonably competent (quasi-) native.[4] In terms of achieving a deep understanding of how psychologically and physiologically depleting the weekly routines of inner city teachers are—whether integrated into recurrent academic year cycles including summer school or not[5]—there was no short cut. There is only one way to get a lived understanding of how poignant, exhausting, and emotionally taxing teaching in a nonselective high-poverty high school really is. You have to keep coming back for more in the corridors and classrooms that most teachers with options avoid like the plague for good reason. Not for a few months but year after year, on top of everything else, you have to take care of your "do nows" and other preparations (especially when inspectors threaten to pass by), keep up on grading and homework assignments, and subject yourself to faculty meetings in which no real issues are discussed even if on rare occasions they might be mentioned.

I felt burnt out when I stopped teaching in the Bronx. I also felt that, as an ethnographer, my learning curve had started to bottom out. It was time for something new. I had studied at the University of Amsterdam and worked for a few years in the Netherlands before becoming a public school teacher in New York. Working as a basketball coach in Amsterdam had brought me into close contact with several poor, racially stigmatized adolescents from, in many cases, Southeast Amsterdam. Off the court, I listened to their stories about life in "gangster"-ridden schools generally identified in the Netherlands as *zwart* (black).[6] Most obviously for these reasons, especially after getting started at Johnson High, I found myself contemplating a comparison of everyday coping processes in nonselective secondary schools in my native New York and my adopted Amsterdam. I knew of no ethnographic comparisons of daily struggles in deeply distressed urban schools on opposite sides of the Atlantic. Moreover, I had been possessed by the corporeal concreteness of everyday life in the kind of setting in which most researchers writing about failing schools never even consider doing authentic fieldwork. I certainly had never heard of a transatlantic comparison offering answers to the types of questions I felt compelled to ask. It seemed obvious that there was a void, and that I should try to fill it.

Just months after being chewed up and spit out in the Bronx, I returned to the lowlands of Western Europe and started doing another nearly three-year stint as a teacher in a devastated school. After a brief introductory period as a basketball coach, the school's principal (*directeur*) hired me as an English teacher and assured me that I had free rein to write about any and all of my experiences. The second time around, from 1999 to 2002, I worked part time because I was also pursuing a PhD in sociology at the University of Amsterdam. My second *adolescent society* (Coleman 1961), which I will refer to as the Delta School, was located in the section of Amsterdam officially known as Southeast (*Zuidoost*). In the informal language of locals, Southeast was the "Bijlmer" (pronounced Bel-mer), and Delta was a school tucked away in the "old" section of the Bijlmer untouched by efforts at urban renewal. The Bijlmer was what people throughout Amsterdam often called the poorest, most dangerous, and blackest side of town. People familiar with the secondary educational system in Amsterdam knew Delta to be the least selective and most troubled school in the Bijlmer and, unquestionably, one of the worst secondary schools in the city.[7]

Given the huge differences in the US and Dutch welfare safety nets and, most obviously, the diverging levels of (child) poverty in American and Western European neighborhoods such as the two surrounding my schools,[8] I want to clarify why (from the perspectives of those I studied) processes of everyday coping in Johnson High and the Delta School might be compared. Just as fellow teachers in New York had regularly characterized their place of work as a "dumping ground," my more critical colleagues in Southeast Amsterdam frequently spoke of theirs as a "garbage can" (*vuilnisbak*). In both cities the adolescents knew very well that they attended neighborhood schools occupying the lowliest positions in their respective spaces of secondary education.[9] While Wacquant (2007; 2004) convincingly details the analytic limitations of the term "ghetto," especially in the context of transatlantic comparisons, students and teachers in the Bronx and the Bijlmer habitually used this word to describe the neighborhoods surrounding their schools; "ghetto" evinced their sense of living, going to school, or working in profoundly stigmatized, poverty-stricken, and ethnically marked residential areas at once symbolically and geographically isolated from higher-status parts of their greater metropolitan areas.[10] The corresponding 1990s hip-hop term "ghetto fabulous," which was used more regularly in New York but also quite often in Amsterdam, shed light on how some of my students temporarily achieved positions that effectively turned institutionalized stigma into a potentially riveting sense of *collective charisma* (that, as we shall see, could only exist thanks to the largely taken for granted *group disgrace* of fellow students denounced as, for example, "nobodies").[11] I hope making repeated use of key classifications such as "ghetto fabulous" will help us keep in mind not only that the worldviews and coping practices of the students were influenced by what went on outside their schools, but also that they overlapped at least in part because of similar positionings within the two overall urban spaces.

What, most basically, is this book all about? Rather than sticking with the stale language of academe, to begin answering this question I propose that we dive straight into the real-life currents perpetually reshaping the vulnerable teens we call students and undermining the forsaken institutions we call schools. In the pragmatist spirit of William James and especially another one-time high school teacher, John Dewey, I want to begin with a detailed view of the concrete problems one student actually faced rather than with a scholarly "puzzle . . . occupy[ing] a realm of its own." Getting started in this way will, I hope, help us stay as connected as possible with the "things of ordinary experience" (Dewey [1925]1988, p. 17) throughout the ensuing journey.[12]

I start with a student I will call Roxanne.[13] The language used by this girl in particularly dire straits illustrates more compellingly than any argument I can muster our need to take seriously the cultural logics, active mental constructions, prediscursive inclinations, and embodied practices of those constituting our most distressed schools. Homing in on a single interview, I hope to bring to life the sources of Roxanne's pride and anxiety, the substance of her happiness and suffering, the incoherence of her habituated response patterns and stated beliefs, the far-reaching power of her neighborhood, and the enthralling micro-level social pressures that—within the relative autonomy of an intensely stressful educational environment—facilitated her complicity in self-destructive spirals. Most important of all, in the language of my students in both Amsterdam and New York, I hope seeing Johnson High and a neighborhood in the Bronx through Roxanne's eyes will help us establish the problems that are most *real* and keep away from *fake* ways of dealing with them.

Roxanne

Ghetto fabulous? That means you just one of these fly people that be comin' through. You from the ghetto and you fly.[14]

Two years into the dark heart of my tenure as a New York City public school teacher, I began systematically recording interviews with, most importantly, students and teachers. Not trusting either my memory or my ability to take sufficiently detailed field notes, I wanted to record exactly how differently pubescents and pedagogues spoke about their experiences at Johnson and their lives outside school. Taking notes on "face work" (Goffman 1967) and bodily presentation, I audio-recorded conversations with students and staff in any number of places (empty stairwells, pizza shops, local parks, homes, and classrooms). I also started working with a friend from graduate school with an exceptionally gentle smile and soothing manner who had become a documentary filmmaker.[15] What we recorded would be poorly conceptualized as outsider-white-academic-meets-minority-ghetto-kid interviews. Aside from the fact that the students and staff sometimes classified me as "not just plain old white," as one fellow teacher put it,[16] they had seen me operating as a teacher for months if not years. If they did not know me personally, they had in many cases heard about me from people they trusted.

For help in finding a range of students who might be interviewed, I asked an especially engaged English teacher for his recommendations. This fellow teacher turned "dean of discipline" and weekend drinking buddy had worked at Johnson for eight years. He seemed especially devoted to his job and his words carried weight. Among those he recommended were Roxanne and one of her friends. He informed me that both of these African American girls were immersed in some of the more dominant cliques within the school. "Roxanne is ghetto," he added. "She is just straight up and down, one hundred percent ghetto."[17]

Five of us—Roxanne and her friend, the other teacher and myself, and the filmmaker with her camera—met in an empty classroom.[18] At sixteen years of age and after having attended Johnson for nearly a year and a half, Roxanne was technically still a freshman—as were roughly half of the students who had entered the year she did. Two silver chains hung outside her sweater and strands of permed hair framed both sides of her dark ebony face. Speaking in her rhythmic, no-nonsense way, Roxanne said she was from "the projects." By this she meant a notorious set of public housing high-rises located a few blocks from Johnson High. (While Roxanne did not talk about family life during our first encounter, in a later conversation she reported that her mother had been out of work for as long as she could remember. Roxanne had not had any contact with her father since she was an infant. Her mother dropped out of another South Bronx high school when she became pregnant with Roxanne.)

Roxanne told us that every single one of her close female friends from middle school had stopped coming to school in order to look after their kids. Roxanne felt that these fifteen-to-seventeen-year-old girls look up to her because she did not have a child and because she came "to school . . . sometimes." When I asked about this "sometimes," Roxanne said she often hung out in the cafeteria instead of going to classes and that she had, at one point, "missed like three weeks straight." When I asked her about why she thought this happened Roxanne said, "It's just me. I'm lazy. I don't like nothing . . . but, I'm coming to school now. I just look at people and be like, I don't wanna be like them. So, now, I'm coming to school."

When I asked where she wanted to be in five years Roxanne took a few seconds to think, then responded: "College. In five years, I wanna be in college, taking something for pediatrician." Here I found myself thinking that her guarded expression revealed at least as much as her words, and that she herself felt that this scenario was highly unlikely. She seemed much more resolute, however, when she discussed plans not to "talk to" (i.e., date, in this context) any of the boys in her neighborhood who did "nothing but hang out, sell drugs, and smoke weed on the corner." Roxanne said twice that she had no idea why her girlfriends tried to hold onto such boys by having their babies. "It doesn't work like that," she said, before adding that these kinds of boys were, in her view, by no means worth holding on to anyway. Just seconds later, Roxanne explained that she would not "walk down the street with" (i.e., give the impression that she was dating) a boy who was "busted" (poorly dressed, not presentable). At this stage in the interview she seemed to take for granted that girls would naturally be attracted to boys because of "money and gear, the way they dress." She added that girls with "game"—or, for short, "g"—could get boys to buy them anything they wanted. "They [girls with g] just be getting them [boys with money and gear]," she said approvingly if not enviously.

Roxanne reported that the day before Thanksgiving, two weeks before our first meeting, she had walked around the corner and discovered a good friend of hers "just laying there, dead . . . shot in the head." Making reference to the two most prominent (and predominantly black) local gangs, she reported that, like many of the killings that took place "every other week" in her neighborhood, this one was related to "some Crip and Blood thing." She said she was growing up in a neighborhood in which guns were "everywhere you go." In a forty-minute stretch, she mentioned six extremely violent encounters in which four people in her direct environment had recently been shot to death. One incident involved a "good" man in his twenties who had just become a father. He broke up a fight, went upstairs to change his clothes, came back down to the street, and was shot to death. "Some guys who still had a teenagers mentality just killed him," she said. In her direct and distinctively cadenced way, Roxanne threw in the after thought that people in her neighborhood were "just killin' each other off."

While visibly distraught by the steady flow of bloodshed she described, Roxanne assured us that the violence in her neighborhood did not affect her. She said she had grown "up over there, and seen things and heard things, so . . . it don't matter." She confessed however that sometimes, when she "think[s] about it," the relentless butchery did get to her. Roxanne's response to my question about what she would most like to see changed in her neighborhood was immediate: "The killing, that's what I would change about my neighborhood, the killing . . . and the gangs."

Roxanne saw school-related violence as far more of a problem for boys than for girls. "The only girls that fight, is jealous girls." These are the "girls who don't have anything." On this theme, when I asked about concrete sequences of events, she added the following: "All right . . . so a girl could look at another girl. Like, say I'm in the hallway, and another girls sees me. If she thinks I'm trying to talk to her man or whatever, she might wanna fight me." With regard to male on male violence among students at Johnson, Roxanne's comments were delivered in a noticeably more rapid-fire, free-flowing way. But what my students in the Netherlands would later call "dirty looks" (*vies kijken*) seemed to remain among the most common triggers of violence: "You [meaning a boy] could just step on their [another boy's] shoe and they wanna fight you. Look at them wrong, they wanna fight you. Anything could just tick 'em off."

When I asked Roxanne what she would change about Johnson High School she again answered almost instantaneously: "The kids." The teachers were not the problem, she argued in the presence of two pedagogues, "It's the kids that make Johnson bad." "All the kids?" I shot back. "No," she replied, "just the bad kids. We do have some good kids in here, but Johnson? . . . Johnson is mainly bad kids."

Without any further prompting, and without missing a beat, Roxanne went from "bad kids" to the issue of school-related stigma. Her tone and bodily comportment indicted that this was a topic close to her heart: "Because . . . outside, people label this school the worst school. They be like 'Oh, you go to Johnson, that's a dumb school.'" After asserting this, Roxanne remained noticeably more defensive than she had been while talking about her neighborhood, objectively more dangerous than her school though it was. "But it [Johnson's reputation, school-related stigma] don't bother me,"

Roxanne said, "'cause, I just go here [attend Johnson], I don't live here." Face to face with people who saw her above all as a student of Johnson High she did not have to say—and perhaps she was incapable of saying—she felt ashamed about her school. With downcast eyes she said, "I don't wanna stay in Johnson. I wanna go to another school." "But," she then added with a shoulder shrug, "I'm here."

In her remarks on sources of dignity and disgrace, Roxanne never once touched on race, ethnicity, or nationality. Indeed the only time she ever said anything to me at all about such topics was when I asked her directly whether, for example, "black kids, Dominicans, and Puerto Ricans" got along in her school. "It ain't no little racial thing up in here, everybody just be with everybody," was her seemingly dispassionate response. Even when I cued it up, that is, race seemed not to be a central concern. Roxanne simply did not frame her experiences in racialized (or ethno-nationalized) terms.[19] Far more urgent for her was feeling degraded by ties to an institution located at the lowest region within her field of urban education. And in response, she degraded—and attempted to symbolically distance herself from—her educational position/institution. It was as if, at least during the interview, Roxanne's sense of self was being "spoiled" (cf. Goffman 1963) more intensely by affiliation with Johnson High than with anything having to do with the racial order or stigma associated with some of the meanest streets and subsidized housing projects in New York.

Trying to get through an awkward silence, at one point I asked Roxanne what students needed to do to be successful at Johnson. Roxanne's response seemed confident and clear: "Just be to yourself, keep to yourself, don't talk to nobody." Instead of once more rather glumly blaming herself for being "lazy," Roxanne spoke authoritatively when she offered the crux of another type of explanation for what had gone wrong during her time at Johnson High. In a wistful, matter-of-fact way, Roxanne reported that things fall apart for Johnson students who get "caught up in the wrong crowd, like I did." Hearing this, my colleague, with just a hint of Jamaican–British "rude boy" demeanor, leaned forward and reentered the conversation. Knowing a great deal about trying to escape poverty in London and downtown Brooklyn, this graduate of Erasmus Hall High School put the following question to Roxanne: "So you're gonna do it?" In other words, are you going to cut yourself loose from the ties that bind and pull inner city teens down? Roxanne's bodily and verbal responses were chilling. With her eyes once again downcast, she mumbled, "I don't know."

Perhaps because of the way my stomach was churning, at this point, I again invited Roxanne to talk about positive aspects of her life. She fantasized, briefly, about past and future shopping sprees [that would be] characterized by impulsive bouts of spending. "I spend money fast," Roxanne asserted, "it's like water 'cause I like clothes." She added that she liked going to parties and movies. But such projections seemed like slender beams of light vanishing into a starless sky. While Roxanne stressed that she enjoyed dancing at parties and laughing about other people's outfits, she rushed to add that the last party she attended ended in a shooting incident in which two people were seriously injured. When I asked if she had a role model, anyone she knew "who she would like to follow," she slowly shook her head and did not make a sound. Pressing again, I asked her about a good day at Johnson and what made it positive. The answer she came around to after a shrug was especially revealing: "I ain't really ha[ve] . . . well you could say all my days is good 'cause I do the same thing every day. I laugh. Play around. That's it. Then . . . go home. I really don't . . . it's the same routine I do every day. So . . . it's nothing."

My attempts to steer the conversation toward empowering pronouncements or some kind of uplifting finale were destined to flop. Roxanne was being candid about the physical vulnerability, emotional wretchedness, and disjointed desires that pushed and pulled in different directions so many of the teenagers in her "dumb" school. The most prominent realities could not be kept at bay.

My conversations with two of her other teachers supported Roxanne's own assessment of her daily routine. Although Roxanne usually made it into the building and to the official class in which formal attendance for the entire day was taken, she spent most of her time in the cafeteria. When Roxanne did make it to class, she tended to be totally unprepared (homework, required materials, etc.). Furthermore, her teachers told me that when she was present, Roxanne usually sat around talking and laughing with other students when she was not disengaged completely. Mainly because of what one teacher called her "attitude problem," the teachers saw no way to help Roxanne catch up academically or "get it together" behaviorally. The teachers said they had no problem with students like Roxanne missing a huge percentage of their classes.

A few months after our first meetings, Roxanne fell off my radar screen. Like most of the others in her cohort who entered Johnson High searching for meaning, direction, purpose, emotional energy, community, and physical well-being, this "internal dropout" broke with her routine and stopped altogether attending the "dropout factory" (cf. Balfanz and Legters 2004) to which she had been assigned.

Questions about Everyday Dealing and Self-Destructing in High-Stress Schools

An alternative view, . . . still struggling to work its way into empirical social science, holds that a person exists in the first place as a being thrown into the world, doing things, including self-reflection and social interaction, while already . . . corporeally engaged.[20]

Keeping in mind the gravity of the problems facing this girl who could obviously talk the "good" talk even if she tended to walk the "bad" walk, let us consider a few possible questions suggested by the dominant research literature on student fates in nonselective, high-poverty schools. Were Roxanne's self-destructive responses most basically the result of her conscious engagement in peer group mediated "counter-school cultural resistance" (Willis 1981)? Did "oppositional (black) culture" lead her to willfully disengage from her school (Ogbu 1978, 1991, 2003)? More specifically, as an "involuntary minority" (i.e., a member of a racially oppressed group and, in this case, a descendent of African slaves), did she feel pressure from her peers to avoid selling out her people/culture by "acting white" (Fordham and Ogbu 1986; Fordham 2008)? Was Roxanne's fate sealed mainly because, although she was able to temporarily switch on a "decent code," she had basically opted for an oppositional "code of the street" (in part because the attractiveness of a more conventional, pro-school set of beliefs had not been thoroughly enough explained to her; Anderson 1999)? Might this African American girl's "oppositional" values be the main force ensuring not just her own educational downfall but also the "downward assimilation" of inappropriately "Americanizing" lower-class immigrant students lacking "ethnic networks" strong enough to act as protective "buffers" against destructive "native" subcultures (Portes and Zhou 1993, Zhou and Bankston 1998)?

As the coming pages illustrate, I take seriously both these ways of posing questions and the many (ethnographic) works that have redeployed and reshaped them over the years. But digging deep into the real-time coping practices of students and staff in my schools will require that we both engage such established questions and ask new ones. Before we lose touch with Roxanne, I therefore want to shed light on the less standardized questions at the core of this investigation. And I want to emphasize again that I began gravitating toward these ways of posing various types of questions about everyday coping not as a theory-obsessed intellectual sitting on an office chair so ergonomically comfortable that it made me forget I had a body, but, rather, while "getting the seat of [my] pants dirty doing real research."[21]

Despite repeated statements indicating that they could be genuinely disgusted with the "ghetto fabulous" practices all around them, why did so many of the students—and especially so many students defined locally as *black*—frequently and fervently participate in bringing about their own (collective) educational demise? Relatedly, why did some lower-class teens in both settings—including boys self-identifying as black in New York and (Afro-) Antillean in Amsterdam[22]—consistently resist the temptation to "wild out"? More specifically, if they sometimes verbally endorsed being "street," how and why did so many (black) students successfully dodge self-destructive here-and-now pressures in their schools? Why, no matter what they said about their goals or beliefs, were the lion's share—but not all—of the teachers in both settings basically incapable of stopping students from recurrently falling into (or choosing) self-destructive and further distressing lines of behavior? Why was a minority of pedagogues in both settings consistently effective in all types of classes? From a slightly different perspective, how did it actually feel to be thrust into everyday transactions in Johnson High and the Delta School? How did it feel to occupy various positions within the different types of routinized face-to-face encounters that, at the micro-level, constituted everyday life in the two schools? For the differently predisposed and hierarchically positioned "players" making up the two fluid, "game-like" overall settings, what did it feel like—right there in the midst of it all—to be conjointly engaged in the "contingent ongoing accomplishments . . . [and] organized artful practices of everyday life"?[23]

I want to expand on this last question. During and long after my time in the two fields, I spontaneously experienced what went on as "chaotic." Only gradually did it dawn on me, as I become more of an ethnographer than a distressed insider, that this was an unacceptably partial and indeed misleading way to characterize everyday life in my schools. Precisely because the various types of interactions were so patterned—or, if you like, because the quasi-autonomous "logics" (de facto "rules") of everyday practice in the two settings were so stringent—what I need to depict actually has little to do with "disorder" in the sense of randomness and a great deal to do with informal yet immanent regularities and the social coordination of skilled coping practices. Thanks in part to reflection on some of the criticisms earlier versions of this book received, and after years of mischaracterizing what is perhaps most important of all, the following emerged as a central concern: Why were the various actors' more or less artful moves so predictably patterned even though they were choreographed by no one?

Whatever merits these theoretically informed questions might have, they will not necessarily help us get a feel for (and may even make it harder to grasp) the urgency of using ethnographic techniques to interrogate what actually unfolds in our most emotionally distressed schools. This brings us to toxicity. One need not be up to date on the findings of neurologists or endocrinologists to know that sustained exposure to high levels of stress diminishes memory, learning capabilities, cognitive performance, decision making, and emotional growth of teens, while ultimately correlating with risk factors for cardiovascular disease, poorer executive functioning (e.g., emotional regulation), and poorer immune functioning more generally.[24] Less well understood is that—thanks in part to the work of Ellisa Epel, the Nobel laureate Elizabeth Blackburn, and several of their colleagues (2004, p. 17312)—scientists are for the first time starting to grasp the "exact mechanisms of how stress gets 'under the skin.'"[25] Concerns about the health-related effects of chronic social stress can no longer be relegated to the speculation or grumbling of do-gooders armed with nothing more than vague associations. This new line of research details precisely why, until further notice, we have to assume that emotional stressors unleashed in stringently hierarchical, notoriously erratic, and at times physically unsafe settings such as our worst (big city) schools are killers.[26]

Just as major scientific breakthroughs are helping us get down to the nuts-and-bolts level of how stress can destroy our (brain) cells, we need to understand in far greater detail the more or less toxic webs of relationships, emotions, and symbolic transactions affecting disadvantaged students (and their teachers). Augmenting insights into the monotone "stressors" one finds in public health research literature,[27] comparative ethnographic investigations centered in high-poverty schools can help specify how different kinds of embodied, gendered, intermittently racialized, and status-related experiences on the ground reinforce ultimately unhealthy ways of life.[28]

Like all scientific methods, the techniques used by ethnographers have many shortcomings. However, instead of being sufficiently informed by the observational data and analysis of long-term insiders, our present day sociological explanations of behavioral responses and outcomes in high-poverty schools tend to be limited either by statistical procedures or by interviews. Administering surveys to adolescents as distressed as Roxanne and then slicing up distinct "variables" will not help us achieve anything approaching an adequate understanding of real-life coping practices.[29] The same basic points can be made with regard to survey interviews (or any kind of interviews not based on extensive ethnographic field work). Aside from the fact that people often lie (to themselves), we should keep in mind that—especially in the case of teenagers confronted with highly charged, fast-paced, and eminently threatening encounters—even people with relevant observations are generally not very good at putting into words what we need to know most: how here-and-now microlevel dynamics and broader contextual effects shape the ongoing in-school responses of differently positioned and predisposed students and teachers. All too often what one elicits in interviews are after-the-fact clichés. Ethnographic interviews such as the one I had with Roxanne were useful precisely because they constituted tiny parts of sustained and direct involvements in the array of routine interactions that influenced everyday life in Johnson High and the Delta School. Preplanned exchanges in interviews were useful, that is, because most of my discoveries were unplanned if not forced—for example, the very "discovery" that while failing to teach I had been doing ethnographic research and generating rapport all along. Most importantly, feeling what the two fields did to the long-term insiders who traversed them helped me avoid the pitfall into which researchers relying on statistical and interview-based methods perpetually fall: overemphasizing the qualities of seemingly self-enclosed, disembodied yet perpetually self-aware "individuals."[30] In short, one might say that being there, and there, for years on end led me to the following insight about basic units of comparative analysis: not, then, students and their moments, but, rather, more or less stressful moments and their students.[31]

Overdoing It? A Note on Language

What is above all needed is to let the meaning choose the word, and not the other way around.[32]

Especially as the term *toxic schools* may strike some readers as overheated, I want to add a few words about my title, phrasing, and writing style. My observations indicate that what goes on daily in schools such as Johnson and Delta does not merely contribute to the reproduction of broader socioeconomic and cultural inequalities[33]; rather, or in addition, I contend that everyday interactional coping practices centered in such degraded institutional domains generate, or at very least powerfully reinforce, ways of life that adversely impact the physical health and emotional well-being of those forced to attend them. The word *toxic* offers, I believe, the most economical and balanced way to speak and think about what is at stake in this study. After all, this is a transnational comparison of coping processes centered in a "comprehensive" school (Johnson) and an officially designated "vocational" school (Delta) constituted by massively disadvantaged teens that, for a range of (historical) reasons, could not be adequately socialized and educated by their parents. And as this book relates, even within such seemingly diverse national welfare regimes, urban contexts, and educational settings, we have not yet hit upon undamaging ways of preparing the truly disadvantaged for adulthood. On top of failing to realize equalizing ways of schooling truly disadvantaged teens, that is, my research suggests that we have not yet developed (emotionally) undamaging ways of doing this. There is every reason to expect, furthermore, that our present-day inability to deal with the kind of chronic anxiety, intimidation, and emotional destabilization I witnessed will have serious repercussions downstream.[34] So it really is not a penchant for "shocking" language or dramatizing moralistic arguments that underlies my choice of title but, rather, the quest for an accurate frame—one that helps us look straight at what is going on. Given how stressful my schools were, I use *toxicity* to alarm. But this does not make me an alarmist.

More generally, while I try to steer clear of hyperbolic and judgmental language, the flat, colorless voice of detached scholastic disinterest is not one I can maintain for long. An engaged, human, exposed writing style continues to feel like part of an attempt to be honest about what I witnessed. A somewhat informal style goes along with my refusal to construct any composite characters, fictional scenes, or imagined utterances. Disingenuous distancing and half-truths would feel treacherous, given the efforts of all the genuine fieldworkers who came before me, the problems facing the people I studied in the Bronx and the Bijlmer, and the efforts that will be required if we are ever to genuinely transform the educational experiences of large percentages of the poor. So while the names of the people and institutions are disguised, I offer sincere language and depictions inspired by the urgency of what the parents and teachers of students attending Johnson High and the Delta School were forced to go through.

The next chapter contextualizes the two neighborhood institutions and demonstrates how I started identifying what became the main themes taken on in each of the empirical chapters at the heart of this book. It also provides a more detailed discussion of both the leading social scientific approach to troubled urban schools and the conceptual framework upon which I rely most heavily. Although readers can find an expanded discussion of my methods in a separate appendix, the next chapter offers a preliminary account of the fieldwork techniques upon which this comparison is based. In the interest of illuminating what students and teachers saw and felt when they entered the two settings, I want to get under way by fleshing out my initial encounters with Johnson High and the Delta School.

ONE

Introduction: Getting Situated

[The technique is] one of getting data . . . by subjecting yourself, your own body, your own personality, and your own social situation, to the set of contingencies that play upon a set of individuals, so that you can . . . penetrate their circle of response . . . That "tunes your body up" and with your "tuned-up" body . . . you're empathetic enough—because you've been taking the same crap they've been taking—to sense what it is that they're responding to. To me, that's the core of observation. If you don't get yourself in that situation, I don't think you have a piece of serious work.[1]

A friend named Jake invited me to check out one of his classes up in the Bronx. That's how it all started. Reclining on the bleachers next to a basketball court after a workout at the Westside YMCA in the fall of 1996, Jake was telling me about one of his English classes and he just popped the question. While he warned me about Johnson High's "bad reputation," his comments and his relaxed delivery had a rather soothing effect. Furthermore, Jake seemed to be genuinely enthusiastic about the life of the New York City public schoolteacher. He mentioned that some of his colleagues had become close friends and that he enjoyed hanging out with some of his students. "Most of the kids are sweethearts," my buddy from the gym told me. Needing to find a job, quickly, I agreed to observe one of Jake's classes.

I may have looked quite young as I entered Johnson High on that fateful first day back up in the "Boogie Down" Bronx. While standing in line with the other students headed for the metal detectors just beyond the building's massive front doors, I heard the following conversation about me. "Is that a new student?" asked one boy standing behind me. "Damn, that nigga's kinda tall," was another student's response. Upon making it through the metal detectors a male security guard (or "security officer," as they preferred to be called) made clear that I would not be checked with the handheld detector that was waved along the bodies of all the incoming students. Arriving at the desk behind the school's main line of defense I picked up my guest pass from a female security officer who explained, with a wry smile, that I could have entered through the teachers' side entrance. The message being communicated was clear cut: the incoming students, not the adults, are treated as threats. Literally from the moment I entered the building, I was exposed to institutionalized pressures not just to identify myself mentally as a teacher but to disentangle myself from the body-based experiences of students.

I went up an empty staircase and started searching for Jake's classroom. While I was walking through a long, bare corridor looking for room 214, the shockingly loud bell rang to end the period. Within just a few seconds, multiple doors opened and the emotional stampede began. *Whoosh!* As kids talked, yelled, screamed jokes, rapped, made beats and sang, a swarm of baseball caps, puffy winter coats, and bright colors engulfed me. I was amazed by the raw energy unleashed when so many bodies moved around through the suddenly quite smallish hallway. The adrenaline shot through my veins. I felt like I had just had five cups of coffee.

Finally I found it, room 214. Just outside Jake's classroom a dark-skinned student with what I took to be a Jamaican accent pretended to hold a gun—sideways—and shoot a victim lying on the ground in front of him. "*Buuyaka, buuyaka, buuyaka*—T[h]ree in da [h]elmet." His companions paid some attention, but on the whole they seemed unmoved by his somewhat playful performance of machismo. Most of them were too busy people watching, just taking it all in. One of the dark-skinned boys making up this vaguely bounded energy circle was banging out dancehall beats on the wall next to the classroom door. The rhythms, the shrieks, the laughs, the distinctive face-work, all the more or less ghettoized gaits, the relative docility of the seemingly meek, the socio-linguistic enactments of ethnonational belonging, the diverse ways of doing race, the gendered and gendering outfits, and the budding bustling vividness of it all were almost too much to register all at once.

Making my way past the small cluster of boys and entering Jake's classroom, I felt as if I had been discharged from a realm overflowing with excitement (tinged with teenage angst) and into an adult's private, low energy sphere of influence. Jake greeted me more calmly then he usually did at the gym and, without giving it much thought, I took a seat in front next to the door and near the ongoing performance of the showman with roots in the West Indies. A few more kids dragged themselves into the classroom. Rather than impolite or hostile, most seemed disengaged. The bell soon rang and the hallway started to empty. The beats, ritualized greetings, screams of delight, laughter, and taunts that had come to life in the corridor all subsided. The tyranny of the bells, I would later come to understand, was supported by mobile teams of security guards and "hallway deans" (as well as two uniformed policemen)—all connected by walkie-talkies.

The class was a disaster, I thought. Jake struggled to get any verbal feedback or to get the students even slightly engaged in written assignments. The kids seemed utterly unconcerned with what the all but irrelevant guy in the front of the room was trying to get them to do. One boy, slouching almost to the point of lying down in his desk/chair unit stared blankly at Jake and the blackboard with nothing on his desk but one black leather glove, which he proceeded to take off and put on over and over again. Two kids seemed to be asleep in the back. One girl came in late, in extremely tight jeans. She talked to a girlfriend, almost perpetually—even as Jake pleaded with her to be quiet. The nonstop chatting seemed all the more bizarre because the two girls were sitting in the front row, just a few seats away from me and almost adjacent to Jake's desk. The presence of a strange adult and proximity to the teacher apparently had no effect. Finally, Jake raised his voice and asked the latecomer with the noteworthy jeans to leave. Nothing. She did stop talking, but she did not move an inch. Jake asked her to leave a second time. Again an awkward silence ensued. "Whatever," she said at last as she slowly got up to leave. Her face expressed a mix of disgust and apathy. As she sashayed over to the door a boy in the back of the room, who had been silent until that point, perked up and said, "Damn she got a fat ass." Jake pretended not to hear this, which surprised me as much as the comment itself.

In Jake's class what I experienced as extraordinary appeared to be entirely mundane. Lesson one, I would later think: While life in the halls is electric and full of meaning, at least under the conditions I was observing, the majority of the kids seem not to focus on or care about the teaching of the formal curriculum or anything else that took place inside classrooms. Lesson two: Getting along in "their" classrooms, many teachers let countless "minor" provocations slide and seemed to find this routine.

Almost as soon as the bell rang to end the period, the hallway scene sprang to life once more. The pupils, seemingly released by the bell, returned to the energizing space on the other side of the classroom door. Left alone, I was confronted by the need to say something to Jake while keeping a straight face. But a most inviting situational way out emerged when Jake appeared happy about the few minutes that he had been able to engage a couple of kids in anything, anything at all, related to Arthur Miller's *The Crucible*.

Looking back now I can say this was the first time that I was sucked into—or allowed myself to get sucked into—the show. Pretending that one teaches and that one's colleagues actually teach is basic to the ongoing practical adaptations of professionals on the ground in such "lousy place[s] to learn anything" (Becker 1972). The summons was at once subtle (just a friendly smile from a genuinely nice guy doing his best) and irresistible (due to my largely unconscious framing of the situation and my preverbal emotional calculus, "playing along" was basically the one possible move open to me). It was already becoming difficult to think, let alone to say anything along the lines of, "Jake, man, that was really pathetic. That was the 'English class' you wanted me to check out? Where most of the kids are 'sweethearts' because they did not actively resist your efforts to teach? Where the hell am I?" Far too embroiled to give it any real thought at the time, right then and there, I (almost) automatically mirrored Jake's goody-two-shoes demeanor. I actually found myself mimicking his posture and state of mind.[2]

After class Jake introduced me to his supervisor—according to the kitschy nameplate on her muddled desk, the Assistant Principal of the English Department. Immediately after finding out about my educational background, she walked us over to another supervisor on another floor, the "AP" of social studies/history. Despite my lack of teaching credentials or experience, this smallish man in a cheap suit asked me to start "subbing" as soon as possible. With a Brooklyn accent as strong as any I'd heard in years, this second supervisor assured me that I could soon become a full-time teacher in his department and that I would have several years to work on becoming certified.[3] The AP asked when I could start. He also began filling in forms that I was to take down to the Board of Education office in Brooklyn. The social studies AP informed me that there were kids "wandering the halls even as we speak" because he simply had no regularly assigned teacher or long term "sub" to put in front of their classrooms.

I agreed to start as a substitute at Johnson High as soon as possible. We agreed that I would—off the record—have my own classes, due to two teachers being out with "long-term illnesses."[4] The supervisor predicted, with another coy smile, that there would be other teachers who would become "ill," for weeks at a time, and that I would therefore have more than enough de facto regular teaching work in addition to the more traditional "sub" work (i.e., "coverages"). Above all, I was able to start teaching in Johnson High for one reason: no one else wanted the job. In the 1990s roughly half of the new teachers exited the New York City public school system by their sixth year (Brumberg 2000, p. 142), and turnover rates were highest in high-poverty, high-stress schools.[5] Mainly because the swimming pool was leaking, I was invited to jump in.

Let us take a few steps back, now, and get a wide-angle view of this major neighborhood institution. Approaching the building, especially when the students were still out of view, Johnson High School looked like a classic early twentieth century American high school. Roughly half a city block long, it was clearly built to last. One could see why it had been viewed, for decades, as one of the best high schools in the city. Indeed long after World War II this proud public institution had been a springboard for the largely Jewish families moving up from places like the Lower East Side. The front entrance, complete with grassy knolls, trees, and an extended concrete walkway leading to a cross street, was neo-classical in style; a touch of the Ivy League just off the Bronx's most beautiful boulevard, the Grand Concourse. At first glance, especially from within and early in the morning, the thick stone building seemed to have nothing to do with the graffiti-drenched tenement buildings, run down bodegas, piles of garbage, broken up sidewalks, and filthy restaurants that had come to surround it. The long corridors on all four floors were immaculate every morning before the students started to trickle in. Johnson could look like an island of civility and order in a sea of degradation and disarray. And in some ways, for some students, it was.

At the same time, the signs of decay were unmistakable. When I arrived there was no playing field, only an enormous and cracked up secondary parking lot that was almost never used. A thirty-foot-high fence surrounded the parking lot that was used by the staff, only a tiny percentage of whom lived in the immediate vicinity. This towering fence along with a multiplicity of gates, gratings, and iron window coverings gave the impression of a besieged fortress. And from the moment one started to witness the hip-hop flavored clothing and postures of the incoming pupils, it became quite evident that Johnson had become a school for urban outcasts. Cliché or not, you know you are in a truly broken down monstrosity of a "school" when you see girls as young as fourteen coming in through a special entrance for those pushing baby strollers. Often with scarves wrapped around their heads, enormous gold-plated earrings, gold-capped teeth, oversized T-shirts the same color as their Nike hightops—sweatpants pulled up to the knee on one leg—these "babies with babies" made their way through a special side entrance toward Johnson's one elevator and the day-care center at the top floor. On some days this center cared for over twenty infants and young children.

Perhaps nothing sent as robust and invasive a message to those approaching the building as the bodily bearing and rhythmic movements of the more "thuggish" students and their associates positioned in front of the students' entrance. (Every morning there were nonstudents who mixed it up with the typically more dominant pupils still at least officially attending Johnson while, for example, letting their pitbulls and Dobermans run around on the grassy areas in front of the school.) Initially without words or sounds, this forewarning was issued every morning as students and staff drew close enough to make out the figures clustering around to the main entrance.

To be sure, other types of signals communicated important messages to those entering Johnson High as well. Clothing, footwear, baseball caps, headscarves, and bandanas mattered, especially when they were embodied adroitly and purposefully deployed in order to "flash" allegiances to specific street gangs (cf. Garot 2010). And of course, to hear the boisterous, ever-repeated calls of the more ostentatious students ("What up, family?" "You aaaiight [all right] dawgs?" "You know how WE do?"), to listen to the synchronized singing, rapping, and beat-boxing almost always audible around the main staging areas, and to perceive the sound of the collective belly laughs of those who felt relaxed enough to enjoy a good "dis" (i.e., the disrespecting of, or the "screaming on" a person or group)—all of this confirmed the power of signals communicated through the ritualized performances of *Bodies That Matter* (Butler 1993).

The signaling certainly did not end here. Oftentimes, while approaching the school, one saw uniformed security guards and regular police stationed just outside the building. This further communicated the same point to those crossing the threshold into the Johnson High: you are now entering a physically dangerous public institution. In the afternoon it was hard to miss confirmation that students and staff were leaving a perilous social arena. Diverse police vehicles (always at least one cruiser, often a paddy wagon) and uniformed officers were deployed in an effort to make the exit areas at least partially safe. From roughly a half a block away from the building, of course, the (informal groups of) kids were left to their own devices.

Officially, year in, year out, Johnson was depicted as being roughly thirty-five percent "Black" and sixty-five percent "Hispanic." A "bilingual"—i.e., Spanish speaking—program at Johnson effectively formed a sub-school within the overall educational environment. "Bilingual" students, who in many cases arrived in the United States fairly recently and who were generally understood to be comparatively less disruptive and aggressive, made up roughly a third of the school population. These pupils tended to be clustered into separate classes and, in many cases, separate sections of the school building. My research focused on the English-speaking segment of the school that was, officially, less than fifty percent "Hispanic." New arrivals from Haiti were formally depicted as "Black," while students from the Dominican Republic—i.e., kids from the other side of the same island who, in many cases, had equally dark skin—showed up in the statistics as "Hispanic." The large contingent of students (whose parents were) from the Dominican Republic, the smaller yet significant percentage of kids (whose parents or grandparents had come) from Puerto Rico, and the relatively small numbers of pupils with roots in Mexico, and Central and South America—all showed up in the statistics as "Hispanic." The statistically insignificant percentages of students from nations such as Pakistan and Bangladesh were thrust together under the label "Asian."[6]

Unofficially, the students with roots in over twenty-five impoverished countries as well as in different parts of the United States (e.g., "Down South") often used their own ways of identifying themselves and each other more or less along ethnic, racial, and national lines. These identification schemes could at times sound static and straightforward (e.g., "She looks black"; "He is Puerto Rican"). They could also appear to be fluid and ambiguous. For example, as Chapter 5 demonstrates, some "Africans" tried to become "black." At times students (generally assumed to be "black" because of their phenotypes and how they spoke) tried to make a point of not being (exclusively) "black" because they (also) experienced themselves as being, for example, Haitian, Jamaican, Panamanian, or, as some half-joked, "light skindeded [sic]."[7] As the coming pages will further detail, racialized (and ethno-nationalized) constructions were inextricably linked not just to various (and more or less porous) racial categories but also to gender regimes and peer group hierarchies. So, when ways of doing blackness or Dominican-ness came into play—and as we have already seen we must not assume the experiential salience of race or ethnicity—they were already tied up with habituated prenotions, and consciously held beliefs about ways of being a "bad boy" or a "fly girl" as opposed to, at the other end of the spectrum, a male or female "nerd."[8] The official "Black"/"Hispanic" split, as well as any other substantialist or *process-reducing*[9] scheme (i.e., any "groupist" scheme that posits ethnic or racial "groups" as clearly bounded substances at rest and implies that such fixed essences can serve as basic units of analysis) fails to adequately represent how situated understandings of race, ethnicity, and nationality actually worked in or around Johnson High.[10]

Even if the previous points must remain murky for now, I hope the next two will be clear straightaway. First, I have no doubt that the school was very close to zero percent middle class. By any reasonable definition—i.e., no matter whether one is inclined to emphasize parental educational levels, amounts of legitimized cultural capital, or family income and wealth— nearly all the teens entering Johnson High were extremely disadvantaged. College-educated parents and guardians with more middle-class jobs either left the neighborhood, paid to send their kids to private (parochial) schools, or found a way to play the overall public school game in such a way that their nearest and dearest did not end up at the bottom of the system.[11] Although the official statistics on poverty rates said little about realities on the ground,[12] it is clear that even kids from stable working-class families almost never ended attending such a "dropout factory" producing diplomas of at best marginal quality.[13]

Second, whether the students frequently put this into words or not, Johnson High did occupy a stigmatized position in a *racialized and racializing* symbolic order. On a typical day approximately a thousand students actually made it past the metal detectors and into the building. Yet in terms of our racialized collective fantasies—i.e., in terms of the pseudobiological, symbolic categories that can of course very be very real in their effects—I never saw a single white teenager even get close to Johnson High.[14] As my depiction of a field trip in Chapter 4 illustrates, the refounding of illusions about complex yet at least partially racialized—and therefore potentially "naturalized"—social orders was undeniably an aspect of the school's "hidden curriculum."[15]

In the end, I stayed on in the Bronx for just over three years until my position—along with those of several other "PPTs" (teachers officially in the process of becoming certified)—evaporated in February of 1999. The state decided to clamp down on the common practice of keeping "ghost students" on the official rolls as a means of collecting money.[16] Feeling quite demoralized and thinking about the opportunity to return to the Netherlands (instead of sitting for weeks or even months in the infamous "rubber room" awaiting a new teaching assignment), I was glad to be let go. Although my union negotiated contract insured that I could have, I did not seek a placement in another school in part because I felt I could take no more.

I alluded above to some of the reasons I went on to become a teacher-ethnographer in the Bijlmer, or southeast Amsterdam. Another set of reasons has to do with a girlfriend who was born in the Bijlmer. Her family originally emigrated from Surinameto the high-rise flats of southeast. While getting to know her mother and other members of her extended family, I repeatedly heard the half-jokes about "making it out" of Bijlmer "before it got too bad." Time and again, the stories about escape from the neighborhood stressed the importance of economic power rather than white racism or ethnic discrimination.[17] At the same time, "communities" and "groups" were often imagined in ways that drew on claims and discourses related to nationality, ethnicity, and race. Despite the existence of some "Dutch blood" in the family, the members made clear that not being purely *blank* (white) could be basic to the collective sense of self, other, and place. At times experiencing themselves as at least to some degree nonwhite, they took for granted that they and their offspring could never really truly be "Dutch."

Due to these and other observations, even before I started teaching in the Bronx, I had speculated about life in racially and socioeconomically segregated schools in the nether regions of educational space in the Netherlands. Once initiated into the world of nonselective New York City public high school teaching, it dawned on me that I might try to do something that, as far as I knew, had never been done: conduct an insider's comparison of everyday life in high-poverty schools on opposite sides of the Atlantic. As an ethnosociologist, as a teacher, and as a New Yorker who had lived for years in Amsterdam, I wanted to know more specifically, *as only insiders can*, whether or not a full-blown European welfare state took the edge off the *hidden injuries* of de facto educational apartheid.

In 1999 I was accepted into the PhD program at the University of Amsterdam. The second half of my fieldwork formally became the rest of the empirical foundation for my doctoral research. I started coaching basketball again. This time, however, I coached in a municipally funded program[18] offered in secondary schools serving "at-risk youth" in three sections of Amsterdam (North, New West, and Southeast).[19] I got back into coaching, that is, not because of any affinity I still had for hoops, but because I wanted to get as close as possible to troubled schools and students. Within weeks it became clear that the school in Southeast Amsterdam, Delta, faced the greatest challenges. This convinced me further that I needed to get as deep as possible into the school in the Bijlmer.

Working nominally as a basketball coach after school, I had originally assumed that I would have to explain why I wanted to snoop around hallways, the cafeteria/auditorium, and in the teachers' quarters hours before the bell rang to end the last period. Yet as soon as the security personnel stationed at the front door (*portiers*), the school's administrators and a few teachers categorized me as a basketball coach, I was granted almost unlimited access. Though I thought I might be pushing my luck, I almost immediately started asking for interviews, observing classes, and even participating in English classes. After telling the school's second-in-command that I wanted to do a comparative study of schools occupying the lowest regions in New York's and Amsterdam's field of secondary education, I was given permission to shadow a teacher for an entire day every week. Instead of telling me to back off,this school manager basically forced one of his teachers to let me shadow him. He insisted that neither he nor any member of the teaching staff had anything to hide.

From the first morning of my in-class shadowing it became clear that the majority of classes were massacring this teacher, a kind man born in Suriname when it was still a Dutch colony, to whom I had been assigned. It was unclear to me why an AP, who knew I wanted to study his school, would suggest that I shadow such an ineffective teacher. What was obvious, however, was that the tone of the classes I observed was set by students getting out of their seats and the teacher yelling at them to sit down, arguments about twenty-five-minute "trips to the bathroom," and seemingly endless bouts of chattering, jokes, insults, petty threats, and nervous laughter. As had been the case in most classrooms at Johnson, the teaching and learning that took place had precious little to do with the official curriculum.

Perhaps depicting a seemingly unimportant anecdote is the best way to sum up what I learned about life in Delta while observing the classes of this gentle-mannered pedagogue. At one point, while several affronts and conversations were taking place alongside his calls for silence, the teacher sighed and looked straight at me. This was rather dramatic in part because he had been pretending I was not there up to that point. I knew the situation—and the feelings of powerlessness mixed with shame, disgust, and anger—all too well. As our eyes met, I lifted my eyebrows and opened my hands in a "what-can-you-do?" gesture of support. Then he clinched his fists, put them down on the desk in front of which he hunched, and dropped his head between his arms. The capitulation, expressed in one of the purest of cross-cultural forms, the kowtow, made other interpretations seem impossible. "You see, they are doing it again," the meek look and strained posture appeared to communicate. "I am crushed and I am ashamed." For a moment at least, the show could not go on. His mask came off. I told him after class that he was doing what he could, and that the disastrous situation was not his fault. What else could I do? I assumed that I had been directed, for some reason, to observe an especially weak teacher. I would soon find out that this was not the case. The methodically dismantled man I shadowed did not return the following year.

Within a few months, due to teacher shortages that were at the time even worse than what I had seen in New York—roughly twenty percent of the classes were simply canceled rather than, as they were in New York, "covered"—I was soon asked to start teaching for as many hours as I could spare.[20] Once again, one of the teachers for whom I was "temporarily" filling in was, as she later made clear to me, pretending to be ill. Upon her return this teacher made the following comment: "I demand respect. And if I don't get it, I go on sick leave." Once more, no formal job vacancy existed—i.e., the official statistics related to these matters had little to do with what was going on, on the ground—because the teachers on long-term sick leave did not officially give up their posts. I began trying to teach, nearly full time, but soon scaled back because of the requirements for the PhD program. After years of exposure to an objectively more dangerous institutional setting in the Bronx, I was surprised to feel intimidated in my new field. I also felt anxious to learn more about power and practice in one of the worst schools in the city I was starting to call home.

The Delta School was housed in a boxlike, flimsy example of unimaginative 1970s cost cutting. The building was tiny compared to the one in which I had worked in New York, and it was visually dominated by a set of high-rise buildings located less than a hundred yards away and connected by the paved walkways and grassy areas which united the various subsections of the Bijlmer. A small playground and a separate building containing exercise and locker rooms was enclosed by a six-foot-high high fence and sliding gate. The Delta School had, at one point, been packed with nearly thirteen hundred students, many of them from middle-class families said to be "Dutch" (i.e., native, white). Up until the late 1980s, the school boasted a prestigious pre-university *VWO track* and an upper level vocational (HAVO) track. By 1999 these more prestigious tracks had disappeared. The at least somewhat stable middle class families had left the neighborhood, and there were simply too few students granted access to these pathway-swilling to attend a school in decline. Nearly all-incoming students entered into the lowest, most stigmatized vocational tracks generating diplomas that were perceived to be all but worthless. Officially, less than five percent of the roughly six hundred students attending the Delta School were "native Dutch" (autochthonous). This category was used to account for a few students from Belgium who, by virtue of their phenotypes and the fact that they spoke Dutch, were not considered *allochtonen* (migrants/ethnic minorities).[21] In other words, to be white was, in practice, to be native. Although the lion's share of pupils had been born in the Netherlands, administrators classified roughly eighty percent of the students as either Surinamese or

Antillean (i.e., from the Dutch Antilles). Administrators and teachers also said, at times seemingly with pride, that pupils (with families) from over twenty countries constituted the student body.

As had been the case in the Bronx, the students' constructions of racial, ethnic, and national identities were often more fluid and complex—as well as far less salient—than the administrators' pie charts might seem to imply. Again, as we shall see in more detail shortly, concerns about gendered peer group dynamics were typically framed less in terms of ethnic categories than in terms of the "gangster" to "nerd" status continuum.

Despite the situated murkiness of how ethnicity, nationality, and race came into play on the ground, Delta also occupied a stigmatized position in an undeniably *racialized and racializing* symbolic order encompassing Amsterdam and the Netherlands more broadly. Like the schools in New West (Amsterdam) populated mainly by pupils with roots in Turkey and Morocco, throughout the Netherlands schools like Delta were generally categorized by outsiders *primarily* as "black." In part because similarly racializing discourses were entrenched in the worldviews of the students and teachers, the predominantly nonwhite character of Delta's social composition was basic to the shared background understandings within which (or against which) everyday (symbolic) transactions emerged. In short I found, once again, the overall implicit pedagogy was based at least in part on racialized differences and, therefore, the pseudo-biological "naturalization" of broader socioeconomic and educational inequalities. And once again it became obvious that such observations demonstrate almost nothing about how racialized identities, worldviews, and claims (fail to) emerge in everyday transactions.

It quickly became clear that the degrees of fear, aggression, and serious violence were much lower in the Bijlmer than they had been in the Bronx. There was an atmosphere of playfulness or lightheartedness that had been largely absent in the Bronx. There were fewer students who seemed deeply depressed and withdrawn. Almost certainly because there was more (thoroughly) subsidized housing and medical care, more robust state-sponsored poverty-reduction interventions, fewer family members behind bars, fewer men on the run from the law (cf. Goffman 2009), and fewer female heads of households being evicted (cf. Desmond 2012a, 2012b), students were also comparatively less mobile in the Bijlmer (i.e., they came and went after the start of semester less often). All of this, but most obviously less geographical and familial disruption plus fewer homeless children meant higher attendance rates and fewer classes thrown into administrative disarray.[22] I was delighted to find no serious gang activity in the Delta School.

There were however serious bouts of physical violence in and around my new school. And the same types of problems relating to nearly constant flows of more or less intimidating, anxiety-ridden disruptions were only too apparent. Once more I discovered that, as had been the case in the Bronx, pupils with darker complexions (typically labeled "black" according to alternative local definitions) were overrepresented among in the most energized, seemingly proud, and ultimately self-destructive peer groups and micro-interactions. Again I saw that teachers were being pushed to, and in some cases over, the edge with regularity. As was the case in the Bronx, some classrooms were consistently productive. Once again, however, during most "periods of instruction" in the Bijlmer, most of my new colleagues and I were unable to actually teach anything for much more than ten to fifteen minutes per forty-five-minute class. The rest of the class time was basically lost to waves of minor infractions and the occasional major commotion. On closer examination, those who bragged at meetings about being able to "handle" specific classes often had even less success behind the closed doors than I did.

This brings us to the frequently overlooked issue of time on task. In terms of percentage of minutes per class on task, I was actually able to teach slightly less in the Bijlmer than in the Bronx. If we take into account (1) the percentage of classes that were canceled in the Bijlmer and "covered" by "subs" and regular staff in the Bronx (both around twenty percent) and (2) the amount of time that was lost to disruptions during "periods of instruction," students at Johnson and Delta spent roughly eight hours a week "on task." In effect, that is, one might say the students in the Bronx and the Bijlmer had a one-day school week. What students learned about most of the time was how to deal with stress, how to cope with informal struggles over recognition and social status, and how to make one's way through the maze of ritualized, more or less energizing transactions that only appeared to be "chaotic." They learned how to belong, foster friendships, and cope with well-policed symbolic and social borders dividing the different kinds of peer-group formations. Again I saw such findings about what actually took place most of the time as a series of bombs lying underneath much of the statistical research based in part on things like officially reported "hours of instruction" per subject per year. Yet again I wondered, as some of my new colleagues did, if the institution I worked in was adequately characterized as a "school."

I ended up working at the Delta School from 1999 until—burned out by the overall experience and extremely frustrated by what certainly felt like "my" failures inside classrooms—I finally gave up just before making it to the end of the 2001–2002 school year.

Oppositional Black Culture and an Alternative Framework

Go into any inner-city neighborhood and folks will tell you that . . . children can't achieve unless we raise their expectations and eradicate the slander that says a black youth with a book is acting white.[23]

Over the past few decades countless theoretical concepts and social scientific approaches have been used to make sense of everyday life in distressed urban schools. However, research by scholars who have generated and reshaped debates about the *oppositional black* (or *involuntary minority*) *culture* approach has the most direct relevance for analyzing what took place in my two schools.

Learning to Labor, Willis's ([1977] 1981) classic educational ethnography based in the British Midlands, celebrated the *highly conscious* "cultural agency" of macho working class "lads." In a nutshell, Willis argued that the lads deliberately challenged the formal, middle-class dominated culture of their school. But this resistance had ironic consequences: instead of helping them oppose class domination, the peer group mediated "cultural agency" of the lads helped ensure that they would do poorly in school and end up struggling to keep blue-collar jobs in Thatcher's de-industrializing political economy. Nonetheless, at least for countless intellectuals on the left, Willis's emphasis on active, willful, and therefore potentially revolutionary "resistance" was preferable to the even less uplifting message that schools stealthily "reproduce" class relations by getting lower class students to buy into the myth of education-based meritocracy (cf. Bowles and Gintis 1976; Bourdieu and Passeron [1970] 1977, [1964] 1979).[24] A genre, and a debate, was born.

The theme of deliberate youthful resistance was extended by the far-reaching theories of Nigerian-born John Ogbu (1974, 1978, 1991, 2003).[25] Indeed within the social sciences, the theories of Ogbu and those more or less openly working within his general framework provide the single most dominant—and perhaps also most hotly debated (Cook and Ludwig 1998; Lee 2002; Tyson 2002; Lundy 2003; Foley 2005; Diamond 2007)—approach to (1) massive failure and occasional success in high poverty urban schools and (2) the actions and achievement of minority and, in particular black, students.

Ogbu's theory rests on a sharp demarcation between "voluntary" and "involuntary minorities." His approach is founded, more precisely, on the emergence of racial/cultural communities that either elected to, or were forced to migrate to the United States. Ogbu stresses the importance of "white" and "black" culture, which he views as adaptations to specific historical circumstances. The most poignant example here is that enslaved Africans in (what would become) the United States—i.e., Ogbu's "involuntary minorities" *par excellence*—knew very well what they were doing when they performed meekness in the presence of "whites," yet derided them and even planned bloody revolts against them when they were not present. Such lessons and practices collectively learned and reinforced over the course of centuries inform Ogbu's ideas about contemporary *black oppositional culture*—a distinctive mix of forms of speech, religiosity, humor, and normative orientations that could serve as a pride-instilling defense mechanism in the face of continuing racism in and out of schools. This distinctively black oppositional culture, involving conscious rejection of inherently stigmatizing "white" attitudes and practices (such as taking advanced-placement classes in high schools), continues to hold back African American students.

Bringing in brutal histories of (de-)colonization, Ogbu extended his historically based arguments about castelike involuntary minority status to putative *groups* such as, most importantly, Latinos in the United States. This set Fordham and Ogbu (1986) up to further refine the specific hypothesis that both African American and Latino students can be "burdened" by peers' perceptions that they "act white" when they try to do well in school.[26] Throwing still more oil on the fire, Ogbu (2003) suggested that African American culture retards the achievement even of more middle-class blacks attending privileged suburban schools.[27]

Subsequent research has produced mixed results, with many researchers associating oppositional culture more with lower class backgrounds—and specifically with Willis's findings—than with racialized subcultures and oppression (e.g., Ainsworth-Darnell and Downey 1998, p. 537). Fryer and Torelli (2006, p. 54) criticized such earlier research widely interpreted as debunking the acting white hypothesis and offered statistical evidence supporting it—especially in the case of Latinos and especially in racially diverse schools. Drawing on both statistics representative for the Netherlands and observations of an elite Dutch high school, Mijs (forthcoming) found no evidence for the burden of acting white hypothesis.[28] Back and forth we go. In two articles offering a particularly fresh and fertile perspective, McFarland (2001, p. 620; 2004) offers empirically rigorous analyses indicating that classroom-based "resistance" is actually understood better in terms of situational possibilities and sanctions emerging from the informal organization of face-to-face encounters than anything related to a "student's background of race and class." No less engaging, Carter's (2005, 2006) sophisticated interview-based findings indicate that maintaining racial identities and related cultural boundaries by means of acting "authentically" "black" (or "Spanish") is important to lower class adolescent students in Yonkers, New York. Fusing insights from Bourdieu and Ogbu, and relying on the notion of nonlegitimized "black cultural capital," however, Carter found that strategic efforts to achieve genuine "blackness" (instead of "acting white") did *not* entail ideological resistance to achievement either in school or in the world of work. As far as she was able to tell, that is, rejecting what they saw as bland, middle-class, mainstream and indeed "white" ways of being did not lead disadvantaged teens going to school just a few miles from Johnson High to adopt "oppositional" beliefs or behaviors.

Dickar's (2008) insider account of a distressed high school in Brooklyn also both supports and contradicts Ogbu's framework. Highlighting that for students the meaningful action was in the hallways rather than in classrooms, Dickar stressed that students could at times associate academic engagement with "whiteness" and find solace in the notions of "black solidarity" expressed most vividly in extra-classroom settings. At the same time, she argued, the steady flow of minor disruptions and more intensely destructive events that basically undermined formal learning processes were not guided by thoroughly oppositional, racially motivated, or situation-transcending beliefs. Rejecting Ogbu's "monolithic construction of oppositional culture," Dickar (2008, p. 79) focused on the tension *not* between racialized (and more academic or more "street") groups but, rather, between "classroom" and "corridor cultures."[29]

Here we begin edging towards an especially influential extension of the oppositional culture approach that remains largely within Ogbu's race-based framework: Elijah Anderson's *Code of the Street: Decency, Violence, and the Moral Life of the Inner City*. At first glance, it seems that Anderson's (1999, p. 9) Philadelphia-based ethnographic examination of "why it is that so many inner-city young people are inclined to commit aggression and violence toward one another" relies mainly on the class-based approach developed in a trilogy of books by William Julius Wilson (1978; 1987; 1996).[30] For Anderson (1999, p. 9), however, what most immediately triggers the self-destructive behavioral responses in question is a "street" cultural "code" understood as a "set of prescriptions and proscriptions, or informal rules of behavior organized around a desperate search for respect that governs public social relations, especially violence." Anderson portrays the "code of the street" as a belligerent mindset spreading from streets into everything from movie theaters and stores to homes and schools. "Decency," which Anderson associates with mainstream values undergirding hard work in the formal economy, traditional (gender) roles in stable families, and achievement in school, is treated as the polar opposite of "the code of the street." In steamrolling the civility associated with "decency," Anderson argues, street-based cultural responses to socioeconomic oppression and racial stigma promulgate aggressive modes of honor seeking that basically destroy face-to-face interactions throughout the central city.

I want to highlight one aspect of Anderson's work that is as significant as it is serpentine. Anderson treats "street" and "decent" as both temporarily situated performances and enduring cultural logics, without specifying the relations between these analytic levels. On the one hand, that is, he relies heavily on the notion of "code-switching,"[31] warning against essentializing usages of "decent" and "street" cultural orientations and stressing that "a person may behave according to either set of rules, *depending on the situation*" (1999, p. 36; emphasis added). Here we find Anderson treating the code of the street as a performance or, if you like, as a mask-like, ritualized way of passing for whatever people feel a certain micro-level encounter demands. From this perspective, acting "street" is a resource most ghetto dwellers can (or are forced to) *temporarily* or *situationally* draw from out of concern for their own well-being.[32]

On the other hand, Anderson presents many ghetto residents, including teenage students, as either unceasingly decent or solidly street (in terms of their clearly racialized identities and belief systems).[33] While relying heavily on the oppositional black culture perspective to make sense of what goes on inside some of the most hateful schools in the City of Brotherly Love, Anderson (1999, p. 97, emphasis added) often depicts the code of the street as little more than an elaboration of Ogbu's racialized group culture based approach: "Alienated black students take on the oppositional role . . . because they are profoundly *at odds with white culture* . . . [and] other alienated students may mimic them because they are such strong models."[34]

Hence, especially with respect to life in troubled big-inner city schools, Anderson arrived at two somewhat diverging conclusions. My findings support Anderson's contention that members discussed both enduring cultural logics and immediately situated performances in terms of more or less "street" ways of being.[35] Furthermore, there was a convergence in both of my schools between more aggressive and disruptive teenagers, generally said to be more "street," and those classified according to local definitions as black. At the same time, my findings also indicate that some of Anderson's key arguments about "the code" are empirically false (cf. Garot 2010, pp. 135, 139, 225–33). More importantly, my findings do not suggest that black students engaged in self-destructive responses mainly because of any racialized identities or any kind of willful cultural resistance. Utilizing a divergent set of conceptual tools and by means of a transatlantic comparison, I therefore aim to clarify the picture with which Anderson's extension of Ogbu leaves us.

The last Ogbu-related line of research I want to mention is an exceptionally fruitful one. I refer now to the extensive corpus of literature on "second generation decline" (Gans 1992) or "downward assimilation" (Portes and Zhou 1993; Portes and Rumbaut 2001) and the contrasting academic success of some (Asian) newcomers to the United States. Let us briefly consider Zhou and Bankston's (1998) examination of the positive educational outcomes of economically and in some ways culturally (e.g., linguistically) disadvantaged Vietnamese students in high-poverty, low-performance New Orleans public schools. These two scholars found that teachers and students had radically different expectations for "nerdy Asian whiz kids" on one hand and for African American or Latinos on the other. (These "model" minority students could hardly be expected to found oppositional in-school identities on positive stereotypes.) They therefore explained the success of the Vietnamese students—and especially the failure or the non-Vietnamese students—in terms of Ogbu's work on cultural adaptations of voluntary and involuntary minorities. This, of course, does not help us understand why nominally white lower class students tend to do far worse in school than these students ensconced in Vietnamese bubbles or, for example, why some "involuntary minorities" thrive. But the problematic use of Ogbu is not at the core of Zhou and Bankston's important work. Most importantly, they demonstrate that the real motor and driver of the successful students' trajectories was a taut, highly organized Vietnamese community network that effectively shielded its own from the "disruptive elements [that] dominate" ghettos and inner-city schools (Zhou and Bankston 1998, p. 13).[36] More specifically, they show that massive levels of *social control* and powerfully regulating feelings of *shame* emerged out of countless interactions within a tightly bound network of Vietnamese families. The resulting "buffer" helped Vietnamese students not just to avoid "downward assimilation" but, in their phrasing, to "Americanize" in "selective" and seemingly rewarding ways.[37]

Newcomers or not, I hope to show that a similar sort of shield—grounded in family ties as well as in networks of stable adults acting in loco parentis (rather than grounded exclusively or even mainly in ethno-national community ties and commitments)—played a vital role in the educational success observable from within my schools. On top of this, as Chapter 5's dissection of the single most dramatic turnaround and successful trajectory I came across in either setting reveals, disciplining the mind by means of learning from self-inflicted bodily discomfort could be a remarkably power-ful way to develop the required levels of emotional self-control as well as other helpful affective and cognitive states and traits.

Here we start getting in touch with the centrality of lived somatic experi-ence and now, with the help of two studies neither enabled nor constrained by assumptions related to the oppositional (black) culture approach, we can start outlining an alternative perspective. This approach will be based on (1) emotional dynamics and bodily exposure to more or less threatening face-to-face encounters, (2) members' practical senses of overall educational settings, and (3) socialization trajectories and social-structural positions in broader urban spaces. The touchstone, for me at least, is John Devine's (1996) harrowing study based on ten years of action research in forlorn secondary "schools"[38] of Brooklyn. This work brought to new heights the ethnographic study of extreme physical violence, security apparatuses, and student life centered in the corridors of our worst schools. Additionally, I want to make use here of Martin Johnson's (1999) study based on no less than three decades of teaching and direct observation in several cities around the UK focused on fear related to continuous disruption and the experiences of teachers inside classrooms.[39]

What comes through above all in Johnson's work is how adults in front of rooms full of teenagers were emotionally worn down by being ignored and frightened by immersion in social tumult. Describing his (1999, p. 4) book as being a teacher's tale about the "small minority of secondary schools in England"—more and less dominated numerically by white pupils in differ-ent times and places—uniformly characterized by their high percentages of "children of underclass origins." Within such settings, it was not any kind of focused resistance but the almost permanent scattering of attention and refusal to take notice of adults that lead to teachers' humiliating capitula-tions.[40] His examples also seem to buttress the assertion that the "silent majority" (Johnson 1999, p. 35) of nondisruptive, nonaggressive students simply could not set the tones in or out of classrooms.[41]

Devine did not study white pupils because no teens classified along these lines attended his thoroughly segregated schools. In relation to those extending Ogbu's theory, then, Devine's most interesting assertion is that the cultural orientations of "native" minorities (mostly African Americans but also Latinos in his schools) did not diverge fundamentally from those of "recent immigrants" (i.e., students from the Caribbean mainly, but also from South America, Africa, and Asia).[42] In support of this claim, Devine (1996, pp. 36, 86) offers numerous vignettes and field notes indicating the pervasiveness and "agency" not of individual students or peer groups but of aggression. This helps make plausible Devine's finding that, in the midst of their daily rounds, native-born students did not even consider the possibility that adults would successfully bring about and maintain well-regulated interactions in or around their schools. Familiar only with schools in which disruption, fear, and violence were always already there, these nonmigrant students had no counter examples of well-supervised educational climates offering, for example, a formal culture against which they might rebel.[43]

For Devine, then, the key to understanding what might appear to be cultural differences between clearly demarcated ethnic groups turned out to have little to do with diverging belief systems and a lot to do with the normalization of belligerence. Newly arrived migrants were still "shock[ed]" by that which went without saying among the more fully familiarized (African American) "natives" (who, when allowed to be calm and reflective, described everyday violence as both "wild" and "normal").[44] Most of the time, like the proverbial light in the room for those whose pupils had already dilated, for the already familiarized threats of violence went to neutral. Relatedly, the data and analysis suggest that the majority of recent arrivals came from places where social control and adult supervision were more effective.[45] On top of this, perhaps the most persuasive challenge to approaches based on ethno-national or racial group cultures came with Devine's (1996, 107–109, 112–113, 138) juxtaposition of African Americans, native-born Latinos and newcomers from various places complaining not just about the violence but how teachers failed to confront students with their inappropriate behavior. Given a chance to consider the "light in the room," one might say, "natives" also seemed to long above all for regulating interventions from responsible adults.

Convinced that the variance was best explained by differing levels of exposure to settings dominated by violent behavior, Devine (1996,p. 34) went on to ponder whether "ethnicity constructs violence or is constructed by it." One might assume, with this direct challenge to so much of the work inspired by Ogbu, that Devine went too far.[46] And in some sense he may have. Devine did not offer evidence that the "agency of violence" in and of itself *created* ethnic identities "from scratch" or allowed students to escape fully the effects of centuries of racial classifications. In another sense, however, Devine's data and analysis do validate a less stringent or absolutist claim about the social construction of ethnicity. That is, when and where ethnicized ways of experiencing self and other became salient they were always both (1) interdependent (i.e., there was no Haitian-ness outside of Jamaican-ness) and (2) profoundly influenced by what mattered most: perceptions about threats and violence (e.g., the notion that Haitians were less aggressive than Jamaicans in a given setting).[47] If we see ethnicity relationally in terms of interdependent enactments and interwoven ways of understanding the world—i.e., as something that people may *do*—rather than in terms of preexisting essences and permanent things that a person or "group" *has*, we can certainly see why Devine would see belligerence as the horse rather than the cart.

Provocative and empirically rich as they are, these works really do raise as many questions as they answer. For example, if there were school-wide "cultures of violence" in inner-city Brooklyn, as Devine suggests, why were even the most aggressive students nonviolent most of the time? And exactly what led some of the natives and newcomers down the path towards aggression on certain occasions? Rather than supporting his own notion of a unified "culture of the underclass" in the United Kingdom, Johnson's work elicits questions about how and why some students become—or temporarily behaved like—tone-setting "rejectionists," docile members of the "silent majority," or anything in between. In the end, while these two authors effectively point the way forward, they tell us surprisingly little about how everyday jockeying for position within and across peer groups contributed to massive failure and distress. Similarly, after reading these two important works, we come away with almost no sense of why some teachers and students are successful in overwhelmed schools.

Having said this, these two investigations based in major cities on opposite sides of the Atlantic also highlight the viability—indeed the necessity—of basing comparative analyses of high-poverty schools not on preconceived ethnicized or racialized group cultures, but on the actual situations in which physically and emotionally endangered students and teachers perpetually find themselves. Whether focusing on noisy hallways or bewildering classrooms, that is, these studies show why analyses might begin with the interactional dynamics encountered by actors conceptualized as *corporally engaged whole beings*. Rather than founding analyses on the explicit interpretations of *spectators* with time to ponder their next moves, in Dewey's language, this points towards the possibility of basing analyses on how *body-mind complexes*[48] were always already preoriented towards possibilities, sanctions, and likely futures related to immediate contexts of action. Especially when taken together, furthermore, these works by Devine and Johnson suggest that the relational contexts in which massively disadvantaged students and their distressed teachers are immersed should be understood *both* as more micro- and as more meso-level[49] structural realties that were themselves embedded in broader webs of interdependence such as the two urban and educational spaces.[50]

With the pieces starting to fall into place, I want to touch upon how a triad of concepts—habitus, field, and capital—can be adapted to ground and develop the analysis of coping processes across the two educational settings. Yet before engaging these *interdependent concepts*[51] associated with the work of Norbert Elias and Pierre Bourdieu,[52] I want to highlight again the crucial turn that began above in the discussion of Devine and Johnson. This is the transition away from overly cognitivist (or mentalist) conceptions of meaning and cultural understandings (so central to the oppositional black culture approach) and toward the more corporeally grounded ones at the heart of the alternative framework informing my work. This shift will continue through the treatment of Elias and Bourdieu, perhaps be most clear in the consideration of Jack Katz's work on moral, sensual, and affective conversions, and be hard to miss in my discussion of Randall Collins's sub-cognitive approach to how situational dynamics energize senses of belonging by marking them with emotional potency.

Attempting to do justice to the ongoing coping processes centered within them but certainly not playing themselves out exclusively within their walls, I approach the two "ghetto" schools as quasi-autonomous *fields* of life with "their own" overall organizational structuring and logics. During the more objectivizing moment of analysis, I try to delineate the distributions of what Elias called *power resources* and what Bourdieu (1986) referred to as more or less legitimized and convertible forms of *capital* (e.g., cultural, social, symbolic, economic, and bodily). Deploying these terms without getting hung up on idiosyncrasies of technical jargon, I will try to show how portfolios consisting of scarce (material and symbolic) resources either promoted the occupancy of relatively low-status positions in the two hierarchically structured social settings or, at the other end of the capital continuum, allowed for "moving up in the world" or maintaining "top dog" status.

Inevitably, stating this brings us to the undesirability of keeping separate the more objectivizing and more subjectivist moments of analysis (i.e., how power chances were objectively distributed and how differently positioned students subjectively perceived and actively constructed their worlds). Adolescents spending large percentages of their waking hours (more or less anchored to specific types of positions) in the stratified social universes I am calling Johnson and Delta unavoidably (further) acquired specific sets of dispositions operating as worldviews. These embedded schemas and embodied inclinations are what Elias and Bourdieu—drawing on work dating back to the ancients and running through such foundational figures such as Durkheim and Mauss—called *habitus* (or socialized *second natures*). Once drilled so deep down that they appeared to be *intrinsic* traits, these largely unconscious practical senses for one's proper "team(s)" and how to "play" the educational "game" contributed profoundly to students" responses.[53] Of course experiences outside the schools influenced students (and teachers) at fundamental levels as well. Indeed, as the portraits of (temporarily) successful students in Chapter 5 demonstrates, there were potentially life-saving *differences* in paths through the two "spaces of play" (i.e., the two educational worlds) that can be explained only with reference to early and extra-school socialization. Yet the second natures observable in the schools could not be explained adequately with reference to socialization processes located exclusively in, for example, surrounding neighborhoods or families.

A central assumption here is that we stand to gain by treating the two high-poverty schools as, in Weberian terms, relatively autonomous "life orders" with their own "internal logics." In Bourdieu's language, I therefore depart from the idea that the two settings can be seen as relatively autonomous fields of life (or overall "social games") with, to some extent, their own taken for granted ways of being and getting things done ("rules"). This does not mean that I conceptualize the two objects of investigation as geographical sites with clearly fixed boundaries. Rather, as a student of Elias's unremittingly "processual" approach, I see them as webs of differently empowered yet interdependent people and dynamic networks of mutually constituting positions organizing ongoing coping practices centered in yet also extending beyond the walls of the two schools. While this gives me no clear-cut answers to questions about boundaries (e.g., Where do the relevant relationships end?), such a relational and dynamic point of departure sets us up to see that the occupancy of positions within the two *worlds* (social structures) depended on objectively unequal distributions of various power resources and produced or reinforced roughly corresponding subjective *worldviews* (largely prediscursive mental structures). This in turn gives us the analytical leverage necessary to pick up on how—in large part because of the bodily dimension of informal learning—students and staff acquired practical senses of (or feels for) the overall "games" they found themselves "playing" at the level of micro-involvements.[54] Certainly, students dealt with micro-level encounters and dynamics that deserve to be taken seriously in their own right (Goffman 1983). The guiding theoretical assumption here, however, is that they were also confronted with and habituated into entire worlds of preestablished hierarchies, de facto rules, (gendered and gendering) roles, and various types of norms, rituals, necessities, and shared background understandings related to ways of "scoring" and being more or less "on top." These cannot be reduced to specific micro-level encounters or treated purely as reflections of what went on in the two "ghetto" neighborhoods.

At various points in each of the empirical chapters I will draw on the work of Jack Katz—a scholar who, like Bourdieu,[55] has found new ways to help sensitize sociologists to the discovery made by the "philosopher of the flesh."[56] In one of his earlier books, Katz (1988, 80–113, 237–73) examined the here and now sensual temptations, moral payoffs, and somatic undergirding of "bad ass," "hardmen," and "bad nigger" enactments. Without denying the influence of wider and historically rooted socio-cultural structures, the primary focus was on releasing stimuli and lived bodies interwoven in the ethno-graphic foreground.[57] Delving into how emotional responses emerge in the phenomenological present, and rejecting out of hand the myth of independent knowing "subjects" representing "objects" in an "external" world, Katz (1999) brought to life (most memorably and instructively) how drivers on Los Angeles highways from time to time feel that they have been "cut-off" by cars that swerve ahead of them but never actually touch their automobiles. This demonstrates that our minds not only continually and unconsciously monitor our whole beings as we cope with such sequences of everyday events, but that this mental mapping of our embodied selves engaged in "normal" routines tends to extend to things outside our physical boundaries, to objects like our cars or pieces of road ahead of us. No matter what our "backgrounds," how we are labeled in terms of "groups," or even whether or not we operate cars, all of us have experienced these types of "mundane [emotional] metamorphoses" (Katz 1999, 309–44) because all of us are, *first and foremost*, porous beings of flesh and blood guided through typically quite familiar surroundings by embodied minds.[58]

It is true, as Katz demonstrates, that such emotional actions and everyday experiences are often actively crafted by self-reflective Goffmanian attempts at impression management and other kinds of "artful" productions. "But," Katz (1999,p. 7, emphasis added) adds, "the self-reflection in emotions is *corporeal rather than a matter of discursive reasoning.*"[59] If while examining emotional reactions we fail to get beneath explicit mental interpretations, if we fail to break through to the level at which competent natives are guided in real time by their immediately felt, primordial senses for the game, we will set up shallow questions and be left with explanations that are "if not exactly epiphenomenal, still relatively superficial with regard to behavioral process and a small part of the variation with regard to causal determination" (ibid,p. 143). As Katz (ibid,p. 344) proclaimed in *How Emotions Work*,

" 'I think therefore I am' arrogantly denies the existence of shadowy back regions." My observations and experiences in the Bronx and the Bijlmer suggest that, especially for researchers focusing on adolescents and teachers in physically and emotionally distressed settings, the implications could not be more important. Ideas matter. Bring in the active mental constructions, conscious beliefs, and strategic performances of sentient beings. But get beneath the fleeting chatter of the thinking mind and especially all the after-the-fact verbalized rationalizations—and base the analysis of real-time coping on what tends to unfold most basically beneath the level of discursive consciousness—or risk reproducing easily racialized clichés about (the "cultures" of) the those born into poverty.

This brings us to Randall Collins's Goffman-inspired version of Durkheim's ritual solidarity theory. Like Katz, Collins exhibits a better eye for micro-interactional dynamics than either Elias or Bourdieu. For our purposes, the real utility lies in grasping how Collins identifies and examines what he sees as the basic mechanism of all social interaction: more or less "successful" micro-level "interaction rituals" based on bodily co-presence, mutual focus of attention, and shared moods. From this perspective, the key ingredient and outcome of successful face-to-face encounters is "emotional energy." By this Collins means the feeling of being positively revved up or invigorated. Less successful interaction rituals can be draining or so neutral in terms of emotional valence that they go all but unnoticed. A central claim here is that qualities typically attributed to individuals are better understood as attributes of (positions within) different types of (chains of) micro-level interactional orders. Building on this core insight, Collins argues that the micro-level orders he dissects provide easily overlooked yet elementary forms of everyday stratification and solidarity.

Collins underplays habitus. He is also too radical in his rejection of extra-interactional fields of relational dynamics. Habitus—which for me includes that which Davidson (2012) calls *emotional styles*—along with other potential power resources that influence rank and therefore shape one's sense of possible moves within hierarchically organized fields, hugely influence *access* to different types of interaction rituals. As we shall see shortly, not just anyone could enter into (and perhaps get juiced up by what transpired in) the reasonably bounded social circles formed by those "getting their thug on" in what were taken for granted to be the most prominent "spots" in the two overall adolescent societies. In this sense there was no (free) "market" for interaction rituals, as Collins's (2004) work might imply. Keeping this in mind while remaining sensitive to Collins's argument that interlocking interaction rituals *cumulatively* charge up or siphon off emotional energy, I illustrate how more or less "successful" everyday rituals contributed mightily to (1) individual's feelings, thoughts, and actions, (2) to vitally important senses of belonging in distinct (and indeed more or less sacred) peer groups, and (3) to the (re)production of the two overall social orders constituted by students who could not bring their other potential power resources into play without at least a modicum of emotional energy and means of concentrating attention. Specifically with regard to violence, furthermore, I will rely time and again on Collins's (2007) ethnographically informed examinations of micro-level determinants of more and less effectively enacted rituals of aggression.[60]

Living Ethnographically, Twice

> The very features of a secularized society, the rationalization of everyday life, have become an object of study for the sociologist, but also a prison for him. He is in the peculiar position of studying the conditions of everyday life, but his data are the product of the conditions.[61]

While I detail them in a separate Appendix, I want to close this chapter with some concrete points about the methods used to collect data and interrogate coping practices based in Johnson High and the Delta School.

My most basic claim on this front can be traced to Goffman's remarks in "On Fieldwork" with which this chapter began and, even further back, to the father of social anthropology, Malinowski. To grasp adequately what it is like to be a competent member of a mini-society like Johnson or Delta, one needs to remain immersed as long as it takes to achieve a practical understanding of a "series of phenomena of great importance which cannot possibly be recorded by questioning or computing documents, but have to be observed in their full actuality," as Malinowski ([1922]1984, pp.18, 21) put it. Genuine fieldwork entails, at certain moments, that "the Ethnographer" put "aside the camera, notebook, and pencil, and join in himself in what is going on." While top notch ethnographic analysis and presentation of data devoid of ethnographic immersion is at least as old as *The Elementary Forms of Religious Life* (Durkheim [1912] 1965), I agree with Goffman (1989,pp. 125–26) that if you do not "physically and ecologically penetrate their circle of response" long enough to achieve a "tuned up body," you cannot claim to have a practical sense for the primordial dimensions of social existence as they are actually felt and lived through.

Switching to sports, sex, dance, music, martial arts, or anything else clearly body-based about which one might have a deep understanding can serve to drive the point home. No matter how refined the measurement methods of contemporary sociologists become, when we reduce the vividness and complexity of felt understandings, real-time competencies, and ongoing practical achievements to (coded) after-the-fact verbalizations (e.g., "We really wanted to work together tonight.") or statistics (e.g., field-goal percentages, minutes of foreplay) we leave out a great deal of what Malinowski famously called the *imponderabilia of actual life*. While surveys and interviews can help, every*body* knows, or at least every physio-psychological system *senses* that there is much more going on in webs of human relationships and practices than that which we can quantify or deduce from interviews alone.[62] In short, rigorous analyses of colossal failure and sporadic success in our most distressed schools are greatly advanced by the techniques associated with *sustained* and *carnal sociology*.

Unlike classical ethnographers (who got stuck on islands), I do not claim to have *discovered* any clearly bounded "sites."[63] Rather, I *constructed* two relatively autonomous fields of ongoing practice and change, or, if you like, webs of interdependent positions and people spatially centered in but not limited to the two school buildings. Given that my fields were conceptualized as contexts of action without clear boundaries, anything influencing everyday dealing and self-destructing—from shifting relationships with fathers to mounting requirements for diplomas to broader cultural structures—might therefore be considered "relevant." Confronted by a host of problems researchers focusing on (ostensibly) well delineated sites might have allowed themselves to forego, I had to identify the range of people, positions, and social forces weighing in on the *problems* and *coping responses* especially visible in the two buildings. When I did not stumble upon them, I had to figure out which entry points allowed me the fullest and most relevant observations in and outside the two schools.

More practically, my approach was based on extended apprenticeships. As a teacher I was forced to acquire some capacity to operate more or less competently as a quasi-native in both institutional domains. I had no choice but to embody and experience the social role that allows researchers to get closest to (if not inside) the phenomena with which students and their teachers have to deal.[64] First and foremost as a teacher trying to make it to the next bell or classroom, that is, I did what one does and tried to hold on long enough to get a practical sense for what the two fields did to those who remained inside them for serious amounts of time. On top of this, and more self-consciously as an ethnographer, I went where very few of my colleagues cared (or dared) to go. If students hung out in places like students' cafeterias where no teachers were to be found, I hung out in those same cafeterias. When students left their schools and neighborhoods, I tried to tag along anywhere from local parks to swanky movie theaters. Doors were by no means always open, but from (purported) gang members to fellow teachers, from students' family members to their (former) boy- or girlfriends, and from the students' potential employers to my former administrators, I tried to talk to "everyone" influencing (or with special insights into) the coping processes in question. I frequented the spaces in and around the two schools that were all but unregulated by adults. When they joked about carry knives, I joked about carrying knives and, for example, asked if I could see how big theirs was. Perpetually resituating myself anywhere from other teachers' classrooms to the students' in-school hideaways, from students' homes to local fast-food restaurants, I put in the kind of time—and gradually built the types of relationships—that few of the other adults involved in the coping processes offered or established.

Especially while in ethnographer mode, I tried to keep something, anything, close at hand so I could write field notes or, short of that, at least a phrase or single word. (As mentioned above, I often used audio and on occasion video recording devices to help capture a necessarily limited selection of the seemingly endless supply of observations, conversations, and events.) While I was often simply too drained to do so after work, especially during weekends and vacations I pushed myself to organize, expand upon, and reflect on what struck me as the most relevant aspects of whatever made it into my field notes or onto a tape. While I focused on what struck me as the most memorable and instructive moments, knowing that seemingly trivial details sometimes prove to be essential later on, in my field notes and reflections I tried to paint as full a picture as possible.[65]

There is much to be said about my direct observations and the hundreds of informal conversations and more formal interviews I had with the people I studied. For now I will report only this: the interviews usually *at once* evolved out of and strengthened relationships based on mutual trust and respect.[66]

Like all the other teachers, in addition to being inundated with informal "shoptalk" (e.g.,rants about dysfunctional colleagues or administrators), I was privy to various types of "in-house" communications and documents (e.g., about upcoming shows to be put on for inspectors, different drafts of texts to be used as propaganda). I also had access to a steady stream of finished products presented to the outside world in the form of everything from upbeat mission statements to official reports for inspectors (including politicized understatements of school-related incidences of violence) to letters for parents to "classroom management" guidebooks. While I only sparingly use evidence related to such documents, observing the gap between bogus texts and harsh contexts forced me to consider focusing on what was, from the perspectives of the exposed, most important.

Main Themes, Empirical Chapters

You can just see it in how he walks, Einstein . . . Nerd![67]

Roxanne was not an outlier. In both the Bronx and the Bijlmer, the so-called "hard," "street," and "ghetto fabulous" students frequently sounded remarkably pro-school. In and out of interview situations, in many cases while speaking among themselves during "naturally" occurring transactions, the apparently "hardcore thug and thugette" students made comments indicating that they wanted to receive a secondary school diploma; that they wanted to continue into higher education; that they considered kids who "dropped out" or frequently engaged in violence to be "dumb." Even the so-called "hardest of the hard," the "real criminals," and "natural-born hustlers" said, *at times*, that it was better to "act normal" (i.e., behave in nondisruptive and nonaggressive ways). Yet, in countless cases, I observed typically more dominant students enacting "street" ways of being soon after making pro-school statements. Furthermore, I found that the students who were more typically labeled "good" (and in some cases "nerdy") could sound supportive of "bad" kids and what were seen as their distinctive ways of being.

This is the most important set of observations from which we start. And clearly, from the perspective of the teacher-ethnographer as well as from that of a (parent of a) student attending such a school, this begs the following question: Why were so many adolescents capable of talking and feeling pro-school regularly engaging in such distressing and (self-) destructive responses?

With this core question in mind, in Chapter 2 we will begin doing what all the incoming students tried to do: deal with preexisting, peer group mediated ways of thinking, feeling, and interacting within overall pecking orders that soon come to be experienced practically as *the natural order of things.* Dissecting the positions and peer group dynamics into which students were thrown it will become evident that some students had far greater access to (and felt far more attracted to) self-destructive ways of being than others did. Building on the comparative analysis of micro-level peer group dynamics and the overall structuring of the two fields, Chapter 3 explores the power of threats and the practice of violence. Here we will see most clearly not only why toxic stress crept beneath the skin of all involved, but also how certain especially dominant students skillfully manipulated the gendered roles and interactional channels leading towards and away from physical aggression. We will also see at this stage how the occupation of specific positions within potentially belligerent interactions governed the violent elites who often appeared as the masters of the two anxiety-ridden universes.

Chapter 4 explores something that is as crucial as it is easy for ethnographers of educational settings to miss. Profiting from walks through ritzy streets of Manhattan with teens from the Bronx as well as from sessions in mellow middle-class pockets of Amsterdam with children of the Bijlmer who could not have felt more out of place, this chapter investigates how stigmatized positions in the two urban spaces contributed to emotional investments in friendships and peer group affiliations that even the students making them at times understood to be self-defeating. More specifically, Chapter Four delves into how feelings of shame experienced outside what the students assumed to be their "natural habitats" reinforced desperate feelings of pride related to even the most debilitating of in-school coping practices.

Focusing on students who at certain stages of their educational careers had been on successful trajectories, Chapter 5 begins by examining how gender regimes, (dis)advantages related to distributions of various species of capital, the (lack of) regulation of bodies, ethno-national (self-) identifications, racial orders, and peer-group hierarchies all reconstituted each other and, in so doing, contributed to tragic individual outcomes. Shifting to an African American young man in the Bronx and an Afro-Antillean-Dutch male student in the Bijlmer (again, members of the gender, racial, and ethnic categories typically said to be most "at risk" in the two settings), the chapter then turns to how and why some pupils remained on successful trajectories. More to the point, this part of the chapter reveals why a massively disadvantaged student, coming to his high school from a homeless shelter while his brothers were incarcerated, was nothing short of triumphant at Johnson High. The chapter then highlights the more modest yet significant successes of a pupil who grew up a short walk from Delta (before being evicted) and who was perpetually invited to join (his school's version of) the "street" elite. More broadly, this chapter explores the ways in which historical trajectories and (early) extracurricular socialization contributed to the more stable and coherent sets of predispositions that could immunize students from the destructive practices and emotional contagions to which they were exposed in and around their beleaguered schools. Here readers will find what worked, to varying degrees, as well as why the keys to success were so rarely found.

While the rattling experiences of teachers are woven into all the empirical chapters, Chapter 6 focuses specifically on the street-level bureaucrats behind all the closed doors. While this chapter illustrates how less effective teachers were overwhelmed, the focus is on the minority of teachers in each setting that successfully micromanaged bodily movements, emotional states, and flows of ideas inside classrooms (until they too burned out). What was the excellence of the continually effective teachers really made of, how did it work in real time, and why was the right stuff so difficult to emulate or pass down?

Each of the empirical chapters ends with a final discussion of the main similarities and differences across the two settings. Pulling together the lessons I learned teaching on opposite sides of the Atlantic, the Conclusion aims to destroy several of most troubling—and influential—myths about everyday coping in high-poverty schools. The final argument is that if we finally stop dodging and mischaracterizing what we are up against—if we arrive at nothing less than a new way of thinking about the ongoing suffering and occasional victories in high poverty schools—we will be able to avoid pseudo-solutions and deal more intelligently with the educational experiences of those born poor.

TWO

Recognizing the Real,
Restructuring the Game

Yeah nigga . . . you better act like you know! We holdin' shit down up in this piece.[1]

Don't front [fake it, pretend to be what you are not], you know I got you open.[2]

Why, even among pupils who could sound "good"—indeed even among pupils like Roxanne who at times felt disgusted with what they thought "bad" students tended to do—was it so difficult to "keep to yourself"? It may be obvious already that the answer lies in the seductions of status and power. But we have yet to begin developing a rich sense for *how* (not) getting "caught up" in the "wrong crowd" actually worked in practice in our two settings. Doing just this while connecting patterned microprocesses to rather sturdy mesolevel (school-wide) outcomes, we can lay a solid foundation for the rest of the comparative analysis.

Where to begin? This chapter starts with entrance areas and then moves into places like hallways and cafeterias before heading back out on to sidewalks for a simple reason: the everyday status struggles setting the tones in the two adolescent societies were based *outside classrooms*.[3] This is not to suggest, of course, that classrooms were meaningless. Most of the time, however, behind classroom doors was not where the stakes were highest or, if you like, where the most physically, emotionally, or cognitively "greedy" (Coser 1973) institutional transactions took place. Peer groups—i.e., the fluctuating and interdependent webs of relations that teachers, administrators, and students often experienced as permanent and self-enclosed—were often broken up in different classrooms. To some degree because teachers at least tried to regulate bodies, moods, and symbolic interactions in what (still) felt most like "their" domains, furthermore, classrooms tended not to be *where the action was*.[4] And by "action" here, I do not simply mean aggression. While the next chapter zooms in on how the excitement and anxiety of physical threats permeated everything that took place in the student bodies and overall environments, this chapter examines more and less intimidating everyday events in the specific subspaces that usually meant the most to those most intensely exposed.

We will start, more concretely, with incidents that might appear to have been generated *mainly* by qualities that should be ascribed to two individuals (and, by extension, to these two individuals' backgrounds). Important as these two students' previously acquired sets of dispositions undoubtedly were, and vital as the portfolios of potentially relevant capitals that they imported into their schools may have been, the incidents in question should be seen *first and foremost* as products of interlocking and highly routinized interactions (or everyday bodily emotional metamorphoses) that could only have taken place within the two overall spaces of play.

Thomas: Not Really Part of the "Real" Team

Real niggaz do real things,
Hangin' with the honies is the song I sing [5]

Thomas was Johnson High's best basketball player. Standing at least six foot six, he was also the tallest boy in the school. Although I never had him in a class, over the course of a couple years, Thomas and I formed an informal, somewhat friendly/somewhat antagonistic relationship with each other. He knew me as the best of the ball-playing teachers in the school, which is not saying much.[6] After one pre-season workout with security guards, a few other teachers, and some boys who hoped to make the basketball team, Thomas and I started talking about prospects for the upcoming season. Because failing two classes or being absent too often could make one ineligible, Thomas knew that many of the better ball players who attended Johnson would not be allowed to try out for the team and that others would be kicked off as soon as their first semester grades and absences started to reach the coach. "A bunch of niggaz in here got game," Thomas assured me in his rather high-pitched inner-city African American vernacular. "Come around [the basketball courts in the park just outside] Yankee Stadium and you'll see a few cats who should definitely be playin' wit' us."[7]

I asked Thomas why, at least in the past two years since I had been teaching at Johnson, he had never failed off the team. He looked down at me as if I had posed a rather stupid, rhetorical question. "'Cause I don't be running through the hallways wit' all these wild niggaz up in here, that's why." Then, in a more considered tone, he continued, "I don't mess with nobody . . . jus' mind my own business." Still sweaty and looking down at his enormous sneakers, he mumbled something about kids "gettin' they thug on" and the need to keep away from "all distractions." When I started to ask him about these distractions, he cut me off. "Niggaz just don't wanna go to class. They jus' stay runnin' through these halls, playin' cards in the cafeteria, smokin' weed in the stairs, talkin' to girls and what not. And plus, you got these niggaz selling nickel bags' til god knows what time at night. Then you know they ain't tryin' to wake up in time for official."[8]

We both knew that some potential teammates were selling more than just five-dollar bags of marijuana. So it was understood that he was making the gang-related drug trade sound more futile than it actually was. Leaving this aside, I pressed him on why he thought even some of the would-be ballplayers sold drugs and "cut" so many classes. Again, he needed very little time to think about an answer and the look on his face implied that he found my question a bit absurd. " 'Cause they wanna be thugs. It's that thug life man, come on. I mean I know a couple dudes that got kids and stuff. But most of these niggaz just wanna be all tight wit' they little thugged out homies. They want that quick cash . . . the gear, the honies [especially attractive girls]. You know, man, they wanna come to school rockin' some new shit [wearing new clothes, jewelry, footwear] . . . take these bitches shoppin'. They just wanna get they thug on." [Pause] "These niggaz ain't thinkin' about no next report card and no coach tellin' them they can't play type shit."

At least in his talk with me, Thomas belittled "thugs" and what he saw as their clearly identifiable and interrelated sets of strategies based on petty friendships. But he also seemed alive to the allure of what he thought "they" were doing. I had come to see that—at least on certain occasions—this type of half-chiding, half-respectful "othering" discourse was commonly deployed. And I got a better sense about why all of this mattered to Thomas when he went on to talk about his future plans. He said he wanted to graduate at the end of the year, attend a "JUCO [junior college] for a year or two," and then move on to a "big time D-1" (Division I) college and basketball program. He evidently planned to take his "wife" (steady girlfriend) to the "middle of nowhere" where they "could jus' go to school" and he "could jus' work on [his] game."

Whether his long-term plans were realistic or not, at least in situations like the one we were in after the workout, Thomas came across as a somewhat levelheaded if not completely calm young man capable of (talking about) using a good deal of foresight. Thomas was not considered at all "nerdy" and he rarely mingled with students labeled in this way. On the other hand, Thomas was rarely found among the "ghetto fabulous" or "(hard-core) thugs."[9] It made perfect sense to me that this unpretentious "baller" usually blended into the neutral backdrop of bland interaction rituals when he was not on the hardwood, and that while talking to me he seemed to want nothing more than to keep away from the "thug life."

I was therefore surprised, a few months later, to find Thomas very much in the spotlight on one of Johnson's main venues.[10] It was the day after Thomas had played quite well in a meagerly attended game in Johnson's gym and he had—I assumed—been invited to hang out with the boys perched at the top of the steps leading up to the main entrance.[11] Grassy knolls on both sides of the steps seemed to pack more or less distinct bundles of students together. The quieter, less loudly (and expensively) dressed students were hovering around each other closer to the bottom of the steps, toward the point at which the front gate met the sidewalk. The loose assemblages of more rowdy and fashionably (i.e., "fabulously") dressed teens occupied posts closer to the main entrance. It was as if those with the flashy clothes, trendy shoes, shiny jewelry, and more aggressive (and otherwise striking) comportment were positioned higher up on the social ladder.

So there was Thomas, if only for a few moments, "on top of the world." The much shorter boys encircling the long-limbed "baller" appeared to be, as the expression went, "big dawgs." Next to the flamboyantly and copiously clad students at the plateau between the top of the steps and the main entrance, that is, Thomas seemed to be wearing rather drab and base "gear." Thomas's "hosts" wore wider jeans as well as thicker and flashier coats, in some cases pulled off the shoulders perhaps for extra "puffy" effect. As if to leave no doubt about their specific—and at once individual as well as collective—identity *claims*, several of the boys seeming to hold court high above the majority of other students flashed their gang-related color.[12] It went without saying that they did this in ways boys like Thomas never would (e.g., red baseball caps, red bandanas either around the head or hanging outside a back pocket). But that the boys encircling Thomas felt more "at home" in the epicenter of this rambling ritual was expressed above all through their confident "gangster leans" and other "techniques of the body" (Mauss 1973).

Alongside those appearing to be "open"[13] and to "really have it going on," Thomas's facial expression and body language were as colorless as his jacket and jeans. Seeming to sense his wobbly place among those presenting themselves as the few, the proud, and the sexy, Thomas hunched over a bit and made no expansive movements. Indeed his relatively flaccid and closed-down bearing seemed to indicate that he was ready to be sent away at any time.[14] Flanking this towering example of humble submission made flesh, the other boys' *ease*—i.e., their mix of "street" flavored macho exuberance and stylized (if not studied) detachment—was essential. From universally understood signals such as the "flashing" of the gang color associated with "The Bloods" to comparatively more rhythmic, loose, aggressive, and quasi-sexualized gestures (punching the air, bumping fists, holding the crotch, raising hands high in the air before offering "pounds" [handshakes] and hugs climaxing in simultaneous slaps on the back), "everything" communicated who did and who did not fully belong in the spotlight. For any of those socialized into the ways of the Johnson High world, it would have been hard not to see that the tall, halting figure was somewhat out of place.

Even in such a "fabulous" crowd, one boy seemed to jump out. Although according to local definitions most of the boys occupying the highly observable observation posts appeared to be "black" (as opposed to, for example, "African"[15]), the most ostentatiously decked out and seemingly radiant presence within the loosely marked-off "roughneck" company was Enrique, an English-speaking boy with (I assume) either Dominican or Puerto Rican roots.[16] Along with a gold chain that reached down to his low hanging and extra-baggy pants, this boy "getting his thug on" kept his hair parted in the middle and made sure his long braids remained visible on either side of his head. Such attention grabbing braids, sometimes covered by an enormous red Yankees cap that went over his ears, had rather definite meanings in this public space. As alluded to above, in this context the red baseball cap announced allegiance to the most prominent (and predominantly black) gang. Especially to those more deeply embedded in networks of slightly older "gangsters" who supposedly "moved kilos" and undeniably "rolled together" in colossal SUV's, the trendy hairstyle was an unambiguous sign of "street" aristocratic refinement. This boy's bodily capital, his sophisticated aesthetic sensibilities, the other (expensive) distinction granting symbols such as his new Timberlands and, most fundamentally, his confident "ghetto fabulous" carriage all indicated that he had what more "normal" (or, as Roxanne put it, "good") kids like Thomas—black as he may have been (perceived to be)—"naturally" lacked.

For a reason I have yet to discuss, especially for the typically inconspicuous and gentle-mannered giant, the high profile experience must have been quite gripping. Even if the window of opportunity would soon shut, to be at the top of the heap and among those performing (and all but forced to take each other seriously as) the really "real niggaz" must have had quite an impact because, as "everyone" knew, things often turned threatening if not violent in such "hot spots." In other words, everyone involved sensed that such (subsettings within) sprawling face-to-face encounters could quickly charge-up volatile and sporadically brutal emotions.[17] Perhaps in part for this reason, my eyes were drawn away from the masses positioned closer to the sidewalk and toward those presenting themselves as a distinct group of "big-money players."

Not surprisingly perhaps, a cluster of flamboyantly dressed and highly animated girls was positioned next to "bad" boys.[18] Without getting too close to each other or to the boys atop the steps, the girls signaled strong affinity with each other and with the "thugged out" overseers. It seemed "natural" that the girls spatially and symbolically closest to those presenting themselves as "pimps and thugs" would have the "tightest" (e.g., most color-coordinated and revealing) outfits, the most stylish haircuts,[19] the most expensive shoes, the shiniest "bling" (e.g., jewelry, watches), and the "loudest" postures. This indicated that, whether handsome and well-built or not, the *kind* of boys who felt comfortable standing around atop the steps had monopolies on the "fly girl" attracting rituals, symbols, and embodied ways of being. Because in part of the proximity of those manifesting as "fly girls," that is, these boys collectively enacted their school's versions of hegemonic masculinity.

So while I began with the boys, this gender-based perspective might just as well be turned on it its head. We might say, that is, that the pinnacle of adolescent manliness had to be on display, and that the boys were forced to "get their thug on," because those effectively claiming the status of "fly girls" were "getting their groove on" in an equally discernible subspace. Either way, it was "on" just in front of the school's main entrance in large part because what was up for grabs in this attention focusing and street-legitimacy reinforcing interaction was the sense that one "naturally" belonged in the cliques constituting the "hottest" males and females. To belong was to have a "hot" self. And the "real" belonged on top in part because, on countless occasions such as this one, the supposedly less "hot" were made to feel that they were less manly and womanly.[20] Those who did not "truly" belong were regularly identified as "fake"—or at least less "real"—and, therefore, as "jealous" (e.g., "player haters").

Here as elsewhere, racial and ethnonational categories certainly came into play alongside those related to gender and sexuality. Most of the girls making up the group adjacent to the boys at the summit "looked black" as opposed to "Spanish," and all involved looked more like native-born New Yorkers than newcomers. They sounded more typically "black" and/or native-born than, say, Panamanian, Trinidadian, or Ghanaian. Yet those positioned as the lowly masses of girls and boys, no matter how they might be labeled racially, were nowhere to be found in the (overlapping) social circles effectively forming high society. And being perceived to be authentically black did not make any girl "fly." There were girls judged to be "fly" who were not categorized as black, and for every black girl near the top of the steps there were at least five black girls literally forced to look up to her. When two girls in skin tight jeans, worshiped for their sex appeal and "street credibility," stood out from the crowd next to the "gangbangers," whether one was deemed a "butter pecan Puerto Rican" and the other a "brown-skinned" girl from "Down South" mattered less than the diverse forms of capital and senses of ease they brought to the encounter and the emotional payoff and symbolic capital they derived from embodying "flyness" in the limelight.[21]

All in all, one did not have to follow any of the verbal exchanges to grasp that, with the possible exception of Thomas's comparatively timid presence, nothing terribly unusual seemed to be taking place within the "fabulous" summit. As usual in such routinized encounters, the short-term success of the "real playaz" was based on getting "juiced" by simply showing up and fitting in. Whether keeping "cool" or getting "heated" themselves, comfortably and conspicuously taking up space *together* in such a "hot spot" was, most basically, what was going on. Authentic fitting in with "All Eyez on Me"[22]—or, better yet, on "us" rather than on the underlings—was enough to temporarily reinforce fantasies of separateness and superiority. Those appearing to be friends and positioned as the more dominant—largely by virtue of the (collective valuation of) portfolios of capital that could be brought into play on such occasions—acted as if they took for granted that they belonged together among the chosen few and that they would remain forever distanced from those held in comparatively low regard if not ignored completely.

Here we get to the crux of the matter: nothing unusual seemed to be going on because "everything" had been normalized previously. Just as we don't usually take note of people using doorknobs to open doors, the gendered and gendering practices of, and the somewhat racialized perspectives on (or ways of making sense of), social cleavages were always already part of the taken for granted background understandings that all the experienced insiders shared. More broadly, everyone slid seamlessly in his or her role because everything that went on followed the "fabulous" fantasy script. With what Schutz called "stocks of knowledge" already drilled into the students' collectivized mental habits, none of the students needed to stop and think about relationships between those on top and students occupying positions toward the middle or lower steps. In Goffmanian language, nothing even threatened to break the dominant *frame* (i.e., the set of mental schemas, prediscursive background understandings) that all the variously positioned insiders had already come to share. So it was just another moment in just another day in the old neighborhood school. The same "routine, every-day," as Roxanne put it. The same types of group-remaking, worldview-reinforcing, and stratification-reproducing ceremonies and responses effectively formed something like links in a chain.

So "everybody" already knew (without consciously thinking about it) that boys *like* Enrique belonged in the elevated social positions where students *like* Thomas could, at best, temporarily pay their respects. The distinguishing jeans, jewelry, gold-capped teeth, and "gangster lean" of the objectively more empowered were all outwardly visible signs of something of fundamental importance to students attending Johnson High: the typically more dominant students' emotionally rewarding self/group image. So passing from one "thugged out" encounter to the next refocused and recharged the relevant symbols, fellowship feelings, and fantasy ideals. At the same time, the "top dawgs" sense of group charisma was reinforced by ways of *not* interacting with (or even getting close to) less-powerful students and their less-invigorated transactions. Without the many pupils modestly humming around beneath or scurrying past the hot spots, everyday life at Johnson would have been radically different for those who imagined themselves to be the "living large niggaz in charge." Those masquerading on one of the school's ceremonial high grounds pulled off presentations of themselves as members of superior and indeed quasi-consecrated *kinds* of students. The boys and girls positioned and predisposed to temporarily do Johnson High's version of "ghetto fabulous" *seemed* to represent the inherently "real," the forever "hot" students and cliques who deserved to go on "holdin' shit down." While it was not completely clear whether those cast into subordinate roles (at times) longed to climb Johnson's adolescent tower of prestige, what I saw coming up the steps was why very few of them could have achieved this feat. No matter what their ascribed backgrounds, those effectively locked out of high profile exchanges were all but forced to let go of any lofty ambitions they may have at times had.

I offered no more than a reverential nod as I "confidently" made my way past the "roughneck" mini-scene and through the giant doors of the main entrance.[23] Then, as the ripples gradually subsided inside an empty hallway, instead of thinking about how thrilling the event must have been for

Thomas, I starting wondering if he would he get "distracted"? Was he start-ing to get caught up in the "thug life"? My mind was returning to what felt like an original, calm state. Then the bell rang.

Less than a month later, as fate would have it, I had a chance to talk to Thomas about, among other things, hanging out with the "thugs." The op-portunity emerged after I covered one of Thomas's classes. Standing at the doorway as the other students left, I asked Thomas if I could ask him some-thing. Thomas agreed and sat down in the chair behind the teacher's desk. I sat in one of the student's desk/chair units facing the board.[24] I should have asked Thomas about how he had been brought into, and how he later took leave of, that memorable scene at the top of the steps. My focus, however, was at once broader and narrower: his safety in the future. I asked him whether or not he was starting to mix it up more frequently with the types of boys he had said he planned to avoid. Thomas responded initially by shrugging his shoulders and speaking in a low-key voice. He offered assur-ances that he was not getting caught up in any dangerous webs of relation-ships. Then, allowing himself to get increasingly worked up, and as if to yet again explain both the appeal of the "thug life" and why he was resisting it, he said the following: "Look, all these dudes wanna like scare bitches into likin' them. And the girls are stupid too, they stay messin' around with all these gangsters, you know what I'm sayin'?" I nodded and he continued. "I'm not trying to do that," he said, waving his hand in a way that suggested disdain. Then he went on, with increasing cadence, "But watch, when I get to college, yo. I'm gonna be long-dickin' these hoes lef' and right." At this he jumped up and pretended to be penetrating the backside of a "hoe" bent over the teacher's desk—his hips going way back away from and then very close to the pretend body.

Graphic and highly ritualized performances of thugged out manliness were hardly new to me by this point. But this was *not* the Thomas I had come to know. I can only speculate as to whether or not my questions con-fronted Thomas with the feeling that he occupied a less than superior posi-tion within the school's sexualized social hierarchy. It seemed, however, that by pushing the comparison with the "hardest of the hard" I may have triggered within Thomas a mix of excitement and a need to recapture a sense of manly pride.

Be this as it may, in many secondary school mini-societies this tall and athletic senior might have been deemed dating material for the most sought-after girls. In a school in which cheerleaders revved up those packed into gyms to see basketball games, he might have found himself in an en-vironment offering steady chances to present himself as an alpha male. But at Johnson, basketball games were failed rituals. And off the court, in and around his school, Thomas and his buddies could not compete with the perpetually recharged and refocused networks of boys who tended to indeed "run things." Thomas came off as a poorly dressed, hushed up, hunched over nonentity—a "bitch-ass nigga" or, as the saying went, "nobody but a body." In this world (of routinized mini-events), this beta male was defined by what he lacked. In mimicking one of the hegemonic "pimp and thug" performances of masculinity, he seemed to be expressing his at once socially situated frustration and embodied desire for a better "self."

Kim: Fitting In, Winning Now

[You] can tell the real by how they interact.[25]

On a cold, drizzly February morning a girl named Kimberly made her way toward Delta's main entrance. I was a couple of steps behind her, and there were about twenty other students ahead of us trying to get into the school's main entrance. As we shuffled toward the crowded doorway, six or seven boys and girls standing beneath a part of the building that jutted out onto the playground formed a semicircle a few yards from the main entrance. As we made our way forward, I could see almost precisely from her perspective how the welcoming looks and body language (e.g., the orientation of feet and shoulders) of these more boisterous and loudly dressed students off to the side seemed to say, "Hey, Kim, join us." Veering suddenly to the left and away from the masses, Kim joined the more exclusively adorned party (which probably entailed being late to, or missing altogether, her class).

Easing away for just a moment might be useful at this stage. Kim might have been just another child of one of Amsterdam's most depressed and stigmatized neighborhoods at the shopping center ten minutes away. But Kim's older brother, who also attended Delta, was universally understood to be an especially hardnosed "gangster." Given the structuring of this quasi-bounded social microcosm, given the symbolic power (prestige) and embodied cultural capital ("fabulous" know-how, skills, practical feel for how to cope, second nature) she brought to the game—and especially given her brother's established position within it—she was "logically" granted full access to the interaction rituals of those presenting themselves as members of the school's "fabulous" power elite. Her rank, or at least her potential to make what were generally considered upwardly mobile moves, was acknowledged in this world. Changing direction suddenly, one might say,

Kim entered the ceremonial core of a larger interaction ritual including all of us who were visible inside the gates of the school but outside the building. Veering off to the right, I pretended to read an announcement posted to the side of the entrance.

So there we were, running late to class and standing in the drizzle. Even though I had already spent over two years in and around Delta by this point, I felt I had to observe just a bit more of this encounter before going inside. In part this was because one of the pupils off to the left of the entrance, Marvin, was in one of my classes. (He also happened to be on the way to prison on drug charges, although I did not know this at the time.) Marvin was preparing a tobacco and marijuana (or hashish) cigarette concoction. The rolled-up piece of hard paper he was going to use as a makeshift filter was prominently displayed between his lips and to the side of his mouth. He had a large North Face–style down jacket on with the hood pulled over his head. His light blue (and seemingly oversized) boots matched the sweater under his puffy coat. He wore gold everywhere, as usual: capped on two of his teeth, a chain outside his sweater, rings on several of his fingers. Legs spread apart slightly more than one would have thought necessary, his large white wrapping paper was highly visible as well. He wanted people to see him preparing to get high instead of going to class. He was, as students literally said in the Netherlands, "doing gangster" (*gangster doen*, a variant of *stoer doen* or, roughly, acting "bad ass").

Remaining outside in the chilly and damp air might have looked rather pathetic to many of the pupils trying to enter the school. But certainly those on line took note of the torchbearer flanked by several other boys and girls generally considered to be more domineering types. Marvin was the star of some kind of show. And there would have been no spotlight were it not for those cast in supporting roles, no stage were it not for the more passive roles played by members of the audience.

Marvin appeared concentrated as he began filling up the wrapping paper with the contents headed for his lungs when, simultaneously, Kim and a few of the other co-stars started laughing quite vigorously. At once, Marvin stopped what he was doing, stood up straight, bellowed out a respectfully exaggerated "Noooooooooo!," and offered an elbow (he was already using both his hands) so as to praise the boy who had made the others laugh. This reinforced several things, including the volume of the laughter.[26]

Such a stretched out "No" was usually reserved to express mock indignation at a moral transgression (and often combined with *"Mi godo"* [Surinamese for "Oh my God"]). I assumed, therefore, that the energy star was pretending to be shocked by how the butt of the joke had been scandalized. The content of what was being said mattered, but the delivery of the overall message was perhaps most poignantly expressed through the expansive posture and lithe movements of the boy in the middle of it all. "Open," as the kids in the Bronx might have said, Marvin initiated body contact in a graceful expression of support for the joke teller while at the same time reclaiming more of the limited attention supply. I was watching a smooth, confident, fun-loving "gangster" performance that almost certainly made co-stars feel themselves part of something special. Marvin's seemingly effortless multitasking evidenced his feel for the game—i.e., a keen sense for how to "score" in such micro-level transactions as well as a practical understanding of his established position in the overall scheme of things. Right down to his self-assured, felicitous, and rhythmic gesturing, the ostentatious joint-roller seemed to embody the role of the "true player" (as he liked to say in English[27]), helping others learn to become marijuana smokers (cf. Becker 1953). Like a well-trained athlete reenergized by being pushed to the fore and getting "into the zone" in the midst of an ongoing competition, his strategic move taking did not require a great deal of explicit thought or planning.[28]

As such, and this is crucial, Marvin *seemed* to be permanently charismatic independent of any shifting external conditions.[29] In reality this "social smoker" needed the spotlight to feel the "right" kind of "high."[30] Nevertheless we can see, I hope, why a strong feeling of group charisma may have become salient for Marvin as well as for Kim—and why a practical sense of authentically belonging to an inherently superior set of students would appear to be independent of anything going on in the immediate encounter. The myth of misplaced concreteness was well founded.

Passing by such "fabulous" peer group (re-)making performances in and just outside Delta, I regularly witnessed students judged to be worthy of high levels of respect offering exuberant greetings to one or more protagonists.[31] Those viewed in such situations as more or less "regular kids" tended to offer at most faint salutations or nods to those soaking up the (collective) "props."[32] What I very rarely observed were those classified during such moments (especially) by the likes of Marvin and Kim as the least powerful "nobodies" saying anything in the direction of grandstanding students. I could not observe those effectively labeled "nerds" get shot down by group/interaction boundary "policing" insiders, that is, because the students typecast along these lines almost never tried to get involved in high status, high visibility performances.

It seemed that Kim "knew" how to stand in relation to the high status others. But it also seemed that doing this required no more conscious thought than the adjustments made by middle class adults clustering around someone telling a captivating story at a cocktail party. Just six months into her first year of secondary school and effectively snatched out of a state of relative indifference, she was already in Delta's "in crowd," and the "in crowd" was already in her.

With so much access to friends in high places, it was not difficult to keep an eye on Kim after observing this encounter. I was able to engage her in a conversation only once, but it seemed to me that this single conversation with Kim was enough. Our dialogue began after one of her friends walked away from her. They had been talking about Kim's shiny new shoes. I asked her about these shoes, first, and then about her new friends and what she thought of her new school. She said she "just liked pink a lot," so she chose to wear it. Motioning to some of the more animated students in the big open space in which we sat (i.e., the "*aula*," see below), she added that she "just liked" hanging out with the "normal kids." With a mix of scorn and being "above it all," she said that she did "not feel at home" around "other kinds of kids." She said she liked her new school because her old one was "so boring and full of fake little kids." In Delta, she said, "there is at least always *something* going on." When I asked if contact with these "normal kids" and all the stuff continually "going on" influenced her grades she looked at me, directly and seriously, and said she would never let that happen.

I also asked one of Kim's teachers and few of her fellow students what they thought of her and her future trajectory. Most of my observations and nearly all of the reports I got from the people I spoke to supported the same conclusion: Kim would continue to hang out with those she and many others saw, most of the time, as Delta's jet set. As the teacher put it, "Kim? Oh, you don't want her [in your class] next year." Another female student switched to an exaggeratedly "street" way of bobbing her head when she commented on Kim: "She comes to school to show off her clothes, I'm telling you. She just got here and she already thinks she's high and mighty [literally, in Dutch, "higher than other children"]. She's going to end up just like Dread" (i.e., her brother, who got this nickname because of his beautifully groomed yet "rough" looking locks).

Dread and I had seen each other around for years.[33] One day after school I asked him what he thought would—and should—happen to his sister now that she was in his school. He seemed to have no problems answering questions about his sister and we started talking as we walked slowly behind a few other boys headed for the Bijlmer's main shopping center. Dread began by saying that Kim should "just act normal." After a little prompting he went on to say that by this phrase, which his sister had also used, he meant things like avoiding conflicts, going to class, getting good grades, and "staying away from the criminals."[34] Mentioning that a teacher had told me Kim was quite disruptive in her class, I asked him whether he thought his sister bought into this pro-school vision. "She knows what she has to do, and she better just go to class and act normally (*gewoon normaal doen*)," he repeated. I followed up by asking whether such behavior befitted a young man such as himself. "Sure," he said, as if he did not understand why I would be asking one of the most feared and disruptive students in the school such a question.

As we walked further, both the character of the interaction and Dread's prognostication for his sister started to change. Dread starting talking about how no one would bother Kimberly because everyone knew what would happen after school if they did (as he said this he pretended to break something over his knee). I asked if this support meant that Kim could, therefore, hang out with "criminals" without putting herself at risk. Seeming uninterested in my question Dread went on to say that he was "afraid of no one" in his school. He looked forward, he claimed, to being physically challenged by someone who was more or less on his "level." After running through a list of especially formidable-looking boys, he added that he would "really like to fight" a boy named Jurgen (an extremely formidable and aggressive boy who will reappear in two of the coming chapters). "We would make a pretty even match," Dread declared, "and I haven't fought him yet." At this one of the boys walking ahead of us told Kim's brother to shut his mouth (implying that Dread wanted no piece of the mightily built Jurgen). This led to some ritual shoving and yelling ("Go ahead and punch me, punch me!"), some chest bumping, a stare down, and finally a stress-releasing mock knee to the midsection from Dread, which made a few boys laugh.

Things mellowed quickly, but Dread remained noticeably more stirred up than he had been at the outset of our conversation. "See . . . they just talk but never throw any punches because they are all *bitches* [in English]," he said rather dejectedly. Trying to bring it back to his sister (and perhaps help Dread get out of thugged out masculinity overdrive and egoistic trance) I mentioned that I had seen Kim hanging out with some of the more "criminal" types. "Of course (in Dutch *natuurlijk*, naturally) Kim's going to be hanging out with kids like that," Dread shot back, "What did you expect (*wat dacht je dan*)?"

While revved up, "thugged out" thoughts found their way to Dread's tongue easily. And indeed, what should we expect? The door was flung wide open and Kim was probably going to continue walking through it. Without romanticizing we can say that by allowing herself to be caught up in Delta's "fabulous" everyday encounters this girl born into a poorly educated family in a highly stigmatized Dutch neighborhood often managed to smile, to enjoy a good belly laugh, to be part of something she considered beautiful and energizing. And to understand the appeal of specific "hot" friendships and interaction rituals is to see them against the broader backdrop of shared understandings about the positions and practices of putatively more charismatic individuals and status groups. Ignoring the call of the "wild" would have required an extraordinary amount of emotional self-discipline and foresight based, as we shall see in Chapter 5, on the types of experiences and relationships that very few young people attending high-poverty schools have.

Feeling High and Feeling Low

You see him over there? He's fabulous because he's such a pretty boy. And you see him, the muscular one? He's fabulous because everybody knows that he'll just punch you in the face. After that he might start to think about whether or not he should have punched you. Everybody in here knows that what I am saying is true—even if they do like to pretend they're not afraid of him (stoer doen).[35]

Yes, the strong gets more, while the weak ones fade.[36]

The area immediately surrounding the façade of a small store constituted the liveliest "hot spot" inside the Delta School. This storefront window opened up into the *"aula,"* the large space that served as cafeteria and auditorium in one.[37] The greater part of this open space (roughly twenty-by-thirty yards) was a sunken area, usually half-filled with chairs and tables, just about three feet below the surrounding walkway onto which the storefront opened. Especially during the two half-hour breaks that all the students and staff enjoyed (or endured) simultaneously, but also during the regular periods of instruction, students flooded into the *aula*.[38] The original idea was that during breaks *all* the kids would get (junk) food at the store and then sit, together, at the tables in the sunken area. This is not how things panned out. Certain students never sat at the tables in the sunken area, others could be found there regularly. And almost perpetually throughout each day, it

was around the storefront—and never down below—that Delta's most ostentatious group-making experiences and boundary-policing performances
took place.

These great performances had to do with the consumption of music as
well as food—the two mainstays of successful parties in the Bijlmer. Next
to the storefront was a soft-drink machine with a colorful Fernandez (a
Surinamese soft drink) display. This soft-drink dispenser was regularly
used—often by three or even four boys at a time—as a collective drum. The
area just outside the store was typically soused, therefore, with different
kinds of Surinamese, Antillean, R&B, (Jamaican) dancehall, and hip-hop
beats. Almost every hour of every school day, those participating in quasi-
autonomous mini-events emerging around the storefront engaged in singing, rhyming, gesturing, or otherwise moving more or less in unison as
rhythms poured out of the enormous makeshift drum.[39] "Coincidently"
lounging around and striking (or trying to strike) "cool poses"[40] right next
to where the most intense action was—but never ending up in the pit—
constituted a well-established accompanying practice. Those that could
appear to be mere spectators functioned as a buffer, or border, for those
making up the inner circle in the area directly around the storefront.

What might be described as the "muscular bonding"[41] rituals in the heart
of this semi-enclosed section of the *aula* were constituted almost exclusively
by more expensively dressed and distinctly "street"-styled boys (who, for example, often kept their heads covered with various types of hats and hoods
although administrators and some teachers were forever waging campaigns
to halt such practices) and comparatively loud and revealingly dressed
girls (who never participated in the drumming, but would at times sing
or dance). Of course students who did not appear to fit in the "fabulous"
frame sometimes ventured up to the store to get snacks. Through their docile demeanors, however, they almost always communicated that they were
there only to make a quick purchase—and that they certainly would not be
hanging out where they did not belong.

The conversations that arose in this spatially elevated, high energy sub-
setting tended not to be about things like homework or future tests. Various
types of jokes, "hard" looks, screams of delight, (mock) threats, distinctively
"gangster" posturing, and laughter were *de rigueur*. The rhetorical worship
of flashy outfits and jewelry, aggressive talk, and anti school sounding utterances ("Come on, let's take off, you don't need to go to your last class!")
were nearly constant.[42] The practices associated with those classified as
"nerds" or otherwise "*neppe kinderen*" (literally "fake children") were almost
never discussed. And here, often against the backdrop of loud beats—and

in many cases borrowing common refrains from American hip-hop songs or R&B videos—"fabulous" group-making "moral entrepreneurs" (Becker 1963) deployed discourses based on the right and wrong kinds of practices, symbols, and collectivities.[43]

Especially in the middle of the school day, the events emerging around the storefront served to reinforce various kinds of potential power resources. On muddled lines leading to the shop keepers' window, the boys judged to be weak (and weakly connected) were frequently elbowed out of the way or "hustled" for sandwich money by more aggressive and typically larger boys. Some girls showed off their clothes or proudly communicated that no one would dare flirt with them at such a venue; other girls were talked down the hall and into the bathroom to be fondled. It was here that I most regularly observed students being slapped around or pounded with fists in front of throngs of their peers. In other words, things could quickly turn ugly if not vicious on this staging area. Seeing a pupil punched or slapped (repeatedly) in front of an especially significant audience—but also various kinds of flirting, grandstanding, and teasing—spelled out unmistakably that at least in such settings the power to dominate was at once material, symbolic, and distributed in radically unequal ways. So it was in this high-energy area that individual reputations were cemented, that visions of social divisions were crystallized, and that the benefits of "truly" belonging among Delta's version of the "street" aristocracy were most vividly brought to life.

The closer one got to the storefront, the more one came face to face with dark complexions. Those categorized as black (e.g., students of Afro-Surinamese and Afro-Antillean ancestry) were overrepresented in and right around this spot. The further one moved into the sunken area the more one was surrounded by students with lighter complexions who, generally speaking, were not said to be–and who did not self-identify as–black. Pupils categorized ethnically as, for example, Hindustani[44] or Dutch were over-represented in the pit. As such, whether one believes that separate races actually exist or not, it was plain to see why racialized ways of understanding were often made salient in this relatively autonomous setting. In part for this reason those familiar with what went on in the *aula* could hardly escape sensing the mutual constitution of racial and social status orders or, in Carter's (2005) terms, the perpetual reblackening of locally dominant forms of cultural capital.

Here again, however, seeing that the curse we call race came into play does not imply overlooking what was experienced as most important most of the time: being "fabulous" rather than "fake." Many of the students relegated to the pit were categorized as (and indeed self-identifying as) black;

and significant numbers of those assumed to belong quite "naturally" in elite social circles were not. In terms of the most frequently and powerfully mobilized principles of social divisions, skin colors, and (ascribed) ethno-national backgrounds tended to be of secondary importance because those said to be "true players" were those who seemed effortlessly to embody the right stuff—especially in such heated spaces. One student indirectly expressed what we might call the *poise over pigment* principle[45] when he discussed access- and practical belong-related issues without even mentioning ethnicity or skin tone: "Look, a nerd could make a big attempt (*poging*) and try to come up to us all dressed up, with a slick hairstyle and all that [the speaker swung his shoulders in an exaggerated and clumsy mock "street" way]. But they just made things worse for themselves. Everybody knew they just didn't have it. [Laughs] . . . So it was like a joke . . . [in a mocking voice] "Hey, check out your friend in the new jeans?" [Big smile] The G-Star jeans were not going to help this kid, you know what I mean?"[46]

How did this microcosm of the Delta world look to those viewing it from the bottom? Of course there were exceptions to the rule. The cloud that usually hung over those in the sunken area did, at times, lift and disperse. The views expressed "down under" could be as multifaceted, fragmented, and contradictory as those observed "on top." There were joyous moments in the pit just as the storefront area could be low key and civil. Having noted this, the occasion depicted below was in many ways representative and, I believe, revealing.

Since we met on the Delta's basketball court, I had carried on a few brief and rather superficial conversations with a smallish boy named Levi—one of the few students with roots in the Antilles who had very pale skin. I felt I could join Levi's table in part because of these informal exchanges and because there was an empty chair between him and a mild-mannered and dark-skinned boy named Marcus whom I had had in a class. Levi and Marcus were sitting at a table with two other students whom I'd seen around for years but did not know. Taken by Levi's perplexed expression and the melancholy demeanor of his associates, I asked Levi if I could have a seat and what was bothering him.

Rather glumly and in hushed tones, Levi recalled a string of threatening and humiliating incidents. In his retelling, the screaming of threats in corridors, the taunting in stairwells, and the disrupting of classrooms was nearly constant. Then, looking over toward the students congregating around the storefront, he declared, "I think the teachers are afraid of them." Although he may not have felt comfortable admitting that *he* was intimidated, it seemed clear that he meant *even* the teachers were afraid of the generally more aggressive students stationed above us.

After proposing that the teachers (too) were afraid of "them," Levi paused and looked at his tablemates, inviting them into the conversation. A couple of them nodded, nothing more. With beats and occasional shouts emanating from the storefront area scarcely audible above the other sounds ricocheting through the *aula*, Marcus did not seem to have enough energy to make himself heard. He just stared somewhat blankly at us and then at the bread crusts littered on the flattened roll of aluminum foil that was his plate. Unable to mobilize those directly around him, Levi launched into a few more examples of the kinds of menacing outbursts that seemed to perturb him. Each of his stories led unmistakably to the same conclusion: "They"—and "their" frequently threatening behavior—kept bothering him and (implicitly) "us," but "the teachers" dared not even try, in any kind of wholehearted or concerted way, to intervene. The narrative seemed to be depressing the other students further, perhaps because they too had heard it many times.

Clearly, Levi did not feel at all intimidated by the others at his table. No one did, as I had come to understand, because no matter how dark their complexions or how they might be grouped along ethnic lines, his friends tended to be utterly nonaggressive. The problem was "them." The problem was what Levi saw an essentially different and clearly identifiable band of belligerent *others*. What was for the ethnographer an illusion—the illusion of separateness, or misplaced concreteness—was, for Levi, a simple and positively known fact. He existed, he was vulnerable, and he was not a thug. They and their kind were, above all, threatening. The unquestionable truth of clearly distinct and permanently separate groups of students was based right in the minutiae of Levi's moment-to-moment and day-to-day experience. And Levi could not figure out why adults working in his school allowed "them" to generate so much fear. "Why don't they [the adults] do anything to get control over this place?," Levi asked at a certain point.

Silence. Marcus and the others at the table occasionally looked up at Levi or at me, but that was it. Certainly there was no attempt to in any-way dispute the evidence, verdict, or accusatory questions articulated by the speaker (and aimed, to some degree, at me). But the silence of those at the table may have been communicating something even more profound than Levi's words. To come back to the native term heard in the Bronx much more frequently than in the Bijlmer, none of Levi's tablemates seemed even slightly "open." Hunched over, sagging, and somewhat caved in, their bodies seemed to be repositories of the social experiences they were—and, by this point, had for years been—going through. I cannot say whether or not they were reduced to hunkering down because they knew there could be no hopeful responses to Levi's group-making claims and poignant questions. What I can report is that none of them were smiling. With their shoulders turned inwards and their heads oriented downwards, it seemed they did not wish to take it all in. These were not postures that expressed self-worth or even being fully present and awake.

Though Levi and Marcus's tables could have been used as a drum, they did not practice pounding out beats. At our table and those around it, there was little movement and certainly no rhythmic, synchronized movement of any kind. There was no song, no dance. No one screamed threats, paraded new outfits, or came off as being terribly sexy. No one made refined moves with makeshift footballs (soda cans, balls of paper), nor did anyone seem to be very athletic or graceful. When they told jokes and laughed, they did so without any expansive gestures. Indeed because of their unassuming postures, meek movements, and restrained ways of covering their bodies (e.g., less loud colors, no puffy winter coats, no hats or hoods), the students such as Levi's tablemates seemed even smaller than they actually were. In part because of how they were viewed from above, the dulled down physical postures of Levi's friends seemed to contribute to their depressing future prospects. The everyday poses of those sinking into their seats therefore looked like biologically based confirmation that the "nerds" and "fake kids" had, as the expression went, "no life." From the lived, carnally based perspectives of the teens making their way around the elevated area, going down into the bowels of the *aula* would have felt like hanging out with soulless corpses—and the students in the pit knew this to be the case.

Students such as Marcus were not comatose and, as Levi's comments illustrated, pupils classified from above as "nerds" were capable of offering rhetorical push back. But while everyone could do this under the right situational conditions—including, as we have seen, those categorized as "100% ghetto"—nobody did this in tones as muffled or with gestures as meek and dispirited as those occupying the lowest positions in this big open space. More importantly, even the humbled attempts at counter-stigmatization I observed in the pit (and similar sub-spaces) revealed deeply ingrained senses of actually being socially inferior. As one dejected pupil put it, "They just think they're like so high and mighty [*dat ze hooger zijn of zo*], but we're all the same . . . right?"[47] Even when during the very moments in which the pupils in the pit talked tough about what should happen in the future, that is, their body language revealed both here-and-now situational pressures and that the "pre-perceptive anticipations, a sort of practical induction based on previous experience . . . are the fact of the habitus as a feel for the game" (Bourdieu 1998, p. 80). Even their cognitive push back seemed to demonstrate that the wrong kind of feel for the game had made its way—and ossified—far beneath their skin.

Sitting in the depths of the *aula* (as well as hanging out in otherwise empty classrooms, and in various other mini-encounters devoid of typically more domineering types), I often heard even those appearing to be the lowliest of the "nerds" do their best to mimic the poses and ways of speaking they associated with their school's upper crust. As they typically appeared to be out of character "doing gangster," this was often done with hints of humor (e.g., in ways that, more or less explicitly, said "Ha, ha, I'm acting 'hard' now . . . but we all know that I'm not"). Occasionally however, among each other, those powerfully classified as "nerds" tried to make "street" happen with straight faces suggesting that being "hard" and "ghetto fabulous" was the shared, taken for granted ideal. More generally, within the least powerful social circles, the most "street" of the boys and girls often appeared to be the big fish in tiny ponds—and the butts of their jokes were also often dubbed "nerds" or "fake kids" in ways that imitated the expressions and movements of the typically more dominant. In brief, many of the (symbolically) less empowered students who duly filed into the places like the pit had internalized the very ways of thinking and feeling that oppressed them and facilitated the further devastation of their schools.

What's the main takeaway from our journey into the nether regions of this wide-open space? Being among themselves certainly helped those effectively locked out of elite social transactions deal with their exclusion. There was some mutual support if not admiration in the pit. But such reassurances of individual and collective self-worth from similarly downtrodden friends were unconvincing. The standing and seating "arrangements" in the *aula* always drove home what everyone involved already understood: the "nerds" formed the least powerful teams, they had no means of scoring, and there was no way for them to change the rules of the game they were forced to play. Switching to another set of native terms we might say that "the sweethearts" (*"schatjes,"* literally "little treasures"), as the teachers called the most docile and least disruptive students, were numerous and—certainly when combined with those often presented as (groups of) "normal kids" or "followers" (*"meelopers"*)—these "nondisruptive elements" formed numerical majorities. But in Delta, energy and symbolic power flowed upward and tended to remain with the few occupying the top positions. In the focused language of the students continually avoiding the pit and (willingly) getting themselves reimmersed in the most frenzied chains of events, the "nerds" were basically forced to feel like a clearly identifiable sort that had been both abandoned and crushed.

Unregulated Spaces, Harder Times

Oh hell yeah . . . he got it goin' on. He probably packin' too.[48]

Let us return now to areas in and around Johnson High such as the cafeteria, staircases, hallways, and sidewalks adjacent to the various official exits.[49] The typically tense moments students spent in these spaces offer clear insights into both the (symbolic) restructuring of the overall social game and the power of micro-level transactions. These were the places where extreme forms of physical violence emerged most regularly. But the vast majority of incidents involving physical affronts and indignities in these bottleneck and/or high visibility areas were comparatively "minor" pushes, slaps, and gropings. Half-full soda cans were thrown on people in stairwells, bundles of papers were knocked out people's hands in hallways, people were spit upon, etc. It became clear that even the "minor" incidents were charged with meaning when they unleashed piercing promises about somebody catching hell "next time."

Class changes provided the most visible examples. During the frantic moments between the sounding of the bells, packs of students often found each other almost as soon as they were released into the halls. Depending in part on where security guards (said to be more or less lenient or "cool") were stationed or absent, those presenting themselves (and recognizing each other) as "fly girls" clustered together and—in pretentious yet seemingly nonchalant manners (e.g., exaggerated movements of the hips)—made their ways over toward the well-known hot spots (e.g., a certain section of a certain floor, the part of the hallway adjacent to a specific stairwell). The boys who clustered and cruised over to these same (or adjacent) sub-spaces appeared to be "gangsters" deeply and durably committed to the "thug life." The macho bopping, screaming, (playful) threatening, beat-boxing, rapping, and "fabulous" gait of those daring to "get their thug on" in public immediately marked them off from those they characterized as "nobodies." Many of the boys and girls who did not perform "realness" in such ways during such intervals typically called as little attention to themselves as possible and certainly did not linger anywhere near the high energy and stress zones of "fabulous" temptation. Cliché or not, from the end of second or third period to the end of the fifth or sixth, when the halls were packed, stepping on shoes and offering "dirty looks" did lead to screamed threats if not actual physical confrontations (slaps, pushes, fistfights) somewhere in the school during nearly every class change. More importantly, perhaps—sometimes just seconds after the ringing of the period ending bell—mini-events or scenes based on the struggle to be "recognized" as a "genuine"[50] somebody emerged all over the school.

These recurring gatherings tended to last only between three to five minutes. In many cases, however, they stretched long into the next period or to the "decision" to cut the next class if not the rest of the school day.[51] Therefore, what went on in the halls and stairwells could propel students into "hot spots" like the cafeteria or out on to the streets. In short, with the scores of bodies packed together in the stairwells and hallways, there was always a distinct possibility not only that things could get "set off" in the school, but also that they could spill over into completely unsupervised areas (e.g., down the block and around the corner) outside the school.[52]

Some of the "hottest" displays of Johnsons' version of the "fabulous" life had to do with parking spots and, once again, music. Especially from around one-thirty to three-thirty in the afternoon, when students started to trickle or flood out of the building, those presenting themselves as "big time thugs" (who in some cases were ex-students and typically twenty- to twenty-five-years-old) parked tricked-out SUVs (which most teachers certainly could not afford) directly adjacent to several of Johnson High's side exits. The roughest of "gangsta" hip-hop lyrics and beats (e.g., the songs of Mobb Deep or early hits by Jay-Z, during my tenure in the Bronx) poured out of these enormous "trucks" when they lined up, usually one at a time, parallel to the long walk way running along the side of the old building.[53] This music was often audible in the hallways, where students would sometimes dance to it (if they did not dare to dance outside). This music could be not just audible but blaring in classrooms facing the sidewalk in question.[54] In part for this reason, the police often asked the people operating the mammoth vehicles to turn down the volume or move. But the volume soon went back up, and the vehicles either returned or were replaced by other, equally striking road machines. For the ethnographer, this added a strongly surreal element to daily life; for the teacher in me it could be extremely frustrating (except when the music was loud enough to cancel out even more annoying sound emanating from the ice-cream truck).

Especially once energy levels got jacked up in the early afternoon, those successfully striking the poses and occupying the positions of the more dynamic young "hustlers" (male)—and those of the more sought-after "honies" (female)—were effectively invited to sit in the colossal vehicles or at least to cluster around them. The girls who seemed to be considering "hustling the hustlers," as well as those who otherwise appeared drawn toward but not completely into the cores of the pulsating "hot spots" typically positioned themselves just outside the "fabulous" epicenters. When no vehicles supplied stentorian beats and melodies, the music that was heard often poured out from the tenement buildings surrounding the school. Sometimes two or more types (e.g., merengue and reggae) of loud music were audible at the same time. Additionally, the more assertive boys often made their own beats without drums (i.e., beat-boxing) while rocking their heads to and fro together as they became caught up in the rhythms they collectively produced. All those within the range of these flowing, sensual, and potentially explosive scenes felt the music and a great deal of singing and especially rapping was done in English, Spanish, "Spanglish," and Jamaican patois. For those coming into view as members of mutually oriented and "fabulous" cliques, at least, the difference between these "hot spots" and the droning meaninglessness of most classroom settings cannot be overemphasized.

In such buzzing subspaces, greetings were ethnically flavored and fused in more or less obvious ways (e.g., "What's poppin', kid?" "My nigga no bigga." "Que paso, mamacita?" "Pero tu sabe! Don't stop, sigue." "G'wan my yut!"). And as such verbalized salutations merged with ways of walking, leaning, and gesturing all involved immediately sensed, most importantly, who felt comfortable taking up space, soaking up attention, and initiating verbal contact in these high voltage settings. No matter how they might identify along ethnic or racial lines, the silence, the meek posturing and bland aesthetic practices of the most docile-looking students off to the margins seemed to indicate that they were not interested in the braggadocio of such "gangster" get-togethers. Rarely if ever greeting those in the spotlight while walking through the cafeteria or making their getaways at the end of the day, for example, the students not "getting their thug on" appeared to be nearly invisible. Those positioned, empowered, and in many cases durably predisposed in ways that made them look like "in-between" students generally found what felt like their kind and moved on (or kept a safe distance) without seeming to be entirely ignorant to the desirability of the kinetic energy unleashed in the cores of the hot spots. But for the more "ordinary kids" as well, "thugged out" greetings and all that went with them were basically ruled out and seemingly unthinkable.

In the interest of fleshing these ideas out further, I want to return to ways of speaking. If all the variously categorized students had been able to talk "propa," there would have been no advantage in it.[55] If this had been the case, ways of speaking would have been endowed with no more meaning than shoe sizes or knowledge of Plato's *Republic*. In reality, properly "ghetto fabulous" ways of speaking served as scarce and therefore distinguishing resources. This was not mainly because of the content of what was so often repeated in staging areas such as hallways (e.g., "I hate these fake-ass jealous bitches out here." "Everybody wanna player hate." "You know how we do! If you don't know you better act like you know, nigga!") but because of everything that came along with being able to speak "correctly." While I will come back to this in a moment, for starters here we might think ways of gesturing that communicated presence and composure, ways of avoiding embodied feelings of linguistic insecurity, and all the techniques of the body signaling affinities with those effectively claiming to be members of high-status groups such as rhythmic handshakes and hugs.[56]

With these points in mind we zoom in on Johnson's exit areas. The body language and ideas of students appeared to be effects of the tension (and either pride or shame) engendered in such sub-spaces. The actual content of the conversations emerging among those who remained close to the bottleneck areas generating the most energy tended to be about violence, sex, music, clothes, bodies, footwear, sports, and dealing drugs. Those who felt at ease in such settings often expressed their thoughts with a good deal of humor and laughter.

Leaning against a gate near one of the main exits immediately after the bell released scores of students, I was able to observe one such lighthearted yet representative "hot spot" conversation. The highly ritualized exchange took place between four seemingly "fabulous" pupils: Rob, Nancy, Mike, and a boy who answered to the nickname Rah Rah (which I have not changed). It began when a girl wearing attention grabbing jeans walked out of the building and passed the group without making eye contact. Mike, holding his crotch, set off the verbal give and take with his rendition of a line all involved heard several times a day, "Damn, yo, she . . . got . . . a . . . fffffffffffat ass." Revved up, cognitively focused, and therefore without missing a beat Rah Rah replied with a question offered in a mock serious tone, "You could hold that down, son? (i.e., Could you handle her in bed buddy?). "I'll die tryin', booooy, I'll die tryin'," Mike replied, as he started dancing around, smiling, and again gesturing towards his crotch. Laughs, handshakes, and knowing looks ensued. These were not brothers-in-arms, forced to collaborate because of intimidation. These were friends having a good time. All the verbal and physical signs of support and mutual orientation were reserved, of course, for the "fabulous" few—not those passing through largely unnoticed. Quickly, Rob chimed in: "Oh shit, that nigga (i.e., Mike) crazy, yo."

And then Rob said, as if only to Mike, "How you gonna go and disrespect my bitch like that?" The joke was that saying "bitch," as all involved immediately understood, was much more disrespectful (or otherwise "crazy") than anything Mike said or did. And for that reason Nancy, pretending to be disgusted, closed off the transaction with, "Oh, see, y'all niggaz ain't right." This customary way to show mock disapproval effectively ended the sequence of events.

Was this an example of black humor or, more generally, of black culture and solidarity manifesting outside classrooms? Were these four African American students consciously switching on "street" codes and opting for black ways of being? Was "ghetto fabulous" cultural capital infused, at least here, with (lower class, rather than legitimate) black cultural capital? To some degree, yes, I would say. The point however, to use once more Bourdieu's phrase, is to keep in mind the *principles of social vision and division* that were most frequently and powerfully brought into play in the field in question. None of the students powerfully labeled as "nerds"—however black, Dominican, African or anything else they may have considered themselves to be—would have dared try to enter such a group-making (or at least group-reinforcing) communicative transaction. Underlying distributions of "ghetto fabulous" cultural capital (both in situ and "worldwide"), economic capital, embodied signs of "hard" self-confidence and "soft" inconsequentiality—all of these were far more important in terms of (re)producing students' senses of place than any racialized (self) identifications or images that at times happened and at times faded away. Most black and nonblack students simply did not dare to speak up during such moments in such spaces. But to feel so comfortable in such a potentially dangerous bottleneck area with "gangsters" all around, indeed to embody the mix of poise and energized alertness that allowed one to partake, artfully, in such a rapid fire humorous exchange—all of this demonstrated that the transaction had taken place not mainly between blacks but, first and foremost, between students who took a firm hold on high-status positions for granted. The gyrating of the neck, the arching of the back, and the sashaying of the girls; the boys' throwing forward of shoulders, the scrunching of the forehead, the "gangster lean" against the gate, the emphasis adding handshakes and of course the almost *drag king*-like "over the top" grabbing of the crotch[57]—all of this was part and parcel of what was being communicated.

Furthermore, and this is crucial in part because it is so easily overlooked, all of this had to be lived through rather than explicitly contemplated in order to be effective in real time.[58] As such, mainly because of the primordial feelings (about belonging, friendship, nobodyness) that remained

unspoken, the worst putative attributes of some docilized individuals classified as "nerds" or "wannabes"—in addition to those already mentioned,
qualities pegged on to those symbolically least able to defend themselves
also included "dirtiness," "bad" hair styles, or the crime of wearing "busted"
[old] clothes—were extended to the entire imagined collectivity of "soft"
and "bitchlike" "player haters." If the "great unwashed" were acknowledged
at all by the well-spoken street aristocracy, that is, it was often a simple comment such as, "Them niggaz jus' stay livin' tiny."

Exceptional Occasions and the Place of Race

"You've got to be real" insinuates that "you've got to be real"
to your black and Hispanic identities.[59]

The blunted eyes of the youth search for a guide
A thug is a lost man in disguise[60]

No students felt strongly about being members of specific groups all the
time. And, during certain moments, the collective mythologizing of the
"ghetto fabulous" as well as the coordinated lambasting of the "normal
kids" and "nerds" did give way. In many cases, these were the moments
when the logic of the wider educational field or pressures from home shook
up normal flows of events. In other words, demands from outside the two
mini-societies and the legitimacy of mainstream cultural capital could return with a vengeance. As Roxanne's comments in the opening pages of
this book indicated, during their temporary falls from grace those typically
constructed as "the fabulous" were forced to see that their ties to "elevated"
peers had been pulling them down all along.[61]

Of the many easily found examples in both settings, the rituals related to
grading at the end of semesters might be the best place to start. Those who
typically appeared to be "fabulous" for several weeks or months at a time often ended up begging teachers not to fail them at the end of marking periods.
This might, for good reason, be seen as highly conscious and manipulative.
But to witness the anxiety of adolescents who had been (extremely) disruptive and disengaged as they started scrambling because they realized what
might happen as a result of failing many if not all of their classes, was to know
that they sensed something upsetting: rather than "holding shit down," they
had been swamped by wave after erratic wave of "fabulous" transactions.
To see even those most frequently acknowledged to be "hard rocks" visibly
dismayed at their poor grades was to know that they, at times, could buy into

the logic of personal responsibility, meritocratic educational systems, and being a "good kid" or, at very least, fear the consequences of failing.

We should keep in mind here that there was much more at stake in Johnson and Delta than in less-distressed neighborhood schools. Wake-up calls in the form of report cards in the Bronx and the Bijlmer were often accompanied by reminders about being years behind grade level in basic academic skills. Facial expressions certainly illustrated how disappointed the typically more dominant students could be when, during parent-teacher conferences, they watched their mothers or aunts (again, men were very rare) cry after hearing about all the absences, the horrible test scores, and missing homework assignments. Questions along the lines of "How can you do this to me when I'm out here working two jobs?" seemed to open the hearts of even the most thoroughly callous teens. I often heard students who typically sounded devoted to the most "street" of cultural codes swear they would "get it together from now on," while their mothers asked me what to do about "losing" their adolescent children to the "wrong kinds of friends." Similarly, the "dropouts" I got to know in the Bronx did not sound at all "fabulous" when they humbly said they were "planning on going back" and "getting a degree."[62] I saw students who typically imagined themselves to be "fabulous" fall apart in front of counselors who were explaining why they would have to transfer to another devastated school or make the shift to special educational. The angry reaction of one of my typically "hard" students was quite instructive. As he stormed out of the counselor's office after hearing the bad news he said, "I ain't tryin" to get no fuckin' GED, in there with all them special-ed niggaz." An antischool "gangster" no more, this student's worldview, his most basic likes and dislikes, and his hopes for the future all seemed to be quite conventional.

The students attending Johnson and Delta also went through reality checks including reminders about older siblings—or their own parents—facing extremely poor job prospects in part because of disastrous educational outcomes. The wake up calls often came from mothers, aunts, and grandmothers trying to make ends meet (in between welfare checks) who literally saw education as the only way to stop adolescents from going "down the wrong track." And, of course, there were the reminders related to extreme violence and incarceration. To be a teen in the South Bronx—and also, albeit to a lesser extent, in the worst subsections of the Bijlmer—was to regularly see (or hear about) the once "fabulous" young people who ended up in jail after a knife fight, as victims of shooting incidents with permanent health problems, and as poorly dressed teenagers with useless diplomas pushing baby carriages through the long corridors of subsidized apartment buildings.

Again, I acknowledge that the furious, numb, and at times tearful responses may have been intentional to some degree. But everything from the somber moods to the viscerally felt categorization schemes (e.g., "I ain't no special-ed nigga") illustrated that when ugly truths about longer term consequences beckoned, when the objective power of the broader educational field pried students out their "hard" demeanors and collective mythologizing, the typically more "fabulous" also proved to be ambivalent about—if not downright appalled by—their peer group allegiances and habitual response patterns. When harsh realities caught up with the "real (players)," their remorse was only occasionally and partially enacted in willful last-ditch efforts to mitigate sanctions such as beatings when they got home.

Here again we see how wrongheaded it would be to base our analyses of more disruptive behavioral patterns on solidified racial identities or situation transcending "oppositional" beliefs. It is true that students defined locally as black were overrepresented among the typically more dominant students rudely awakened from time to time in both settings.[63] However, the presence of so many black (and native) "nerds" as well as of so many nonblack, nonnative born "fabulous" students (from all sorts of ethnic "groups") illustrates why we should avoid viewing peer dynamics, self-destructive coping practices and eventual wake-up calls *mainly* through the ethnicity/race-meets-culture prism. Here again we find that the all but irresistible seductiveness—and only occasionally revealed (long-term) costs—of "realness" is what mattered most. As this analysis of exceptional events further indicates, from here on we should ask *not* whether ethno-racialized distinctions and performances mattered but how they became salient in the foreground or withdrew into the backgrounds in the two overall game-like settings perpetually restructured most significantly by *real- vs. fake-based principles of hierarchization* in both settings. [64]

So to do justice to how race mattered is to understand how "realness" mattered most, most of the time. As we will see in Chapter 5, for example, for newcomers to the Bronx from places like West Africa, leaving behind all that was "soft" went along with being classified as "black" (or, if you like, effectively pulling off blackness). But becoming "black" was never just about achieving a higher position on a purely racial hierarchy. This chapter illustrates why "moving up in the world" for such newcomers was mainly about becoming something most (native) black students were effectively barred from becoming: "fabulous." Similarly, many first-generation immigrants to the Bronx from supposedly "soft" parts of the world achieved access to more dominant slots (in interaction rituals) almost immediately.[65] In the Bijlmer some of the most disruptive students I encountered were from Ghana. While these "gangsters" cannot be singled out as newcomers any more than most of the students attending Delta, they certainly seemed to harden as they grew into occupancy of their dominant social positions. In the Bijlmer, furthermore, I discovered students of European ancestry (and "white" by local definitions, unlike kids from Turkey who might be "white" in the United States but were not in the Bijlmer), who were perceived as being "completely [Afro] Surinamese." All the way down to the core of their aesthetic, linguistic, and bodily predispositions, these "Dutch" (i.e., white) pupils were perceived to be typical of teenagers imagined to make up Delta's largest ethnoracial and ethnonational "community" (cf. Anderson 1991). We might say that the phenotypically white kids who occupied more dominant positions successfully pulled off, or were swept up in the process of doing, the local version of "street"-flavored blackness. Or we might just say they, like all the others with a path to their school's version of the "fabulous" life, did what felt right.

Crucially, this does not mean that everyone could always slide from one type of ethnoracialized performance or imagined national community to another with equal freedom. A relatively light-skinned girl whose ancestors came from Puerto Rico could not pull off blackness (in the sense of being/doing African American-ness) as easily as a dark-skinned girl whose (grand)parents came from the same island. Only the darker of these two students would be able to successfully make (or be forced to make) blackness stick to her one moment and then make "morena" (i.e., a Puerto Rican girl with relatively dark hair, eyes, and skin) happen for her in another. At the same time, especially if they had access to the energy-producing rituals of the "fabulous," both of these students might proudly enact their responses to seeing the Tito Puente (i.e., a phenotypically white Salsa musician) float at the Puerto Rican Day parade while sporting a "100% Boricua" T-shirt adorned with a Puerto Rican flag.

Discussion: Moments and their Students, Remaking Two Worlds Apart

There exists a correspondence between social structures and mental structures, between the objective divisions of the social world—particularly into dominant and dominated in the various fields—and the principles of vision and division that agents apply to it.[66]

We act and have to act as if mischief were not afoot in the kingdom of the real and that all around the ground lay firm.[67]

This chapter can serve as the foundation for what lies ahead because it documents how, why, when, and where those granted access to the more prestigious social positions (in interlocking chains of micro-level interactional structures and in the two overall pecking orders) were continually seduced into contributing to their own educational downfalls and, more broadly, to the ongoing destruction of the two learning environments. This chapter indicates that those enchanted by their school's version of the "(ghetto) fabulous" life did not "believe" in what they were doing in the sense of any consciously held, disembodied "belief systems" that somehow transcended (micro) contextual dynamics. It was not because of some sort of fixed ideological commitments (related to permanently salient racial identities) that "just keeping to yourself" and avoiding the "wrong crowd" was nearly impossible for those—like Roxanne and Kim—who were judged worthy of invitations to the almost nonstop "fabulous" parties. Rather, when those invited to the "real" mini-events located for the most part outside classrooms[68] felt the tug—i.e., when they were invigorated and focused by the actions of those they experienced as members of distinct and inherently charismatic groups embodying legitimate authority—what could otherwise appear as the "right" thing to do was not at all obvious.

Perhaps this does not go far enough to really bring the main point home. The countless moments in extra-classroom settings could be as enticing for the teens thrust into such stigmatizing, objectively inferior, and physically unsafe neighborhood schools as the signals sent by a powerful seductress, the raptures of a cocaine- or gambling-induced frenzy, or the "infinite" highs associated with *The Varieties of Religious Experience* (James [1902]1982) can be for many adults. But we might also take examples less easily associated with "character flaws." The seemingly trivial moments detailed above regularly operated on them the way being "cut off" on a congested highway occasionally operates on us.[69] None of us really have any idea how "inhumanely" we would have behaved if, as teens or even as (young) adults, we had been stationed inside Abu Ghraib and, while people were being tortured to death in the next room, forced to cope with comrades forcing prisoners to strip and form human pyramids (cf. Gourevitch and Morris 2008). Finally, in terms of something both intimate and ever-present for many of us, the relationship between our knowledge about the need to eat less fattening foods and the situational dynamics and social relationships "hiding" behind our own ever-expanding waistlines could be used to demonstrate this chapter's main insight.

Black or not, having "good" beliefs (when there was time to "think straight") often failed to help those positioned and predisposed to get further caught up in compulsive, distressing, and ultimately self-defeating practices. Once the feeling broke through the surface, once it grabbed the adolescents by the gut if not thereunder, many of them were done for the next "period of instruction" if not for the day. During these ultimately noxious moral and sensual conversions, something deep inside them was awakened and what they wanted and knew to be "right" under other types of conditions became largely if not completely irrelevant. With or without consent, they were compelled.

So those staging dominant selves really were dominant most of the time, but only because they were swept up in webs of social transactions, practical and deeply habituated perceptions, and ultimately destructive emotional flows that they did not themselves create. Those judged to be worthy—because of past experiences turned into sets of (potentially activated) dispositions operating in the short term as embodied power resources—could not ignore entirely the call of the "wild," and they often found themselves intensifying it. Like coals constantly shoveled into a huge oven, everyday interaction rituals continually fired-up ideas about separateness and made the struggle to belong to a quasisacred community (the "fabulous") while keeping away from the profane (the "[fake-ass] nerds") feel like the way to go. Those invited into the "fabulous" circles of response and camaraderie were basically forced to prop up certain kinds of "selves" and to classify one set of students and practices as charismatic. They were forced to desire authentic belonging within these higher ranking social formations merging fantastic and realistic elements. The pressures to go on doing this were almost "everywhere" and counterexamples tended to be fleeting and comparably weak. Having said this, the constant reminders that they were "real" and that they hated "player haters" demonstrated that the teens most ardently and frequently making "fabulous" happen also—at least on exceptional occasions—felt lost, afraid, and desperate.

We need to keep the *primary* analytic focus on interdependent *positions* rather than on the (qualities spontaneously, ritualistically, and essentially attributed to) *people* temporarily occupying them. We have keep thinking relationally, that is, and we need to begin *not* with things (e.g., peer groups, personalities, or racial identities conceptualized as frozen substances) but with ongoing micro- and meso-level processes. To the degree that the spontaneous analyses of students (and teachers) were based on myths about rugged, self-acting individuals with fixed traits ("He just got it going on." "I don't pay no attention to nobody, I'm just fly like that.")—or about groups conceptualized as clearly distinct things-in-the-world ("Them niggaz is just straight up thug life for life")—thinking sociologically requires an epistemological rupture with the worldviews of natives. Myths matter. They are data. And we have just seen that idealized "I/we" images can be very real in terms of their consequences. However, breaking with native analyses and ways of speaking where necessary, we must keep in mind that as the more and less dominant positions were filled by an ever-changing mix of individual students, the emotionally energizing rituals of "realness"—and, at the opposite pole according to the most frequently and powerfully mobilized vision of social divisions, the stigmatizing rituals of those labeled and made to feel "fake"—continued to *reflect and reconstitute* the two fiercely hierarchical status systems. We need to remember why expelling five or ten "ringleaders," as the deans in the Bronx did from time to time, or "pushing" a great many students "through the system," as teachers and administrators in the Bijlmer did, changed next to nothing. After a few days in the Bronx, or after the summer vacation in the Bijlmer, things went back to "normal."[70] No single individuals or even cliques determined what happened. Within the two systemically segregated contexts of action, it was the pre-established power positions and the everyday interactional norms that were the main problem, not any of those ritually constructed as more or less "problem" kids (or teachers). With the preexisting hierarchical structure of the sociosymbolic system always already in place, and with the well-established norms and roles of interaction routines continually reordering (or "renormalizing") what only appeared to be "chaos" on the ground, steady streams of incoming "up and comers" were more than willing to take over the vacated posts. This point can be seen more clearly if we keep in mind that even those who appeared as the highest of "high potentials" (mainly due to their previously acquired sets of more "street" dispositions) had no means of actually "getting their thug on" until they found their way into dominant posts in face-to-face encounters which offered the "right" disposition triggers or *releasing stimuli*.

As this suggests, when I allude to *more or less "dominant"* students in the coming chapters, I hope readers will understand that—in the final analysis—we should not reduce *processes* (of identity formation) to anything *static* (such as, in their terms, a permanently "fabulous" or inherently "nerdy" teen). I hope it will be understood that, in using such terms, I make use of a shorthand for the ongoing dynamics in webs of relations (or processes-in-relations) detailed in this chapter—and that I do not reference some preconstructed, self-enclosed, and self-acting entities somehow capable of remaining uninfluenced by the slots and roles they occupied as they traversed their fields. Relatedly, I hope my use of such (coupled) terms will not give the impression that "the dominant" were merely "comrades in arms" who only had meaningful ties to other well overbearing types or that "the dominated" were perpetually trying to find refuge from their oppression by huddling together (and avoiding their tormentors). To be sure, the students in both settings experienced the varied textures of heartfelt friendships that cannot be simply reduced to the shared—or, in some cases, divergent— status positions they tended to occupy.

The main dissimilarities documented in this chapter related to how— despite the far more extensive security apparatus in and around Johnson High—everyday interaction rituals in the Bronx tended to be more harsh, erratic, intense, and dangerous than those in the Bijlmer. This brings us onto the next chapter's terrain, where the most upsetting aspects of these differences become more central. From how daily transactions at once reflected and reordered (practical senses of) the two overall status systems—and with a grounded sense of how even the most mighty of players and teams were overpowered by what transpired moment-by-moment "where the action was"—we can now home in on the "hottest" and most decisive moments produced in the two potentially lethal settings.

Another way of bridging to the next chapter is this. As Goffman (1967, 95) once declared while in full Durkheimian mode, the "secular world is not so irreligious as we might think. Many gods have been done away with, but the individual himself stubbornly remains as a deity of considerable importance." At least in the contexts being compared here, exactly the same might be said of the "fabulous" peer group. And, while we might associate the staging of a "hardcore thug" persona or the consecration of "real" communities with the "rhetorical, performative, and aesthetic practices through which people upgrade the reality caliber of the stories-they-live-by"—or, if you like, with the "cultural production of the really real"—we must keep in touch with how the social construction of "incontestables" was underpinned by the most pressing and *undeniable experience[s] of the sensuous body.*"[71] Because the teens longing for *communitas* were gendered beings of flesh and blood in objectively unsafe worlds, from this foundation-laying analysis of muscular bonding and boundary policing we must turn to physical vulnerability and, for example, the irrefutable facticity of a boy cutting girls' faces.

THREE

Episodic Violence, Perpetual Threats

So the nature of war consisteth not in actual fighting, but in the known disposition thereto during all time there is no assurance to the contrary. . . . In such condition there is no place for industry, because the fruit thereof is uncertain, and consequently, no . . . arts, no letters . . . and, which is worst of all, continual fear and danger . . . [1]

He ain't a crook, son. He just a shook one.[2]

Two girls had their faces slashed one bright Bronx morning while trying to enter one of Johnson High's side entrances. The first girl's face was shredded without any warning at all. A hooded boy approached her—perhaps with a box cutter—and slit her cheek open. While the second girl may have had a couple seconds to react, she did not escape a similar fate.

I want to reexamine this incident in order to begin considering something that, up to this point, has been underappreciated: how occasional outbursts of extreme physical violence related to more routine or "everyday" threats and, more broadly, how these interrelated aspects of belligerence influenced everything that went on in the two schools—especially in the Bronx but also in the Bijlmer.

As the previous chapter showed, the status hierarchies in both schools usually concentrated both rewards and risks on what students typically associated with "real" ways of being. For reasons we already started to see, therefore, extremely perilous encounters in Johnson and Delta were almost always elite (or "fabulous") affairs; "nobodies" and "normal kids" did not get "beatdowns" because they rarely tried to rise up and claim any of the (symbolic) goods that could be had. Before we get any further into threatening encounters, it might therefore be useful to clarify a few central points related to power ratios and positioning. First, those typically positioned as what we might call "dominant dominants" brought into play certain power resources that slightly less established actors—i.e., "dominated dominants"—could not always mobilize or deploy.[3] Second, those typically positioned at (or very near) the apex of these relatively autonomous worlds often defended not just their positions, but also the symbolic underpinnings of these positions (e.g., the visions of social division, the prevailing ways of "recognizing" the "real").[4]

With regard to aggression in our two schools, the main questions suggested by this relational and processual way of thinking are the following: How exactly did threats and violence relate to *different types of more or less dominant positions* and the various types of power resources that allowed individuals and peer groups to occupy them? And, how did the actual actions of violent elites relate to the conservation or transformation of *the two overall settings*?

Now, not because it was terribly typical but because it was so instructive, let us return to the double slashing. What did this outburst of exceptional brutality disclose about everyday threats, more customary modes of doing violence, and the "normal" social and symbolic ordering of life in Johnson High?

The classroom out of which I operated the morning of the double-slashing happened to be directly adjacent to the side entrance the girls tried to enter. And on that morning, as the bell rang to end first period, a security officer named Joe was stationed just inside that door. Joe was a friendly man in his late 20s with whom I regularly played basketball after school. He was exceptionally popular with all types of students in part because he often risked reprimands from his supervisor for allowing students to enter the school through side doors. Sensing that Joe had been rattled, I asked him if he was all right. He explained that he had opened the door after hearing the two girls scream. Looking out into the morning sunshine he saw both girls buckled over with their hands on their faces, blood squishing out on all sides. He had rushed them to a colleague down the hall before returning to his post, bewildered.

Ordinarily, news and rumors about even extreme incidents of violence did not travel very fast in Johnson High. And when the information finally did spread, it was often communicated matter-of-factly.[5] But things were different this time. Several pupils had seen the girls hurried off to the dean's office before they were sent to the hospital and word was spreading quickly that the slashing had taken place at Joe's door. By the time the bell rang to start second period nearly a dozen students were peppering Joe with questions. They continued to press him for details until he admonished them to "Go to class!" with more sternness in his voice than usual. As the crowd slowly dispersed the students' comments, expressions, and bearing indicated that they were struggling to integrate the new event into their preexisting mental maps. One girl seemed to be shielding a girlfriend who was covering her face, crying, and repeating the words, "Oh my God." While easing away from Joe a typically more dominant boy I had gotten to know in a class the previous year looked at me, bit his inverted lips, and nodded his head disapprovingly as he walked off to class.

I tried to tune out the entire affair and get through my second period. But my students were obviously perturbed and over the course of the forty minutes we spent even less time on task than usual. When my second-period class finally came to an end I rushed out to see how Joe was doing. I also wanted to find out if he had heard any news about the girls over his walkie-talkie. Joe's only news was that his stomach was still upset. "This is too much for me, man. They was just some nice girls . . . tryin' to come to school, you know what I'm sayin'? I can't deal with this shit, for real. This is too much," he said scratching his head and looking up at me from the top of the desk/chair unit where he sat. Within a couple of minutes a throng of students—nearly all girls—came over and began pressing Joe for more details. Had he seen the boy who did the cutting? Was the attacker alone? Was anyone on the other side of the street that might have been with the attacker? What exactly did the girls say about the boy who had cut them? What color was his hooded sweater? Was he wearing a red baseball cap? How deep had they been cut?

The telling phrase, perhaps, is "just some nice girls." These were no "thuggettes." I left Joe to talk with the students and stood by my open classroom door. During this part of the day the ground floor was usually packed and unruly. Other than the buzz around Joe, however, the hallways were eerily quiet. I was amazed both by the almost complete absence of sound and the dumbstruck looks on the students' faces. It was becoming obvious, at this stage, that some of the clearly gendered "rules" of acceptable (e.g., "gangster" on "gangster") violence had been broken.

After having had more time to think about responding to the angst and gloominess spreading through the hallways, I decided to transform my third-period class into a makeshift group therapy session. I began by asking the students to help rearrange their desks into a circle. Arranging this new set-up did not unleash any of the usual jokes or complaints. With everyone inside, I shut the door and opened up a conversation about the double slashing and school-related violence more generally.

The impromptu session was extraordinary for several reasons. Most obviously, those who often seemed to be inherently and permanently dominant were on the defensive from the start. Like the "thug" who had been biting his lip in the hallway after talking with Joe, the "gangsters" in my class seemed to be at a loss for words. There was almost none of the usual chattering, eye contact, or posturing. The situational means of gaining credibility by doing/being "gangster" had vanished. I was observing the *typically* dominant boys during *atypical* moments. Neither their situation transcending belief systems (if such things exist) nor their (racial) backgrounds had changed. The "normal" rhythm and chain of events had, however, been broken.

More surprisingly still, the unusual movements and solemn comportment of the typically disempowered "nobodies" suggested a newfound dignity. Those who rarely dared to speak above a whisper in class derided gang initiation rites (e.g., cutting your way into a gang) and everything they represented. "How they could do something like this Mr. Paulle?" asked Maria, a tiny, doe-eyed girl originally from Central America. "They animals. I'm telling you," she continued, looking away from me and toward some of the usually more outspoken boys. "Pero . . . I don't care what nobody says, they just animals." The uncharacteristically brazen body language announced that was a new Maria talking—a Maria on the winning side of a conflict-ridden exchange of emotional energy.

Maria stared for several seconds directly at a few of the "playaz"—especially the one who typically took on the role of the ringleader, at least in our class, Cory. With Maria looking on in silence, the mood in the room seemed to defy Cory, Sean, Juanito, and Demetrius to speak. The "thugs" looked down or off to the side. They said nothing. Then James, a usually ill-at-ease and soft-spoken boy with an unfashionably disheveled afro, also seemed to come out of his shell for the first time. "It's sick," James said. "How they gonna . . . c'mon now . . . slicin' up girls' faces like that. They all sick."

The momentum lay with those who usually appeared as the "softest" of nonentities, and so the conversation continued. Over the course of around twenty minutes I heard more from several students typically forced into "nobody" roles than I had heard from them in the months. Those who spoke out seemed disgusted and frightened. But they also seemed to relish the moment and their newfound room for maneuver. It became clear that all the students associated the incident with a gang initiation. (One way to become a Blood, it was said, was to the draw the blood of a person wearing red.) As Joe's comments had indicated, the students found the incident especially unnerving at least in part because the victims were not viewed as particularly dominant types. Several of the girls mentioned how awful it was that the victims "had to be" female. On top of this, students found it dismaying that any kind of extreme violence would take place on school property so early in the morning. A more dominant girl explained that the projects, and especially the stairwells in the projects, could be dangerous that early in the morning—in part because junkies were often still awake and making their rounds. But one was said to be safe in the direct vicinity of the school at this stage of the day (when so many "gangsters" were at home or still making their way toward the school). Even if they had been wearing some red, the students felt, the victims could not be said to have taken on any unnecessary risks. Especially for those least likely to get involved in harsh violence—nondominant girls—the cauldron had just become a few degrees warmer, and much less predictable.

So even Cory, normally the master of ceremonies, quieted. It must be mentioned here that Cory never actually told me he was a Blood. Not while in his house to film an interview, not while hanging out in between classes—never. As Garot's (2010) work suggests, he may have decided not to present himself to me as a gang member in part because, during such interactions, he genuinely did not feel like he was one.[6] Cory knew I was in regular contact with his mother (about homework, and, for example, her attempts to juggle a day job and the evening classes she took to become a certified nursing assistant). And with me at least, Cory's mother liked to portray her son as just another nice boy destined for college. I told her about the missing homework, the failed exams, and the disruptive behavior. But I also played along, and I think Cory knew and liked this. At the same time, Cory did not need to explain to any of us that he sometimes felt like, and was certainly perceived to be, a Blood. Signs like his oversized red baseball cap and the intricate handshakes with the "rough necks" flashing "colors" were hard to miss.[7]

So there Cory was, hushed by a situation not of his choosing. And when he finally started talking, while remaining sullen and withdrawn, what he said was revealing: "Look, growing up around here," Cory muttered, "at some point . . . you know it's gonna be on, right?" After a pause, and with the entire group in a circle focusing exclusively on him, he continued. "And that's when . . . when they comin' for you, I mean . . . that's when, you don't wanna be standin' out there naked-like, all by yourself."[8] I think we can assume that all involved heard this as an excuse for having "joined" a gang. Cory also seemed to assume that the slashings were gang related, furthermore, and he seemed to be parlaying the general need for protection into a rather indirect defense of those who went through such rites of initiation. (I do not think he was saying the girls would have been protected if they had been in gangs.)

In something akin to a breaching experiment, a new "lived order"[9] was collaboratively and practically accomplished. Cory was made to feel ashamed, perhaps for the first time inside the walls of Johnson High, about his affinity with the "thug life" as well as, more particularly, his (symbolic) ties with an organization that pressured children into cutting other children's faces.[10] "Called out" by Maria and the other provisionally juiced up moral entrepreneurs, in this fleeting situational order Cory had bare exposure on his mind and instinctively he sought the cover that comes with fitting into a morally righteous community.[11]

Cory and his "thugged out" associates, then, were not suspended *mainly* in webs of significance they spun themselves, if I may paraphrase Geertz's (1973, p. 5) famous rendering of Weber. Rather, *first and foremost,* they were caught up in an almost never-ending web of threatening relationships and bodily practices that operated on them *beneath the level of explicit interpretation.* The slicing of human flesh altered the balance of power and the types of responses that could emerge, not in theory, but in lived through and somatically sensed practice. When the ordinary chains of events and habitual responses were temporarily broken—when Cory was transformed at the level of primordial feelings—he sounded like a Mama's boy, not like an avid proponent of the code of the street. On this occasion, the "normal kids" and "nobodies" made clear that they did not buy Cory's mea culpa. The majority of pupils sucked their teeth, rolled their eyes, or nodded their heads in disgust. These responses amounted to another challenge. This time, however, Cory mustered nothing in return. Juanito's body language signaled push back, but neither he nor Sean nor Demetrius tried to defend themselves verbally from the concerted attack. The conversation seemed to continue as if Cory and "his boys" could simply be ignored. Our session started to wind down quickly after another usually muted female student posed the following question: "Now how you think those girls gonna feel when they look in the mirror for the first time?"

One might argue that all of this amounts to something both hopeful and disheartening. Those who typically showed up as hapless victims appeared to be the judges in some kind of dreadful, bloody contest. This might be said to recall how Gandhi galvanized the long-silenced and (in our popular imagination) nonviolent masses after the most shocking incidences of imperial brutality. The hope, then, is that nonaggressive struggle might create a new, lasting, less violence-prone order. Yet here we arrive at the most tragic part of this story. No one led the masses in any real revolt because, outside of the isolated encounters such as the one that took place in my classroom, there were no occasions for any such unified revolutionary action. The basic conditions for substantive change being absent, within just a few hours, the "normal" chain of events regained their grip. By the afternoon those occupying the same "old" dominant positions once again dominated the corridors and exit areas. Back came the proud bopping through the halls, the self-important greetings of the "street" aristocrats, and the "thugged out" howls of delight and scorn. In my classrooms standard "ghetto fabulous" operating procedures swept away the cathartic effects of a statistically freakish event. As such, this uncustomary incident revealed something important about why the *logic* of the field was so resilient. Back in the normal state of affairs, certainly from the perspective of boys like Cory who wanted to move up in (or stay near the top of) the world, it might well seem that engaging in "wildness" was the best way to be realized as well as protected. And for most of the students and staff members like Joe, the social order that was reinstated so quickly after the double slashing must have appeared as the way things had always been and the way things would forever be.

Trying Not to Remember: Denials from Above and from Below

> If one of these guys hits you right, like in the aula or something . . . and especially if somebody else sees it happen . . . like a girl. [Pause] Look, you are not going to forget that.[12]

In part to illustrate some key contrasts with Johnson High, I want to turn now to an incident of extreme violence at Delta. A boy named Patrick, a "quiet" third year student, appears to have been unwilling to offer up a piece of jewelry one day as he left school. He was stabbed twice. He lost so much blood trying to crawl back to the school that he nearly died. A trauma helicopter landed on the Delta's playground and whisked him off to a local emergency operating table where his life was saved. The doctors told an assistant principal that it had been a very close call. Patrick, whom I did not know, stopped attending Delta after this event.

The next day, the stabbing seemed to be the only thing people were talking about. From various types of students to the assistant principal, I got basically the same story over and again. An ex-student and a current student had been responsible for a string of robberies. The boy who still attended

Delta would telephone his companion outside the school when he spotted someone with an expensive piece of jewelry who was vulnerable. Needless to say perhaps, they were not targeting the most powerfully built, well-connected, and respected types. On the other hand, the weakest of the weak did not have (or did not reveal having) things like gold chains that might attract attention. The ex-student waiting just outside the school used a range of weapons, including a pistol, to demand jewelry even if it was tucked inside the unsuspecting student's clothing. On the day Patrick was mugged, "only" a knife had been used.

Immediately in the wake of the stabbing, the typically less-dominant students admitted freely to being shaken by the events that had taken place the day before. This was hardly surprising. However, the day after the stabbing I sat near another adult in a classroom with six or seven "thugged out" boys and one especially powerful girl named Leslie. One at a time each of the Afro-Surinamese and Antillean boys reported that they were not intimidated by the event and not at all concerned about school-related violence. "Afraid of what?," one boy asked before punctuating his question with a long and loud suck on his teeth. As usual, Leslie's hair was pulled back tight and she wore pants that seemed to be made of some kind of painted on leather and plastic blend. She wore three or four chains outside her sweater, gold-plated earrings, several gold rings on her fingers, and a gold-covered tooth. Except for the fact that she was very short, she looked like one of the revealingly clad hip-hop goddesses that might be found on the set of a Snoop Dog video. Her bearing and direct eye contact signaled that she was not going to be avoiding anything. "Of course I'm more scared now coming to this place after what happened. We all are," she announced in a nearly hostile tone. "I mean . . . what do you expect? This kid almost bleed to death." The collection of boys wiggled around on their chairs. They appeared to be disconcerted by Leslie's commanding performance. "If this could happen to a calm [rustige] boy like Patrick, who never went looking for problems," Leslie continued, "it could happen to anybody." After catching her breath she continued. "These street kids [straat jongeren] are walking around outside the gate [of the school] with guns and knives and God knows what else. Everybody in here is afraid. Period [punt uit]."

The "bad" boys' collective bluff appeared to have been called. They did not take Leslie on. An awkward silence followed. We all sat around looking at each other for a few seconds. Finally, one boy got up and left the room. Two others let out a nervous laugh. Leslie eased back in her chair, perhaps sensing that her claims would not be challenged because everyone knew that the proverbial "emperors" were indeed "wearing no clothes."

It seems that, as an especially dominant student—and perhaps most importantly as a girl—Leslie felt she had the space to directly undermine the routinized performances of the normally dominant boys. Less eminent and securely established students—and especially most boys even slightly less secure in their positions within the overall scheme of things—would have almost certainly been reluctant to let their shields down, act as concerned citizens, and make themselves vulnerable by weighing in honestly on such a question. It took one of the "flyest" of "fly girls" to show how seemingly dominant boys were locked into their "afraid of what?" postures. While Leslie seemed very much in touch with signals of fright emanating from her little body, the boys caught up in "hard" ways of being appeared subjectively cut off from the messages that might otherwise have welled up from their bodily cores.[13]

Patrick's stabbing was revealing for another reason as well. Immediately after this event, Delta's administrators went into overdrive. They understood that the students would have been less edgy if a "bad" kid had been stabbed. Perhaps for this reason characterizing the botched robbery as "senseless violence" in an internal memo, the principal asked teachers to discuss the event and the feelings it generated the following day during the second period. This was surprising to me because all I had seen, up to that point, was the "we have a great school, now let us make it even better" propaganda.

If you do not feel capable of discussing this incident with your second-period class tomorrow please share this with the administration. We understand. None of us have been trained or prepared for this. We will try to find someone to support you. Some of the main themes that should be addressed are the following: What can we do despite our *feelings of helplessness*? Emphasize that senseless violence occurs at the end of a chain of events that begins with kids having a big mouth, fighting, and robbing each other. Emphasize that we as a school community must show through our behavior that we collectively reject senseless violence. Only in this way can we oppose it. Try to convince students that they can share information with us. Doing so is not an act of betrayal but of self-protection. We can only address this problem if we work together. *Senseless violence starts small in every class. The good must unite and form a front. This is a very difficult task . . . and I know that what I am offering is not very substantial.* I hope that you will be able to draw from your character, your humanity, and that you will be able to strike the right chord with the students. Show them that this event has influenced you on an emotional level. As human beings we are all the same in this respect. Be strong, [the name of the director of the school]

Johnson High, which had roughly twice the population of the Delta School, produced at least three times as many cases of extreme brutality per year as the school in the Bijlmer. Yet during my three years at Johnson, the school's administrators never responded in any such fashion to any of the severe acts of violence that took place in or around the building. No (assistant) principals ever "publicly" communicated their feelings about horrific episodes or their thoughts about how teachers might help students deal with (the reactivation of) trauma. While teachers responded individually, as I did in my own meek way on the day of the double slashing, the policy of the school managers amounted, time and again, to denial: pretend nothing horrible has happened, just get on with it.

Blaming the administrators in the Bronx for failing to react would be easy enough. But the adults who were supposed to run Johnson were themselves run down by the steady flows of violent transactions with which they were, in addition to everything else, forced to cope. While their (non-) responses might for good reason be interpreted as highly conscious coping strategies (i.e., avoid damaging the "good name of the school"), they should also be seen as the more or less automatic defense mechanisms of bureaucrats so emotionally battered that they could not soften enough to permit such schoolwide displays of "weakness." If the systemic underreporting of "incidents" and diverted gazes of administrators did not make students or teachers forget acts of extreme violence, the lack of responses "from above" in the Bronx did reveal one of the most significant differences across the two settings: extreme violence was far more "normalized" in Johnson than it had been in Delta.

Publicly Exposed, Privately Disposed: Crowds and Gender Regimes Matter

A moral holiday comprises a free zone in time and space, an occasion and a place where the feeling prevails that everyday restraints are off; individuals feel protected by the crowd, and are encouraged in normally forbidden acts. Often there is . . . a heady feeling of entering a special reality, separate and extraordinary, where there is little thought for the future and no concern for being called to account.[14]

Male students were responsible for the lion's share of all forms of violence in both educational settings, and students at Johnson were particularly upset about the double-slashing depicted above because it contravened their gendered senses of how "normal" violence should be done. However, while I saw girls fight with fists in both settings, and heard about many more fights between girls in both schools, a clear difference between the two settings related to the *sexual division of labor of extreme violence.* I never saw or even heard about a girl doing any serious beating—let alone any cutting or stabbing—over the course of my three years in Delta.[15] In short, under the "right" conditions, especially the putatively more "thugged out" girls in Johnson did engage in extreme violence while their counterparts in Delta, it seems, did not. The admittedly limited and secondhand evidence I was able to collect suggests that this difference related to dissimilar types of bodily vulnerability due to much larger and more intense assemblages of "spectators" (in places like hallways) in Johnson High. As I mentioned above, well over twelve hundred students had attended Delta when it was in its prime. But less than six hundred made it into the building—with its comparatively wide halls and many open spaces—each day by the time I arrived. Johnson High was, by comparison, still quite full and the halls and stairwells of the far older building were much narrower. From the entrance to the cafeteria to the side exits, Johnson contained many more potential bottleneck areas in which situations were likely to become "tight."

Of course, with so many other "internal" and "external" processes influencing more or less belligerent responses, it would be unreasonable to assert that greater density and more intense crowds in the Bronx *caused, by themselves,* greater levels of (girl on girl) violence in and around Johnson. Furthermore, my data certainly *do not* suggest that fighting ever took place simply *because* of audiences. What I want to suggest here, nonetheless, is that relatively greater density in Johnson High mattered in part because it translated into a greater likelihood of (comparatively more intense) crowds forming instantly. While recalling that many factors played important roles in the processes to which we will now turn—and keeping in mind that what happened before crowds formed was critical—I want to explore the possibility that greater density (1) increased the chances that male and female students in Johnson High would be collectively humiliated (in especially energizing and attention focusing ways) and, therefore, (2) promoted becoming violent (on another occasion, such as after school, whether crowds were involved or not.) So let us return now to emotional reactions based on *bodily exposure* while introducing a new theme: *crowds.*

Two girls got into brawl in a hallway during my second year at Johnson. One girl pulled a hair extension out of the other girl's head revealing what several pupils in the vicinity characterized as a "bald spot." It seems that a great deal of laughing and screams from a crowd of observers ensued. One eyewitness account convinced me that, as so often happened, the "spectators" shaped the emotional environment and, therefore, determined the lived-through meaning of the spectacle.[16] The girl who felt she had been scandalized ran home, covered her head with a scarf and a baseball cap, and returned with a knife (or a box cutter). When the girl who had pulled out the extension emerged from the relative safety of the building, she was immediately attacked. According to several accounts the slashed girl's teeth were visible through the side of her mouth, but that may have been more hyperbole than factual reporting. What I was able to confirm is that the girl who was slashed had to have her face patched together in an emergency room after the incident. I never had a chance to talk to her after the incident because she—like the two girls disfigured in the double slashing incident—never returned to Johnson. The slasher, who perhaps felt she had to take revenge (in front of yet another crowd), never entered the building again either.

According to the after-the-fact reports I was able to gather from several students and colleagues, the two rather disruptive and somewhat "fabulous" girls had been "good friends." Perhaps, if I had spoken about the incident with the girl who sliced open the face of her former friend, she would have sounded as if her actions had resulted from a street "code" such as the one outlined by Anderson.[17] But surely this cultural logic was, above all, situated; and the situational dynamics were not basedon consciously held beliefs relating to racial identities or deliberate decisions about "switching" between "decent" and "street" orientations or personas. Rather, the key lay in what was going on primarily beneath the level of explicit mental representations and interpretations: the meshing of bodily vulnerability and collective energies unleashed by crowds. This gruesome response was also related, it seems, to a shared sense that some girls (living Johnson's or the South Bronx's version of the "fabulous" life) could, under certain conditions, engage in such beastly displays—a sense, I would argue, rooted deep in the unconscious minds even of those vulnerable beings who could express it in words.

To sum up: there were far more incidents of extreme violence involving males and females at the more thoroughly "packed" school in the Bronx, and virtually none involving females at the school with the wider halls in the Bijlmer. Although formalized administrative responses to extreme violence could be strikingly different across the two settings, the overall school-community reactions ended up being quite similar: denial was rampant and, in terms of both more internal and more external pacification, no one seemed to have much to offer those left behind. And finally, at least in part because significantly more bodies were fused into the "tight situations" emerging in places like corridors in the far larger and more densely populated school in the Bronx, crowds appear to have played more central roles in triggering extremely violent events—including those we might associate with macabre moral holidays for girls—at Johnson High.

Failing to Make "Real" Violence Happen

Some background conditions may be necessary or at least strongly predisposing, but they certainly are not sufficient; situational conditions are always necessary, and sometimes sufficient, giving violence a much more emergent quality than any other kind of human practice.[18]

Just as we used the extreme to shed light on the normalized above, I now want to examine more routinized forms of aggression, in part to bring more sharply into view the meanings and impact of extreme violence. Against the backdrop of occasional yet severe bursts of butchery, bringing everyday anxiety and intimidation to life can help us achieve a visceral sense of how threats reflected and reinforced peer group mediated status struggles. Drawing heavily from the work of Katz and Collins, I try to depict the ways in which differently positioned and predisposed actors dealt with "ordinary" threats and less extreme forms of violence as they arose and declined in real time.

Stephano, a short, not noticeably handsome, and slightly chubby boy who was in one of my classes, started walking away from the storefront area and toward the (non-"nerdy," close to the "hotspot") place in Delta's *aula* where he wanted to sit down and have his lunch. He carried a drink in one hand and a sandwich in the other. Suddenly the taller and much more powerfully built Jurgen pivoted away from the group he was in and blocked Stephano's path. After a brief pause, Jurgen punched Stephano in the chest hard enough to generate a clearly audible thud.

Everything seemed to stop. The twenty to thirty students scattered around Jurgen, and his most recent target looked on in silence. I looked up from the pit of the *aula* where I was sitting with a few students who almost always avoided the storefront area largely because they associated it with the Jurgen's of their world and these types of encounters. Apprehension seemed to well up from my gut while it spread through the dispersed throng of eyewitnesses. Like objects pulled by a powerful magnet, our minds were drawn directly to the event in question.

The smaller boy responded by pretending that the affront had been a meaningless gag. Mustering what dignity he could, Stephano flashed a meek smile at the bully and tried to walk past him. But his worried expression and jerky gait gave him away: he was in physical and emotional pain.

Stepping to the side Jurgen once again blocked Stephano's path. Perhaps Jurgen sensed that Stephano's movements had not expressed an adequate degree of subservience. Maybe Jurgen felt pumped up by the onlookers and the act of pounding someone's chest. Jurgen may even have been consciously making a point to others or retaliating for something Stephano had done in the past. An even bigger and far more genuine smile emerged on Jurgen's face. His movements were supple and confident. Boom, boom. Two more plainly audible punches landed squarely on Stephano's open chest. His upper body was visibly rattled by each of the thumps. This time "oohs" and "aahs" arose from the crowd. It was as if all of us formed a fully captivated theatre-in-the-round audience. Stephano stood his ground and tried to keep grinning. Jurgen looked down at his victim for a couple seconds. Then, still smiling, he gave Stephano (and the onlookers) a knowing wink, said something that I could not make out, and slid cheerily back to the "fabulous" clique with whom he had been standing near the storefront. Stephano looked squarely at his final destination—a place to sit that was off to the side and far enough from the storefront to be out of the spotlight. He sat down, alone, and appeared to be wholly focused on the sandwich and drink beside him. There would be no immediate escalation, it seemed.

As soon as Stephano retreated into the background the students resumed their conversations. "Did you see that?," the girl sitting next to me whispered to her girlfriend at our low- status, low-elevation table. "Yeah," the other girl answered. "He was faking it, but you could tell it hurt." Discreetly observing Jurgen and his friends joking around in the hot spot she added, "They think they own this place." The two girls assumed that Stephano had, in Jurgen's eyes, been trying to "act too big" and that Jurgen therefore wanted to "teach him a lesson." They agreed that Stephano was "no sweetheart" and that, this time around, he had received the treatment he had often inflicted on others in the past. While no match for Jurgen, the soft-spoken girls maintained, Stephano was without doubt one of the more aggressive boys. When I asked them about everyone returning so quickly to business as usual, they confirmed that such events were "normal." No one was very surprised by what happened because such "thug" on slightly smaller "thug" beatdowns materialized several times a day.

I waited a couple of minutes, not wanting to add insult to injury, and then made my way over to Stephano. His eyes were still watery. I plopped down beside him and asked if he was all right. "Oh, you mean Jurgen? I don't care about that—he doesn't bother me," he replied, fighting back tears. He then looked away, an obvious cue for me to leave him alone and I did.

Weeks later, Stephano disrupted one of my classes even more than usual. After repeatedly asking him to calm down I demanded that he leave the room. When he finally did so I tried to talk to him in the hallway. Again I could not get through. We agreed that he would come to my room immediately after his last class and that I would give him an extra assignment. He showed up, late, and I explained the punishment. Seeing that he was less agitated, I asked him if he wanted to talk about what was going wrong. Although it may have been a ploy to escape the drudgery of the extra assignment, when I asked him about Jurgen attacking him in the *aula* he seemed to open up. He told me that Jurgen was not the only one. Apparently over the course of his two and a half years at Delta—as well as in his neighborhood—this aspirant "gangster" gained just enough access to the "hot" social circles to be elbowed, slapped around, and punched by the even more dominant and aggressive types at the epicenter of these interaction rituals. Looking down at the empty piece of paper on his desk he said, "Sometimes I just want to get a knife or something. And I know where I could get a pistol. Make these boys stop bothering me. I wish I could . . . make myself do something like that. The worst part is that they all know I never will."

Stephano was ashamed, evidently, about not being vicious, unstable, or desperate enough to protect himself by means of extreme violence. But above all he was humiliated by the fact that those he saw as genuine "gangsters" assumed this to be the case. As such, the threats and minor beatings traveled only in one direction and—given that Stephano was predisposed to travel down the only path he saw to being a "somebody" in his stigmatized school and neighborhood—there was no reason to expect that this situation would change in the foreseeable future. I wondered if Stephano was the type who would, one day, snap or, as the girls in the pit seemed to imply, just go on terrorizing much less dominant types on "off Broadway" stages.

Back in the *aula*'s sunken area after the punches to the chest incident I knew I would get nowhere with Jurgen while he was still grandstanding with his entourage. But soon after the incident, encountering him alone in the hallway, I remarked that I had seen what happened in the *aula* and asked him what was up with him and Stephano. "With Stephano? Nothing," Jurgen replied with a shrug. "Stephano's cool," he added, "I was just playing with him." Had Stephano really done nothing he found offensive? Could it be this simple and random, a public form of light amusement? Seeing that I was perplexed, Jurgen insisted, "Mister, look, you know, we were just playing around . . . so, it was nothing." I reminded Jurgen of what he had shared with me when I took him out to lunch in the center of Amsterdam. There, in a Chinese restaurant, he had told me about receiving beatings from his older brother. I reminded him that he did not associate the beatings he took with "playing around." Jurgen's expression became more serious. He put his hand on my shoulder and looked directly at me like my grandfather used to when he really wanted to get a point across. "Mister," Jurgen said, "why do you get all nervous about these types of things? This is just how it goes." Jurgen turned on his heel and walked away from me. That was our last substantive conversation.

The bully was wrong in at least one sense. Stephano did not associate his pummeling with playfulness. And during my years in Delta no one had ever "played around" with Jurgen or any of the other boys in dominant positions (who seemed to be inherently aggressive and short tempered) in this way. No one dared do this because, as students perpetually said, such "wild" types lashed out (or immediately started things in motion to ensure violent reprisals after school) first and considered possible longer term consequences later.

On the other hand, of course, Jurgen was right. This was just how it went. These "ordinary" beatings, these endless indignations and ephemeral satisfactions, these ethnicity (re-)making performances of "craziness" and "I'm not the one to fuck with" masculinity, were part of the daily rhythms into which he had settled. Furthermore, while they never showed up in official reports on school violence or pedagogic climate, "minor" incidents such as Stephano's thumping massively influenced the day-to-day experience of being there and (not) being "real." Countless transactions such as this public display of muscle, ferocity and (ritualized) unpredictability fueled the sense that students like Jurgen were "naturally" dominant. Among the socially ambitious, such interactions also fired up the practical sense that being tightly integrated into the school's elite—rather than being a subdominant, less than "truly hard"-type like Stephano—was far more urgent than doing homework, going to class, or getting a passing grade. The longer term was often swallowed up by the here and now largely because of such *pressing* matters.

Jurgen may have been right about something else as well. For students like him there was little reason to be "nervous" about such daily hammerings. Jurgen had not been challenging any of those really close to him in terms of the various forms of power that allowed one to be a genuinely dominant member of the upper crust. And all the boasting aside, the other members of the violent elite almost never "played around" with Jurgen.[19] The key here, as we will see more clearly in a moment, is that students like Jurgen quite accurately predicted that the underlings they terrorized would never mobilize the situational means required for "successfully" doing serious violence.

Cool Threats: The Incorporated Ease and Situated Courage of Dominant Dominants

Watch their . . . street display and you will be struck by the awesome fascination that symbols of evil hold for young men who are linked to the groups we often call gangs. . . . And if we examine the lived sensuality behind events . . . we are compelled to acknowledge the power that may still be created in the modern world through the sensualities of defilement, spiritual chaos, and the apprehension of vengeance.[20]

Not all the boys capable of defending themselves from bullying and mobilizing serious threats were large or powerfully built. Julio, a second year Delta student with a moderately handsome face, was tiny, maybe five-foot, three-inches tall. He was much shorter than Stephano and not terribly muscular. To understand why size did not matter in this case is to grasp something basic about how fear and violence worked in both settings.

When Julio smiled, which was often, it seemed like he had a mouth full of gold teeth. A lot of the kids wore bright and color coordinated outfits, but his not very strapping frame seemed forever clad in the most striking outfits of all. One certainly did not need to hear him speak to understand that he felt entirely at ease hanging out with the most erratic of "criminals." And hang out he did. From the storefront area in the *aula* to the school's entrance to the most "happening" subsections of stairwells and corridors—as if by an invisible umbilical cord, Julio seemed connected to the hottest of spots. What is more, he seemed somehow disconnected from the frenzy. It seemed that the faster things moved for others, the slower they moved for him. His calm presence and cool refinement, even in the eye of the tornado, seemed to allow him to elevate mundane "fabulous" encounters into exciting public affairs.

Here we edge closer to the main reason Julio seemed to personify Delta's version of the "hardest of the hard." It was *something in the way he moved.* The boys in Delta could believe any number of things about (more or less "gangster") ways of moving, but in real time few if any could match Julio's poise and unforced swagger. No one, it often seemed, could spit into a corner while leaning on a wall, flash a confident smile, and then parade through the *aula* holding his crotch with quite the same degree of "street credibility." Julio's seemingly effortless gestures appeared at once graceful, understated, and electrifying, leading me to envision this most "dangerous" of "gangsters" as a kind of "thugged out" Fred Astaire.

One incident stands out. Toward the end of the night at one of Delta's school dances,[21] a student named Roy asked Julio's girlfriend, Vanessa, to dance. Sporting an exceptionally tight sweater with a particularly low neckline, Vanessa had been standing in one of the most visible spots alongside her "big-time player" boyfriend, who perhaps made it up to her shoulder. Cracking jokes and appearing to be "above it all," they had not been dancing in the *aula*'s pit (even though, for once, the pit was cool and the "nerds" were nowhere to be found). When Julio walked away and the much taller and more forcefully built Roy approached Vanessa, décolleté and all, there is no doubt that many eyes were on them. In other words, while the typically more stylish and status-rich were grinding on each other with loud music in the background, a boy unquestionably embedded in one of the most dominant peer groups in the school had summoned up the audacity to make public advances on "Julio's girl." This was not just any exchange between members of Delta's aristocracy. It was an exchange *automatically framed* in terms of the nightclubs, racy outfits, hot sex, and serious violence of more adult members of the broader "fabulous" and "gangster"-dominated world outside the school. In short, for all insiders, this was a significant high-society event.

Vanessa did not dance with Roy. In all likelihood he never imagined that she would. Roy was not so much asking for a dance as enacting the type of highly ritualized provocation that have unleashed swordfights and duals among members of court societies across Europe for centuries. There is much to be said for seeing this provocation, and the response it generated, in terms of the kind of "code" that Anderson (1999) traced back centuries yet associates with the "street" violence of alienated, inner-city black teens. Again here, however, what mattered most were real-time situational dynamics, emotional flows, and prediscursive bodily practices. Immediately upon hearing the news, Julio made a few phone calls. The cavalry—mounted on scooters and bicycles—arrived within minutes. Some, I was informed, were ex-students, but all were "crazy Antilleans."[22] What I could see for myself was that these young men with puffy coats and heads covered by hats and hoods certainly looked like the types you would not want waiting for you outside a party. The "back up," looking at once businesslike and fiery, waited just outside the gate, staring at the door Roy would sooner or later have to use.

The next half hour was nail-biting time. Julio seemed, however, to remain amazingly self-composed. Initially he staked out a position next to the exit, beside Vanessa and several other jet-setters. He appeared to take in the whole scene, calmly yet attentively. Then Julio left the building and repositioned himself facing the building's exit with his back to his friends. About fifty students and staff formed a jagged semicircle around, but not too close to, the one boy standing right in the middle of the pending storm.

Vanessa did not appear to enjoy the Helen of Troy role nor the drama the evening was generating. Standing off to the side of the exit surrounded by a collection of Delta's other divas, she alternated between making aggressive gestures and covering her face with her hands. The girls around her listened conscientiously but regularly glimpsed over their shoulders to see if Roy was coming.

Everyone knew it was on. Roy would have to come out of the one and only door. I asked a colleague with twenty-five years of experience what he thought we should do. As he saw it there was no way to completely regulate what would happen because neither the teachers nor the two policemen—accompanied by a dog and a paddy wagon—could control all of those involved. Somehow, this conflict had to be resolved, and especially given the likelihood that several of the boys involved were carrying weapons, it was preferable that this should happen inside the school's gates. If things got out of hand, especially outside the gates of the schools, several boys might end up in intensive care.[23]

The crowd edged closer to the "hustler" and his entourage behind the bars of the gate and off to stage left. With Roy nowhere in sight, the focus of attention was singular and intense. Julio just stood there, by himself, with one thumb in the pocket of his baggy jeans and his tongue out to the side of his mouth. No one dared approach him. I would later think of curtains being pulled back to reveal a brilliant dancer striking a pose under a single beam of light just before the music started. This tiny warrior was the sacred object in our outdoor church of thuggery.

Finally, Roy emerged with his clique. The dark-skinned boys in Roy's entourage may have all been "Surinamese," as one informant implied. Similarly, Julio's supporters may have all been "Antilleans." Yet it would be misleading to suggest that the two groups of boys "were identified as" Antillean and Surinamese. They were identified, first and foremost, as subsets of "thugs" (or "gangsters" or "players") and as regulars in elite circles that were by no means constituted exclusively by adolescents associated with any one ethnicity.[24] So while the relational ties supporting Roy and Julio might *seem* to be based *primarily* on experiences or invocations of common ethnicity, it was only at the *second level* that mobilizations within the overall pool of potentially violent elites related to ethnic boundaries. This was, fundamentally, a gendered conflict (revolving around one of the "flyest" of girls) between "fabulous" representatives of factions of the school's dominant class. Only secondarily was this an affair that reflected and reinforced racial orders or practical senses of ethnonational belonging.

Roy led his crew consisting of three other students a few steps towards Julio. In almost perfect unison, as if a conductor just out of view had orchestrated their movements, Roy's friends drifted off to the right—as far as possible from the larger number of boys who had come at Julio's request. Like cornermen looking on from behind the ropes in diametrically opposed corners, the two sets of boys peered into the central area where the main antagonists at last confronted each other directly.

We all watched. Except for a few whispers, everyone was quiet. Standing just outside the exit I had a nearly perfect vantage point. Roy towered above Julio as he drew closer. The stare down got underway. There was a subtle jerkiness to Roy's movements. His shoulders, eyebrows, and forehead seemed tense. Julio, by contrast, seemed to be in his element—loose as could be. Except for looking up and adjusting his feet slightly toward the taller boy, Julio did not seem to move when Roy approached him. With his thumb still in his low hanging pants, one leg straight, one leg crooked, he seemed completely undaunted. Julio seemed almost to pity the larger, slightly ruffled boy. The emotional energy simultaneously translating into and resulting from the two boys' stances seemed to flow in Julio's favor. For a couple of awkward, protracted seconds nothing was said. Everything, it seemed, was being communicated by the boys' more and less self-reliant postures. Then the silence was punctured. "You're afraid, ain't ya?" ("*Je bent bang eh?*"), the tiny boy said to the larger one, two years his senior, in a voice just loud enough for the hushed spectators to hear. Julio delivered his line with a faint smile and continued looking straight into his counterpart's eyes.

Roy mumbled something back that I could not quite make out. At this Julio immediately sucked his teeth, loudly, and continued staring at the taller boy. Then, in a flash, something clearly expressed the taller boy's capitulation. This "something" is hard to describe in words, although I think it was clear to all the transfixed observers. The seemingly more fluid and ennobled Julio appeared to be feasting on the suddenly more submissive and recoiling boy's energy. Julio's words may have been effective, but it was his poise and Roy's flinching, his stiffness, and his averted gaze that communicated what was going on. The taller boy's vitality seemed to evaporate and the balance of power suddenly tilted radically in Julio's favor. We all knew it was over. Julio had delivered the equivalent of a knockout blow. Like a dog with its tail between its legs, Roy backed off in an utterly dispirited and nonpretentious manner. I could not see Roy's face as he made his way over to his comrades. But the facial expressions of Roy's associates confirmed what we all knew. The boy representing their group had been symbolically thrashed, and they too had been somewhat disgraced. Although Roy had thrown in the towel and the winner had been effectively announced, the looks also made clear why Roy's friends would stick close to the paddy wagon as long as Julio and his associates were nearby.[25]

The star of the show did not shout any promises about later that night or "next time." Still appearing to be utterly relaxed, as if such challenges on his school's most grand of late-night venues were akin to a Sunday afternoon walk in the park, Julio turned on his heels and swaggered elegantly over to his friends on the other side of the gate. His crew welcomed him with hugs and trendy handshakes. After cracking a couple jokes and piercing the night air with a few howls of delight, they disappeared into the darkness.[26]

Apparently relieved, several members of what had been the audience began almost immediately using humor to deal with what they had just observed. Offering animated and rather light-hearted renditions of frequently heard refrains—"Nooooo, boy, Julio is no joke (*geen grap*)"—speakers seemed to express not only their approval of the tiny boy's winning actions but also to imply that they might have dealt with such well-recognized situations in similar ways.[27]

"Julio is a force of nature!" I wrote in my field notes the next day. To this I added nothing about positions—i.e., nothing about either access to more "fabulous" habitus forming experiences in the past or to the here and now situational means of pulling off threats—just "I can't imagine a kid remaining so cool." Of course, I saw that superior connections to "gangsters" (fostered in and out of Delta) were crucial. But when I wrote these notes it seemed to me that, beyond his general ability to maintain strong ties with (slightly older) boys who could be counted on to administer violence, the key to Julio's performance lay in something personal and fixed. This brought to mind a native concept frequently deployed in the Bronx: "shook." Even seemingly hardened and dominant kids could turn out to be "shook ones" if they proved themselves to be incapable of handling the microdynamics of (potentially) violent situations. All the never-ending bluster aside, according to this macho mythology reproduced by gangster hip hop artists, the *all too common* "shook ones" turned out to be "cardboard crooks" "fakes," "punks," and "bitches" who "ass out" instead of adequately demonstrating the "cold-blooded" instincts of the "stone-faced killer."

I now see that, romanced by a potentially violent ritual, I fell into commonsensical ways of thinking about Julio and, by extension, about those occupying truly elite positions and Delta's overall pecking order. I want to take a moment to be as clear as possible about why I got this so wrong—i.e., why I slipped into this naïve, decontextualizing, essentializing, "hero-worshipping" (mixed with "scapegoating") state of mind that Elias might have associated with *Zustandsreduktion*.[28]

Let us go back to what might seem to be a single power resource unrelated to the way Julio used threats to distinguish himself: his pants. Everyone saw the type of pants Julio wore and how he covered them in graffiti. Wearing a pair of such jeans was not chiefly a matter of money; and the stores selling such pants were well known. Nor did the graffiti demand a great deal of specialized craftsmanship. What mattered was how the jeans were worn. Few if any could let their pants sag in quite as "right" a way as Julio. Few if any could wear their pants three quarters of the way down their backsides while exuding so much elegance. To work the jeans, or make the jeans work, was to "nonchalantly" glide out of an exquisite "gangster lean" and into a gallant stiff-leg/loose-leg walk through Delta's most "thugged out" spaces.

This seemingly frivolous example illustrates, we might say, the first of the secret weapons in the little general's arsenal: his corporeal poise and know-how.[29] It was his knowledge about (or sense of) how to carry himself in just the right way that made his pants, gold teeth and all the rest look so hot, hard, and happening. Because this could not be faked, especially during the high pressure encounters that produced countless "shook ones," this embodied feel for the game helped boys like Julio *establish and maintain their coalitions* and, therefore, reign supreme in the realms of the "real" violent elites. More broadly, Julio's elegantly composed presence and way of taking up space can help us understand the decentralized, day-to-day mechanisms by which the dominant dominated in the here and now (and, as we saw in the previous chapter, by which they tended ultimately to dominated by their own domination). Crucially then, rather than anything Julio could put into words, it was this tiny boy's incorporated sense for how to cope that set the bar too high for the vast majority of aspiring "criminals"—in part because his "g(ame)" seemed to be inborn. In terms of "scoring" right now, the masses of less beneficially positioned and predisposed would-be "true players" spontaneously assumed that few if any could compete with a boy so naturally "gifted."

Yet this somatic poise and knowledge, *this difference that really made a difference,* was social through and through. What we all observed was a *second* nature, something that had been learned (in part over the course of roughly eighteen months) in just the right positions within just the right "spots." It was almost impossible to duplicate what looked like Julio's natural "talent" not because of his chromosomes but because in and out of Delta the slots at the top of the social ladder that gradually produced the relevant learning moments (i.e., drilled in the right corporeal and cognitive habits) were so scarce. Time in the school (quantity) was not as important here as the quality of the learning processes that fostered the inclination towards just the right stance, look, walk, and gesture. Moving through thousands of social miniencounters, one "gangster" handshake and "real nigga" grab of the crotch at a time, Julio came to embody just the right type of *feel for the game.* Many if not most others might have acquired the same skills and inclinations had they had access to these situations, but they did not. Failing to grasp this, it appeared that Julio's "excellence [was] a thing inside of him which he periodically reveal[ed] to us. . . . [and therefore] his . . . habits become reified [in our minds]. "Talent" is merely the word we use to label this reification" (Chambliss 1989, p. 79).

This brings us to another easily overlooked asset in Julio's capital portfolio: emotional energy. Even Julio's social trajectory turned flesh and forgotten—i.e., his most "fabulous" of historically acquired dispositions and cultural know-how—never operated outside of the (symbolic) structuring of an overall game and countless micro-situational encounters within it. And these nearly perpetual face-to-face interactions were what made this tiny warrior feel ten feet tall. This explains, to a large extent, why Julio was so often drawn back into Delta's equivalent of VIP rooms. What he found (and co-created) there, in the here and now, was something he desperately needed: the "electricity" that accrued to those occupying the most privileged roles and hottest of posts, the stuff that made students with high potential dispositions actually seem charismatic in everyday transactions and feel fearless when their dominant positions were challenged.[30] Even when the right situational means for deploying his feel for the game were absent—i.e., in boring classrooms or while alone—Julio's body and unconscious mind were forever tuned up by "gangster" rituals never more than an hour away.

Once again we see that more was "given" to those who already had. Julio came across as so lionhearted and endlessly cool most immediately because of his social position within a web of relationships. Elite positions had provided the "learning moments" that taught him how to manipulate tense moments and, more than ever on the big night, we juiced him up by making him the center of our narrow attention space. Roy's public challenge and Julio's knockout counterpunch had everything to do with how the spectators were charging up the more and less skilled manipulators of threatening encounters. Without the audience there would have been no stage upon which to dramatize the initial challenge, no spotlights for anyone to get under, and no riveting performance of an energy star capable of rising above the cowardice of (slightly) less "real" boys who could only dream of dancing with a girl like Vanessa.[31]

Flesh in the game

The relation to the world is a relation of presence in the world, of being in the world, in the sense of belonging to the world, being possessed by it, in which neither the agent nor the object is posited as such. The degree to which the body is invested in this relation is no doubt one of the main determinants of the interest and attention that are involved in it . . . (This is what is forgotten by the intellectualist vision, a vision directly linked to the fact that scholastic universes treat the body and everything connected with it, in particular the urgency of the satisfactions of needs and physical violence, actual or potential, in such a way that the body is in a sense excluded from the game).[32]

I now want to shift the focus from observations of violence involving students to my own experience of violence as a teacher. In so doing I will rely on my own mind-body complex as chief investigative tool. I engage in sociology *from the body* not because I want to make the narrative about "my own" experience. Nor do I do this because I am primarily interested in the plight of teachers in high-poverty schools. Rather, this mode of investigation generates unique insights into how students and teachers actually deal, in real time, with waves of what may appear to those standing on the shore as "external" threats.[33] I will describe how, as a physically engaged, quasi-native pressed further into action, I felt (or, if you like, how *das man* feels) as a porous and whole being-in-a-violent-world. Inspired by Merleau-Ponty[34] and his many students, I use this "ethnography from the gut" to document how interlocking chains of "mundane" threats emotionally metamorphosize—and worm their way deep into—the bodies and consciousnesses of those who regularly participate in such schools run amuck.

During one of my final days as a teacher in the New York City public school system, I was called upon at the last minute to cover the class of an absent teacher. It was common for untenured, uncertified, and unconnected teachers to be forced into taking last minute "coverages." I would have roughly three minutes to go through the crowded halls and stairwells to another part of the building, collect the absent teacher's substitute lesson plan, and then go back down two flights of steps to the classroom. As often happened the absent teacher had not left any trace of an "absentee lesson plan," although three such lessons were supposed to be in each teacher's file at all times. I had to hustle the annoyed department chair (AP or Assistant Principal) to give me something, anything that related to the subject that the class was supposed to be on. "Why didn't you come earlier?" the AP asked. "What am I supposed to . . . have everybody's absentee lesson in my back pocket?" The piercing "late bell" rang as I rushed to get down to the floor where the class was to be held. I could not cover my ears because I was carrying a number of books, a heavy shoulder bag, and handouts. Coming out of the stairwell, sweating, and hungry for the lunch I had planned to eat during this period, I made my way through the lively "thug" dominated hallway scene that was still "poppin'" directly outside the classroom to which I had been assigned. The "gangster leans" and baggy jeans made clear what kind of atmosphere existed just outside "my" classroom. There were no "security officers" in the area. There were no guards, that is, who might take it upon themselves to whisk the "bad boyz" out of the hallway after the late bell had sounded and the new period of instruction had officially begun. Intimidated, like most teachers were by such situations, I did not even consider taking it upon myself to try to clear the hall.

Arriving inside the classroom a few moments late, I breathed a sigh of relief. I sensed almost instantly that the small class was made up of mostly quiet, well-behaved types. This was not by any means always the case when one walked into a room for a coverage. Knowing that their teacher was absent, the pupils were already prepared to have yet another (incredibly dull and easy) absentee lesson plan dropped on their desks.[35]

I dumped my bag on the absent teacher's desk and started to distribute the handouts. "Again?" asked a girl sitting next to the desk, "Mister, we already had this one like how many times?" The girl's manner was not at all aggressive. She seemed to be simply fed up with yet another ritualized and institutionalized farce. As I pondered a possible response I felt something graze against my back. I heard a strange crashing sound behind me and then a student mumbling "Oh shit," as I spun around toward the open door. I immediately realized that a rubber trash container had been thrown against my back. I peered into the hallway to find a small group of "thugs" looking back at me. One of the students, a light-skinned boy with curly black hair— who I assumed to be of Puerto Rican rather than Dominican ancestry—had his eyes wide open and fixed straight upon me. He stood slightly closer to me than the rest of the "gangsters" clustered around him. "What," the boy said while thrusting his chest out. "You don't know who threw it. Whatchu gonna do?" The students inside the classroom would later confirm that this boy was, indeed, the one who had thrown the container. As I never learned his name, in what follows I will refer to him as "C."

I had no idea why I had been singled out. What I grasped, straight away, was that C had never been a student of mine and that I had no history with him. It was not really about us, in other words, as much as it was about the gazes and the posturing of the "rough necks" in the hallway. C was pumped up, in the spotlight, and clearly caught up in his "thugged out" role. I had been pulled into C's attempt to generate recognition.

Staring at the "ghetto fabulous" boys in the hall, I found myself thinking that C was right. There was not, I felt, much that I could do. As shame, anger, and fear welled up inside me, I tried to give my assailant and his acquaintances a cool and confident look before I retreated into the classroom. As we have already seen at several turns in this chapter, the feeling of being exposed drove the desire to cover up and achieve protection. Pathetic or not, this required no reflection. This reaction had little to do with my socioeconomic background and sense of ethnoracial identity. It had to do with a sense of being penetrated. I too was a conscious being. I also reflected and crafted my performance consciously, to some degree. But at a fundamental level, I responded prereflexively to the emerging network of sanctions, opportunities, collective emotions, and overlapping meanings that was far beyond my control. I was in real time and space; C's socioeconomic position and possible ethnicity were utterly out of the picture. He seemed like a small but venomous person that I desperately wanted out of my life. Seeking physical well-being and not about to start a fight, I ended my foray into C's circle of response with a nod of my head. I have no idea why I nodded the way I did, or what it may have meant to anyone else. It just happened. Closing the classroom door behind me I felt that it—the door—was much more than merely my buffer between the security of the classroom and the unpredictable, bestial atmosphere of the hallway. I experienced the door as a godsend, a manifestation of that which protected the good from the evil.

Within minutes, C kicked the door open, violently. It made a crashing sound as it whacked a desk just inside the classroom. C poked his head inside the open doorway. After taking a quick look at his victims, the aggressor left my field of vision and returned to the hallway. Above all, this ramped up the practical sense of being penetrated even though I had not been touched. Everything else was secondary; feeling drained and hollowed out as well as perforated, I found myself simply checking to see if a security officer had shown up, meekly asking C to "chill out," and then closing the door. The logic of my response was most basically lived through, not thought out. "You can handle this, just stay cool," was a part of the conversation going on inside my head. But my stomach seemed to be conveying a very different message—and one that was harder to ignore. Possessed, it seems I was capable of doing no more than once again meekly closing the door. Too ashamed to look at the students in the room, I went back to my desk next to the door. I felt *emotionally* transformed: I hated C and his friends, and I very much wanted to cause them bodily pain. Luckily, no situational means for doing this were or could be made present.

A few moments later C repeated the trick. This time he kicked the door open and barged into the room, all in one movement. Now flushed with fantasies about grabbing this little "demonic fuck" (to use a term from my most Malinowski-like field notes) and throwing him out of the room on his head, I did nothing but look at him until he disappeared, again into the hall. As I started to close the door I noticed that it was starting to crack through the middle. While slurping up what felt like the last drops of my emotional energy, my tormentor was destroying precisely what I experienced as my sheltering outer layer. Inside and out, it seemed, things were literally falling apart. I am at a loss for words to describe the chemical aspect of my reaction, but I was gripped by something that made me feel quite nauseous.

Afterwards, released from the grip of the situation, walking down a flight of steps and finding a security officer seemed like what I should have done straight away. But in the heat of the moment, leaving the classroom to search for a security guard or dean never showed up on my radar screen.[36] Was it some practical sense that the competent soldier should never leave his post? Was I unconsciously "choosing" to play some kind of John Wayne-ish inner-city schoolteacher, protecting the innocent from the wild elements? If the body-based experience of being emotionally shattered by here and now threats and violence made thinking up coherent responses impossible for a stable middle class adult, what did it do to teenagers left behind?

With the door shut once again, there were a few seconds of relative serenity. The class was quiet. At this point, Robert[37]—a soft-spoken dark-skinned boy from the Dominican Republic—almost jokingly suggested the obvious: "Mister, why don't you leave the door open?" His words may have been slightly mocking, but his body language and facial expression were empathetic. I was amazed, suddenly, that I had not thought of doing this. When I hesitated to come out from behind my desk, and probably because I appeared as nearly comatose, Robert got his massive body out of the comparatively tiny chair unit and edged over to the closed door when, again, it shot open. This time the door whacked into Robert's extended right hand. Oddly, I could not help thinking not just about the damage to Robert's hand but also how much it would cost to replace the door and lock that were being ruined. Some kind of weird commodity fetishism had taken hold of my somewhat 'unhinged' mind. Later I would wonder if my stomach was so upset because I had smelled the odor of my own fear.

Although his hand must have hurt, Robert seemed to remain calm. Serenely yet sternly, Robert peered out into the hall at the much smaller container thrower/door kicker and his "rude boy" retinue. Robert then wedged the door open and went back to his desk. From C's perspective, Robert's intervention amounted to an affront. The challenge, of course, was related to more than just the action of wedging the door open. The obvious message, which required no words, was this: "You are a little punk. You would never be doing any of this if your boys were not watching you, and there to protect you. Stop this nonsense and leave us alone." With the door open, C peered into the room, staring intently at Robert, who had returned to his seat. Ignoring the aggressor, Robert seemed to concentrate on the handout I had given him. C entered the room and began yelling insults and threats at Robert. "I'm gonna do this punk ass motherfucka . . . that's my word . . . hate these fruity niggaz out here . . ." When Robert did not respond, C began to screech more threats while holding an empty metal trash container directly above Robert's head. C then put the metal container back on the ground, stood next to the seated Robert and screamed, "I'm gonna make you my bitch after school!" While screaming these remarks, C held a sharpened pencil in his right hand as if it were a dagger. Saliva sprayed into the air around him as he shrieked. At one point his head tilted backwards slightly and bluish veins stood out on his pale neck.

Several of C's acquaintances were peering in from the hall. All of the kids in the small class were watching the epicenter of the action intently. Emotionally and cognitively, all of us were captivated. I dared do no more than form a weak barrier between the aggressor and Robert; I moved over between them, and when we touched it was only because C lurched toward Robert, not because I initiated contact. I did not consider using my size, weight, and strength advantage to push C away from Robert or out of the classroom.

Throughout this sequence of events, Robert seemed to be alarmed and keenly alert, but also calm. He accepted C's authority in the here and now, but somehow communicated that this state of affairs would not last. For a second or two after the promises of impending violence nothing happened. C broke the eerie and intensely charged standstill with a final upper body lurch towards Robert. But he pulled back before making contact, and Robert did not react. Then, after C bit his lip and looked down at Robert one more time, it was over. Perhaps C felt that the social order had been restored, that the ritualized marking off of the more dominant had been achieved, and that the challenge inherent in Robert's oppositional look out into the hall had been successfully met. C departed.

The crowd in the hallway dispersed and I assumed that C would not be back during the rest of my "coverage from hell." At once drained and uncontrollably tense, I went back behind my desk and tried to come up for air. Silence. Time to reflect. Had all this been my fault? Did the students find me pathetic? Was I an embarrassment to the teaching profession, an irresponsible adult, a man who had allowed himself to be manhandled by a bunch of little punks? And most urgently, was Robert really in serious danger? Would the pencil turn into a knife? Would C be forced to keep his word and "catch somebody," as the expression associated with stabbing went?

I could not even begin to understand how Robert and several other students in the classroom managed to engage the assignment I had given them. Was this a bizarre coping strategy, a sort of "I'm ok, we're ok" performance? Or were they simply not nearly as distraught as I was? Whatever the case may have been, had an observer peered into the room from the corridor during the moments that followed, the classroom would have seemed well behaved and productive. But for Robert, for myself, and I would imagine for several of Robert's fellow students, these moments were nerve-racking. As if to prove to myself—and the class—that I had not been shaken to my core, I tried to eat my lunch. The queasy feeling, rather akin to the muscle pain that often announces the coming of a viral infection, made taking in nourishment vaguely disgusting. And yet, in a response perhaps as strange as Robert's working on the assignment, I ate. After eating, and with a profound sense of being even more out of touch than when I started trying to "comfort" myself with my lunch, I walked around the front of the classroom. When would this period end? When would the effects of that explosion of nervous energy and destructive emotions finally stop manifesting in my body?

Several minutes had passed when, for some reason, I looked out into the otherwise empty hallway. I saw C approaching. Or, more accurately, I saw "another" C coming my way. C did not merely look different. He was different. His walk and bearing made clear that the storm had passed. He approached in a strikingly meek and mild way. Upon arriving, he offered me a silent handshake. No "gangster" handshake, just a conventional and rather limp one. He barely dared to make eye contact with me. While observing our handshake, Robert suddenly stood up and looked at C with a quite aggressive gaze. Robert, who had remained seated and avoided eye contact with C during the most intense moments of the encounter, also seemed to have been transformed. C offered the far taller and broader Robert the same type of humble handshake he had offered me. The olive branch was being extended. The two boys exchanged knowing nods. No words were spoken. C's new physical presence was still more "street" than it was "nerdy." He still had something of a swagger—the stiff-leg/loose-leg walk. But the hyperactivity, the aggression, and the quick, nervous movements were gone. C's torso and shoulders were now oriented in and downward instead of outward and toward the ceiling. He now seemed to be not only a much smaller but also a demoralized, rather piteous figure. After the handshakes, C quickly made his final exit. Another awkward silence ensued. Then a girl seated not far from the damaged door coldly spoke the following words: "You know that don't mean nothin', right?" The fact that she had seemed to be emotionless throughout the entire encounter and that she had said nothing before that point somehow added extra weight to her comment. She seemed to know very, very well what she was talking about. I immediately sensed that she was right. C's peer group and the pressure of the after-school scene at one of the main exits might spur him to follow up on his promises. Perhaps because on some level I felt ashamed about not having come to his aid the way he had helped me, I told Robert I would pick him up after his last class at a less frequently used exit. I told him I would make sure it was safe for him to walk from this exit to my car before I came in to get him.

Hours later I was still feeling the aftereffects of the ordeal as I walked out of the main exit to collect the shelter-providing vehicle. As I hit the street, I was relieved to find neither C nor members of his "thugged out" clique anywhere in the vicinity. I started to relax. Within a few strides I felt a hard object pressed against my ribs and heard a high-pitched voice ordering me to produce my wallet. The fight or flight instinct took over, again. With the foreign object pressed against my body I very literally felt how to cope. I turned and discovered a small boy with a ski mask pulled over his head. I spun around and grabbed the boy's wrist with my left hand. I found myself squeezing the kid's slender wrist tightly, even after I noticed he was holding a harmless wooden block, instead of a gun or a knife. As I turned and made these discoveries (i.e., what I was doing, what was in his hand), I felt the urge to use my right hand to pummel him. But the urge to turn and clobber passed almost as quickly as it had come over me. This too was instinctual. The brakes were applied almost as quickly as the fight-or-flight engine had been revved up. Slowly, my horizon widened. The smiles on the faces around the exit area made it clear that I had been the butt of a joke. It also became clear that I had been using the nail of my thumb to dig into the flesh of the boy's wrist. My mildly violent response to the smallish prankster's provocation was instantaneous and had everything to do with the fact that I was still rattled by what had happened earlier.

As the primary emotional impulses (defend yourself, turn, hurt him) and the almost instantaneous emotion-controlling counterimpulses (do not hit the child, not too deep with the thumbnail) faded, the kaleidoscope of secondary emotions and thoughts started to arrive. I began to feel aware of being embarrassed and angry. What the hell was I doing with my thumbnail in this kid's forearm? With a mild nudge I released the boy's wrist. I tried to muster yet another confidant smirk and dignified walk as I headed for the car. For some reason, I found myself hoping that my walk would be perceived as calmer, tougher, and more dignified than those of the others who had been the butt of the same joke. I slowly came to see this hope—that I would measure up, that I would produce a relatively manly man image—as bizarre. The idea that I might have held the wooden block and the hand that had pressed it against my side and walked directly to the dean's office arose only much later. First and foremost, I was concerned with my own bodily well-being and how my movements were being perceived. It seems the situation so focused me on the somatic aspect of my being, and so made me feel that I was going to pieces, that concentrating on my "I've got it together"/tough-guy-teacher walk was the best I could do.

While still reeling, I finally began feeling safe only when I was inside the car and had locked all the doors with the flip of a switch. With my flesh finally out of the game, one thought rushed to my mind: I would call in sick the next morning.

The coast remained clear, and I picked up a very thankful Robert. He was visibly distraught, more so than he had been in the classroom. During the five-minute ride to his eight-story tenement building on the other side of the Grand Concourse he explained to me, while nodding and looking down at his feet, that he was "tired of all this shit." He went on to tell me that he had been forced to transfer to Johnson High from another notoriously unsafe local high school in the South Bronx. His old high school had a highly respected football team that he had wanted to join, but because of a violent incident involving a cousin, he had been forced to leave. If he had remained at the other school, he might have become a target for revenge in his family member's absence. As we pulled up to his building, he informed me that if the boy who had threatened him ever happened to walk down his "block by accident," he and his "people" would "put him in the hospital for a few

months. That's my word Mr. P. We gonna hurt dat nigga for real, watch."
Before he closed the door to the car he looked down at me and offered an
informal and typically rhythmic late 1990s South Bronx salute, "Get home
safe, yo. Thanks for the ride." "Yo" at the end of a sentence and in this context implied equal status and warmth. It might be read as something like
"friend." First viscerally then discursively, we were "grouped."

I had a few brief conversations with Robert in the following days, my
last in the Bronx. We would see each other in the hallway and report that
neither of us had seen C, and that neither of us wanted to. I thanked him
repeatedly for his aid on the spot and he thanked me again for the ride
home. Robert continued to express concern about my welfare: he assured
me that his hand was all right, that C would never bother him, and that he
would be fine after my departure. I could not tell how deeply or durably
Robert had been impacted by the whole affair. But the very fact that our
connection was strengthened indicated that the sequence of events had influenced him to some extent. I asked him if encounters such as "ours" ever
made him a little bit crazy. "Mr. P.," the kind-hearted giant answered, "this
wasn't nothin' special. It's punks like him all over the place so . . . I'm used
to dealing with these types of kids. Don't worry about me man, you just take
care of yourself." There may have been a bit of extra bravado in this statement because, to some extent, Robert cared what I thought of him. We were
forming something that, unfortunately, was nothing special for many students in both settings as well as for some teachers, especially in the Bronx:
a friendship based both on the emotional rawness of being simultaneously
threatened by a clearly definable enemy and the tenderness of being mutually supportive.

Cruising down the FDR Drive and taking in the tranquility of the East
River in the leather bucket seats of the touring sedan my stepfather had
given me, I retreated to the apartment in a low-stress residential area that
one of my stepfather's business associates rented me at well below market
value. I decided to call in sick the next day. Cashing in on a range of privi-
leges that began flowing my way before I was born, that is, I did what my
students could not: I extracted my whole being from the wildly stressful educational setting without having to worry about sanctions. Although under
the right conditions nearly all of the teens could express the desire for safer,
less frantic, better-regulated educational experiences—in part because their
parents would not allow *them* to take a ("mental health") day off—they had
no socially acceptable way to give themselves even a few hours of respite
from the intimidation cursing the entire student body in their high-poverty
school.

Discussion: Bringing Out the Worst

One sees the bear with flying feet. One is always going through the woods in one state of anticipation or another, and the perception of a menacing bear is constructed by the gingerly manner in which one is already walking.[38]

If we really want to understand students in toxic schools, we need to start by getting in touch with how their bodies are prediscursively gendered and endangered. Instead of rushing to blame students for specific actions or more general tendencies, we need to get a grounded sense of the degree to which their *observable behaviors* are *stress responses*. Of course, in the scenes depicted above, explicit thoughts came into play and backgrounds mattered. Mainly because of their previous experiences and gradually acquired capital portfolios, some students (like Stephano) were especially predisposed to go on thirsting for the high-status posts that more powerful types (like Vanessa, Cory, and Julio) were all but forced to occupy "naturally." While Jurgen's culturally "street" performances and potentially racialized ways of making "gangster" happen were to some degree intentional, there is no denying that he had gradually acquired a comparatively violent habitus which prestructured everything he did in and around his educational world. Previously conditioned students were sentient beings capable of consciously reflecting on—and to some extent modulating—their emotions. But, as we just saw, a middle class white *teacher* shielded his entire life from violence and stigma could be transformed, quickly, into something of a "belligerent" (capable of digging a thumbnail into a small child's wrist). And lower class black boys like Cory (who at times seemed close to the ideal typical gang member in the South Bronx) and Jurgen (who was as "street" as they come, as we will see more clearly when he is profiled in a later chapter) were at times at least ambivalent about, if not ashamed of, the violent coping practices associated especially with more dominant boys in their schools. So the place to start our analyses of the threats and violence perpetually founding and reflecting status struggles in schools such as ours is *not* mainly with consciously held (oppositional or racialized) beliefs or even (underprivileged) backgrounds. Rather, we need to begin with immediate, viscerally felt, and nauseatingly cumulative senses of being frightened, tightened, hardened, beaten down, revved up and stressed out in the public institutions black and nonblack parents *with means* fight to keep their own flesh and blood from having to experience directly.

In emphasizing this core similarity across the two settings, I do not want to downplay the harsh reality that the school in the Bronx was far more violent than the school in the Bijlmer. Nor do I want to make light of how the greater levels of fear and aggression maintained an overall emotional environment—and power ratio between the (potentially) belligerent and the rest—that was dramatically less healthy in the failing American "ghetto" school than in the one buttressed by a European welfare state. Nonetheless, the first point that must be made here relates to a profound similarity across the two settings: No matter what any of the students believed, the anxiety related to threats and episodic outbursts of brutal violence was always both "out there," in the educational settings, and "in there," beneath the flesh of the exposed. While there was far more intense violence in Johnson High, the contaminating and corrosive effects of even a small number of extremely harrowing incidents (such as the stabbing of Patrick in the Bijlmer) were significant, and everyday threats remained endemic to both schools.

As we saw at several turns in this chapter, then, while the most pressing problems confronting the students certainly related in part to actual violence, the ongoing experience of bodily vulnerability was tied up with all kinds of (seemingly trivial) reminders that one was immersed in an environment riven by threats large and small. As a result, putting aside such concepts as late modernity and advanced post-industrial cities, we find that born-poor adolescents on both sides of the Atlantic are being compelled—ultimately by state law—into uncivilizing (if not de-civilizing) institutions of late barbarity.[39] Especially in the Bronx, but also in the Bijlmer, because threats and violence were "already" out there and deep inside pre-alerted and braced bodies, fear always retarded (or actively reversed) the processes through which social constraints gradually become emotional self-constraints. Albeit in different dosages, here we find in both settings institutional toxicity in its least diluted form.

This brings us to a finding that can be especially hard to see when race-based lenses color too strongly analyses of "groups" in the schools of the poor students. No matter how they were categorized along ethnoracial lines, the more docile male and female "nobodies" tended to remain peaceful. In other words there were busloads of (native-born) black kids (as well as other teens many researchers might classify as "involuntary minorities") in both settings who were not at all threatening. While those labeled black were overrepresented among the most aggressive groups, a blanket concept like "oppositional black culture" (or some kind of burden of acting white related to historical adaptations to racial oppression) does not explain when or how certain students turned threatening or why others remained non-aggressive. While violence flowed much more clearly along gendered fault lines, and while (potentially) violent conflicts were often ethnoracialized to varying degrees (as we saw with the encounter centering around Vanessa), what I saw and heard about was not so much "black on black" or "brown on brown" violence as dominant male vs. dominant male aggression related more or less directly to access to the "hottest" girls.

The potentially violent confrontations of elites in the two schools had everything to do with sex in another sense of the word as well. In both schools, as was indicated in Vanessa's attraction to Julio, many of the "hottest" girls (or those in positions which insured that they would be judged most attractive) demonstrated appetites for the "hardest" of the "bad boys."[40] Again here, "ghetto fabulous" thuggery trumped concerns about ethnicity-race by a long shot. I cannot say whether this resulted more profoundly from a yearning for "street" resources (and hence shopping sprees), the desire to feel protected in unsafe settings, or some other kind of thirst for local prestige related to being "hot." But the weight of the evidence suggests that the (sexual) tastes of the (supposedly) most attractive girls perpetuated the ways of doing belligerence undergirding the two overall pecking orders and the everyday moment-by-moment destruction of the two educational environments. In short, while shifting and ambiguous constructions of ethnicized boundaries could at times become salient, gender regimes were always strongly related to power struggles and ways of doing "real" violence.

In "naturally" defending their exceptionally privileged positions, the most dominant of dominant boys ended up not "opposing" anything so much as conserving the status quos and overall logics of their respective adolescent societies. Of course many of their actions can be viewed as oppositional from the teacher's perspective. But, as this chapter further revealed, the students most likely to scream that they were "running things" had the fewest means of easing into safe and stabilized bodily-emotional states. Those most inclined to brag about "holding shit down" actually had, that is, the fewest moments to "gather themselves," to unravel the stress, and to take stock of how their compulsive here-and-now reactions related to what they themselves said they wanted (in the future) during many of their calmer moments. As such, those who tended to appear as the masters of the two universes ("We got shit locked-down up in this piece") were in some crucial senses the most enslaved of all. For the majority of less aggressive students forced to observe the proud parading of the most pumped-up and erratic boys—and let us remember that these were students with no counterexamples and no way of even seriously considering making investments in other adolescent status systems—the message was that one should try to attain "true gangster" ways of being. If these seemingly legitimate ways of "scoring" could not be attained, the message was that there was only one ("wanna-be") player to blame.

With regard to one dominant boy's seemingly effortless ability not just to score regularly but to remain calm in a maelstrom of potential violence, this chapter reveled something important about informal socialization processes that once again highlights the centrality of the immediately lived through and fully embodied present. Julio's "gift" did not come though some kind of abstract self-confidence building discourses or any "breakthroughs" related to big ideas. Rather, practical mastery of threatening encounters emerged out thousands of moment-by-moment engagements. The metamorphoses that made a difference came in tiny bits and pieces, for example, though countless little "Wow, I did that" moments which, in turn, led to going a bit further. It took a lot of learning moments in just the right positions to create what appeared as a "natural" like Julio, but the mundane transformations did add up to something that looked like inherent excellence.[41]

Relying on the use of my body as the main research instrument, in this chapter's final vignette we got all the way *inside* a sequence of threatening circles of response. In terms of actually doing violence and being violated in real time, here we saw clearly that which is at once *most fundamental and most often overlooked* in the vast majority of social scientific accounts of physically distressed high schools: the moment by moment *somatic experience* of anxiety and intimidation.[42] But it was not only when I examined what the field did to me (and C and Robert) that the basically pre-discursive and literally embodied character of menacing experiences was revealed. We also saw how the suffering and shame of the less dominant dominant boys (Stephano) was at times drilled into their mental habits via their bodies. Less obviously, perhaps, we also saw that Julio and Jurgen enjoyed mobilizing violence and successfully enacting threats not merely because of what this *signified* (i.e., alpha male status, unchallenged relationships with revered females, strong ties to "true gangsters") but also—and perhaps *mainly*—because of the immediate experience of pulsating energy and rushing blood. All of these cases suggest, one might therefore say, that while fluctuating ideas related to cultural "codes" (and more or less salient ethnoracialized aspects of belonging) were significant, what we really need is to get beneath them. We need to keep in mind that none of Julio's, Roy's, Vanessa's, Stephano's, C's, or my own thoughts would have made any sense—and indeed none of them would have *even been possible*—without the bodies that placed our sensing, cognizing beings in the world. Silent as they may have been, situated bodies provided the taken for granted ground zeros for, and directionality of, emerging feelings and thoughts. There were no skills, there was no knowledge, and there were no values, beliefs, or meanings that somehow influenced actions *outside* of the underlying somatic experiences in which the collaborators and contestants found themselves.

In sum, extending the analysis of moment by moment peer group (un-)making and everyday seductions of status in the previous chapter, this chapter indicates that being physically unsafe and emotionally destabilized brought out the worst in the students: their scattered mixes of compulsive fears, aversions, and fantasies. Their attention and thoughts were "always already" hijacked, that is, by poorly regulated interaction rituals and bodily states that pushed and pulled them in ways making a purposeful life guided by any explicit values and interpretations all but impossible. Perhaps even more clearly than the previous one, therefore, this chapter indicates why we need to ease away from overly mentalist approaches and toward understandings of real-life coping processes based on destructive emotional metamorphoses and the frenzied energetics of precariously embodied minds.

A critical reader might argue that getting so close to the gendered and gendering transactions that naturalized interpersonal brutality and relegitimized the two status systems was a great way to conceal broader (and ultimately even more oppressive) structures of power.[43] Such a reading would miss entirely the point of comparing what actually took place inside my failing "ghetto" schools.[44] There is, however, something to be said for the idea that we have, up to now, paid too little attention to the myriad ways in which students experienced inequalities within the two broader urban realms (and, relatedly, within the two broader fields of education). The next chapter steps outside the two segregated neighborhood schools in an attempt to further consider why students made emotional investments in ways of playing their educational games that, at times, they themselves understood to be damaging if not potentially deadly.

FOUR

Exile and Commitment

You were born into a society which spelled out with brutal clarity, and in as many ways as possible, that you were a worthless human being.[1]

Oh, you from over there by Walton [Avenue] yo? A'ight [respectful handshake and direct eye contact], them niggaz is real.[2]

The students attending Johnson High and the Delta School were growing up poor in two of the world's most opulent cities. They lived in rundown neighborhoods near some of the most esteemed residential areas on the two continents. Together they formed "dumb" schools in cities known for first-rate educational institutions and high concentrations of intellectual capital. As such, the adolescents could not help being reminded from time to time of the lowly positions within the two broader urban spaces into which they had been born—and these reminders contributed at times to profoundly stressful insecurities. Yet the more dominant teens in both settings also *tuned out* such depressing signals by *tuning into* here-and-now rituals of "realness" (Chapter 2) and, in some cases, by chasing cheap thrills and compulsive aversions all the way from threatening everyday transactions to the razor's cutting edge (Chapter 3). Furthermore, as we have already started to see, students in both settings developed pride by embracing potentially disgraceful aspects of their own habitus and neighborhood habitats.

The term "ghetto fabulous" has more than hinted at this complex process of (collective) self-degradation and self-aggrandizement.[3] Up to this point, however, I have not considered how proximity to the (basically white or native Dutch) *haut monde* bled into students' practical understandings of belonging. Walking with students as they moved in and out of wealthy sections of the two metropolises can help us understand with depth and clarity the insidious tug of "ghetto fabulous" *communitas* which at once shamed and shielded them from the effects of living and going to school in the Bronx and the Bijlmer.

A few straightforward questions can serve as helpful guides here: How did crossing what were often perceived as class and color lines in the their native cities influence the students' feelings about "I," "us," "them," and the possibility of "making it" in the future? How did students' experiences in upscale sections of the two cities inform their more local points of reference and everyday pursuits of emotional "payoff" inside Johnson High and the Delta School? In speaking to these questions, I hope the vignettes in this chapter communicate—and perhaps even validate—the students' necessarily fragmented mixes of emotional intricacy, irrationality, denial, and realistic judgments.

Inheritors and Non-Inheritors at the IMAX

For us to go back there is to be submitted to an insult again. The Quarte Mille is an insult. We take it as a slap in the face . . . This poverty is experienced as a shame. It is a shame.[4]

A small group of teachers, including myself, took a group of about twenty tenth-graders to a high-tech movie theater in Manhattan. We were going to see *Amistad*, a Steven Spielberg film about slavery and rebellion, at the IMAX theater located just a few blocks from Lincoln Center. All the students had been in my class for at least one semester and I thought I knew the ones that actually came to class quite well. (I had recorded interviews with a few of them, talked with several of their mothers or guardians, and visited one student's home.)

From the teacher's perspective the main storyline went something like this: although we had been worried about behavioral problems, nothing went very far awry. We traveled down to Manhattan by subway, we watched the film, and we tried to engage the students in discussions about what they had just seen on the way back. We were disappointed when the engagement never got past the "Wow, what a boring movie" stage. On the ride back to the Bronx, for example, a teacher asked four of the students sitting in front of her what they thought the movie was really all about. There were several blank stares, but no responses. Finally, a student responded by talking about a movie she had seen the week before on TV. There would be no conversations about oppression or the struggle to achieve full humanity.

For most of the students the highlight of the excursion seemed to center around playing (or watching the fellow students with money to spend play) what struck me as an incredibly modern shoot 'em up videogame. In the game, zombies came out of graves. One or two people with guns had to stand in front of a sort of shoebox movie theater and blow the bad guys to bits before they got too close. The action was intense. The graphics and special effects were vivid. And the sound, especially for those in the little booth, was jarring. As I had not really noticed the new generation of videogames in these types of establishments, I too was genuinely impressed. At one point I gave it a try. It seemed fun to play alongside Cory—in part because he so frequently made my attempts to teach pathetically ineffectual, and in part because of his status as one of the most feared and respected boys in the school. The students seemed to get a kick out of watching him efficiently obliterate the zombies while spitting out epithets in a somewhat humorous fashion: "What de fuck you think this is nigga? . . . Gonna blast yo' ass, motherfucka, blaaah blaaah. Step the fuck back bitch. Clown-ass motherfuckers." The zombies got to me almost immediately. When the zombies finally got to Cory he pretended that it was my fault, and that he was angry with me for not being able to shoot straight. "Mr. P," Cory said loud enough for his classmates to hear, "you is one lousy-ass partner man."

Part of the fun was, no doubt, that while his language remained thuggish and proud, Cory was clearly less loud and intimidating than he might have been. Although still a "gangster" in terms of his underlying style, in the new setting Cory seemed to have been transformed into a rather mildmannered hoodlum (for entirely different reasons than he was after the double slashing discussed in the previous chapter). His tone was more lighthearted than belligerent, and he made the predictable jokes one might associate with a rather light Hollywood comedy. Intentionally or not, he seemed to communicate to the others that one should remain somewhat reserved in such "classy" establishments. The other typically more dominant and often threatening students were doing the same.[5]

Compared with Cory's gentle-gangster performance and the action of the video game, for most if not all of the students, the film was a downer. Judging by their moods and comments after the film, I assumed that they were not endowed with nearly enough informational or linguistic capital to understand most of the film's references. I wondered if they felt insulted because they sensed lacking this. What I saw was that they did not have good senses of self during or after the confrontation with the form of edutainment the other teachers and I had selected.

From the perspective of the urban ethnographer, several things happened on the way into the ritzy Cineplex that were far more telling than anything I have described so far. First off, the natives of the South Bronx became relatively tranquil the moment we emerged from the train station and into the affluence of West 66th Street. The more "fabulous" pupils swaggered in far less distinctive ways than they usually did "back home."[6] All the students pretty much stopped talking to each other. They came across as tourists, just taking it all in. In fact, the deference expressed in their postures and movements suggested that they felt like visitors who sensed that "their place" was less high ranking.

Soon after we arrived at the theater in what to many of my students may have felt like the heart of whiteness, one teacher went in to get the tickets while the students and the other teachers stood out in front. A couple of students, another teacher and I ended up on one side of the main entrance. Most of the students clustered together on the other side. The students huddled together, perhaps because the unseasonably crisp winds were penetrating their jackets. The status differences that usually divided them seemed to become less stringent in this foreign setting.

Then a large yellow school bus rather suddenly stopped directly in front of the theater. I heard one of my students crack a joke about "the cheese bus" arriving (i.e., a bus that looked like a huge block of American cheese). The load of pupils from a prestigious private high school located in the northernmost section of the Bronx started filing out of their bus, walking right past my students, and strolling directly into the large lobby of the movie theater. At this point I think we all felt a bit awkward—students and teachers—because we were waiting outside while this was, evidently, neither necessary nor "the done thing." But instead of going in we gawked. It was as if my students, the other teacher, and I were the paparazzi who dared not go inside as the stars glided in on the Oscar night carpet.

My students carefully observed their "well-bred" counterparts. They appeared to be fascinated by the rich kids' mix of preppy, grungy, Kurt Cobain–influenced, skateboarder-ish styles. Many of the wealthy kids made a point of wearing sneakers so old they looked as if they might disintegrate with every step. Their jeans did not sag (i.e., they were pulled up "too high") but often dragged along the ground and were therefore shredded. None of them had the jackets with loud colors or shiny new baseball caps that my students adored. No gold teeth, no gold necklaces, no flashy earrings. The hairstyles were all a mess—from the viewpoint of the kids from the South Bronx.

Given that "each society has its own special habits" (Mauss [1935] 2006: p.79), it seems fair to say that my students found the privileged kids so exotic at least in part because of the markedly different "attitude of their bod[ies]." From the standpoints of my students and colleagues, more precisely, the poised facial expressions and languid movements of those unfazed by the affluent surroundings as they got off the bus seemed to communicate that they were of an entirely different kind. Perhaps their corporal poise resulted primary from socialization in culturally and economically elite families. It may also have evolved out of repeated experiences in such upscale neighborhoods and establishments. However, as surely as the ease of *The State Nobility* in France results in part from years of (informal, bodily-based) learning in elite *lycées*,[7] and as certainly as the poise of the most privileged teens in the United States is in part incorporated in places like elite prep schools (Khan 2011, pp.81–84), the "natural" composure of the adolescents making their way past my students resulted at least in part from their everyday experiences in schools atop New York's fields of secondary education.

My students seemed to scrutinize most carefully their counterparts appearing to be of African (American) ancestry. Two of these darker skinned students, one girl and one boy, had dreadlocks. And there was also a girl with a rather large, bushy afro. While there was one student at Johnson High with dreads—an incredibly exceptional boy we will meet in the next chapter—literally every girl with kinky hair at Johnson had a "perm" (i.e., artificially straightened hair). A girl with an unkempt afro was unthinkable. How could this be, my students seemed to be thinking as they pored over these most baffling of bohemians.

What I was witnessing, I would later think, is at once endlessly complex and amazingly straightforward. The complexity had to do with substantialist categories such as "black" and "white" simultaneously being reinforced and losing their grip as my students came face to face with the undeniable fact of white privilege and the irrelevance of race. Analytic pairings like white/wealthy on one hand and black/poor on the other were at once being strengthened and weakened. All the while, and this is the straightforward part, senses of *not belonging* in opulent and predominantly white surroundings were being further seared into my students' collective unconscious. Whether class was trumping race or not, objective positions in educational and urban space were instilling subjective senses of "us" vs. "them." The unplanned experiment offered a chance to feel something my kids had already been forced to feel any number of times: a New York moment spelling out that there would be no escape from areas like the South Bronx. When they left the "hood" they were often made to feel even more "ghetto," and certainly much less "fabulous," than when they stayed "where they belonged."

Another lesson I took away from this excursion has to do with the surprisingly orderly, predictable atmosphere. Even during the "hottest" moment of the trip, it was clear that no one was going to become aggressive. Five or six "thugs" nearly on top of each other, getting in and out of the smallish videogame booth, trying to grab one of the pistols or put coins in the slots before the movie started so they could perform in front of a meaningful audience—not even this threatened to spark an aggressive exchange.

The previous chapters already indicated that crowding did not *cause* violence. Those forced into the roles of "nerds" never attacked anyone, not even if they were packed into small spaces. The interplay of deeply rooted inclinations and the releasing of specific kinds of micro-situational stimuli *among those positioned toward the top of the two status hierarchies* were responsible for triggering *crowd-related* violence. But what did *not* happen even during the moment of the fieldtrip when many of the usual triggering stimuli and necessary conditions were present helps us take the analysis a step further. Because the students felt (or were made to feel) that "wilding out" would be inappropriate in such an upscale setting, even among the potentially more volatile and aggressive, the belligerent predispositions were not "turned on" by the mix of micro-situational pressures that usually did trigger at least some threatening behavior. Like most adolescent boys and young men, it seems, while the typically dominant male students had no problem with violence in certain types of settings (e.g., a boxing ring) they were far less predisposed toward or ideologically supportive of the use of violence in other types of settings. The difference was not about feelings about violence as such but, rather, that my (especially male) students were effectively forced into (institutional) environments in which threats of serious physical violence were pervasive and, therefore, normalized. Here again the grounded observations not only lead away from analyses based on firmly rooted, situation transcendent normative commitments but also suggest the need to observe down-and-out adolescents in genuinely safe environments (for months at a time) before jumping to conclusions about "their" (black) cultural condoning of belligerence.

After the trip I kept hoping some serious conversations about slavery would spring up in our class. But like Jake's earlier attempts to get his class involved in discussions about *The Crucible* (he also took them to the film), all my attempts to get the students focused on the slave trade fell flat within a matter of seconds. Then it was back to the usual mix of students trying to get some sleep and ongoing conversations about what really mattered: e.g., the infinite status clues related to sneakers, flirtations, "dirty looks" in the hallway, and physical threats.

I was nonetheless intrigued by an apparently offhand remark a student made in our class soon after the field trip. I did not note the exact phrasing, but it was a variation on a question I often received when students looked up from textbooks depicting horrors like dark-skinned human beings in chains on auctioning blocks: "Why did y'all do that to us?" As I had done before, I tried to use "us" and "you all" to charge up the conversation and allow some sustained cognitive focus. Instead of dodging the emotion, that is, I tried to use it. And once again, I found that not even a question loaded with such powerful pronouns (us vs. you) could jumpstart a meaningful, sustained conversation about the most corrosive of institutions.

Maybe what the teachers saw as the "problem" of disengagement did not relate mainly to the movie being too cerebral, wordy, and slow for the students. Perhaps the students were not emotionally settled or physically comfortable enough for a potentially painful investigation into the barbaric depth of their ancestors' subjugation, the holes they were in presently, or what would be required to climb out of them. For the students, faced with the demands of here-and-now insecurity as well as with bleak messages about their futures, further distracting one's self from dealing with the (historical roots) of one's ongoing oppression—i.e., getting aboard the flight to the "fabulous" fantasyland—could seem anything but "problematic."

From this perspective, one might say, it is the "progressive" young teachers and adults more generally—not the pupils—who tend to be incapable of engaging what needs to be engaged. Taking kids to see "uplifting" films and trying to facilitate in-class discussions about overcoming racial oppression might be useful in terms of alleviating senses of (white, middle class) guilt or scoring at cocktail parties. But such "consciousness raising" interventions both derive from and potentially strengthen the old intellectualist fallacy that exposure to critical (historical) analyses and (further) explications of wholesome values can, by themselves, somehow "empower" truly disadvantaged adolescents. The subtext, of course, is that nothing needs to be done about things like ongoing socio-spatial isolation or, short of that, regulating the frenzied, chronically stressful, and at times deadly chains of interaction rituals by which students such as those we took to the IMAX theater are continually yoked.[8]

In short, "failed" fieldtrips can teach adults hard lessons. Self-righteous attempts at "giving something back" and "making a difference"—or worse, to help "emancipate" them from "mental slavery"—were, in the students' language, "a joke." But if we pay close attention to the students' reactions to things like viewing *Amistad* in a wealthy neighborhood, we might catch a few glimmers into why so many urban outcastes contribute to their own further subjection and how we can move past pseudo-interventions in the future.

Ronny's Sense of Place

Born in Curaçao, Ronny came to Amsterdam at age five. From that point on he lived in the high-rise section of the Bijlmer with his aunt, who had been incarcerated in the Netherlands for trafficking cocaine. Ronny was, physically at least, in my English class during his final semester at Delta. He did not seem to care enough about my class even to resist my attempts to teach it. Observations of Ronny's other classes, and conversations with other teachers, generally confirmed this conclusion: when Ronny was in class, he was just hanging out. Like so many others, the formal aspects of life in school (grades, tests, assignments) seemed to mean almost nothing to him. As gentle as he may have been (when I observed him), what really made Ronny tick was maintaining strong ties with what he saw as the more attractive young people in and around his troubled school.

By the time I got to know this first generation Dutch-Antillean boy, he was already eighteen years old. He had a kind, warm, winning smile. His skin was dark, and he kept his afro low. Ronny was not terribly handsome, but he had an athletic build and his eyes lit up when he grinned. He had the endearing habit of placing both of his large hands on his head and looking down when he laughed. And during his last semester at Delta, he seemed to laugh quite a lot—mostly about girls with certain types of bodies and boys' (failed) attempts to get to know them better. To the delight of the other boys in his class, Ronny regularly made remarks along the line of "Mmmm, look how that thing follows her around when she walks," while, for example, clinching his fists as if he were suffering some horrible pain and straining in his chair to look out of the open classroom doorway as girls with certain types of bodies and outfits strolled past. Appropriate or not, I often laughed at such rhythmic performances of working class, Afro-Caribbean-Dutch manliness. And my laughter seemed to make Ronny beam with joy.[9] "Ok, Mr. Paulle, sorry, let's get back to work now. . . . seriously," Ronny once said with mock seriousness towards the end of such an occasion. Although he almost never raised his voice, the jokester did like to wear loud colors. And although he seemed not to need to be in the spotlight very often, except to make a light-hearted (and sexist) joke, the gold chain around his neck, like his gold tooth, seemed to be visible almost all the time.

Despite its exceptionally small size, Ronny's class was characterized by as much low-level disruption, humor, aggravation, nervous excitement, and pointlessness as most of the others I taught at Delta.[10] Although things never became physically violent inside the classroom, three of the most frequently wound-up boys regularly yelled taunts across the room and the majority of the others, including Ronny, often carried on conversations even during my attempts to regain order. Getting the boys to bring their books, do any homework, or pay attention to a formal task proved nearly impossible. From traditional textbook-based chalk talk lesson plans to working in pairs translating hip-hop and dancehall lyrics to reading and translating excerpts from Martin Luther King and Malcolm X speeches, nothing seemed to move them, or hold them, for more than a few minutes. And getting them to write anything, anything at all, was like pulling teeth. Drained, sometimes after sending one or two of the "worst offenders" out of the room, I often found myself falling into what might be called a "fuck-it mentality" (Duneier 1999, p. 60), letting the remaining boys get into their gossiping, joking, bragging, and boasting.

Two of the nine students were incarcerated that semester. One boy, Marvin, who seemed to be the most disrupted and (often frantically) energized of all—i.e., the boy who was described rolling a joint in front of the school in an earlier chapter—was locked up on a drug charge. The other boy, Ronny's closest friend—the even more sharply dressed Marcello—was incarcerated for stabbing someone. Ronny contended that Marcello had been attacked "for no reason" while hanging out with a few slightly older men whom he had also "grown up with." Marcello had acted, Ronny said with a serious face and open hands turned up to the sky, "purely in self-defense."

I found this hard to believe. No girl, gun, or gold was involved? Not even an insult or failed joke? I had heard scores of stories about slashings, stabbings, and shootings by that time, but I had never heard about any extreme physical violence just happening. As the school year slogged on, however, the only information I had was from Ronny and from a school manager. This manager shared with me only that Marcello had indeed stabbed a young man on the street near where he and Ronny lived, and that I was to prepare a final exam for him to take behind bars.

Ronny fulfilled the token requirements for my class as well as for his others. Soon thereafter he glided down the aisle and picked up his diploma in front of a crowd of other students, their families, and their friends. In the heat of August 2001, Ronny and I agreed to meet so that I could give him copies of the pictures I had taken at his graduation and so that he could tell me more of his story. Ronny seemed fine with me recording parts our conversation, but he was especially keen to see the pictures I had taken of him and his lady friend dressed to the nines at the commencement ceremony. (They were the typical stand against the wall and strike a "hard" pose type of pictures that made me think back to picture taking rituals I had seen, as a teenager, on 125th Street in Harlem and on Fordham Road in the Bronx.) One picture was especially memorable. While his female companion put her leg over his, he looked deadpan into the camera, draped one arm around the girl and allowed the other arm to hang at his side exposing a clinched fist. I did not know this Ronny—the "thugged out" lover boy. So I was very interested to see what he would say about this shot.

But I was keen to give Ronny the pictures for other reasons as well. I had ordered some extra prints of pictures taken during the big event for a few of Ronny's friends, including Marcello. And I wanted to give him the pictures because I found what I knew of his story so touching. Ronny had shared with me that he was the first person in his family to receive any kind of diploma. Yet, as I confirmed on the big day, no family members took any pictures because none were present at the ceremony. This seemed odd. How could it be that not even his aunt showed up? And, of course, there was the stabbing incident involving Ronny's dearest friend. Was Marcello safe now? Would Ronny, who often seemed to be Marcello's shadow, be safe now that Marcello was back in the neighborhood? And what had really triggered Marcello's deed?

By this time I had already had two extensive extra-school conversations with Ronny: one with a group near the school and one as the two of us walked from the school over to his apartment building about ten minutes away. Between our school and his apartment building he greeted several people, more than once offering a warm smile or a "box" (the fist-to-fist greeting ending with a pat on one's own chest above one's heart.) His wittiness, his smooth gait, and the confident way he leaned against the mailbox as we said goodbye made it all too clear: he was not actively constructing or representing a feeling of belonging, there really was no shame in his game on that day and he felt completely at home in these surroundings.[11] "Ok, take it easy," he said as we departed. "Oh, Mr. Paulle, you know how to get to the Metro from here, right?" I responded with a distracted "Yes," while looking at a girl on a bike with training wheels swerve at the last moment to avoid a concrete column. "Hey, what are you looking at," Ronny said with an excessively serious face, "she's way too young for you man!"

Ronny agreed to hang out, for the first time, in my neck of the woods. I lived on a congested street in West Amsterdam close to the Vondel Park. I suggested that we meet at the Blue Teahouse in the middle of the park. Before going in for lunch, and with a strong sun bearing down on us, we decided to take a little stroll. We started speaking about Ronny's past and the extra-school forces with which Ronny contended while still at Delta. According to Ronny's calculations the majority of his neighborhood friends and acquaintances, around his age or slightly older, were "dropouts." Many of them dipped and dabbed in the drug trade, especially the boys. Those involved usually sold cocaine, and sometimes heroin, to local junkies. In some cases, they smuggled the "stuff" in themselves by swallowing "little balls" of cocaine before return trips from the Dutch Antilles. This was, Ronny explained for the first time, what his aunt had been caught doing. He stressed that many of the mostly male and mostly small-time dealers and smugglers had no formal address. Their female acquaintances would allow them to store drugs and weapons in their apartments, and offer them temporary shelter, in exchange for gifts and a small percentage of the proceeds.

We went on to discuss what he saw as the good and bad aspects of his primary school. Ronny said he felt sorry for the teachers that he and his friends had often brought to tears and "sent home stressed." He did not know exactly why, at some point, he stopped "acting like a kid," and started "acting normally," in school.

Perhaps nothing was as instructive on that day as what Ronny expressed without words soon after we sat down to have lunch. I had just pulled out the pictures and we were laughing about the outfits people wore to the graduation when the waitress came to take our order. As fate would have it, she heard what we were discussing and she was also a recent graduate. "Oh," she said to Ronny, "you just graduated too." Ronny was visibly caught off guard but in good spirits and he smiled as he answered her question in the affirmative. "Me too," she said. And then it came: "HAVO?" The HAVO is a Dutch secondary education track, the one this extremely middle-class Dutch girl had just completed. Although it is not the highest track in the secondary system, the HAVO is high enough to grant admission to a BA program. "No," Ronny said, with a less than luminous grin uncomfortably superimposed on his face, "VMBO." He looked from the girl to me to the ground. I also looked down, instinctively, at my feet. I could just make out his faltering gestures. With his shoulders slumped and his back rounded, he crossed his arms in front of him before apprehensively putting his hand on his forehead. I felt my body stiffen and grow queasy. The VMBO was the "prevocational" track, under the HAVO level, that did not allow graduates to move directly on to college. Ronny lied, literally, I think we can say, in an attempt to save face. He knew, and he knew that I knew, that he did not in fact have a VMBO diploma but an even lower IVBO diploma, or a "local"

VBO diploma that was not even recognized at the national level. His "piece of paper," as the students often put it, was worth even less than the generally stigmatized VMBO diploma.[12]

"Oh . . . umm . . . what would you like to drink?," the waitress managed to ask. The "Oh. . . . uum" was more awkward than the utterance of the word "HAVO" a few seconds earlier. The rhythm and rapport with which our encounter began had come to a screeching halt. We were now caught up in a ritual headed in the wrong direction. Clumsily, we placed our orders.

But the damage had been done. During that half-second or so in which we made eye contact, before we both looked down, I saw that Ronny had been dealt a body blow. This Ronny on the ropes was even less familiar to me than the ladies' man striking the prefight pose in one of the pictures. The gregarious and outwardly oriented young man who had walked through his neighborhood greeting old friends appeared frail, insecure, and introverted. His expression conveyed desolation and hopelessness.

As we waited for our food and drinks, the atmosphere seemed to be full of potential mishaps. What would happen next? After the fact I would think about all the euphemisms of Dutch education experts confidently prattling on about how lower vocational tracks are good for "youth who have trouble with theoretical learning" and who "want to work with their hands." The message, of course, is that the lower vocational education is ok for *them* in large part because *they* do not know any better. What I saw in Ronny's face before intuitively looking away was not the ignorant suffering of a kid who knew no better and felt good about the educational track onto which he had been forced. What I saw was a young man with an accurate sense of the difference between the waitress's more prestigious track and his own. Ronny was aware of what was happening on the micro-level, but the sting emerged from his sense of the underlying status differentials between him, our waitress, and most of the people in the unfamiliar surroundings. The distance between what felt like his kind and my kind came as plainly into view as the grass, trees, and bike path we could see from the upper level of the Blue Teahouse.

Perhaps on some elementary level Ronny also sensed that the verdict the school system had passed would come back to haunt him whenever he ventured into non-marginalizied enclaves where pre-BA level diplomas were taken for granted. He had been proud, back in the Bijlmer, that he had received any diploma at all. In the universe I had dragged him into, his academic past came to feel like a disfigurement, or a botched tattoo, that should be hidden from view. The ceremony, the pictures, my congratulating him—it all seemed rather vacuous after the call to order imposed by the waitress and by the configuration of the city itself. "Stay where you belong, where your kind belongs" was the undeniable subtext of the event. And this message was pregnant with connotations about race as well as class.

Thankfully, the ice melted quickly in the summer sun. We started to recover while eating our sandwiches. Ronny didn't hold a grudge, and he was polite with the waitress as we left. Yet Ronny's awkwardness and perhaps shame, and my own awkwardness and shame, were not completely left behind as we headed away from the teahouse. "That was a really good sandwich, thanks," the gentle soul offered. Awkwardly, I slung my arm around his back and rested my hand on his shoulder as we began taking another walk. Observing Ronny's lack of a status shield, perhaps mixed with his lack of a sense of "ethnic honor" (Weber 1978, p. 390), made me feel guilty about having put him in a situation in which he would have to pay a steep price for some (now degraded and degrading) pictures. After having seen Ronny confident and relaxed just outside his home, watching him get humiliated just a few minutes from my own apartment gave me a newfound respect for something a dark-skinned Surinamese boy in Ronny's class had said to me during the group discussion in which Ronny had taken part. Referring to changes related to sweeping urban renewal projects, he said: "The Bijlmer belongs to us. They are trying to change it, but it will always be ours." Thinking about this comment and to a degree feeling what Ronny felt, I got a taste of the visceral state that can accompany the following straightforward bit of explicit mental content: The Bijlmer had to belong to them because they could never "belong" outside the Bijlmer. In the throes of this "Ah ha!" moment, there was no questioning of any underlying classification schemes or "social constructions"; the divide between (darker skinned) Bijlmer kids on one side and privileged (white) kids like our waitress on the other was as taken for granted as the solidity of the ground upon which we walked.

We tried out different park benches, trying to keep in the shade. Beads of sweat formed on my forehead as I turned on the tape recorder I dared not use in the teahouse. In what struck me as an exceptionally open way, Ronny further sketched a picture of his past and present. About the future he did not have a lot to say. His story about growing up in Southeast Amsterdam and attending an overwhelmed primary school was similar to others I had heard before. He portrayed his aunt as a kind woman with a mild temperament. Ronny told stories of growing up in an apartment through which lots of friendly adults passed. As he remembered it, there was a steady stream of parties, loud music, and good food. There was joy, rhythm, warmth, and in terms of caring and love, a degree of stability in Ronny's pre- and extra-Delta life. There was also, however, the stint in jail for trying to smuggle cocaine into the country—something his aunt had done, Ronny said, to try to get out from under a mountain of debt. Ronny had questions, furthermore, about why there was so much partying when there was often no money to pay the rent or fix the washing machine. (Ronny half-joked about having to wash his own clothing by hand in the bathtub.) And I had questions, of course, about why Ronny grew up without either of his parents and what happened to him when his aunt was incarcerated. I was concerned, more generally, about the much darker side of Ronny's social capital. From the perspective of someone like myself (who would have liked to see Ronny move on to a continuing education program, learn some marketable skills, and follow the winding path to a stable job), Ronny had been, and still was, immersed in a sea of destabilizing relationships and experiences.

Pulling the strands together we have to say that Ronny grew up experiencing joy and warmth and a kind of emotional stability. At the same time, disorganization, ambiguity, the informal economy, and incarceration were also at the core of both his family life and his street life. In his stories there were no disciplined people getting serious degrees and working hard to make it in a post-industrial urban economy. While the small-time dealers were the only types emerging as Horatio Algers, the "dropouts" and the pregnant teens grinding it out on welfare were commonplace. Ronny had no family members nor even friends of friends who might help him through the tribulations of the Dutch educational system after having successfully navigated it themselves. He had no mother who regularly worked, came home to cook and talk about her day, check up on his homework and speak, when necessary, to teachers in fluent and confident Dutch. In this narrative there was no stable father, older brother, or uncle to help him deal with the perplexities inherent in becoming a man in a high-poverty neighborhood. (Ronny never told me what happened to either of his parents. He knew I wanted to know, so I never felt the need to press him for more information about them.)

In short, Ronny had been fully exposed to the pressures intrinsic to the only residential area he could call home. The disinherited boy's life trajectory, in and out of Delta, made achieving even modest success in either the educational or the economic field seem unlikely.

Disheartened, I turned off the tape recorder and put it in my bag. I started closing off the conversation and thanking him for coming to my neighborhood. Perhaps feeling that we had been forced out of the superficial mode we had at times found ourselves in, I asked if his friend would be safe now, after getting out of police custody. "Marcello's got problems now," was Ronny's direct answer. "And you, will you be alright?" I asked. "Me," he said smiling, "I never stabbed nobody . . . so I don't have anything to worry about." This rather revealing comment may have primed me to go into more detail about what led up to the stabbing incident. I looked at Ronny, and I said, "Tell me, tell me how your boy ended up stabbing somebody?"[13] At this point, perhaps feeling that he was engaged in a genuine human connection rather than playing the ex-student/informant role, Ronny appeared to lay things out for me for the first time.

"Look, Mr. Paulle. . . . We grew up in a rough neighborhood, you know what I mean? I mean . . . look, when your mother is getting high, you know . . . when she has a habit . . . and when the welfare check is just . . . it just disappears, right?" Ronny looked right at me. I was trying to get a sense of whether he was talking about Marcello or about himself. Ronny looked down at his feet. "I mean it's that same old story Mr. Paulle. When you're not eating like you are supposed to be eating, and when you have to go to school looking all dirty with the kids laughing at you and everything. You know what that does to these guys, right? These guys . . . they want to wear gold and look good." Ronny paused, perhaps making up the story as he went along, perhaps deciding how much to reveal, and perhaps coming to grips with the fact that he was coming clean. Then he continued, "So Marcello was tired of all that." "I hear you," I said, trying to sound reassuring and to get him back in the flow. "Right, so . . . that's when guys just start getting into things . . . you know, just start going street. . . . trying to get something together, you know, hustling. And then he started getting some real money together, started buying clothes . . . you know, taking girls shopping." Ronny looked at me again, "And that is when I couldn't tell him . . . I mean . . . what was I gonna tell him then?" Ronny paused, and while I was thinking back to Marcello's fancy outfits and gold chains—and looking at Ronny's gold a little more skeptically—I wanted to reassure him that I was not sitting in judgment: "I got it . . . and that's what led up to the stabbing?"

Sitting on our park bench, Ronny exhaled, closed his eyes, and then opened them to look out at the trees in front of us. "Look . . . when you're young and when you start making money and all that, eventually, you know, people are gonna start trying to take things from you. You know, they want to take your money, your gold, whatever. So you get challenged. They were just like, 'We are going to rob you.' And I guess Marcello, I mean he was out there working, you know, hustling every night. And if somebody robs you, you know, other people are going to find out that you got robbed and sort of like see if you did anything about it. And that's when, at some point, I guess that's when it just happened."[14]

Ronny appeared dignified as he looked out across the empty field directly in front of us. His posture and expression made it clear that he was finished. Ronny may have felt good about getting this off his chest, I thought. He may have felt that he needed to feed me some interesting lines after I bought him lunch. Either way, I knew I would never be able to verify what I had just heard. But even if only a small fraction of what he was telling me was true, the question for me was how such a dearth of nurturing relationships and experiences could have produced—to borrow my friend Jake's term—such a sweetheart. I was awed by Ronny's gentleness even more than what I took to be his candor. I felt compassion for this young man born into so many more troubles than I had been forced to face. The heat may have been getting to both of us and I would press him no more. I thanked him for his time, and we said our goodbyes with cordial smiles and handshakes. "Thanks for the pictures, Mr. Paulle . . . and the sandwich. Next time my treat." Indeed it was an "old story," but I felt honored to that he should choose to let me hear it. I do not want to be overly sentimental here. But I will report that in my own secular way, and only in my own head, I thought, "God bless you, my son. Go in peace." I ended up saying something more like, "Take care Ronny. Keep in touch."

I see now that I should have been more vigilant about keeping lines of communication open. After a string of intermittent and rather superficial phone calls, I lost touch with Ronny soon after he "temporarily" stopped attending his continuing vocational education program. He told me he was working part time at a "store," but was so evasive about this job that I doubted whether it existed. Pondering his precarious connection with the formal economy I thought back to the two-week apprenticeship Delta organized for him in his final year. During this brief period he was confronted with racist working-class shop-floor jokes. "Why don't you drink more milk? You might turn lighter," one lost soul apparently remarked. Ronny told me he responded by stating that he did not want to get foot-and-mouth disease (which was causing a stir in the Netherlands around that time). Boasts about his strategic use of humor aside, he reported that his apprenticeship was a disaster. Add to this his thick accent, his poor reading and especially writing skills, his nearly worthless diploma, and his largely negative social capital, and one has to assume that Ronny is probably down and out right now. I figured Ronny stopped returning my calls because he had stopped going to school and did not want to get a lecture from me. If this is the case, I can only hope that the call to order that emerged from our meeting in the park did not contribute in any way to the adoption of coping strategies as risky as those put into practice by Marcello.

Although Ronny did not always appear to be smart in the classroom, his quick humor and his advanced social skills did not imply an especially dull brain. Contrary to the logic inherent in the Dutch school system, there is no reason to conclude that he regularly fell into his school's version of the "fabulous" life because he lacked the intelligence required for even a modicum of success in the educational field (e.g., the equivalent of a high school diploma, the attainment of some marketable skills). Nor is there any reason, significant as race and racism may have been in his life, to think his actions in school were significantly influenced by a fear that others would think he was "acting white" if he applied himself. And as we have seen, there is a great deal of reason to suspect that Ronny was *not* steadfastly committed to (ideologically) "resisting" the "middle class culture" of the teachers or school. We get closer to the truth when we say that this potentially "soft" young man was—from moment to moment, in and around his neighborhood school—strongly oriented towards "scoring" socially with some of the "hardest" of his fellow students because of his practical sense that he (and his non-"nerdy," Bijlmer-based friends) really had no other way to "play." There is every reason to expect, that is, that Ronny arrived at his stigmatized secondary school with a socially constituted sense of inferiority outside "his" Bijlmer and a faith in "fabulous" ways of playing what looked to him like the only game in town. Even if on some level he may have known about the risks inherent in such social ties, his friendship with Marcello—his being a member of Marcello's "fabulous" team—could feel not just like it was worth the potential trouble, but like it was "everything."

Even Jurgen Softens, a Bit

For reasons we only started to explore (e.g., the seemingly unprovoked attack on the smaller Stefano in the *aula* recounted in the previous chapter), for years, Jurgen appeared to me as an enigma. During one-on-one conversations in and around Delta, Jurgen could sound utterly conventional about "good" (pro-school) and "bad" (disruptive, aggressive) sorts of student practices. During a calmer moment just outside the Delta's *aula*, Jurgen told me how important it was for students to "keep their hands to themselves" and "not talk back to teachers." He described what went on in the highly regulated classroom of an extraordinarily effective teacher—including his own nondisruptive behavior, which I observed for many hours while sitting in the back of my colleague's class—as "normal."

And yet, throughout the time I got to know him, indeed during the years I found it hard not to observe this dark-skinned and remarkably muscular boy with a closely cropped afro, Jurgen struck me as truly fearsome, highly impulsive, and as thoroughly "hardcore street" as they come. Several times I saw him lash out against students who appeared to be, at once, his prey and his all but irrelevant playthings (e.g., elbowing students aside while making his way toward Delta's crowded front entrance). Never a "shook one," as they said in the Bronx, Jurgen appeared to be entirely "thug life for life." Skipping classes and strolling through hallways or hanging out in various high visibility areas, he seemed to be more convinced than all but a few other extremely dominant students that everything was progressing quite well even as he contributed—perhaps more mightily that anyone else in the building—to the destabilization of his school. With his multiple gold chains, tight T-shirts, baggy pants, macho bearing, and cocky grin revealing two gold teeth, Jurgen seemed to be the embodiment of the Bijlmer-version of the highly aggressive "bad boy."[15]

The other students told and retold stories about beatings Jurgen had dished out. One of the more famous encounters took place when a number of students from another school came to Delta to confront him. Like a modern-day Beowulf, Jurgen rushed out of Delta's *aula* to meet the challenging group the instant he heard about their arrival. According to the legend, there was no plotting, no coalition building, he just walked out on his own. A small group of Delta students followed him, less to offer support than because they wanted to see what would happen. About exactly what took place next I have heard different things. According to all the renditions, however, all but one of the boys who came to take revenge scattered quickly when they saw the fierce symmetry of Jurgen approaching them. The one that remained, as an upper level manager there at the time confirmed, was taken to the hospital by ambulance after Jurgen whacked his head with a motorcycle helmet until he lost consciousness.

The stories about the incident stressed the importance of how spontaneously Jurgen responded to the challenge and how quickly he became brutally violent. First and foremost, in the eyes of many of his fellow schoolmates, Jurgen was "fabulous" because he was so unrestrained, fearless, and vicious. In Jurgen's case, access to Delta's power elite did not depend on being ostentatiously dressed or lavishly bejeweled. He was not terribly handsome or distinctively styled, and he did not need to be. One Delta student described Jurgen—and attempted to offer a bit of contextualization—in the following way: "He was raised in the street and he practically lives there now. Kids like him come to school to have fun, talk to the girls, and just wreak havoc (*gewoon om een bende van alles maken*)."

Perhaps triggered by this "raised in the street" comment, I asked Jurgen if I could take him out to lunch outside my University of Amsterdam office. I may have sensed that getting insider's knowledge about Jurgen's domestic/neighborhood situation might be easier if he were removed from it, and it was simply convenient and sort of thrilling for me to meet him in the center of town. For Jurgen it was less than a twenty-minute metro ride to the station near the Dam and the Red Light Distinct, and he agreed. I met him outside the station, asked him what he felt like eating, and we wandered over to a popular Chinese restaurant.

As soon as I had spotted Jurgen standing outside the metro station, and certainly once we started walking, I was struck by the non-thuggish posturing and movements of the boy who had once bragged to me about being part of, arguably, the Bijlmer's most feared street gang.[16] Jurgen did not seem completely mainstream, for lack of a better word. (As was the case with Cory in the IMAX theater, hints of his flamboyant "ghetto" stance and gait were still observable.) But clearly this was not the sure-footed "hard rock" that I had often observed—and frequently had one-on-one meetings with—in and around Delta. This was the kind of Jurgen that manifests, it seemed, in such unfamiliar and peaceful settings.

After making our way into the restaurant, we started with small talk. Soon enough it became clear that Jurgen felt somewhat comfortable talking about his family background and reflecting on life in his neighborhood (the subsection of the "old" Bijlmer characterized by high-rise apartment buildings whose names all began with the letter H). At times with an arm slung around his plate as if to protect it from attempts someone might make to take a bit of his chicken, Jurgen shared with me the following.

His family was from Suriname but he grew up in the Bijlmer in an apartment with his grandmother and a brother fifteen years his senior. Except for the age difference, this came as no surprise to me because the other student who commented on Jurgen's family situation had already told me that his grandmother "didn't even attempt to discipline (*opvoeden*) her two grandchildren." I told Jurgen about this comment and asked if it was true. He remarked that his grandmother "cooks and waits at home for her welfare check. She never says anything to us, never asks any questions." Jurgen also made clear that before and during his years at Delta, he spent an enormous amount of time with a network of boys and young men from his neighborhood. Much earlier, in a conversation inside Delta, he had referred to this group as the "Hoptile Boyz." Back in the Bijlmer, that is, in the domain in which he seemed to reign supreme, "all gangsters" was Jurgen's assessment of this informal group. When he told me about them for the first time, in Delta, he held both his fists up to my face as if we were boxers going toe-to-toe—and seeming to offer a pretty good emic description of tribalism—he added, "You got problems with one of them, you got problems with all of them." In the restaurant, I was the one who had to bring up the possibility that he was talking about the Hoptile Boyz and that some of them might aptly be classified as "gangsters." Jurgen denied nothing, but the flair that made him such an enigmatic figure was gone. He was low energy.

I had been informed that Jurgen's older brother was a "big-time dealer." When I brought this up in the restaurant Jurgen explained, seemingly without emotion, that this was in fact the case. He seemed utterly matter of fact when he went on to tell me that his brother came back from prison and "started dealing cocaine again on the same day." Jurgen repeatedly assured me, however, that he never got involved in more than "little things," like selling stolen mobile telephones, muggings, and grabbing money out of cash registers in small Bijlmer stores. He said he did not get involved in anything "heavy," as he put it, because he was certain his brother would "kill" him if he did. "My brother is dangerous," Jurgen said, "really dangerous." As he said this, he looked up at me. What I saw, for the first time, was a vulnerable young man. Instead of anything related to romanticized or even neutralized (e.g., as he put it when I asked him about beating Stephano, "this is just how things go") discourses on violence, his expression seemed to convey that the beatings he had received from his older brother were simply atrocious and perhaps traumatizing.

I had trouble believing Jurgen was steering clear of any drug-related "hustles" for several reasons. Most obviously, Jurgen had continued to come to school with expensive new outfits and shoes during the extended period that, as he confirmed, his brother had been in jail. During those months, furthermore, in part because I offered to take pictures of him striking a "b-boy stance," I had repeatedly seen Jurgen showing off wads of cash much thicker, it seemed, than what one might get for a few stolen telephones. I assumed his grandmother was not supplying him with fat bundles of 20 and 50 euro bills any more than occasional "small-time" stunts were. But even as he softened and opened up, Jurgen seemed no more willing to tell me the sources of his income than why he so intensely feared his brother's wrath.

Whether or not he was deeply into the local drug trade, a glimpse of what was most likely on the horizon for Jurgen came a couple months after our meeting in the center of Amsterdam when he encountered the world of legal work. One of the requirements for the "prevocational" degree that Jurgen was on track to receive was the successful completion of a two-week unpaid mini-apprenticeship (*stage lopen*). In his case the apprenticeship was with a construction company. Jurgen came to work late. He soon began misplacing tools that he had borrowed. Before the end of the first week, the verbal shouting matches had started and the foreman told him not to return. With no time left to find another apprenticeship, one of the upper level school managers (i.e., the man who had told me about Jurgen knocking a boy unconscious with a motorcycle helmet) created one for him, at least on paper. This ensured that Jurgen would receive his ceremonial diploma and be allowed to move along on the lowest vocational track in the Dutch system. While some of the other students in his class were getting their first taste of the working life, Jurgen and a few other boys who had also been sent off almost immediately sat around school and made jokes. As fate would have it, more than one of the other students was associated with the Hoptile Boyz. The school manager who had manufactured the "job" for Jurgen and the others put it this way: "Look, nobody is going to be well-served by holding these guys back for another year here—least of all the teachers and the other kids. They are going to be somebody else's problem in a few months, and we are all going to just get on with our lives (*wij gaan gewoon lekker verder*)."

Jurgen seemed to feel good about how his life was unfolding in and directly around the Delta School mainly for the following reason. Surrounded by (slightly) less-dominant students in Delta's "hot spots"—at once feared and more or less worshipped by any number of "underlings" operating from positions such as the ones Stephano occupied—Jurgen resembled some kind of high priest of thuggery or warrior-king holding a knightly court. In and directly around his school he went from one validating, invigorating interaction to the next. While almost perpetually reenergized by central positions in interaction rituals poorly if not completely unregulated by adults it was difficult for him to even consider what might be going wrong. In and out of school, he went from one more or less effervescent situation to the next in which being physically strong and impulsively ferocious translated better than just about anything into the field-specific form of symbolic power known as "realness" that was the main stake up for grabs in the educational setting he terrorized. Repeatedly going through the immediate full spectrum first-person experience of (Delta's version of) the "thug life," strengthened if not catalyzed by more or less "fabulous" associates and onlookers, the Jurgen I usually saw seemed singularly concentrated on embodying "hardness." Except for during exceptional moments in well-ordered classrooms, that is, this was the superior self he was able, if not forced, to prop up in the here and now. After further destabilizing his school for years, after being forced onto the lowest educational track, after acquiring almost no academic skills, after living alone with his grandmother for months while his older brother was behind bars, and after getting thrown off the shop floor during the first week of his apprenticeship, everything seemed to be working out fine as long as Jurgen remained in the "fabulous" flow. Right up to and soon after the time I took him out to lunch in another world, that is, Jurgen seemed to be feeling pretty good about destroying his school and, quite possibly, his own long-term life chances.

My time with Jurgen in the famous center of Old Amsterdam helped me solve the riddle that my observations in the Bijlmer had produced. Even in this forcefully built limiting case—and as violent as Jurgen's set of dispositions may have been—his in-school bodily states, feelings, thoughts, and responses must be conceptualized primarily as effects of shifting (micro-situational) contexts of action rather than as anything having to do with seemingly fixed personal attributes.

Discussion

Resignation is indeed the commonest effect of . . . the teaching performed by the order of things itself . . . next to which the intentional actions of domestication performed by all the ideological State apparatuses are of little weight.[17]

The explicit ideas that "progressive" pedagogues saw as extensions of formal curricula did not generate much of the desired "consciousness raising," as this chapter indicates. Yet the teens attending Johnson and Delta could not help but absorb many of the implicit messages issued by the incontestable fact of vastly more and less desirable neighborhoods (and neighborhood schools) within New York and Amsterdam. The students could not easily put into words how such materialized differences conveyed messages about painful pasts and unpromising futures—about "us" and "them." This does not mean, however, that they were impervious to the frames and sensitivities pregnant in the at once spatial and social divisions of the two national capitals of economic and cultural might.[18] More to the point—from the geographic locations of ritzy establishments and the (racial) compositions of different neighborhoods to the carriage of "grungy" (black) adolescents attending elite schools and the diploma received by a gregarious waitress—the same core communication could seem at once built into the basic *physical* and *social structures* of the two *divided cities*[19] and cemented into the students *mental structures* and *unconscious minds*: you and your kind will never belong outside the ghetto.

Despite the fact that concentrations of wealth and levels of inequality are less extreme in Amsterdam than they are in New York, then, this chapter highlights above all another clear similarity across the two settings. In ways all the more potent because they were so stealthy articulated, strong senses of *not belonging* in (what were experienced as) predominantly white and wealthy domains constrained and enabled the students' underlying emotional commitments and cognitive framing vis-à-vis various types of in-school "crowds" and coping strategies. The symbolic and emotional effects of growing up poor and attending schools like Johnson and Delta are as real as the movie screens beneath the images projected in IMAX theaters. And the shared sets of background meanings and underlying moods fostered by the segregated situations into which my students were born remain effective, like all those "silver screens," in part because they were at once right in front of everyone and effectively hidden from view.

What we find here, if I may switch metaphors yet again, is at least part of what tilled and made fertile the fields into which the "fabulous" seeds were strewn. But to conclude that this was simply corrosive would be to miss half of the picture I am trying to depict. Here we locate the backdrop against which—to take an example relevant among many teenage urban outcastes on opposite sides of the Atlantic—the greatest unifying and energizing force of the previous quarter-century emerged. This force, of course, is hip-hop music—with which the term "ghetto fabulous" is closely associated—and it started in places like the Bronx and spread to places like the Bijlmer in part because it served to counter stigmatized senses of place such as those we just observed.[20] In short, how exactly one should regard the moment-to-moment workings of these "behind the scenes" necessities must remain an open question. But to ignore how they influenced the poorly born students' crafty constructions of virtue mixed with feelings of shame would be to offer a radically incomplete account.

As such, harnessing the insights from this chapter as well as the two preceding it, we can say the following: at once geographically expansive, schoolwide, and micro-interactional dynamics of *stigmatization* and *counter-stigmatization* increased (1)the likelihood that both sets of students would commit to what they themselves—at times—were capable of depicting as the "wrong" (or risky) types of peer groups, friendships, and in-school coping practices; and (2)the chances that even those students most frequently reduced to "nobody" status would care a great deal about the stakes up for grabs in the prestige-based "spaces of play" we are calling Johnson and Delta. In other words, especially for those deemed worthy of invitations to the "wild" parties, the ambiguous pride of place, as well as the sting of stigma as concrete as brick and mortar helped make the two schools' versions of "ghetto fabulous" almost impossible to resist.

While filling in the two material and symbolic backgrounds, this chapter documented something else about urgencies emerging in lived through foregrounds that educational ethnographers might easily miss—especially if they take time "in the field" to mean time in or very near clearly bounded institutional sites rather than in the wide range of exchanges and relationships relevant to actual coping processes. When my students were in highly pacified and more middle-class (if not highbrow) settings that did not lend themselves to hardening, even those who could seem durably (and ideologically) committed to what is discussed in the research literature as black or street "opposition" more or less automatically relaxed into relatively docile stances. From novel points of view, then, this chapter illustrated once again the applicability of what might be called the Goffman principle: *not students and their moments but, rather, moments and their students.* If oppositional black culture—or, for example, the "poverty of their minds" (Patterson 2006)—was primarily responsible for generating all the antisocial behavior usually on display, why were even the potentially most disruptive and aggressive boys like Cory and Jurgen so "soft" in the IMAX theater and along the canals? Here again, it seems, we need to draw clear distinctions between sturdy yet *varied* sets of dispositions (informed in part by things like residential and educational apartheid) and the actual triggering of *specific* kinds of primordial feelings, perceptions, and responses in different interactional contexts.

Especially given the unyielding prevalence of culture-based explanations for what goes in our most distressed high-poverty schools, it might be worth closing here with the following. Left-leaning and inclined toward "social engineering" as they may at times seem (when viewed from the United States), no Dutch government officials have ever made serious attempts to increase the chances that poor students in cities like Amsterdam would end up attending middle-class schools. In fact, they barely even talk about such issues (cf. Vink 2010). Similarly, though nearly all the teachers at Johnson commuted from middle class places like the Upper West Side of Manhattan, suburban New Jersey or Westchester—i.e., the commute was not a problem for them—during my years as a teacher few if any of the relevant policy-makers in the "greater metropolitan area" even engaged in debates about granting lower class kids in areas like the South Bronx sustained access to predominantly middle-class public schools in less impoverished residential areas. As such, the interwoven influences of urban space and educational isolation detailed in this chapter should ultimately be treated as inseparable from the (in)actions of generations of policy makers on both sides of the Atlantic. Likewise, the insidious effects of urban space detailed here should not be seen as existing somehow outside of the countless (in)actions of the (putatively progressive) intellectuals, journalists, civic "leaders," and voters who have continually supported education reform efforts attempting to "make separate but equal work" (Kahlenberg 2004, p. 4). If we must speak of the *cultural* determinants of behavior leading to the devastation of schools tucked away in our most impoverished urban neighborhoods, this chapter highlights why we should at least mention the adults—and their (institutionalized) peer groups—that have averted their gaze from the costs of isolating those born poor in schools like Johnson and Delta. Even if (racially) privileged urbanites increasingly associate the isolation of students attending high-poverty neighborhood schools with natural processes (e.g., "it's like the weather, you can't do anything about it," "it has always been this way"), we should recall that "savage" (Kozol 1991) inequalities in our massively segregated systems of (neighborhood) school are to a significant extent the manmade (unintended) consequences of those caught up in categorizing, quantifying, planning, and otherwise "seeing like a state" (Scott 1998).

FIVE

Survival of the Nurtured

Give me that man that is not passion's slave[1]

Troubles of the world had me in a cross-face. Chicken-wing, sickening, liver so off-base . . . So you can stop and refresh. . . . Breathe in, breathe out, let it heal all your exit wounds. Something inside said that's the move and maybe today, I'll restart fresh and new.[2]

For students at both Johnson and Delta, talking from time to time about doing the "right thing" turned out to be relatively easy and common. Yet moving consistently towards beneficial longer term goals remained difficult and rare. Whether they were typically juiced up or worn down by the positions they occupied (in chains of interaction rituals) within their adolescent societies, that is, both sets of students had more difficulty maintaining positive lines of behavior than simply invoking conventional refrains about avoiding "distractions" or "getting caught up in the wrong crowd."

Thus the main question examined in this chapter: What did it take to dodge negative pressures and stay on the "right" course in the two schools? Here the goal is to see what was "behind" success as well as to detail how consistent execution actually worked on the ground. A sub-question relates to the concerns, frequently voiced in the respective national discussions about "urban" education, that African American[3] and Antillean Dutch males (from the island of Curaçao)[4] are especially "at risk." How did two boys, one self-identifying as African American and the other as black/Antillean, overcome destabilizing family-, domestic-, and neighborhood-related influences and thrive in Johnson and Delta? To this, building on the insights generated in the previous chapters, we can now add the following: How did these two boys achieve academic success even though they were granted access to—and basically forced to acquire something of a taste for—the "thug life?"

Of course, among the relatively small pools of students who did exceptionally well[5] in Johnson and Delta, only a few allowed me to delve deeply into their past and present lives. So readers will have to decide for themselves how representative or generalizable the findings in this chapter are. What this chapter offers is depth. While one might say that I focus "only" on four cases (the temporarily successful Derek and Brindisha, the ultimately successful Raul and Simi), each of them involves hundreds of interactions. These repeated transactions helped me attend carefully to how primary socialization processes centered outside the two educational systems related to the more or less successful coping strategies that emerged in the two schools.[6]

Although I think it can fairly be characterized as alternative, I certainly do not claim that my approach to successful adaptations is new. In fact, as this chapter makes clear, my ethnographic experiences led me more or less to the approach favored by the most revered of American educators, John Dewey. Dewey (1922, p. 67, emphasis added) saw clearly that "Thought which does not exist within *ordinary habits of action* lacks means of execution."[7] Engaging in polemics with what he saw as out of touch intellectuals indulging in mentalist myths, yet above all as a pragmatist educator concerned with getting the job done on the ground, this former high school teacher asserted that continually exposing *mind-body* complexes (or *psychophysical* wholes[8]) to nurturing social experiences that fostered capacities for self-discipline was the *only* way to insure that truly beneficial habits would take root and remain sturdy enough to generate consistently desirable behavior. Searching for the keys to success far away from the proverbial street lamp, it was the empirical realities I bumped into—not the attractiveness of any theories or concepts—that led me to see how Dewey (and later, in remarkably similar ways, Elias and Bourdieu) had pointed the flashlight in extremely useful directions.

"Uplifting" as aspects of this chapter may ultimately be, the first thing we need to understand about paths to potentially life-saving outcomes in toxic "ghetto" schools is that they were hard to find and full of obstacles. For a variety of reasons, that is, many students who were for a time on quite promising trajectories ended up derailed if not damaged beyond repair. The opening section therefore explores the temporarily promising trajectories of Derek and Brindisha. Starting with how these two were sidetracked will set us up to appreciate more fully Raul's somewhat erratic yet ultimately successful habitus formation process and journey through the Dutch educational system. This, in turn, may help us recognize the profound significance of Simi's struggle to get from a homeless shelter to one of world's most prestigious universities.

Derek

Derek had an unfashionably rounded afro when he moved with his parents from rural Ghana to urban America at the age of fourteen. He showed up at Johnson wearing out-of-date jeans and speaking English haltingly, with a strong West African accent. Unassumingly, he made his way from one classroom to the next. Without fail, every day, he brought the right materials to class in a large backpack. Often seeming to tune out what took place around him, he remained more focused on the work I assigned than almost anyone else in any of my classes. He did his homework thoroughly—i.e., he did assignments that almost none of the other students in his new educational environment even attempted, remembering to hand them in even what I forgot to ask for them. Often, during such moments, he offered a warm and gentle smile. In short, he came across as one of the friendliest and most diligent students I ever got to know. Although Derek was years behind in terms of academic skills, like nearly all the teenagers attending his new school, it seemed initially that this strikingly handsome newcomer might make great leaps in short periods of time. At very least he seemed like he might be part of the roughly twenty percent destined to graduate from Johnson in four years. That was in 1997.

Doors started to open for Derek and he soon began playing around with an increasingly "gangster" presentation of self. His jeans got baggier and started to sag more. He started to distance himself from those referred to (by boys generally taken for granted to be the manliest of "hard rocks") as "soft" or "nerdy (ass) Africans." At first with a shy smile, then with a more serious demeanor, he also started adopting the colloquial speech of the "roughneck" students who, when classified along ethno-racial lines, were usually said to be either black, Jamaican, Dominican, or Puerto Rican. At one point, trying out and seeming to delight in his new performative repertoire, Derek went out of his way to impress upon me what he looked for in a girl: "If she got a phat ass, yo. I'll fuck her—no digity [no doubt]—you know what I'm sayin' dawgs?"

I knew enough to know Derek did not have "it" yet. The accent could still be heard, the delivery was still awkward, the body language was still consciously mimicked rather than "natural." And Derek knew that I knew he was not there yet. The look in his eye made clear that the entire act was meant to be slightly tongue-in-cheek. At the same time, Derek was on his way to competently embodying a "harder," more "street" self. While in what now appears to have been a transition phase, Derek asked me—rather jokingly—to call him by his new name. "They call me Cookie now Mr. Paulle," Derek said with a bright smile. Then he continued, "You know why? Cause I'm so sweet."

First with humor and then in more serious tones, I tried to discuss with Derek the risks inherent in the path he was on. Despite the rapport I at least thought we had built up, my warnings about "thugged out" social circles and getting swept up in self-destructive fantasies about manliness seemed to fall on deaf ears. More with his actions than with his words, Derek made clear that he felt his star was rising. Excluding a mix of energy and newfound confidence, born-again "ghetto fabulous" I'm tempted to say, "Cookie" seemed certain that his social ascendancy was due mainly to his looks. As Derek put it, "They tell me I don't look African. They tell me I look black." I know exactly what he meant. While some kids at Johnson had typically West African features, Derek was not one of them. A strikingly handsome face and non-African phenotype opened up space for this dark-skinned newcomer to at once embody "realness" and become black.

As the months rolled on, the gossip I heard in my classes and in the halls confirmed that this classically square-jawed, athletically built boy was perceived by symbolically empowered members of the opposite sex to be "a hottie." Looks were important here, but if what had started out as a playful experiment had not turned into second nature, Derek would never have become "official" dating material in the upper echelons of his adolescent social order. Derek had incorporated the type of feel for the in-school game that brought short-term rewards as well as long-term risks.

The more Derek seemed to be charged up by interaction rituals generating "street" and "fabulous" solidarity, the less he seemed able to focus on anything related to the official curriculum and, of course, the more his grades and rates of attendance plummeted. And, after a period in which Derek at least appeared to be enjoying his introduction into the "thug life," he seemed to fall into a depression. The smiles evaporated. Gradually, Derek even became noticeably more edgy and hostile toward other students. His bearing and facial expressions—i.e., that which I had experienced as being the most innate and permanent aspects of his personality—were nothing like what they had been when he arrived in the Bronx. The "sweet," fun-loving "gangster" period had evolved into something much more ambiguous and far gloomier.

During the start of my last academic year at Johnson, in the fall of 1998, a colleague and friend named Terrell[9] called Derek into his cubicle within the dean's office while I happened to be sitting in there with him: "You . . . got sent down here again? Come here and have a seat, Derek." With a few keystrokes Terrell sent a copy of Derek's most recent report card and attendance record to the printer on the floor next to his desk. He placed exhibits A and B on the corner of his desk where both he and Derek could see them. Sitting in the corner I was taken by the almost glazed look in Derek's eyes. Although he might simply have been stoned, Derek seemed inexplicably detached from the reality check Terrell was trying to deliver.

Sitting opposite his ex-student and looking for a sign that he might be getting through, Terrell spoke with more of his old British-Jamaican accent than he normally did. "Look at you," he said before pausing for a slow, loud, suck on his teeth. "Look at how you're just fucking everything up. You think this is some kind of a joke don't you? You know, when you came to this school you were soft as could be. That's right, I knew you when you came up in here with your busted afro and paper-thin coat. And you know what? That's okay. 'Cause you *are* soft Derek." Terrell paused again before continuing in his rich baritone. "Deep down inside you're soft . . . just like me. And that's why you can make it." The dean's face edged closer to Derek's as he said these words. Derek neither drew back nor made eye contact. He seemed to remain focused on an upper corner of the wall opposite him. He said nothing. The look on his face remained eerily blank.

"Derek!" Terrell finally yelled, "do you hear what I'm saying? . . . If you stay soft and stop fuckin' things up . . ." There was another pause. It seemed Terrell was searching for words. Then, with a muted tone, he continued, "Say something Derek, let's talk this out . . . How are you gonna turn this thing around . . . Derek?"

There was no response. At this point Terrell seemed to just let it rip completely. "You think you're really cute don't you? Man, listen, I've seen fifty Dereks come and go and let me tell you something, straight up. If you don't get your shit together, and I mean like real, real soon. Oh man." Terrell glanced down at the space on the floor between his shoes and Derek's, then swiveled on his chair and looked up at me. "Bo, you wanna try to say something to him? He can't even hear me. I'm just wasting my time."

In my own way I had, for many months, been trying to communicate exactly the same message. At this point, it seemed, nothing was going to help—not more (self-important) "advice" from a middle-class man generally judged to be white and not this rant from an alumnus of high-poverty high school in downtown Brooklyn whose skin was darker than Derek's. In and outside Johnson High, the positions Derek occupied had come to occupy him—and we had no means of loosening their grip.

Just before I stopped teaching at Johnson in 1999, Derek attempted to rob a young man who was reportedly sporting a flamboyant gold chain. Derek approached with a gun and, perhaps before he knew it, was himself shot in the stomach. He was, according to all accounts, the father of a six-month-old baby at the time of the shooting. The baby's mother, a native-born "black" rather than "African" girl, according to local definitions, was also an ex-student of mine. More importantly, the (alleged) mother of Derek's baby—a spontaneous, humorous, and seemingly confident girl who did literally no work while occasionally passing through my classroom—was about as explicitly "ghetto fabulous" as one could get.[10]

Another student, whom I had come to trust fully, and who also hailed from Ghana,[11] put the calamity in perspective during an interview in a local pizza shop. She explained that Derek's parents both worked two jobs. They were, in her words, "never home." In and out of school, Derek was left to fend for himself, she said, surrounded by "thugs" and amazing amounts of what she and Derek certainly did not have a lot of in their Ghanaian villages: "stuff" (clothing, jewelry, footwear, etc.). The majority of the young people who hung out in front of the building in which Derek lived were, she claimed, "Bloods" and "hustlers."

This interview indicated that everyday life outside Johnson High significantly influenced the rise and fall of "Cookie." At the same time, Terrell and I were able to see the train wreck happen in slow motion from within the school. More importantly, the way mutually interdependent power resources related to race, ethno-nationality, gender, body, and peer groups played out in Johnson facilitated the development of Derek's self-defeating feel for the school and neighborhood "games" he found himself playing. The co-creation of "realness" and what transpired daily in Johnson High more generally contributed significantly, it seems, to this once promising student's educational derailing and, most likely, to the birth of his child and very nearly to his death. There may have been dignity in his temporary rise. And, stretching a bit perhaps, one might argue that (especially early on) his social ascendency was based on a conscious attempt to achieve authentic blackness. But Derek took for granted that countless "nerds" in his school were black, and what he wanted was recognition of something granted to many of those he did not see as black: "realness." And certainly, Cookie's fall from grace had less to do with willful (black) cultural rebellion than with physical immersion in settings lacking supervision from stable adults. While in part proud, intentional and related to explicit ideas about blackness, his "bad boy" behavior was most basically a prediscursive stress response triggered by a noxious brew of socio-emotional, physical, and cultural pressures far beyond his control.

Brindisha

Brindisha moved to the Netherlands from Suriname with her parents and her younger brother when she was three years old. Upon arrival in the Netherlands, she lived in the Bijlmer and was surrounded by extended family members, friends, and acquaintances—nearly all with working class "Hindustani" backgrounds. After her parents broke up, and toward the end of her time in primary school, Brindisha moved to a small town "far away from Amsterdam." Talking together in an otherwise empty classroom as we occasionally did after school, she once conflated whiteness and nationhood in a way that was common in the Bijlmer yet unheard of in the Bronx.[12] She told me it felt "strange being around so many *Nederlanders* and so few brown people." Pale skin, which had been rather exceptional if not exotic in her subsection of the Bijlmer, was the new default setting. In rural Holland, more immediately than anything else, her brown skin made Brindisha stick out in a crowd. Yet, Brindisha went on to explain, the feeling of being out of place soon dissipated. After a while she came to enjoy attending her school far from the capital city. As she put it, "Everybody just acted normal. Everybody was calm and we all hung out together. It was really nice. I mean nobody really teased anybody and I didn't feel weird or anything like that."

Brindisha did well in her new primary school. Heading into secondary school, she was placed on a secondary-educational track (MAVO-HAVO) slightly above the national average which, if completed successfully, granted direct admission to the system of four-year colleges (BA level). Then, in the summer before her second year in secondary school, she moved back to the Bijlmer.

Brindisha could not recall why her mother decided to move back to the Bijlmer. She did however remember that—initially—she had been excited about returning to her old neighborhood. Soon after the move she started attending Delta. Her mother also started to spend a good deal of time with her new live-in boyfriend, who also came from Suriname and had roots in the Asian sub-continent.

Moving from a school dominated by nonvocational students in a small town to one dominated by lower level "prevocational" students in one of the poorest neighborhoods in the Netherlands came as a shock. Life in her new school was, Brindisha said, much more stratified and tense. "All of a sudden it was this group over here, and that group over there . . . and, you know, some kids really thought they were high and mighty (*hoger*). They really tried to keep the other kids small you know, saying 'Shut your mouth, you stupid bitch,' and pushing and yelling. And they did the same thing to the teachers, too." Looking right at me she continued, "I don't think they act normally at this school. Do you think they act normally here?"

While Brindisha never reported being involved in extreme violence in any school, it seems one especially strong, loud-spoken boy at Delta, who was also a student in one of my classes, had the habit of terrorizing her. "Yuk!" was her reply when I insinuated that the bully's behavior might have had to do with his confusion about how to express a romantic interest. "No, I'm serious, he hits me, really hard. I'm not kidding. He throws me against the walls and laughs at me in front of everybody." She had already spoken to my supervisor about this boy's behavior and I did the same after one of our conversations. But the supervisor, who in theory could have taken disciplinary measures immediately, did not make any attempt to stem the continuing attacks.[13]

Even in the harsh educational climate in the Bijlmer, Brindisha was one of the least disruptive and hardest working students in the school. As was the case with Derek early on, simply dropping an assignment on her desk was—even in a rowdy classroom—enough to trigger comparatively long intervals of unbroken attention. The penmanship alone demonstrated that she did her homework with precision and high levels of sustained concentration.

Nevertheless, it was while things were still going well for her academically that Brindisha and I started having occasional after-school talks. As the months rolled on, at a certain point, it became evident that Brindisha was increasingly upset about something. She seemed not to be "herself" and she was clearly looking for help. Unlike the Brindisha I thought I knew, she stopped doing homework and often left materials for class at home or in her locker. Although never really disruptive in class, she seemed increasingly incapable of paying attention—even during the special moments when there was a relatively calm and productive atmosphere. Her grades nosedived and, while she still smiled politely from time to time, Brindisha appeared to be increasingly demoralized.

Seeming to fall further and further out of kilter, Brindisha started asking with more regularity and urgency if we could talk after school or after class. We developed a good deal of trust in part because she saw how frustrated and ashamed I was when the mix of peer dynamics in her class and my inability to overcome them made it basically impossible for anyone to learn.

Then it came, the conversation. First Brindisha shared with me that she was seeing a special counselor at Delta. In an indirect way initially, Brindisha then told me why: her mother's new boyfriend was sexually abusing her. (I confirmed with her, and later with the special counselor who reported to my supervisor, that I was not the only one who had heard about this.) Although she felt that she did have something of a support network in the school, she rather lifelessly picked up and dropped her shoulders when I asked her if talking to the counselor was helping her cope. While I thought about police and a shelter, Brindisha rather numbly explained that the abuse—and the fear of going home—came to dominate her life almost totally during her mother's extended vacations to Suriname. During these especially hellish intervals, she said, she was left alone in the apartment with her tormentor. She dared not say anything about this to her mother.

"That's when everything just fell apart," Brindisha said referring to the first of her mother's trips to Suriname, while looking down and toying with a piece of paper on my desk. When her mother returned home, Brindisha explained, her grades picked up a bit. The downward trend was, however, very evident. I lost touch with Brindisha when she left Delta after failing to advance into the fourth year. Transferring meant she would be allowed to go to the next grade in another new school, but that she would be demoted to a lower vocational track.

When Brindisha did well in school, this was not mainly because she thought the right thoughts. Even in her distressed and distressing new school, she continued to do well after her return to the Bijlmer because she was physically and emotionally safe at home, and because her gradually acquired and remarkably docile dispositions "fit" the formal requirements of the educational system. With regard to her educational ruin, Brindisha's story puts in a rather hideous light something Bourdieu wrote—almost certainly with the hidden injuries of class in mind rather than anything related to domestic violence—about segregated schools of the *banlieue* (outer city) in France: the "school system often inflicts wounds that are likely to reactivate basic traumas."[14] The exact degree to which basic traumas at home were compounded by comparatively minor yet almost constant ones in school is, in Brindisha's case, unclear. The main cause of this one-time academic high-flyer's crash landing, however, is not. I have to believe that she was one of the countless girls exposed to the (quasi-sexualized) violence of men in domestic settings and, on top of this, abused physically and emotionally by (in the vast majority of cases) male students in poorly regulated high-poverty schools. The one institutional setting that might have helped her was further stressing her out.

Explanations of failure based on tantalizing riddles about the interface of ethno-racial "groups" and headstrong ideological "resistance" remain so prevalent, this case again indicates, because intellectuals remain disengaged from the mutually reinforcing stressors at the core of what is damaging student bodies and destroying our worst schools. Brindisha's story also demonstrates why researchers continue to focus on the outsides of bodies (e.g., skin tones) and what can be easily put into words (especially when ideas about racial "groups" and ethnic "communities" are cued up in interviews or on surveys) rather than on what is communicated "silently" from within vulnerable student bodies. It took months of interactions (including those allowing her to observe me being put to shame in her class) for Brindisha to feel safe enough to reveal what no survey or "in-depth" interview could have: first and foremost, Brindisha's fate was sealed because her whole being was at risk everywhere she went. And once her fall got underway during her time attending Delta, no pro-school ideology or positive ethnic identity was going to slow it.

With something of a felt sense for how narrow and bumpy the roads less traveled often were, it is time now to detail how two boys managed to remain focused despite both their affinities with certain aspects of "street" culture and the pressures emerging from their destabilized domestic situations.

Raul

Raul was born in 1986 on the island of Curaçao. His mother took him and his older sister to the Netherlands before he started primary school. His father remained in the Dutch Antilles, and still lives there today. For the most part Raul grew up (in "neighborhood D") with his mother in one of the high-rise apartment buildings for which the Bijlmer is well-known throughout the Netherlands.

From the time of her arrival in the Netherlands until she was diagnosed with cancer soon after he graduated from Delta, Raul's mother had always been regularly employed. As will be discussed below, his mother's background and stable work experiences translated into positive influences on Raul. Her steady employment also meant, however, that Raul had a great deal of unsupervised time between the end of the school day and the time he was expected home for dinner in one of the most dangerous residential areas in Amsterdam. As we pieced together the puzzle of his socialization trajectory during our many conversations, it is therefore no wonder that Raul usually began with the "bad" influences from his neighborhood.

Raul repeatedly stressed that "street kids" completely dominated everything going on in the section of the Bijlmer in which he grew up. Mainly for this reason, Raul said that feeling frightened was part of everyday life for all the kids he knew. "I think that was normal for the kids growing up in neighborhood D," Raul once asserted. Later, at the age of eighteen, when Raul looked back on his ten years in the "old Bijlmer," he spoke about criminality, drugs, fights, and "sexual intimidation." Raul witnessed "a lot" of girls being sexually harassed. He felt, however, that the sexual intimidation knife cut both ways. "I saw a lot of girls showing off their bodies . . . asking for it, even if they had no idea what they were doing." Sexist cliché or not, this brings us right to that part of life in his "street" dominated world that Raul found most difficult to resist. Time and again he came back to the interdependence of what he saw as sexual intimidation, charisma, rounded backsides, and how having the right moves at the right house parties influenced degrees of recognition from powerful peers and explained the allure of the "ghetto fabulous" life.

Growing up in his neighborhood, Raul tended to hang out with a set of slightly older boys. He often described them as being either Surinamese or, more frequently, Antillean.[15] Coming of age in environments governed by this network of boys and young men, Raul saw "no way" not to get "swept up in the street" (*opgaan met de straat*). And yet Raul claimed that from around eleven years of age, he started finding ways to avoid some of the "street" activities his friends were getting into. "When they came by and asked me to come play football with them after school," he once explained, "they were really asking for much more than that." "Playing football" meant stealing from the stores, maybe beating up another kid for fun, and possibly mugging somebody with a kitchen knife. These are all guys who are dealing coke now, if they are not locked up. And you could see it on them even back then. So it wasn't just like come *chill wit' da boys* [in English]."[16]

The streets may have been most mean, but Raul's home life was far from stable. When he was thirteen years old and a first-year student at the Delta School, Raul woke up one morning to the sound of inexplicable male voices in his living room. He walked into the room and found his mother crying. His mother had not paid the rent for months and it had finally come to this: the bailiff and the movers were taking action. Raul and his mother were being evicted. The local authorities took not only his Nintendo, but, to his surprise, also the dishes, pots, and pans. "Everything we had built up," he said while snapping his fingers, "gone." As fate would have it, two relatives from Curaçao who happened to be visiting witnessed the entire event. This led to stays in a string of apartments—with and without his mother—in various parts of the Bijlmer. To hear Raul retell the story was to know that he was deeply scarred by the experience of being ousted from his home.

According to Raul there were also "bad" influences present within his extended family "back home" on the island of Curaçao. Raul characterized half of his family as "more or less bad . . . lots of drugs, violence, prison . . . they were just restless (*druk*) and loud." To this characterization he was quick to add, "but we were a tight family, regardless."

Raul seemed to have been especially tight with one of his slightly older cousins from the "bad" side of the family. During a conversation about this "hustler," Raul turned to me and said, "He just had that *flavor*, you know what I mean? You know what he told me once? I will never forget it. He said, 'Raul, *game recognizes game.*' That was his way of just telling me that he knew that he had it, that he had *game*, that he was a *true player* . . . and if you did not have it, all the *players* knew right away that you did not count. And he was telling me this, you know, because he did not think I was a *nerd* or something." We shared a smile and I tried to keep him in the flow, "And you think you got *it* partly from hanging out with him [when you made trips back to Curaçao]?" Again Raul's response was almost immediate, "Not so much. I mean I didn't spend that much time with him. I had it just from *chillin' with da boys*, too [in Southeast Amsterdam]. But we would go back for months, almost every year, and I was just with him and his friends all the time . . . and at first I was like . . . yeah, *they got it going on* . . . and then, so, I guess it just came naturally. And, you know, I guess he was just telling me he saw it, in himself and in me, too, . . . that thing that people recognize." This cousin, who Raul says had become a *"big-time dealer,"* was shot to death less than eight months after Raul graduated from Delta in 2002.

What Raul considered "good" in his life related to what he saw as the other half of the family, his primary school, and a few neighborhood figures. Most important by far here, however, was his mother. Raul stressed that "she was strict when she needed to be" and that she "never had any habits [e.g., drinking, drugs]. She," Raul once said, "just has it together."

As mentioned above, Raul's mother always had regular work. This does not make her exceptional. Being a college-educated woman and living in the heart of the high-rise dominated "old Bijlmer" does. White or black, native or newcomer, there were very few adults living in the high-rise flats who had any type of post-secondary-educational credentials. Raul's mother graduated from a BA-level teacher-training program in the Dutch Antilles, where she taught for several years before coming to the Netherlands. Unlike newcomers from the Dutch Antilles, furthermore, Raul's mother spoke utterly flawless and lightly accented Dutch. Her English, like Raul's, was also exceptionally good. She left education and became a social worker after resettling in Amsterdam.

My conversations with Raul's mother left me with the impression that she was a dignified, friendly, and confident woman. She also struck me as, culturally, the most middle class of all the parents and guardians I met while carrying out research on either of the two schools. After speaking with her, I saw Raul through a very different lens. I began to see him as a part of a rather elite immigration flow.[17]

This portrait of a "together" woman with exceptional educational and linguistic capital raises questions. For example, what caused the disorganization and debt that led to Raul's worst childhood memory? Perhaps part of the answer to the riddle is that over the course of two decades, Raul's mother spent a small fortune on at least one, and sometimes as many as many as three trips per year, often with Raul, "back to Curaçao." Raul and his mother were quick to point out that going "back home" did not feel so much like a vacation as an extended therapy session. They felt isolated not just from their family members, but also, and more generally, from anything like a warm, loving, laid-back, rural community. As Raul's mother put it the time we ran into her in a busy shopping area in the Bijlmer, "People don't even know what it is to relax here, it is just go, go, go. If I don't go back home and relax, I'll go nuts over here." To this need to take it slow one might add, as Raul did when I pushed him on the topic, that his mother always worked poorly paid jobs despite her educational credentials. This one-two combination might lead many single parents to get behind on rent and credit cards. And this debt, in turn, might even be said to explain why Raul's mother never made an effort to leave one of the most distressed neighborhoods within Southeast Amsterdam.

The family-based and, relative to most families of Delta students, exceptionally positive social and cultural capital resources do not end here. When I met Raul, I was surprised to hear that his sister was on a university track in an elite secondary school on Curaçao. Soon after I got to know Raul, his sister left the Antilles to study psychology on an MA trajectory at a Dutch university.[18]

Raul also pointed out that his neighborhood was not wholly negative in its influence. Raul's face lit up during one interview in which he told the story of a "guy with sense" who also grew up in his native neighborhood D. "I was around twelve and he, I think, was sixteen," Raul explained. "That's when I started to hang out with him. I would just watch him. He was the oldest in his family, with two other kids, and a single mother, Antillean. He showed me how he was by how he acted, by things he did . . . and did not do. He just made it clear that the street life was not going to really take you anywhere. He had that style, the street body language.[19] But he was also really smart. I just saw in him that there was another way. His younger brother, who was my age . . . [pause] . . . he went on the *ghetto life* path and he [the older brother] couldn't do anything about it. He [the younger brother] went *street*. The older guy is now an engineer. He has a family. They came back to visit sometimes. It's beautiful to see . . . the man has seen so much shit and he has it together, you know, he just has it all." At this point I asked what happened to the younger brother. "I don't know," Raul shot back. "I heard he was locked up on some drug charges, but that was a while ago . . . he should have been out by now. I haven't seen or heard from him. I mean I don't live in neighborhood D anymore so . . . but you know he is not doing as well as his brother. I promise you that." This prompted me to switch the topic a bit, "So that's where you're going, in the direction of the engineer with the family?" At this Raul laughed a bit and then replied, "I hope so. And with a *fat* car!"

Unlike the vast majority of Delta School students, Raul did not attend a primary school in Southeast Amsterdam. Along with his mother, initially, he traveled forty-five minutes to get to an out-of-the-way school every morning. When I asked him to describe his primary school, the first thing that came to Raul's mind was physical safety. It was, he said, "totally peaceful." As if I needed convincing about how nonviolent his primary school was after being at Delta for three years, Raul stressed that, "There were really never any problems or fights." Then, in a statement that might again remind us of Devine's (1996) key claim about the "agency" of violence "constructing" ethnicity in schools, Raul added the following: "Even with all the different cultures mixed up in there, we were like one big family." Raul seemed not only to relish his years in primary school, but also an especially warm relationship with his last teacher there—a man who taught Raul's class for two years in row. With regard to both his favorite teacher, whom he classified as a middle-aged Dutchman, and his primary school, Raul once summed things up in the following way: "He just gave me so much self-confidence. He told me that I might be president one day, and I think he believed it. You know, this is what gives you the strength to think long term. . . . And it was just day in, day out, you know, calm and *relaxed* in that school. I mean it, Bo [apparently I still had a look of disbelief on my face as he said this], there were no conflicts, no aggression, no discipline problems, zero."[20]

A World of Difference

When I asked Raul about his first impressions of Delta his energy level shot up. Again, the somatic dimension of life was central to what he wanted to get off his chest: "Shock. It was unbelievable. When I first got there, my mouth just fell open. I had no idea . . . I was like, how is this possible? I felt like my whole world was just falling apart. (*Je wereld stort in elkaar.*) Most of the other kids did not feel this way, because they had seen nothing but chaos in [primary] school. It was not any one thing, it was everything, aggression was just in the air. Intimidation, sexual intimidation, girls walking around almost naked . . . kids getting robbed, guys coming up to you like, 'Hey, buy a sandwich for me,' girls pushed into giving blowjobs in the bathrooms, kids screaming at the teachers . . . I had never seen anything like this. You know, I mean, it was really threatening. Not just teasing, but really threatening the teachers. Bo . . . a world of difference . . . I just stared with my jaw on the floor until [smile and pause] I did it myself (*Ik bleef met open mond gewoon kijken . . . tot dat ik het zelf deed*). You have no idea what you're doing, and then you're doing it, too. So you see how easy it is to get swept into the *wrong flow*." I pressed him on how this felt. "When I started doing it, it felt great," was Raul's relaxed reply. "I started getting attention from girls, and from popular guys, now I was no longer the quiet guy nobody paid any attention to."

This kick was, evidently, more powerful than anything else during Raul's initial period of immersion. As such, from his own more mature and disengaged perspective, Raul's first two years at Delta did not go at all well. Emotionally and cognitively entrained within interlocking chains of "fabulous" interaction rituals, it seems, he became disengaged with what his teachers tried to do and drifted into a more "street" way of being. Soon enough, Raul also slipped down from the top of Delta's four-tiered vocational track.

Within this new world of affordances and sanctions, Raul was able to cash in on his smooth interpersonal skills, his good looks, and his "game" recognized by others with "game." In the all-important court of the popular girls, he came to be judged as one of the more desirable boys. Demonstrating why he felt at the time that everything was coming together for him, Raul said the following: "Look, when you date a *hot* girl and word gets out, the *cool* guys just start coming up to you and . . . some of them just give you a look . . . some of them want to shake your hand. Anyway, I was, you know, by that time . . . [smiles] I was a little *player*, a little *bad boy*." In the middle of a conversation in my home, while reflecting on these types of ritualized micro-encounters, Raul once paused, look straight at me, and said the following: "*Ghetto fabulous is like a religion.*"

But as if some kind of mystical spell had been broken, by his third year Raul settled back into his previous, nondisruptive behavioral repertoire. His grades quickly improved as he became, in his own words, less "annoying" in class. This was when our paths crossed for the first time. It usually required no more than a firm look from me or any of his other teachers to get him to stop participating in the nearly ceaseless distractions generated by classmates. Yet his attention was often fixed on the more disruptive students, including Roissa, his girlfriend. Even after regaining a good deal of his "old" composure, Raul never severed ties with the more "street" types in his classes. Often seeming to enjoy being distracted in class, he disregarded as many homework assignments as he (half-heartedly) attempted, and he regularly failed to bring the proper materials to class.

But the steep fall had been avoided. Despite the fact that Raul continued to enjoy access to the "fabulous" life in his school and neighborhood, he did no more than peer over the edge of the cliff. Raul stayed out of serious trouble during his "bad" phase and, as a more "together" third year student, started to turn away from destructive in-school coping practices even though he was still seen as the type who should be invited to the "hot" parties (hosted by his girlfriend). By the time I asked his teachers how they felt about Raul—at the end of his third year—nearly all of them had only positive things to say.

Looking back on his last two years at Delta, Raul summed up his mixed bag of internalized habitudes in a telling way: "So . . . you see, I'm in the middle. I've always been in the middle somewhere. Not a gangster, not a nerd. That's why, even when I was twelve or so, I was telling those boys I didn't want to go play football with them. I knew what they would get into, even then. But I also have that street in me. And the *players*, they can see it, like a sixth sense, in a *nanosecond*." Raul's slide stopped and this son of certified teacher turned social worked graduated on the second highest of the four vocational tracks.

Life after Delta

After leaving Delta things once again fell apart for Raul. During our intermittent phone calls, Raul's mother started openly expressing fears that Raul would end up without even a "starter's qualification."[21] Around this time, soon after his revered cousin was shot to death in Curaçao, Raul shared with me that he was rattled by the thought that his mother might die of cancer.

I could tell, even in conversations on the telephone, that Raul was feeling increasingly insecure, confused, angry, and ashamed. Not surprisingly perhaps, it was during this phase that I began having trouble connecting with Raul. First his phone number stopped working, then his mother's number stopped working, and neither reached out to me.

No less than five years later, when he was twenty-four years old, Raul called me and we reestablished regular contact. He apologized for not getting in touch with me, in part because he had wanted, he claimed, to invite me to his mother's funeral. With confidence and clarity, Raul recalled the period during which his mother had grown increasingly ill. During this trying time, Raul failed out of two post-secondary vocational schools in Amsterdam. As an adult looking back more in remorse than in anger, he reported that he temporarily "lost touch with reality" and tried to anesthetize himself with alcohol and marijuana. (*"Ik probeerde mezelf lam te blowen en te drinken in de hoop dat ik de pijn niet zou voelen."*) After his mother's death, he moved about as far from the Bijlmer as one can go (Leeuwarden) in the Netherlands, and lived with his sister. There Raul started attending yet another post-secondary vocational school. He went on to receive the "starter's qualification" his mother had been afraid he would never obtain. He also went on to finish a vocational degree. (An MBO 4, which is comparable to an associate's degree in the United States.) Raul got back in touch with me in part because he was proud about having a one-year renewable contract with an agency providing social services and, above all, about being enrolled part time in a BA-level post-secondary program[22] that prepares people for middle- and upper-level management positions in the social-work sector. He is on course to become a professional with better educational credentials and career prospects than the average Dutchman. Despite the blatant and upsetting racism to which he is exposed in the city he now calls home,[23] Raul said that "Leeuwarden has been good to [him]," and that he is looking forward to "helping people, like [his] mom did." Today Raul lives on a tree-lined street on the outskirts of this mid-sized Dutch city with his college-educated girlfriend and their baby boy. He told me, in his garden, that he was saving up for a nice car.

As he saw clearly enough himself, growing up in the high-rise a stone's throw from Delta, Raul was basically forced to develop an appreciation for the "thug life." Raul was capable of slipping through the many cracks—or gaping holes—in Delta and other poorly regulated educational settings. But this young man "in the middle" averted disaster and got back on track. Like the relatively stable "weekend warrior" who dips and dabs with cocaine without becoming addicted, it seems Raul could "have a sniff" without doing himself too much harm. If his internal steering mechanism ensured that while he would be susceptible to the thrill of veering toward the edge, time and again it also guided him back toward a safer path. The comparatively massive amounts of cultural capital he inherited and, perhaps even more importantly, because of his socialized capacities for emotional self-control and foresight, Raul regained his footing in Delta and beyond.

Simi

Simi was born in the South Bronx in 1982. As was common among African American students of Johnson High, Simi and several members of his family frequently moved back and forth, for months or years at a time, between the South Bronx and "Down South." The later, in the case of Simi's family, meant small-town, deeply segregated Virginia and North Carolina. Simi said very little about his father other than that he was, as he put it, "African." Although an interest in all things African had become important in Simi's life by the time I got to know him, it was clear almost immediately that his biological father had nothing to do with Simi's upbringing. Because of his father's place of birth, Simi's two older half-brothers[24] often jokingly called him "the African." Simi was reluctant to go into detail about his mother, other than to mention that she had moved back and forth between New York and Down South much of her life. When one of Simi's older brothers came home from prison, we sat together in Simi's bedroom as he told me that their mother and his father had both been in gangs. Simi just looked at me when his brother said this, he said nothing.

Simi told me, and later one of his brothers confirmed, that various members of his family had, over the years, turned to the ultraviolent drug trade "just to provide, just to get by." His two older brothers saw their father gunned down in broad daylight in front of the housing project in which they lived. Simi spoke of his brothers seeing their father's "brains on the mailbox." When Simi was nine and living Down South, both of his older brothers were incarcerated. One for attempted murder, the other for a serious drug-related offense. By the time he was eleven, Simi reports, his life was "totally unstructured" and "really goin' downhill fast." Leaving school early and "just goin[g] back for lunch" became normal. Simi said that he and his friends frequently "played" with loaded guns inside homes as well as out on the street. In his own words he was, at this stage of his life, "just wildin' out, smoking weed, drinking loads of beer and wine, smoking cigarettes . . . just, you know, tryin' to hang out with the thugs and just be all thugged out."

Simi started selling drugs with some of his childhood friends. First an adult they knew gave them "fake stuff, just to see if we could like really get rid of it."[25] With their first mission accomplished, the same adult then started "putting [Simi and his friends] on for real." Around this time, Simi also started getting into trouble with the local authorities for relatively minor infractions. Simi and a few friends had broken another boy's jaw in an incident involving a stolen bicycle. This incident got Simi "into the system." Before his mother was notified about her son's impending court date, Simi intervened in a heated argument she was having with a female neighbor. The neighbor received a rather severe beating, and at the behest of the arresting officer, Simi's mother went to the police station with her son. "When she found out about the other stuff too, that . . . oh man, that's when she just flipped. She was like, 'What! Oh, no, no, this here is jus' goin' all wrong.'" Convinced that Simi would soon be sent to a juvenile detention center, and, Simi claims, unable to bear the thought that yet another of her children might be "locked up," Simi's mother sent him across state lines and back up to the Bronx without giving notice to the local authorities (which led to several "failures to appear" in Virginia courtrooms).

At age twelve Simi found himself living with one of his older brothers. Just out of jail, Simi's eldest sibling was "already hustling again" and looking to buy "bulk" (i.e., at least a kilo of cocaine) to bring Down South to sell where profits were much greater than in New York. Feeling that New York was far too "hectic," as Simi recalled, the older brother brought him on one of his trips to North Carolina to stay with a longtime friend of the family. (At this point his mother was still residing in Virginia.)

The relationship with the longtime family friend and this woman's new boyfriend was, in Simi's words, "disastrous." "She tried to give me structure . . . you know, 'Why your pants so low?'. . . but to me it was just like she was trying to put me down, like." Simi soon stopped attending school regularly and longed to be with his mother and brother. "The only safety I had was my brother," Simi said, referring to the psychological protection he felt when in the presence of his brother who occasionally ventured down to North Carolina to distribute cocaine. "He was everything to me." When his brother was in the area, Simi sometimes moved in with him temporarily. One day the woman offering Simi shelter casually mentioned to Simi that his brother had been "locked-up again." Simi now had two older brothers in jail for attempted murder and he would not see either of them for several years. Simi said he "cried for days" and longed to "get back up with [his] mother."

Unable to rejoin her, Simi fell into the same patterns that had motivated his mother to send him away: "hanging with dealers, skipping school, weed, drinking." Soon the arguments in his foster-care living situation became too much for his mother's friend. Although the fights never cascaded into any physical violence, she began locking Simi out of the house. "I would come home and they would just not let me in, they wouldn't answer the door." Simi recalls coming home one night and stealing a large American flag that was hanging outside a local Laundromat. Balled up in the flag he slept in front of a closed door.

Around this time, Simi's girlfriend, Rachel, became pregnant. Fourteen years of age, Rachel decided to keep the baby against her mother's will. Her mother made it clear that she was not prepared to contribute to the financial costs of a baby in her house. It was also during this phase of his life that Simi was reunited with his mother. Simi later reported that he felt he had no other way to "provide" than to start, once again, doing what his mother was doing from the house in which he lived: selling drugs. Simi reports that he started "stealing" crack and heroin from the supply that his mother was selling in order to "get baby stuff." I asked him if he thought his mother knew that he was doing this. "Yeah, I think she knew," he said. "But she understood. . . . I mean, she had taken care of her kids by selling too."

Simi and Rachel "broke up" during a fight they had in the maternity ward immediately following the birth of their son. "We knew it was all downhill after that," Simi told me in what appeared to be an utterly nonsarcastic statement. But it seems Simi continued trying to support his child financially. Simi also began what would turn out to be years of attempts to gain custody of his son. From the start there was no doubt in Simi's mind that his child would be better off with him and his family than with Rachel and her relatives. Simi told me that he regularly and openly discussed these feelings about what would be best for their offspring with "my baby's mother." But sensing that no judge would ever grant him custody as long as Rachel did not want to give up their son, he felt that his was a losing cause.

Several trips across state lines and intermittent stays in various settings came to an end when Simi's mother was briefly incarcerated. She felt lucky not to have been convicted of any major felonies and, Simi says, she "learned her lesson." She wanted "out of the drug game for good," Simi reported. She decided to collect Simi and his younger brother and move into her mother's house in the Bronx. This escape strategy "fell apart," Simi says, because "there were some problems" related to his grandmother being a substance abuser. (This was his only mention of any grandparent.) Simi, his mother, and his younger brother ended up in a homeless shelter in the

South Bronx. When we drove past this shelter on one of our drives around the various neighborhoods he knew so well, Simi told me that he spent most of his first year at Johnson High living in "that place. It was like rock bottom." In a later interview Simi added, "Everybody in there knew it wasn't no way but up from there."

"Structure"

Despite feeling frustrated about his son remaining in what he saw as an unstable situation, despite having had very poor grades the year before, and despite living in a homeless shelter, Simi's did well enough at Johnson High to earn a place on the Honor Roll during the ensuing school year. Not only had Simi ceased drinking, drugging, stealing, fighting, "wilding," and "selling," but he had become a straight-A student. Nothing communicated so far would lead one to expect that Simi might be capable of such an achievement. Yet, Simi had by this time, gotten "structure." What we need to do now is turn back the clock and detail what exactly it was that made Simi's turnaround possible.

In retrospect, Simi thinks, the incarceration of his brothers was not altogether negative—for them or for him. This is where Simi begins the story of his triumph. In jail, both of his brothers became "5-Percenters," a sect associated with the Nation of Islam (also known as the "Black Muslims"). For the first time, his brothers were exposed to what Simi called a "black viewpoint." Bits and pieces of his brothers' experiences trickled down to Simi. Today Simi associates the Nation of Islam with more than just faith, ideology, black pride, and Malcolm X; for him the Nation of Islam is also, and perhaps most fundamentally, about discipline, self-control, and the piecing together of broken black lives.

From two different prisons, Simi's brothers began describing their new experiences and newfound (religious) ideologies. They also started sending home literature (including the "Final Call," the Nation of Islam's newspaper), cassette tapes with lectures, and information on various types of exercises. Simi reports that, from eleven years of age on, his brothers' communiqués started to help him get a grip. Through them he started learning about "what you could and could not eat," and about how his brothers were forced to memorize entire "pages of information" related to "their own calendar and number systems." His brothers had to be able to "repeat a whole page of stuff," Simi said, "whenever someone asked them to." Negative associations with drinking alcohol and sugary soft drinks and with eating candy and pork entered his consciousness for the first time. As Simi put it, "You know my family was all into the pork thang [smile]. And so, *before I got full control over myself*, I would still go into the kitchen when nobody was looking and eat some pork . . . I mean, I had to eat somethin'." But later on, [smile] it was like, I could be mad hungry but . . . no more temptation. I could just walk by it and not even be tempted."

This may sound like a detail of minor significance. For Simi at least, it is not. Simi often integrated digressions on his changing dietary habits—part and parcel of his changing bodily regimes—with remarks on nothing less than "a new way of seeing the world." Fasting during the month of Ramadan, which Simi said started to do "with" his incarcerated brothers at eleven years of age, illustrates this point. Simi's quest to get control over his life was, to use the old version of the Dutch word from which "life" comes, founded on a learning process at once social and very clearly based inside his *lyf* (body).[26]

What we have seen up to this point might be said to represent the first step on a long march. But the mix of increased (body-based) self-discipline, reflexivity, (racial) pride, and religious zeal that Simi (and his brothers) derived from an interest in the Nation of Islam was certainly not enough to protect him—or one of his brothers—from getting into further trouble. Nor was Simi's introduction to Nation of Islam enough to insure his success in school. Fortunately for him, there were far more profound, prolonged, intimate, and empowering experiences still to come. By far the most important of these healing influences came from, again in Simi's own words, his "spiritual parents."

Kitty, Ben, the Store, and "The Community"

Kitty and Ben were a couple who owned and operated a small store near one of the homes in which Simi had lived with his mother in Virginia. Interested in the scents and sounds emanating from the store, Simi first wandered inside when he was twelve years old. The store was full of African and Afro-Caribbean art, music, drums, incense, vegetarian food, healthy drinks, and references to Marcus Garvey and Haile Selassie. Ben and Kitty "were more than just into their blackness," Simi once recalled, "they were very serious about the Rasta way of life."

Initial conversations with Kitty led to visits to Ben and Kitty's home and, soon thereafter, a job for Simi in the store. "So," Simi at one point explained, "I started working in the store and, you know, I had that responsibility, right? I mean they didn't close for no religious holidays [laugh] and so, I was, like, working all the time. I was, like, waking up at like seven in the morning to get there on time, clean up, and do all kinds of stuff in the store. I had to know how much everything cost and where it all went. I had to know about the food, and the drinks, and what what was for. I loved it, though, you know, I couldn't get enough of that place."

Simi's mother intuitively felt "cool" about her son being with "good people" and Simi started spending nights as well as days with Ben and Kitty. In the store, in Kitty and Ben's home, and in their residential "community," Simi was consistently immersed for the first time in nurturing social contexts rich with black pride and scholarly books. "So you know, for me it was like a whole new world opening up," as Simi once put it. "I mean just being around adults was like, wow. I had . . . before that . . . I wasn't never really around adults like that. It was always just kids, you know, just messing around." "And you liked it?" I asked. "Yeah, man. I mean, more than just 'liked it,'" Simi shot back. "They was . . . man, I was lovin' what they had going on out there. You know, it was like a whole community of people just steady looking out for me and just . . . it was all love out there . . . wasn't no stressin' and no fights or nothing. They was part of . . . you know not all Rastas smoke weed, right? Did you know that? They were part of a Rasta sect that didn't smoke no weed. They didn't think it was healthy. And . . . you know, they really started challenging me to think about who I was and where I was . . . I mean where I wanted to go. Good food, everything . . . [smile] man, I was lovin' it out there for real."

Looking back, Simi emphasized that Ben, Kitty, and many of their friends had extensive and detailed knowledge "about history and whatnot." As he saw it, "Ben and Kitty, they, like, they gave me the bigger picture. Just talking with them, their books . . . if I didn't have school they would be like, 'Why don't you go to the library?' And they were cool about Rachel having the baby, you know, it was part of their religion not to believe in abortions. They were just like, 'Okay, how are we gonna handle this situation as best we can?' They were breaking it down for me, like, 'Why are you spending money on phone cards to call Rachel when you could spend that money when you see her on baby clothes?' And, I mean, they was type [sic] critical about school, too. They didn't really think the schools I was goin' to was about anything. They were like, 'What does it mean to be black?' and whatnot. But they were still pushing me to do good in school, though. They changed my life deeply, no question." Here, fusing insights from Gramsci and Malcolm X, we might speak of organic intellectuals instilling in Simi a profound sense of black pride. By the time I met Simi, there was often no awareness of "I" outside of a larger nonwhite "we"—a community that could be united in the struggle against race-related modes of continuing oppression.

On his way to hitting full stride, Simi began doing something that became, for him, extremely significant: grow dreadlocks. He reported that the initial decision to grow dreads had more to do with respect for Ben and Kitty than with "being serious about being a Rasta." But by the time I met him his long, funky, and authentic-looking—rather than overly neat—dreads were central to his self- and group-representations. His hairstyle was knotted up with the fact that he listened to "Conscious Reggae" instead of the infamous "Gangsta Rap" that was so popular among students attending Johnson.[27] His dreads, for him, were an outward sign that his dietary habits were evolving once again. Simi had become, in his own words, even more "health conscious . . . I mean, I just went ahead and cut out any and all junk food." He also became a strict vegetarian. He switched from fasting during Ramadan to what he called a "Rasta fast" (i.e., sundown to sundown, one day per week). Simi continued this once-a-week fast throughout his time at Johnson even though this required, as he told me, an enormous amount of self-discipline once he left Ben and Kitty's sphere of influence. He did this, he once rather casually remarked, "to like . . . prove to myself that I had that . . . that control over myself."[28]

So off and on, while twelve and thirteen years of age, Simi worked either full- or part-time at the store. During these years he also spent a great deal of time with Ben and Kitty outside the store. The sense of trust between Simi's two "families" was so great that, at one point, Simi's mother asked Ben and Kitty to travel from Virginia to North Carolina to collect Simi and bring him back. During another extended period, Simi's mother stayed in North Carolina and Simi lived with Ben and Kitty. In general, when Simi was primarily in the care of Ben and Kitty, he kept out of trouble and did quite well in school. In one instance, Simi's vastly improved report cards so impressed a judge that he was willing to throw Simi's earlier offenses and failures to appear out of court. The judge let the new Simi off with a warning.

Before he returned to the Bronx, then, Simi was starting to get back on track. It must be stressed, however, that what Simi once called "circumstances" initially offset the healing influences. For example, when he was removed from Ben and Kitty's direct sphere of influence—and while living close to Rachel and with his mother while she was selling drugs—things once more went awry.

On a visit back Down South after he started attending Johnson, Simi was stricken when he discovered that the store was gone and that Ben and Kitty had moved without leaving a trace. He is to this day sorry he was never able to inform the people who so diligently acted *in loco parentis* about what started to happen during the next stage of his life.

When It "Clicked"

Even when we first got to know each other, Simi saw that Johnson High was a gang-ridden, stigmatized, erratic, and often extremely violent place. He, like several other students with experience in schools Down South, was of the opinion that institutions like Johnson High were much more distressed and distressing than anything one would find in rural Virginia.[29] Perhaps for these reasons, Simi often became visibly dejected when we discussed what occurred in and around Johnson High. During such moments he would regularly send his dreads flying by looking down and nodding his head. Like Brindisha and Raul, Simi understood how disastrously wrong things could go in his school in part because he had spent time in far less distressed educational environments in the past.

Nevertheless, while making his way back and forth between Johnson High and his homeless shelter during his first year back in New York, Simi went through some of his most positive changes. As he put it in an interview, "When I started going to Johnson, that's really when it all started to come together for me, that's when it all started to click." The recognition of his academic abilities and the staunch support of several (mostly white) teachers were not the only reasons Simi often had positive things to say about Johnson High. Simi felt proud of, and a sense of solidarity with, both his school and co-students. Like a sociologist who sees underlying oppression and (micro) configurations of structural forces instead of "deviant" individuals, Simi repeatedly emphasized that he considered even the most disruptive and violent types in Johnson High to be "[his] people." He often spoke, usually in quasi-religious terms, about redistributing wealth and reconstructing society in such a way that the temporarily lost flock might be brought back to their utopian home.

It was also while he was attending Johnson High, and soon after his mother stopped selling drugs, that Simi released himself from the sense that he had to "sell" to provide financially for his son and his son's mother. Simi might be accused of choosing for himself and his future, during this period, rather than trying to find a legal or illegal way to provide financially for his child. According to such a reading, this fifteen-year-old child abandoned his child. One might also find it unreasonable to expect a boy from such an destabilized family and social position to do more than try, as Simi claims he often did, to get custody of (and to partially provide for) his son. No matter how one interprets his response to becoming a child-father, with a past so full of overwhelming emotional demands and with a residential situation so dangerous and stigmatized, one can see why Simi might have

experienced his new school as a sanctuary. Thanks largely to his newly developed intellectual skills, his newfound self-respect and his unheard of levels of self-discipline, being in school often felt good to this student claiming
to be on a communal, quasi-religious, "mission."

Johnson High did not feel like a sanctuary to Simi only because (early
on) he compared it to a homeless shelter. Long after moving into an apartment building, on his way to an extra-early and noncompulsory class one
morning, Simi thought he would walk through the small park between his
apartment building and Johnson High. A much larger man tried to pull him
behind a tree and, Simi claimed, sexually abuse him. He escaped, he said,
only because a passerby made a distracting sound and his attacker looked
away for a second. Simi dropped his book bag and sprinted to safety—*inside the walls of Johnson High.* For teens in areas such as the South Bronx,
the after-school hours (from roughly 3:00 until 6:00 p.m.) are widely known to
be some of the most violent of the entire day. At around 3:00 p.m., while
I was getting ready to leave the building, Simi often started asking me detailed questions about things like the role of Philadelphia in the American
War of Independence.[30] Sitting together, bent over his "advanced placement" textbook, he exhibited a laserlike and seemingly interminable focus.
It was I (unfamiliar with the details packed into the textbooks used in selective classes), not he, who had trouble paying undivided attention in these
impromptu study sessions. Simi's school days were longer than mine, and
he returned at the end of them to a frenzied and loud (i.e., sleep-reducing)
apartment building in a viciously dangerous neighborhood. But before this
teenage son of the South Bronx went to college he had a greater capacity
to stay focused on detailed texts than I did at nearly twice his age and after
having received a Master's degree.

My first trip to his apartment in particular gave me a sense of why Simi
felt so at home inside Johnson High.[31] One place Simi was never found,
after school or at any other time, was the basketball court and park directly
opposite his apartment building. This park was "regularly" the site of severe
violence. Simi reported that during the years he resided directly opposite
this "playground" area, there were several near fatal stabbing incidents. He
also avoided hanging out in front of his building. Simi reported that the
rotating sets of young men who stood in front of this early twentieth century tenement were almost completely made up of gang members and drug
dealers—typically in their late teens and early twenties. When I visited his
apartment, I saw him offer cordial yet guarded greetings to the young men
who seemed to be stationed in front his residence. Then, passing through
another space in which Simi never lingered, we practically had to step over

teenagers smoking marijuana in the filthy stairwell. They seemed utterly unmotivated to get out of our way. Garbage bags, some of them open, had been placed in the halls. A brew of old graffiti (some of which may have seemed colorful and creative when it was new) and filth seemed to be everywhere.

I started seeing Johnson as even more a safe haven when, sitting on his bed, Simi told me that gunshots—as well as blaring music (hip-hop, R&B, salsa, merengue, and reggae)—could be heard deep into the night from his bedroom facing out into the echoing courtyard. The advanced placement classes and less "thugged out" interactional niches in which Simi spent most of his time in school seemed quite harmless by comparison to nearly everything else going on in his life. Given the internal resources he had cultivated—through his own continuing efforts as well as through the earlier one's of his "spiritual parents"—Simi's distressed and objectively unsafe school functioned for him as a combined refuge and launching pad.

Simi also started to feel good about Johnson High because of the friendships he made with like-minded (or at least utterly peaceful, nondisruptive) students and with supportive teachers. One of the pupils in this clique was Rita, the girl he half-jokingly started to call his "wife." (Originally from Ghana—and like Derek in the early days—Rita was one of most softspoken, reserved, and hard-working students I ever came across.) For better or for worse, several of Simi's teachers (myself included) started telling him not only that he could graduate with honors, but that he might want to pursue academic scholarships from prestigious universities. Tracked into the advanced classes and empowered by a realistic sense that better things were on the horizon, Johnson seemed to Simi like an empowering island of predictability and serenity.

In class, as one might expect at this stage, Simi's demeanor was nearly always austere and pensive. He rarely smiled at or even made meaningful eye contact with anyone he did not trust. Even in classroom settings dominated by frenzied transactions and students (i.e., in his nonselective classes as opposed to the advanced placement ones), he sat quietly and looked at the teacher, the blackboard, or textbook. His alert yet soothing demeanor constantly communicated to everyone that he was a threat to no one and there to learn. Always appearing self-composed, he never made jokes in class and, if he laughed at one, it was under his breath and without any potentially provocative physical orientation towards the jokester.

Making his way through "thugged out" hallways and stairwells, Simi tended to stick close to a wall and keep his gaze fixed straight ahead and down. In spaces such as this he seemed to have a gift for taking it all in while deflecting attention. No matter where he was—the cafeteria, an entrance/exit area, an assembly—Simi seemed never to look directly at any potentially hostile students. The overall effect of his ascetic carriage, uncompromising silence, and avoidance of the "wrong" kinds of eye contact was unmistakable. He perpetually diffused what might have developed into "wild" situations before they began. What were zones of temptation for so many others, seemed to have no effect at all. Between 1996 and 1999, every hour of every day that I observed him in and out of my own classes, Simi modulated his gestures, his emotions, and his speech such that, as the expression goes, "trouble never came looking for him."

Simi had not become impervious to the symbolic power of the "ghetto fabulous." He retained his "old" aesthetic dispositions and, if only on this front, a strong distaste for what others called "fake" ways of being. However subtly (e.g., though comments about the well-dressed at once "getting their thug on" and "having it going on"), he seemed to sense that the "true players" really did have more sex appeal, charisma, and rhythm than the "nobodies." In this sense, we might say, Simi was culturally "street." But these types of feelings and thoughts played quite minor roles in his life no matter what situation he faced. Even as he recognized the "real" to some extent, Simi was neither positioned nor predisposed in ways that stimulated or even allowed for getting caught up in compulsive and ultimately self-destructive responses. To observe Simi in the frenzy of daily life in Johnson High was to see a young man who "naturally" and persistently played the game in positive ways. In a school dominated by teens twisted and torn by incoherent sets of pressures and desires, Simi personified the fit between a coherent set of dispositions and the formal demands of the educational field.

Life after Johnson

Simi went on to receive over a hundred thousand dollars in academic scholarships and, in four years, a BA in African American Studies and Education from Brown University. While he went through college, I tried to monitor how he was doing as well as how he felt about his time at Johnson. In the summer before Simi's junior year at Brown, he and Rita joined me for a stroll after brunch in my mother's Upper West Side apartment. Nodding his head in disgust, Simi returned to his central theme: Johnson's real problem was not the outbursts of physical violence, but, instead, the day-to-day disruptions and lack of "structure." (This is a distinction that, as we have seen, I would not want to push too far.) Making our way from Amsterdam to Broadway on West 111th Street, with Rita silently tagging along beside us, Simi returned to the lack of social constraints toward self-constraints: "I used to be vexed up in there because of that. That's what just like kinda . . . fucked everything up . . . just that, that everyday chaos. Kids steady messin' up they classes, not doin' no work . . . runnin' round, screaming, wildin' in the halls. Oh, God. That's what messed it up to me." Rita finally chimed in. "Yup," she said. "That . . . was really the worst problem. It wasn't really the violence. I mean I got attacked on the way home from school [in what appeared to be a genuinely nonschool related incident]. I know that's when I was really afraid, not in [Johnson High]. It was jus' that daily stress."

I started to see Simi as much more of a fellow traveler than as an ex-student when, just before he graduated from Brown, Simi sent me an e-mail including the following fragment: "I was working in a public high school in Providence. It is kinda like their version of [Johnson]. I had some real good experiences there beneath the chaos. One day you told me, 'People talk about Dewey and the child as an active learner, but Dewey wasn't talking about all that in the midst of chaos.' I believed you then and I believe you even more now." But Simi's frustrations in Providence were not confined to his experiences in local public schools. At some points, as one might expect, he felt extremely out of place in such an elite academic setting.[32]

Simi finally won custody of his son. As he put it in an e-mail, he presently lives in the South Bronx with Rita and "one [kid] from my side, one from her side, and one from the both of us." The last time I saw them together, roughly a decade after meeting them, Rita was trying to figure out whether to pursue a promotion as social worker or go to graduate school. Simi was teaching history and social studies at a new "urban academy" run by one of my former colleagues. The young couple was spread thin financially and taking care of three kids was obviously taking its toll. They both seemed drained. They also seemed to be a stable couple, excellent parents, and young professionals who really were pillars of their community.

Discussion

Youngsters issued from the most disadvantaged families are eliminated because they lack the habits and inclinations demanded. . . . [What is required is] a regularity of life, a sense of discipline, a physical and mental asceticism that cannot take root in . . . conditions marked by chronic instability . . .[33]

I want to conclude by highlighting what I see as the most vital insights provided by the juxtaposition of these four profiles. Certain aspects of

Brindisha's story and especially the early stages of Derek's highly intentional transformation into "Cookie" strongly support the use of concepts and types of analyses associated with major contributors to current debates on failing urban schools.[34] At times augmenting these ways of thinking and speaking, as I hope to show now, we might be well advised to take together the different aspects of all four cases presented in this chapter—including those aspects that cannot be explained well when viewed primarily through the prism of distinct racial (or ethno-national) "groups" and highly conscious cultural "resistance."

Even after being forced to acquire something of a taste for the "street life," two of the three boys self-identifying as black and featured in this chapter did not remain engulfed in harmful coping strategies. The keys to success had little to do with being a native (Simi) or newcomer (Raul, Derek). Unlike Derek and even more dramatically than Raul, in Goffman's famous terms,[35] Simi stopped getting caught up in the *staging of a "real" self* even though he remained exposed to the "usual" cast of characters and temptations leading so many to continue playing along with (increasingly) tragic acts. *The "fabulous" I/we image producing show*—the process of collective positing, continual propping up, and trying (desperately) to live up to a "thugged out" self—*did not have to go on.* Simi appeared to be free from nearly all preoccupation with how one was evaluated by audiences of peers. He liked "fabulous gear," yet he did not suffer from the cravings for props (shoes, jeans, gold) that so often seemed to solidify senses of "real" self and facilitate risky behaviors such of the one that nearly cost Derek his life. Indeed Simi's deeds and words indicated that he was comparatively less concerned with staging *any* kind of essentialized self (e.g., the good student, the future college whiz kid, the holier than thou revolutionary type). Once his own immediate physical safety was secured, as it usually was inside Johnson in part because of how he carried himself, what he genuinely seemed to care most about was focusing on the official curriculum right now and remaining on a path leading towards a useful contribution to his (imagined) community in the future. At a much more primordial level than that of some kind of thinking Machiavellian subject out to manipulate the impressions others had of him, Simi seemed to care about healthy developmental processes that would allow him to give others the kind of gift his "spiritual parents" had given him.

Inevitably, Simi was attuned to the overriding moods into which he was thrust. And he was by no means happy all the time. However, when the worst was being brought out in those around him, Simi remained calm, discerning, and amazingly concentrated. If we cannot say Simi was fully immunized from the anxiety and intimidation unleashed by everyday transactions in and around his school, it seems fair to say that—due primarily to healthy experiences turned "thick" flesh—for him the toxicity remained at dosages too low to do lasting damage. Rather than being pushed and pulled by detrimental thoughts, beliefs, and feelings, Simi seemed to have an exceptional ability to dodge negative social pressures while making choices that helped generate more well-being for him and those around him.

Here it seems that the language of "choice" is justified even though it can become misleading if we start to see too many of Simi's actions as results of explicit calculation.[36] We might therefore do well to remember that—like a great musician striking just the right chord at just the right time while harmonizing in just the right way with "everything" going on a jam session— right there "in the middle of it all" Simi did not have time to explicitly "think" keen focus or calm detachment before enacting it. Rather, a composed presence and gentle strength emanated (almost) automatically from this product of sustained experiences in a web of relationships so intensely transformative and meaningful that Simi used (quasi-) religious terms to describe them.[37]

So what were the keys to Simi's triumph? In answering this question, we must not underemphasize the positive effects of Simi's conscious, collective, and color-related sense of self. There can be no doubt that, in Simi's case, explicit ideas about race and academic achievement mattered.[38] Having said this, if we really want to do justice to sources of Simi's coping practices and how they worked in real time, we have to be clear on the social structural, collective emotional, and material (e.g., body-based) learning processes that (1) undergirded his explicit mental representations and (2) allowed them to be effective. It was not primarily the content of any explicit ideas (associated with figures such as Marcus Garvey, Haile Selassie, or Louis Farrakhan) but, rather, sustained immersion in well-regulated environments supervised by emotionally stable and somewhat bookish adults that, most fundamentally, put Simi in a position to (help himself) succeed. Potentially uplifting ideas about spiritual regeneration and racial pride (passed on to Simi by his brothers) did not noticeably improve Simi's situation until he started spending huge amounts of time in the care of Kitty and Ben.

Most fundamentally then, although this might have been too painful for Simi to spell out in plain language, it was getting away from the adults that meant the most to him and being part of a sturdy string of emotionally stabilizing and self-control enabling interactions regulated by his "spiritual parents" that gave Simi a toehold.

It is not a coincidence that in six years across the two fields the adolescent I came across with the greatest ability to use foresight and sustain concentrated attention had also gone through a uniquely civilizing process of *body-based learning*. Even more obviously than in the case of Raul's trajectory,[39] the somatic dimension of informal learning is in Simi's case not another "variable" we might "bring in." Body-based emotional metamorphoses were the foundation of his educational success and, more broadly, his emancipation from destructive social pressures and habits or mind. Seeing this does not at all imply downplaying the massive influence of Ben and Kitty. It was largely within the "spiritual" environment they maintained that new *techniques of the body* really took hold and, along with the content of the narratives to which he was exposed, helped Simi develop a more heightened sense of somatic awareness and emotional self-restraint. Sermons do not make saints and even the most righteous spiritual ideas alone would have done little to help Simi given the depth of the hole into which he was thrust. Emotional self-control based on new corporeal regimes and social relationships seem, by contrast, to have been precisely what helped him begin and remain on his "mission."

Derek's decline, Brindisha's tragedy, Raul's avoidance of disaster, and Simi's triumph might be said to teach us, above all, two things. First, if the students did not experience their lives in the two schools mainly through the filter of explicit mental representations, then we should not base our analyses of their more or less successful trajectories on any thoughts (about race) that they can easily put into words. And second, if by far the most successful student felt the effects of emotional stability and social control most rigorously *through his body*, then all of us should consider the possibility that calming bodies and regulating emotional states should be the core of every high-poverty high school's curriculum. In other words, we need to at least seriously consider the idea that the keys to helping massively disadvantaged (pre-) adolescent students have little to do with ideas. Difficult as the shift may be, as Simi's U-turn indicates, we (education) intellectuals should consider opening up to the self-control generating power of mundane emotional metamorphoses and the utility of the one heuristic device that students always already use no matter where their minds may wander: their bodies. Here again, my sense is that Dewey's reasoning, reputation, and rhetoric might help:

> Men are afraid, without even being aware of their fear, to recognize, the most wonderful of all the structures of the vast universe—the human body. They have been led to think that a serious notice and regard would somehow involve disloyalty to man's higher life. [Our] discussions [should] breathe rever-

ence for this wonderful instrument of our life, life mental and moral as well as that life which . . . we call bodily. When such [an] . . . attitude toward the body becomes more general, we shall have an atmosphere favorable to securing the conscious control which is urged.[40]

The main dissimilarity this chapter highlights has to do with the formal structuring of the American and the Dutch fields of education. Given the lack of "structure" with which he was forced to contend at the time, had Simi been tracked at twelve years of age (as is the practice in the Netherlands), he almost certainly would have been placed on a low-level vocational trajectory. Instead, Simi ended up at a *comprehensive* high school with, for example, advanced placement classes. Across the United States most disadvantaged teens attend such schools meant, formally, to turn out graduates who are "college ready." This is, thanks to Kitty and Ben's intervention as well as to Simi's incredible resilience, exactly what happened in our most spectacular case. Simi maxed out his academic possibilities, went straight to college, and graduated in four years with marketable skills and a steady job.[41] This raises an obvious question about the comparatively early—if not cruelly premature—formal selection moment in the Dutch system (cf. Van der Werfhorst and Mijs 2010). Are lower class kids getting tracked "efficiently" because of their (innate) "abilities" or being punished because they have been denied emotional self-control generating experiences supervised by stable adults (cf. Moffit et al. 2011)?

Raul ended up in a *vocational* school granting access only to more vocational and, in Amsterdam at least, to more high-poverty education. Throughout big cities in the Netherlands, the vast majority of disadvantaged teens end up being tracked into such secondary schools. One might suggest, once again, that the system worked. Raul graduated on time from one of Delta's higher tracks and is now working on a BA while holding down a promising part-time job. Yet Raul, who had no major problems in a less impoverished primary school, was very nearly thrown off course twice—first during his initial period at Delta and then again, after graduating, in a nonselective postsecondary vocational school that he considered to be even more "wild." Raul's second slide had to do with many things, but it ended only when Raul started attending a less segregated school far outside Amsterdam.

Whatever one thinks of the American dream of high schools capable of making even deeply disadvantaged children "college ready," Simi's case can offer us a number of truly important lessons: If they are granted sustained access to healing socio-emotional environments, if they are equipped with coping skills engrained deeply into their adaptive unconscious minds via highly disciplined bodily practices, and if they are endowed with even mod-est amounts of cultural capital—the educational trajectories of countless twelve-to-fourteen-year-old "lost souls" headed into our worst high schools might be saved. And this, in turn, might be the single most promising way to turnaround such "lost" educational institutions. Relatedly, instead of rely-ing on the "measuring" and "systemic" tracking of *substance-like things* with putatively fixed and decontextualized intellectual attributes, our predictions about the *ongoing processes* we call individual (twelve-to-fourteen-year-old) students should be informed by what might happen in terms of emotional and cognitive (neuro) plasticity if those born poor were granted access to genuinely nurturing experiences. In terms of our successful cases, closing off Simi's path to college because of scores on exit exams at the end of primary or middle school might have done incalculable harm. And a similar point can be made with reference to Raul. At least from his mother's perspective soon before she died, Raul's path toward college and stable employment was more hampered than it was expedited by the "early" tracking system in the Netherlands. As things stand now it seems that lower class teens granted opportunities to develop sufficient levels of emotional self-control and to acquire even a certain level of "legitimized" cultural capital may be better off in American-style comprehensives than in typically Dutch vocational high schools. For the other ninety percent or so who are granted none of the above, the opposite may hold or, more likely, the formal differences simply do not matter very much at all.

Especially seen against this backdrop of what worked for Raul (a "to-gether," cultivated mother) and Simi (a rather intellectual set of "spiritual parents"), Brindisha and Derek's misfortunes reveal that years of stabilizing social influences can be all but nullified by comparatively short bursts of exposure to *environments inadequately regulated by adults*. I do not deny that Brindisha's Hindustani background mattered or that Derek was so "soft" when he arrived because he was from a village in West Africa. Yet my re-search indicates that this holds for children and teens no matter how we classify them—and no matter how they categorize themselves—along ever-changing ethnic lines. "Newcomers" or "native," what the students attend-ing schools like Johnson and Delta need most are what the vast majority of privileged teens get from their parents: access to physically safe, reasonably well-regulated experiences that serve as the means for developing relatively high levels of emotional self-control and cultural capital.[42]

All this talk of adult supervision brings us to teachers and, therefore, to the domains within the two schools were these "street-level bureaucrats" made their last stands. Unlike Kitty and Ben—who were in positions to offer massive dosages of one-on-one tutoring to Simi—the adults stationed in front of Johnson and Delta's classrooms were vastly outnumbered. Largely for this reason, as the next chapter further reveals, such adults typically have almost no access to the solidarity generating experiences and transformative body-based learning techniques that helped Ben and Kitty come to Simi's emotional rescue. Yet I suspect that Simi remains a high school teacher in the South Bronx today in part because he knows there is reason to hope that, in more and less segregated schools, the type of medicine he received can be offered even to young people on trajectories as sickening as the one upon which he was originally placed.

SIX

The Tipping of Classrooms,
Teachers Left Behind

Listen. Don't try to be a hero. Do your time here, get your [state] certification, and get out [to the suburbs] before you become too expensive. Don't get stuck . . . like I did.[1]

Look, it's simple. Either you have it or you don't. Did you ever read *The Call of the Wild*?[2]

From influential research papers to popular opinion pieces in major news-papers, quite a bit of attention is being paid to the impact that "good" (or "high-value-added") and "poor" teachers[3] may have on their disadvantaged students. My research on classrooms also suggests that the value of excel-lent teachers—and the costs of incompetent ones—should be incorporated into national discussions about high-poverty schools. However, given the prevalence of popular dogmas on this topic, I want to be clear about where my findings and analysis diverge from what is making the rounds.

In leading academic and public debates, teachers often appear to be self-enclosed, thing-like substances that simply *are* either strong or weak. While it is readily admitted that few teachers excel in their first year or two, and that screening for those who will later exhibit the right stuff is extremely difficult,[4] little is said in these popular debates about exactly how class-room teachers (fail to) *become* highly skilled and why they might remain vulnerable (to burnouts) even after having achieved this. Instead of rely-ing exclusively on the "cleaned" data sets underpinning statistical variable based research, my experiences in the Bronx and the Bijlmer suggest the need to bring into these discussions evidence on the situated learning and coping processes that can be observed on the ground in strategically se-lected settings. My nearly six years in classrooms indicate, in fact, that it might be a good idea to base our analyses of different types of teachers on how rampant fraud and massive levels of stress in and outside specific classrooms regularly (1) wear down *potentially effective* teachers to the point that they may appear (on paper or to the eye) to be *inherently* incompetent; (2) make the determination of (potentially) excellent teachers by means of quantitative evaluations enormously problematic[5]; (3) guarantee that turning even dedicated high potentials into consistently effective teachers will be extremely difficult; and (4) ensure that few highly effective teachers with options will remain in our worst schools (even if they can expect to be paid significantly more than many of their colleagues).

This brings us from the seemingly permanent attributes of teachers to developmental processes involving interactions with students. Detailed empirical work has challenged the longstanding notion that students engage in disruptive classroom behavior mainly because of their socioeconomic or racial backgrounds. While relevant contributions have come from many quarters,[6] two back-to-back articles by McFarland (2001, pp. 620, 665; 2004, p. 1250) deserve special mention here. Taking aim at the dominant paradigm, McFarland argued that "both Willis's lads and ear'oles [were] only able to [engage in disruptive behavior] when teachers [provided] them social opportunities." Starting the analysis with immediately observable symbolic interactions, McFarland tried to replace the assumption that "minorities and lower-income students rebel in class" with the finding that "instructional processes and social (network) resources enable students to disrupt . . . classroom affairs." Reminding readers that the "social dramas" unfolding in classrooms are "not chaotic, but ordered," he added that "most any student will breach tasks and attempt to control the classroom if they are afforded the social opportunities and have the necessary political resources at their discretion."

Most importantly in the following sense, many of my observations in Johnson and Delta support McFarland's central empirical claim: With truly masterful teachers supervising them, here and now situational dynamics basically ensured that nearly all students remained at least nondisruptive if not productively engaged; with less effective adults at the helm, most students were capable of contributing to the destruction of their "periods of instruction." However, this corroboration of McFarland's findings requires critically reexamining two key aspects of his influential interventions into the classroom "resistance" debate.

First, sound as McFarland's descriptions of what teachers *ought* to do in front of a classroom may be,[7] his findings reveal little about the immediate relationships between specific kinds of classroom situations on one hand,

and the skills and predispositions that actually enabled (or constrained) real-time responses of teachers on the other. The crucial omission has to do with McFarland's assumption that the actions of teachers (and students) result from *explicit mental representations*.[8] Because the actual responses of teachers in classrooms need not be any more influenced by conscious deliberations than the adjustments of athletes in the heat of action (cf. Paulle, Van Heerikhuizen, and Emirbayer 2012),[9] I suggest instead trying to get as close as possible to *how* those standing in front of classes more or less successfully brought about the predictability and productivity that, as nearly all my colleagues in both settings agreed, should characterize classroom settings. In other words the present chapter attempts to drill down beneath overt interpretations to the bedrock of situationally embedded somatic states and how more or less competent teachers pre-reflectively coped while already absorbed in various kinds of classroom dynamics.

The second concern relates to something McFarland failed to acknowledge even though it is quite straightforward: while it may be true that most teens can act up under the right interactional conditions, and while (social-class and racialized) backgrounds may not be as "over-determining" as many have suggested, the lives adolescents lead can strongly incline them toward problems with self-regulation and maintaining focused concentration on anything related to official curricula in classrooms. Teachers used revealing language to get at what they saw as the relevant personality traits and attitude problems—*druk* (restless, busy bodies) and *rustig* (calm, docile) were the paired terms most frequently heard in the Netherlands; in New York teachers spoke habitually of kids who "just don't wanna listen"). Drawing from the idiom and insights developed in the previous chapters we can say now that—along with the fleeting effects of immersion in here and now micro-level involvements (e.g., boosts of energy received just before walking into a classroom)—the ways in which students' engrained sets of emotional predispositions (which led them, for example, to react more or less explosively, to be more or less in touch with signals from their own bodily cores and their immediate surroundings, to see classroom settings in generally more gloomy or in more optimistic ways, and to recover more or less quickly from strong emotional triggers) mattered a great deal in terms of the contestations and collaborations that emerged in classroom environments. In short, ongoing (extra-classroom) interactional effects as well as habitus—and especially the experiences and relationships turned durable dispositions making up *emotional styles* (Davidson 2012)—mattered. The delightful experience of teaching a room full of kids as stabilized as Simi or Raul (by the time I got to know them) had very little to do with the experience of trying to teach students as emotionally overburdened, as incapable of using foresight, and as frequently despondent as Brindisha and especially Derek toward the end of their times in Delta and Johnson. As we begin building on McFarland's work and attending carefully to life in classrooms, we need to keep in mind how the presence of more or less *potentially* disruptive (and aggressive) students always prestructured what my colleagues were led to experience as their "personal" victories and failures.

Beginning with the continual strain breaking down those who certainly appeared to be the "weakest" teachers and then moving on to those who got stuck (as I did) at the level of "ordinary" proficiency will, I suspect, help us appreciate more fully what went on in the rooms of the roughly one in five teachers in Johnson and perhaps one in four in Delta who might be called "super teachers."[10]

The Wearing Down of the Weakest

It was just another day at the stress factory. I had stopped hassling my students to do anything productive. Assists from a few frail allies had helped generate perhaps fifteen productive minutes, but the usual chains of routinized disruptions had basically smashed my lesson plan and frayed my nerves. With the bell to end the period still a few minutes off, the students sat around waiting to be released. I slumped behind my desk and my mind wandered, aimlessly.

Curious about the sounds emanating from the hallway, I walked toward my classroom door. Directly across the corridor a small cluster of mostly male students had gathered. They seemed to be uncharacteristically early for their next class. Suddenly, three or four of these boys with their backs to me banged several times, hard, on the closed door immediately across the hall. One girl stood especially close to the door-bangers, but she did not pound on or even approach the door. The instant the boys finished their hammering, they dashed down the hallway through a set of swinging doors and out of sight. As if pulled by a magnet that drew her chest first, the girl positioned closest to them followed excitedly behind. Before she made it to the swinging doors, however, a noticeably vexed female teacher (in her late twenties and of Afro-Surinamese descent), Raquel, opened the classroom door and yelled, "Mary-Anne, I saw you." Mary-Anne (also of Afro-Surinamese descent)—clearly one of the more boisterous girls as my observations in places like the *aula* had previously made clear—came back to the doorway and tried to speak to my irate colleague.

Raquel was in no mood for chatting. "What do you want now?" she bellowed. Raquel's wild eyes and expression seemed to indicate that she was "losing it." A few words were exchanged and Raquel attempted to end the conversation by closing the door. A standoff ensued when Mary-Anne wedged herself into the doorway.[11] I could not follow all of the verbal exchange, but it was obvious that Mary-Anne tried to explain that she had not been part of the banging. The teacher refused to be drawn into the verbal exchange and continued trying to shut her out. Mary-Anne would not budge.

The temptation, perhaps, is to see "chaos" breaking loose at this stage. Yet these can, usefully I think, be seen as players slogging their ways through the second of four acts in one of McFarland's recognizably patterned (if not well-ordered) mini-dramas.[12] In this case the stars of the show were a revved-up girl who felt she had been wronged and a visibly upset adult who felt not only wronged but—as my experiences with the "trash-can thrower" indicated—that her body-space was under attack. While the "seriousness and extent of the breach" had not yet been determined, the face-off was edging toward a full-blown "crisis," and it was anything but clear how "redress" and finally some kind of "reintegration" might occur.

Then it came, the physical cue and emotional reaction that mattered most. Rather gingerly, as far as I could see, the distraught teacher pressed against Mary-Anne's shoulder. There was, for the first time, direct body-to-body contact. Almost instantaneously and in one fluid motion, Mary-Anne dropped her bag from her right hand and took a swing at the chin of the much taller teacher. She missed her mark only because my colleague instinctively snapped her head backward. In an instant Raquel and Mary-Anne grabbed each other by the neck with their left hands and drew back their right hands. At just that moment, a boy from inside Raquel's classroom thrust himself between the two combatants before any blows could be delivered.

As if frozen during the flash in which all this happened, I did nothing to separate the adversaries. My inaction had *nothing* to do with any conscious mental deliberations. After the deeds were done, and feeling vaguely ashamed about not having proven to be the (manly) type who spontaneously breaks up such circles of disastrous (female) energy, I joined the pupil from across the hall in his successful attempt to keep Mary-Anne and my colleague from doing any more damage. I found myself consciously trying to present an authoritative presence, that is, after a much smaller teenager had already brought the negative spiral to a halt.

Raquel's next class was cancelled and, within a few minutes, a conversation ensued in the office of the school manager who most frequently dealt with such incidents. Raquel, the administrator with twenty-five years of experience, and I were joined by another veteran teacher who seemed to know quite a bit about Mary-Anne's situation. The manager and the other teacher tried to convince Raquel, whose neck was still visibly red, that Mary-Anne should merely be suspended, rather than expelled. According to the second teacher's argument, Mary-Anne deserved to be treated as exceptional case. This, she told us, was Mary-Anne's "last chance." As she had already been kicked out of her previous school, another expulsion would make it all but impossible to place her anywhere outside of the special-educational system. Both the other teacher and the administrator more than implied that they could understand why Mary-Anne might have felt she had been falsely accused and that Raquel may have acted in haste. The teacher who had just dodged the right cross saw things differently. Wide-eyed and still clearly upset, Raquel argued if Mary-Anne returned any hint of legitimacy she had built up with the other students would evaporate. Although less than obvious perhaps, the implication here, I think we have to say, was the following: "Okay, I might not be a great teacher—but either you lose her right now or you lose me well before the end of the school year."

The manager sat and listened. Then the decision was made. Mary-Anne would be expelled, immediately. Shoulders slumped and alone, Raquel returned within minutes to her empty classroom. After several months at home, as the same administrator informed me, Mary-Anne did end up in school for children with "special needs"—usually a sentence that remains binding for the remainder of a student's life in secondary education.

Before this incident occurred, I had observed several of Raquel's classes. They were hopeless, among the worst I ever observed anywhere. The continuity of petty disruptions had been hard to believe or stomach. At one point I planted a tape recorder above a bookcase before the start of one of her classes. I wanted to find out if the level of disruption might possibly be any lower when I was not there. There was no difference. Again, against the fully audible backdrop of disruptions, Raquel's more or less frantic pleas for quiet were pitiable. Again, less than five minutes of the period was spent on task. As my own observations and conversations with teachers positioned in adjacent rooms confirmed, minute after minute and day after day, waves of disruptions rolled through Raquel's classroom. The door-bangers who showed up early for their next class had been primed to shatter this woman's attempts to teach even before they got underway.

Raquel felt this more deeply than anyone. Long before the bout with Mary-Anne I had interviewed her after yet another disastrous class. Kids had been yelling, wandering around, simply ignoring her and, occasionally, mocking her attempts to return to the official curriculum. Raquel's transparently empty threats, disjointed movements, and insecure attempts to single out individual actions stemmed the tide for—at best—thirty seconds at a time. Whatever tools might have helped one begin climbing out of what she certainly experienced as "her" hole, Raquel did not have them. When we talked, after the bell saved her, Raquel told me she felt ashamed about having a colleague observe such a class. Trying to be supportive, I assured her that I also had sustained problems in my classes and that my chief concern was with how she was dealing with what she had to face—not with anything that might be construed as personal shortcomings. Her comments boiled down to one core idea: she felt that she was being pushed very near the breaking point and that she would inevitably start looking for "a regular office job, sooner or later." She also explained that she had come to Delta with high hopes after feeling very "out of place" at another school where nearly all the teachers were "*Nederlanders.*" She had wanted, desperately perhaps, to make this work.

I checked in again with Raquel a few days after the decision to expel Mary-Anne. We plopped down on the couch outside the manager's office where we had sat together after she dodged Mary-Anne's sucker punch. Still seeming somewhat fazed, Raquel told me that despite the shortage of teachers at Delta, she would start looking for another job immediately. Raquel barely made eye contact with me.

There were reports that my former colleague from across the hall at Delta ended up a social worker. What I confirmed was that she did not return after the summer vacation. As far as I could tell, neither Mary-Anne nor Raquel's ever came back to visit. The relatively minor social altercation proved powerful enough to push a troubled student into special education and a beleaguered teacher over the edge.

––––––––––––––––––

To get a better "read" on the role Raquel played in this drama, let us consider a counter example. I had been substituting at Johnson High for two weeks and I was observing the generally tranquil class of a nominally white teacher in his mid-thirties, William. The class had not been underway for very long before it was punctured by a bang on the closed door. After moderately berating the members of what he later called a "wolf pack" roaming the halls, William put a small rubber garbage container in the doorway to keep the door from closing completely and returned quickly to the lesson plan.

Within minutes two boys appeared. Under the weight of their leaning bodies the door opened almost to the halfway point. "Can I help you with something, gentlemen?" William asked. "Let me check if it's any honies, yo," one boy said, as if only to his hallway running mate. The boy who did not make any comment looked at William and then receded into the hall. "Look, I'll see you later, okay," William offered in a firm yet somewhat serene way to the remaining intruder.

There was an uncomfortable pause. "Eh, yo, check it, why you don't come out here and talk to me for a hot second," the remaining hallway wanderer asked a girl sitting close to the door. The girl smiled shyly, and then whispered something to another girl sitting next to her. "Excuse me, sir," William pronounced in a less acquiescent voice as he walked over to the door, "that'll be just about enough." At this point, the other boy in the hallway called out, "Yo, Bri, man, let's be out, son." Smiling widely, Brian displayed multiple gold teeth. The "bad boy" seemed to enjoy the abundant nervous energy he was soaking up in the center of the limited attention space. His friend called him again, more urgently this time, "Eh, yo, let's be out son."

Brian and William were just inches from each other. The teacher put his hand on the door and gently applied a bit of pressure to it and, indirectly, to Brian's shoulder. "Let's go buddy, c'mon," said the teacher in a way that seemed to communicate that nothing extraordinary would happen and that the ritual now required that the curtain come down on the "thugged out" act. "Eh, yo, man, I'll go when I'm ready. You see I'm trying to get my groove on, right?," Brian blurted out while looking at William as if to suggest that he finally noticed the teacher's presence for the first time. Several members of the class laughed out loud, others hung their nodding heads. I could see from the teacher's body language he was not applying more than symbolic pressure to the door. What I could not see, at the time, was whether the opening "breach" was going to erupt into a full-blown "crisis" or fizzle into a "redress" (in the form of an exit).

The standoff continued. Still pressing lightly on the door and looking directly at Brian, William was clearly frustrated and upset. Yet compared to Raquel during the earliest part of the encounter with Mary-Anne, William displayed a level of composed self-possession and level-headedness that seemed somehow to close off pathways to escalation and drain the energy out of the conflict. William was no pushover. He walked toward Brian and stood his ground. But William never did anything that unnecessarily jacked-up tensions. Certainly, no direct physical contact was made but William never even raised his voice. He just stood his ground, spoke in clear ways, and looked straight at Brian—perhaps inviting him to deal emotionally with the fact that he was engaging a real human being rather than some abstract notion of a "teacher."

But we cannot leave our comparison here. Compared to the more "in your face" tactics that highly effective pedagogues sometimes successfully deployed during such encounters in the Bijlmer, as we shall later in this chapter, William made the rather tame moves that were effectively open to him given the objective distribution of power resources between teachers and potentially aggressive students in Johnson High. Through his calming tone and noninflammatory bodily techniques most crucially—and in ways that were highly suitable given the overall social world as well as the more immediate web of co-created tensions with which he was confronted—William confidently communicated that it would all end peacefully.

Finally the other boy returned to the doorway and grabbed Brian. Still looking at William, Brian allowed himself to be pulled back into the corridor. As William reached down to remove the garbage container so as to allow the door to close all the way, Brian could be heard yelling in the hall, "Fuck that bitch, son . . . I hate these fucking teachers out here." The teacher walked over to the blackboard and picked up a piece of chalk. "Okay," he said, perhaps trying to calm his own nerves as well as ours, "where were we?" William was somewhat rattled to be sure, but he had dealt effectively with a potentially explosive situation and he seemed to rest assured that—during the rest of the period—there would be no fireworks in his room.[13]

So what is the main takeaway? What I observed was a man who acted from a comparatively well-composed emotional state that was rooted in a confident posture and soothing movements. *Bodily based poise*, not anything he could easily put into words, *was the foundation of his felt understandings and responses*. Even though it had to remain in the shadowy back regions, this was the core gift William gave to his students. Indeed precisely *because* this immediately lived, prefamiliarized, and comparatively composed body remained outside the spotlight of his discursive awareness when he concentrated on Brian—i.e., because it functioned like the "darkness in the theatre needed to show up the performance" (Merleau-Ponty [1962] 2002, p. 115; see also Cromby 2008, p. 13)—this silent source of wisdom enabled and unified the moves William made as well as any discursive interpretations he may have had about how to modulate emotions as they welled up inside him.[14] Here we see what Raquel lacked. Already beaten down and riled up when the bang on her door came—already fed up with feeling crushed by challenges such as the one she would now have to answer—she found herself ignoring the very "rules" she might have articulated when she was in the leisurely position of the "Monday Morning Quarterback." Already living through a *diminished visceral state* before being yanked into yet another destructive emotional contagion, this teacher with a *comparatively ineffectual feel for the game* reacted compulsively (as did Mary-Anne, who paid the highest price of all for a series of mindless responses to what had originally been a rather trivial incident). Obviously, while William slowed down the whirlpool of negative reactivity, the less-effective teacher inadvertently stirred things up. Less obviously, before anything else, the teachers did this because their differently socialized bodies were not just in the world, but also co-generative of practical worldviews and real-time reactions. The wear, the tear, the skill, and the confidence manifesting *at once* in the two teachers' *felt bodies* and *subjective mental experiences* were the hidden sources of their more or less appropriate ways of being in banged-on worlds.

Getting as close as possible to the absorbed coping of a deteriorating replacement and an effective teacher who held on after so many of his kind departed,[15] we have seen why the overall power ratios and microlevel rituals manifesting in corridors only *seemed* to muscle their way into classrooms *randomly*. These opening vignettes also reveal that, even in the case of the most "golden" of rules,[16] here and now reactions shaping career paths of teachers and students often had nothing to do with explicit mental representations.

The Overwhelming of the Ordinary

I want to transition now to those appearing in both settings as average or normal teachers. Ascribing a unified view to members of such a social category is problematic. It is nonetheless fair to say, I believe, that the bulk of teachers were ordinary in terms of effectiveness and that they saw their workdays first and foremost in terms of transactions with exceptionally "easy" classes (that allowed one to "come up for air"), the all too common "difficult" classes (that often came two or three in a row), and "killer" classes (powerful enough to preoccupy minds frequently even though they were only dealt with physically on occasion).

Right up to the end of my time at Delta, I made no bones about being an ordinary teacher. Admitting this in the Bronx—i.e., confessing that you were made to feel like cannon fodder several hours of every workday—was far more permissible than in the Bijlmer. In staff meetings, during lunch breaks, and in interviews, nearly without exception my Dutch colleagues steadfastly avoided acknowledging that they were being swamped (even after my observations had made plain that they were no better at maintaining positive interactions in their classrooms than I was).[17] On the other hand, several of these same colleagues in Southeast Amsterdam did suggest that I talk about teaching "difficult classes" with a woman named Joanne. The first time this happened I did not make much of it. But by the second or third time I started to sense that their injunctions, often slipped in on the edges of remarks, might be loaded with meanings I should try to unpack.

Hunting for Joanne I finally caught up with a woman I had taken to be a secretary. I approached this reserved if not dour middle-aged office worker, and soon found myself sitting with her in an empty classroom for the first of two extended interviews. Initially, during our first and most productive sitting, Joanne seemed depleted and a bit withdrawn. There was something tragic about her, I thought, and it seemed at first she was not going to let her guard down. Clearly, however, she understood why I had been sent to her and part of her wanted to tell me her (school's) story. I did little more than explain my concerns and ask if I could record the conversation. I pressed record and off she went—with very definite ideas about the things I needed to hear and the order in which I was to hear them.

"In the beginning," Joanne recalled—i.e., at the outset of her two-decade career as a classroom teacher and long before she worked her way up to a mid-level administrative position—there was an unofficial agreement among all Delta staff. There would be no single class consisting of more than one or two "slightly naughty kids" (boefjes). "Then," she explained, "the magic number went up to three."

Joanne paused and fidgeted as she said this. She looked out the window in the direction of the trees blowing in the wind. Every once in a while she looked right at me, rather schemingly. Either she was trying to figure out if talking to me candidly was "safe," or she was trying to gauge the degree to which I was capable of grasping how crucial her historical account in fact was, it seemed. She continued, "And as the school kept going downhill [pause, shrill laugh . . .] we started sending three, four, five really difficult kids (echte moeilijke kinderen) to each class." Looking right at me, she pressed forward. "What could we do?" she asked. "That's just what was coming in." (Joanne knew that I, like all the other adults in the school, knew about the Bijlmer's and Delta's steep decline since the 1980s.) There was another suspense generating pause. But the floodgates had broken and the rest, apparently, had to come rolling down, "And now . . . now? Now we don't even try to spread them around anymore. . . . There is no more informal agreement."

Gathering momentum as she talked, the pauses and perhaps the internal strategy sessions ceased. Joanne went on to explain why, after managing admissions for Delta full time for a number of years, she had come to see fraud and hypocrisy almost everywhere. The exit exams at the end of primary school that were used to track pupils and rank schools (and, by the way, to gauge the possible effects of segregation)—all bogus. The way the educational inspection agency worked to cover up what actually went on in overwhelmed schools as long as administrators went through a few paper-pushing rituals—a farce. The information about emotional/behavior problems of students passed from "feeder" schools to her own, the lectures about how worthless diplomas were going to help kids in the future, the start of the academic year pep talks to teachers about turning their school around, policy changes debated in parliament—the fix was in, she rather convincingly argued, and it was all one huge scam. Greater "transparency" in theory had led time and again to more deception in practice. She laughed when I asked if she was exaggerating. But the chuckles were replaced with detailed examples strung together by coherent institutional analyses. She was damning her school and educational system intelligently, as only long-term insiders can. And she was damning it carefully because she cared about what teachers faced behind all the closed doors in her school. Joanne wanted me to connect the dots, from systemic breakdown to the "individual" failure of those still stuck in the position she had escaped.

Perhaps sensing that we could use a reprieve from the gloom and doom, I invited her to talk about what might help. Joanne brushed this aside. This woman had spent countless hours wasting away in forsaken classrooms and no less than twenty years of her professional life in an institution coming apart at the seams. She had lived nearly her entire adult life in Southeast Amsterdam while it was in steep decline. She had seen temporarily replacements like me come and go for decades. She was far beyond the stage of pretending any flavor-of-the-month pseudo-interventions would turn the tide. She knew all the rhetoric, of course, but she was not going to get sidetracked with newspeak about group-based learning projects, intercultural textbooks, conflict mediation specialists, per-pupil funding schemes, increased accountancy through more rigorous testing regimes, individualized learning trajectories, teacher training programs customized for "urban academies," or better compensation packages for teachers labeled especially effective. Fully aware that a few of her remaining colleagues could "handle" even the most "difficult" classes, she wanted to talk about the real stuff: the structural overburdening of her neighborhood school and the overwhelming of most classroom teachers left behind. Almost in slow motion, she had seen how the classrooms of Delta were pushed well beyond the tipping point and, by the time she sat down with me to reflect, this was all that mattered. Because she no longer taught, it seemed, she could tell the truth without losing face.

So to me, Joanne sounded like a wise old teacher-administrator in the Bronx with nothing to lose or gain. But while colleagues in the Bronx were more forthright about (their own) struggles inside classrooms, I never heard such a detailed historical account of Johnson High because no one I spoke to in New York actually experienced the decline of the once respected institution from the inside. Having said this, one dialogue I had with an especially insightful ex-teacher turned administrator in the United States did speak to Joanne's structural analysis in a potentially helpful way. In an e-mail exchange concerning the "average inner-city high school class," he offered an especially articulate and revealing depiction of what most pedagogues in Johnson thought they faced. "In a typical universe, your classroom," he wrote, "there are twenty-five interacting particles . . . the kids. One particle is really fucked up, the kid who might well throw a chair at a teacher. Four particles are just royal pains in the ass. Fifteen are followers who will conform to the environment . . . enhance chaos or preserve order. Five are basically not going to cause any problems no matter what. The five chaos creators can only be addressed by teachers pursuing individual relationships with kids, proactively, and backed up by an administration that's got their collective back . . . the other fifteen followers will occasionally need clear discipline."

Had the magic number of "pains in the ass" and occasional "really fucked up kid[s]"[18] been just two, as it seems to have been during the early days at Delta, things might have been different. But, according to the logic of this account, classes in schools like Johnson were typically overburdened by five or more (potentially) extremely disruptive if not aggressive teens. Of course, teachers in the Bijlmer tended for good reason to be far less afraid than my colleagues in the Bronx that one of their students might do something like throw a chair at them. Here again we see that the biggest and most primordial area of divergence between the two settings related to levels of threats and fear. Nevertheless, the two administrators on opposite sides of the Atlantic were using almost the same numbers and (noticeably nonethnicized) categories to stress the importance of how compositions of students usually translated into tipping points in classrooms. Furthermore, the analysis advanced by the American administrator highlights in memorable fashion something that was vital in both settings: the *lack of support for teachers* attempting to (proactively) build relationships with—and regulate the actions of—the most frequently disruptive students as well as those emerging as more average types who usually only played along overtly when destructive mini-dramas were already underway.

Sticking with this "lack of support" theme as well as with the example of what a "fucked-up kid might do," I want to flesh out a crucial area of divergence and a main underlying similarity. The union representative for teachers at Johnson High often bragged about attending meetings with the principal and AFT big shots. This senior colleague—who seemed to enjoy telling me about the leather seats in his Jaguar and who repeatedly assured me, in a condescending way, that it took "several years to become a master teacher"—was, as repeated observations made clear, less effective in his classes than I was in mine. Despite the fact that his close ties to the Assistant Principal of our department kept him more than an arm's distance from many of the more difficult teaching assignments, this ineffective long-term insider ended up coming to work for weeks in a neck brace after a chair was thrown at him in one of his classes. Even for this most "connected" of characters, there was nothing even resembling "collective back-up" or support from above when it mattered most. Especially for the less masterful types and especially at Johnson, being a teacher meant, most basically, feeling endangered and forlorn.

What actually took place in Johnson and Delta when ordinary teachers found themselves in a room dominated (numerically) by four or five "pains in the ass" and anywhere from ten to fifteen (less emotionally overburdened and aggressive) "followers"? If the specific variations were infinite, the patterns were nonetheless clear. And here the similarities across the two settings seem much more profound than any differences. Depending in part on the students' perceptions and feelings about their teacher's level of composure, energy, and concentrated focus, there were usually several casual conversations going on at once. If only in the interest of being heard, talkers were often inclined to raise their voices. Against the backdrop of continuing conversations, sometimes dotted with calls for quiet, someone might walk in late or, for example, a boy might put his feet up on a desk, and a girl might stand up and half-jokingly threaten a boy she had a crush on for having thrown a piece of paper at her. With the paths provided by the typically more disruptive students, those filling the slots of the "followers" often became more fully distracted, inappropriately stimulated, and troublesome. During such points, even minor disturbances or silly jokes could quickly spiral into bouts of nervous laughter, screams of delight, and occasionally serious threats. The hum of challenges to the teacher, the buzz of challenges between students, the teacher's more or less effective attempts to regain focus—and the inescapable mood that contributed to the reproduction of the established social and moral order—all of this could became more or less intense. Compared to what was experienced in classes stabilized either by virtue of selective student compositions or the interaction rituals that emerged only in the presence of extraordinarily effective teachers, in these classes, nearly all the students' senses of physical and emotional security deteriorated. There were lots of lighthearted and emotionally neutral transactions, but strife is perhaps the best word to describe what usually emerged. The mini-dramas did not make the players happy, most of the time. Sustained and fruitful concentration was, like serious reflection, nearly impossible.

For ordinary teachers dealing within such classroom environments the most pressing of all real-time questions was *not* whether one ought to engage. Like it or not, one was already (and had for some time already been) engaged. Even doing "nothing," you could not help but take a stand and be observed. When discriminations and adaptations were hesitant, like moves on a dance floor or basketball court, they flopped. Already in a diminished visceral state, the elemental question was "What is important enough that it demands immediate attention?" now that the action is already speeding along (in a more or less disastrous direction). Right there in the midst of it all, worn down to varying degrees by weeks or months of heavy exposure, as an average teacher you contemplate your next move *after* the look from the soft-spoken girl in the first row informed how sturdy, poised, self-assured, energized, and concentrated you will feel if you take on those tormenting her three rows back (but, in doing so, ignore the kid walking over to the window). In real time and space, deliberations about the appropriateness of taking bold steps took place with ordinary teachers already in midstride and, in all too many cases, giving themselves away as street-level bureaucrats who were simply not up to the multiple tasks at hand.[19]

As we will see more clearly when we detail the actions of my highly effective co-workers, the various movements "beneath the radar screen" as well as the feelings and self-images inhabiting the teacher's conscious mind needed to work as a unified team, pulling together toward a common goal. While this did at times happen—to varying degrees and for varying amounts of time—in the classrooms of more ordinary teachers, this was not continuous because it was not "automatic." Habitually getting out of anything approaching an optimal flow, the lack of coordination (if not the obvious clash of unsynchronized moving parts) often gave rise to disjointed, compulsive, and (horrifically) unconstructive responses. Putting their trained eyes to use, students intuited immediately what was happening (and were primed to go after bleeding jugulars). Teachers hammered themselves for "allowing" it to happen, again. Taking all of this together, one might say, we find the oil that more ordinarily types habitually threw onto the preexisting fires responsible for their "burnouts."

I do hope, moving forward, we can keep this in mind. From the way Raquel walked back to her empty classroom after being attacked to the way the union rep avoided eye contact while sporting his neck brace—it could seem on the inside that "everything" demonstrated what we might call the harsh *abandonment* of the adults working in both schools. From the perspectives of those former pedagogues capable of articulating historical overviews as well as from those in denial and concerned mainly with slogging away in the subterranean bowels of the two neighborhood schools, teachers in both high poverty schools were basically left to fend for themselves. Under these conditions, consistently providing "clear discipline" to "the followers" was far more than the vast majority could manage.[20] Proactively developing healing relationships and calming interactions with the most emotionally revved up and damaged individual students proved in nearly all cases to be a pipe dream. Fifteen out of forty-five minutes on task and simply making it to the next bell, the next weekend, the next vacation—that is what ordinary teachers were hoping to achieve. When so much stress and self-doubt are allowed to compound, hour after hour and day after day, even links that are not especially weak will eventually give.

The Success of the Superlative

Intelligent activity is distinguished from aimless by the fact that it involves selection of means—analysis—out of the variety of conditions that are present, and their arrangement—synthesis—to reach a desired goal.[21]

Given differences in levels of fear, violence, and overall social breakdown, it was easier to be a highly effective teacher in the Bijlmer than in the Bronx. There were, however, a number of countertendencies. Potentially disruptive students in the Bronx missed far more of their classes than their counterparts in Amsterdam, where attendance rates in classrooms usually ran between twenty percent and forty percent higher. Additionally, there could be a light side to the darkness of teenage angst that was more prevalent in Johnson High: comparatively higher levels of fear often reduced amounts of horseplay and chatter in the Bronx.[22] Similarly, whether due to greater levels of fear in Johnson or not, there were more students in the Bronx who simply became despondent. This could be unnerving as well as depressing, especially when it manifested in students staring glassy-eyed and wistfully at walls for several minutes at a time. It could also have a distinctly quieting if not stabilizing effect.[23] Finally, falling asleep in class was also a more common and socially accepted practice in the Bronx than in the Bijlmer. Teachers knew that many kids in the Bronx were in poorly regulated situations at home (or in shelters or wherever they were "staying at"). They also knew that letting (the typically more disruptive) students sleep could engender greater chances to "reach" those predisposed and positioned in ways that allowed them to engage the formal curriculum.

One last remark before we pull-in tight once again. My interest in these witch-doctor types did not stem from the fact that they looked, at first glance, like ordinary teachers. Nor was I particularly interested in how the presence of highly effective teachers drove others, most notably in the Bijlmer, to deny just how badly their classes were going. I found the most effective teachers intriguing mainly because they were capable of generating the only consistently healthy learning environments most of the adolescents I studied had in a typical day. Furthermore, in some cases after initial periods marked by emotional conflict, even the most frequently disruptive students seemed to be fond of uncharacteristically steady periods of instruction as well as those managing them. I checked this finding again and again every way I could in both settings and there can be no doubt about it. Even the students who most frequently engaged in the sorts of behaviors that generations of researchers have associated with staunch (class and/or race-based) "cultural resistance" tended to feel good about being in the care of master teachers.

From Easy to Exit

So there we sat, sipping tea in the lounge area off to the side of the teachers' cafeteria at Delta. Gerrit almost always avoided this room. He preferred to grade papers or simply eat his lunch alone in his own classroom during the moments that teachers usually congregated in this space. I had seen this excellent and often quite humorous teacher in action and I was excited about my first interview with him. I sensed a genuine click. I also sensed that Gerrit was not only highly intelligent, but that he would be straightforward about why so few teachers were anywhere near as effective as he was and how I might be able to join his club.

This native of Amsterdam did not share many insights into why he and his kind were capable of doing what they did. He tended to personalize things—"Janna is just a very weak teacher, she can't handle it . . . Johan, well, he is wonderful, one of the best"—rather than even try to put into words what was behind the different types of adaptations. "It really isn't so difficult," he said with his legs crossed on the couch and looking as if he were in his own living room. "And," he threw in, "we barely have any grading to do because they are all so incapable of writing very much or doing much homework." The steady streams of fellow teachers reduced to tears, shaking cigarettes, and early departures seemed not to influence his opinion.

So the keys to the Ferrari were not going to pass hands quickly, and it remained unclear to me if they ever would. What did seem clear, from Gerrit's comments, was that the quality of teachers at Delta had gone down radically. "It used to be better," he said at one point. "We used to have a really good team [of teachers]. Now," he added, looking at a new colleague, "well . . . now it's a different story." Although the dominant tendency was to personalize, Gerrit conceded that during his decade at Delta it had become "much harder to do your work." And at one point in the conversation he even said something that I would later hear several teachers say, no matter how successful they were: "If you can teach at Delta, you can teach anywhere in the Dutch school system."

Gerrit was not just an excellent teacher, he was also a university-educated holder of a "tier one" teacher's certificate and quite confident in middle class social settings with, for example, parents. In other words, because of his typically middle-class types and amounts of cultural capital, Gerrit was the kind of teacher who was sought after by managers of selective schools notwithstanding the fact that his years in the system made him relatively expensive. Moreover, something was telling this man with options to get out.

During my years at Delta, Gerrit started working part time, and then full time, at a much less distressed secondary school closer to the opulent heart of Amsterdam. Gerrit stressed, after his final move, that there were many black kids from poor families in his new school. Some even came, he said, from the Bijlmer. He was implying, of course, that he had not stopped fighting the good fight. And, for what it's worth, I agreed. I saw Gerrit as someone who had put a massive amount of his life's energy into "my" school and as someone who remained a great teacher. I felt this way even after I observed a few classes in the new, far more selective, peaceful, and altogether healthy pedagogic environment in which he told me, during a break, that he enjoyed being "more able to actually teach."

There was nothing terribly illuminating about this statement or anything else he put into words on that visit. Yet I was taken by the message expressed in Gerrit's tone and carriage. He seemed to be a much happier person in his new surroundings. Teaching at Delta had, evidently, meant taking countless little blows, everyday, for years. To see the lighter, softer, more contented

Gerrit in his new school was to grasp why he followed in the footsteps of thousands of teachers who made the same type of stress-reducing, vibrancy-improving change. Even this highly successful teacher who genuinely did not seem beleaguered at Delta experienced this *de facto* promotion as something he "should have done years earlier."

Natural Authority

In the Bijlmer especially, where I did not teach a full load and had more time for such things, I spent many hours watching the "super teachers" operate. Indeed, I did everything I could think of to become a member of their elite corps. Nevertheless, right up to the end of my nearly six-year stint in "ghetto" schooling, when I tried to make my version of the same moves in nonselective classes all involved sensed almost immediately that I was (and would remain) run-of-the-mill.

Thus the poignancy, for me at least, of the remarks made by a fellow English teacher in Amsterdam who was explaining what he saw as the "natural authority" that most of his colleagues lacked: "Look . . . it's simple, " he told me while we sat together in the tiny English department office. "Either you have it or you don't. Did you ever read *The Call of the Wild* by Jack London? That's it. Take a pack of dogs up near the North Pole. Hungry, vicious dogs. Now, let's say a new dog comes along. He wants to join the pack. What happens? All the dogs watch him come over. The dominant dog, the leader of the pack, goes over and . . . you know . . . smells the new dog. Within about five seconds all the dogs know if the new dog will be accepted into the pack or if he is that night's dinner. That's it. You walk in, the kids try you out, and everybody knows within fifteen seconds. [The students] think to themselves, either we are gonna have to work in here or we're gonna destroy this guy and do nothing. You get them immediately or you don't get them at all. If you don't get them right away, I'm telling you, you are not gonna get them three months later." This same colleague told me he had extremely tough times with classes early on, until he "broke" them.[24] This colleague's comments and delivery made me think about disparaging remarks I had heard effective teachers in the Bronx make about "rookies" wanting the "kids to like them."[25]

This male teacher could be rather edgy. This was especially difficult to miss when he proudly lent me a book about soccer hooligans in his native city, Rotterdam. Unlike Gerrit, for example, he seemed to have generations of working-class roughness running through his veins. He kept a poster of the wrestler known as "Rowdy" Roddy Piper pointing menacingly into the camera next to the entrance of his classroom. He boasted, more than once, that his pupils joked about the wrestler reminding them of him. Be this as it may, what went on in his classes was extremely well regulated, predictable, and productive. Even the "hardest or of the hard" (e.g., Jurgen, whom I observed regularly in this master teacher's class) seemed to enjoy—or at least take for granted the normalcy of—what took place.

This pale, brawny man who could have passed for a retired wrestler looked nothing at all like the women—Kindra—who came to personify "natural authority" for me. Kindra, whom I frequently observed, was a tiny dark-skinned woman with Hindustani roots. Doing her Saturday morning grocery shopping, she might have appeared meek. In the flow, she was larger than life.

From the moment pupils started walking into her room until after the bell rang to end the class, at the slightest hint that an intervention was necessary, this miniature person with a commanding presence literally hissed at the students while seeming to freeze them with ice-cold looks. If necessary, she made hissing sounds and threw these looks hundreds of times during each period of instruction. "Anthony . . . *sssht!* . . . read number . . . *sssht!* . . . thirteen . . . *sssht!* . . . for us." When this did not work, she raised her voice and increased the speed of her delivery. And if even this did not settle down those in her charge, she jacked up her energy level—without losing her composure, but immediately and high enough to meet every incipient obstruction. "What did you come here to do?," I more than once heard her demand, sometimes just inches from students' faces. "Didn't your mother raise you better than that?"[26]

We could all say this, but very few could make such utterances work. The students accepted this from Kindra in part because her delivery was so compelling but also because such tongue-lashings were almost never necessary and, most importantly, because they knew how it felt to be in her class when all went according to plan. Such outbursts came, therefore, as a shock. And somehow, when the shock came, nearly all the emotional energy that was created by the burst flowed to her. She was emboldened; they were flattened. I wish now that I had somehow filmed it. Whenever the situation called for such responses, with an intensely unitary focus and seemingly unbreakable confidence, she virtually propelled herself into the direct physical proximity of anyone doing anything that might lead to a substantial interruption.

The hard shell came off and stayed off whenever the moods in her classes were tempered and the stream of actions constructive. Moreover, when there were no disruptive energies brewing—when all the thoughts, feelings, and actions flowed in the single stream she had in mind—she seemed to become an inherently gentle soul. The students who looked up from their desks saw warm smiles and twinkling eyes. From behind her desk, when things were progressing harmoniously, she made soft-spoken and restrained jokes. She was able to put the kids to work and, in silence, take care of any administrative tasks or grading she needed to do. Things usually moved slowly and steadily in her class.

When all was going well, when it seemed like the students were incapable of getting out of their seats or even talking, she often walked around the room patting them on their shoulders or rubbing their backs. In fact, when things were going according to plan, she made more physical contact with the students than any teacher I observed in either setting. Peering over the shoulder of a pupil with a question about an assignment often evolved into a sort of impromptu neck massage. When things were at their best in her classrooms, the bodies of the seated students seemed to be tilted over the desks at just the same angle.[27] During these moments, her air of rigidity and coldness melted away completely. When she said to shift from a textbook to a workbook exercise, or to look up at the blackboard, the comparatively[28] *erect and alert spines* seemed not just to move almost in unison, but to move together in ways that—as McNeill (1995) might have predicted—generated senses of fellowship. She aimed for their conscious minds to be sure. But Kindra seemed to "reach" her kids principally at the level of their postures, muscles, brain stems, hearts, and guts.

During such moments, the positive energy—at once hers and the students'—was unmistakable. Even the typically more scattered and "street" kids usually indicated on such occasions that they wanted to please their remarkable teacher, and that it felt good to be part of a collective, constructive process. Observing this, I sometimes had to stop myself from laughing. I felt like I was in on a big and glorious secret. Again, as Goffman might have put it: not students and their moments but, rather, moments and their students! The social hierarchies structuring the broader adolescent society did not evaporate any more than the students' internalized sets of dispositions. But it could feel as though there were no "thugs" or "nerds" or anything else outside of what went on, most immediately, in such calming and attention focusing situations. For me, taking it all in from the corner of the room, "tough love" went from cheap cliché to priceless practice. Appearing to be the firm yet friendly aunt we all wanted, Kindra "effortlessly" maintained the kinds of atmospheres in which all students thrive. Whether any of her students ever finished high school or not, what they got in her room was undeniably healthy.

Did Kindra care more about what she was doing than most teachers? Was she more relentless that ordinary teachers? Did she seem inherently to possess more "grit," "zest," and "enthusiasm"?[29] And did the kids pick up on this. Emphatically we have to answer these questions with: Of course! The point, however, is that it is easier tobe passionate about something that goes well than about something that recurrently blows up in the your face. It was obvious that Kindra enjoyed the tension-free, solidarity-building moments she so regularly brought into being. She liked feeling that her kids liked her. This was part and parcel of her "compensation," we might say. Largely because it felt so right (and energizing) to have things on track, the "drill sergeant with a heart of gold" (Goldstein 2005, p. 27) did not give up an inch until she achieved the mundane emotional metamorphoses, bodily states, and shared cognitive focus she wanted. And once she had what she wanted, she made sure the students cashed in on a good sense of self and the delightful feeling of fellowship.

In short, Kindra succeeded in making it feel good to act, feel, and think like a "good" kid. In her room at least, the adolescent body-mind complexes proved again and again to enjoy (or at least no resist) being "malleable site[s] for inscribing social power" (Shusterman 2002, p. 18). No matter what the color of their skin, the "dark sides" of the second natures of students who could seem to be ardently "oppositional" were neutralized through, most basically, processes of *muscular bonding* (McNeil 1995) and attunement to soothing emotional transactions. Staging a (more or less racialized) "wild" self did not feel like an option. Once in the grip of the mundane metamorphoses she facilitated, in Kindra's classes there seemed to be almost no clinging to the "fabulous" ideal, no stigmatizing of "nerds" and therefore none of the delusion, greed, and insecurity that often *seemed* to be inherent in their lives and fixed in their personalities.

So what was her secret? Part of it was that this petite pedagogue, like several others of various shapes, sizes, and complexions in both settings, found ways to micromanage the currents and countercurrents of emotions *before* things got out of hand. While they all had their own styles, this is a common thread linking all of the highly successful teachers I witnessed in action in the Bronx and the Bijlmer. As Freiberg (1999, p. 82) notes, "prevention is eighty percent of classroom management."[30]

But every teacher in either building could agree that this was the goal. The point is to understand why, in *her* classrooms, this limiting example of the successful schoolmarm seemed to be able to sense, down to the smallest detail, exactly what demanded attention as well as what needed to happen and how this could be brought about. Why didn't Kindra experience any of the uncertainly, or exude any of the hesitancy or ambiguity, that sealed the fates of average teachers. And what made it all look so easy?

Just as the well-trained skater cannot represent consciously (or even unconsciously) how she keeps her balance on ice, my mentor in Amsterdam was incapable of thematizing what allowed the embodiment of her own excellence. After one of my in-class observations, I asked her about making scores of *"sssht"* sounds in less than three quarters of an hour. "Oh," she replied. "Did I do that? It's funny, you know, sometimes . . . I'm not even aware of doing that." She was not aware of what her highly adaptive yet largely unconscious dispositions were helping her achieve because the fit between her pedagogic habitus and the demands of the classroom sub-field allowed her to inhabit the "flow" (Csikszentmihalyi and Csikszentmihalyi 1988). Humming along in the bounded mini-universe of her expert activity, she not only intuitively picked out what had to be salient, she began immediately doing what needed to be done. There was no wavering because no time was "wasted" on (cost-benefit or comparative) analyses or explicit consideration of any rules. There could be no brain freezes because she never followed any scripts. Like they say of great cooks, she was the recipe. There was nothing but a steady flow of proficient situated responses based on a superb sense of what exactly needed to be "picked out" of the unfolding situational dynamics.

So the key is what I did not see. Whether born with some kind of innate abilities or not, by the time I started observing her, this woman had already gone through countless emotional, bodily, and cognitive learning experiences—both positive and negative—which reinforced excellent reactions and hindered ineffective ones. For sociologists interested in excellence, as Chambliss might therefore point out, concepts like "superteachers" and "natural authority" are as useless as "talent" or "gift." Such terms lead us away from what we need to know: why and how some of the pedagogues' *specific habitus*[31] formation processes are qualitatively better than others. Somewhat longitudinal as my data are (e.g., I felt the effects of longer term immersion and was in both settings long enough to see that most average teachers failed to become great ones), they do not allow me to speak to this question.[32] Kindra and several other highly effective teachers in both settings assured me that they had picked up their exceptional skills on the job. But they may have been playing nice or trying to keep me from giving up. I have no idea.

What I do know is that before and during my time in the two schools there was an exodus of excellent teachers who turned out to be irreplaceable. Some, like Gerrit, did not seem terribly distressed when they left.

Others from the elite corps were clearly burned-out by things going on in and especially around their classrooms. The vast majority of us who took over the posts of the exceptionally competent teachers seemed to be forever bumbling over thin and bumpy patches of ice. While we were repeatedly drained by inopportune positions within failing interaction rituals, the ever declining population of teachers like Kindra went on orchestrating successful ones and, therefore, spending most of their time stockpiling the emotional energy that, if necessary, helped them halt *nascent* interruptions. Try as we might to imitate their confidence-engendering inner-steadiness and equanimous concentration, we could do no more than wonder at colleagues like this tiny, sharp-edged figure who skated elegantly through classically structured, teacher-centered classes revolving around chalk talk and homework checks. I may be overusing the ice-skating metaphor, but I like it because it can help us once again get a sense that the that milliseconds and embodied wisdom were crucial. If you had to think you were going to be too late. Just as in ice-skating—the right twitches, comportment, and grace have to be deeply habituated for the proper coordination of the various aspects of the self in movement to work. Where others went down (and often became paralyzed by fear no matter what they believed), Kindra glided not mainly because of her ideas or ideals but because she had gradually acquired a superior feel for the game.

The final issue that must be addressed in this treatment of highly effective teachers is a less uplifting one. Excellent or not, all my colleagues had to deal with the fact that their institutions were basically being overrun and none of them could cleanse themselves of the destructive emotions pervading the overall atmospheres in which they spent a good deal of their waking hours. This was especially obvious in Johnson, where just making it from one classroom to the next could be extremely frightening and demoralizing. Denial of the risk of extreme physical violence might have been adaptive in the short term. It certainly helped my colleagues to focus on the tasks at hand. Yet even in the less violent of the two schools, teachers could not avoid occasional bouts of horrific suffering any better than their students. Two examples will make this point.

In the Bijlmer, a former semi-professional athlete turned teacher named Mitch went into an office to talk to a mother who was apparently furious about how her child had been treated after he run into the school after a late bell and refused to identify himself. The eyewitnesses to whom I spoke confirmed that Mitch had done no more than hold the boy against a locker as he tried to run away. He used force, I was later informed, only because the student was trying to run away from him. In the office, things went haywire and the parent bit through the skin on Mitch's shoulder.[33] I was in the crowded hallway when Mitch emerged from the office, with his clothes in tatters. Appearing to be more ashamed about his clothes than his open wound, several teachers tried to comfort him. One colleague started to curse the "beast" who bit Mitch as he was taken away to receive a tetanus shot.

Animalistic or not, this was civilized in the extreme compared to the worst example of school-related violence in New York. Relatively early on in my time at Johnson, the friend who had introduced me to high-poverty schooling—Jake—was murdered by one of his ex-students and an accomplice. After Jake buzzed them in to his apartment building they tied him up, tortured him for the code that went with his bank pass, stabbed him to death with kitchen knives, and made off with $700. Jake's ex-student received a twenty-five-year sentence. The accomplice was acquitted. Before the police found his body, I left a Monday morning message on Jake's answering machine asking him why he had missed work and not even gone through the trouble to call in sick.

In both ponds the rippling effects of such stones were enormous. Even if they took place far from their (peaceful) classrooms, such intermittent attacks on co-workers (and stories in the media about many more, nearly always in high-poverty high schools) shaped everything the pedagogues did in both settings—including, of course, "burnout."

For these and other reasons, during my years in Johnson and Delta, many of my seemingly invincible co-workers either went on extended "sick" leave or moved on to less distressing institutions. Whether they were ideologically committed to remaining in their overwhelmed schools or not, the wear-and-tear to which they were exposed often led them to—as one successful teacher put it after nine years—"abandon ship." It would be more accurate to say that teachers in such distressed educational environments have been systemically cast away and made to feel guilty for failing to accomplish missions that were indeed all but impossible.

Discussion

[M]inor civil servants . . . those charged with carrying out the so-called "social" functions, that is, with compensating, without being given all the necessary means, for the most intolerable effects and deficiencies of the logic of the market—[including] more and more in recent years, primary and secondary teachers—should feel abandoned, if not disowned outright, in their efforts to deal with the material

and moral suffering that is the only certain consequence of the economically le-
gitimated Realpolitik.[34]

In film after film on both sides of the Atlantic Ocean, the real action in
high-poverty schools has taken place when the lone—and increasingly heroic—teacher takes on (nonwhite and ideologically resistant) students inside classrooms. This is not only because the *Dances with Wolves* (1990)
narrative is second nature to so many consumers and producers of cultural
goods.[35] After all, some teachers are extremely successful and it is above all
inside classrooms that long-term public investments should gradually generate more informed, skilled, stable, curious, and self-disciplined students
as well as, ultimately, more equitable, democratic, and cohesive societies.
If we needed to begin this empirical investigation by showing why *ordinary
classroom settings* tended *not* to be where students' emotional energy and attention was charged up and focused most intently, we had to finish with the
incalculable inefficiency manifesting in these *supposedly autonomous spaces*
that should have been the hearts of the two educational institutions.

For very good reason, teachers trying to redirect the predictably pattered
social dramas destroying classrooms in Johnson were more hesitant than
they were in Delta. Given the different balance of power between teachers
and potentially disruptive (and aggressive) students, especially the more
self-assured and energized classroom teachers in the Bijlmer had moves
open to them that were effectively closed to teachers in the Bronx. We cannot however say that being in classrooms in the Bronx was simply harder
for teachers or more damaging for students. Ironically perhaps, the greater
levels of fear, absenteeism, and overall social breakdown could make it
comparatively easier for teachers to "reach" (at least some) students in classrooms in the Bronx. Furthermore, although the majority of my former colleagues in Amsterdam denied it (at least while they still worked at Delta),
fears about violence and all kinds of daily jolts made it tough to teach there
as well.

I think it is fair to say that the most elementary similarities this chapter
turned up were rooted in how the injuries of de facto socioeconomic apartheid led systemically to the same kinds of hidden classroom curricula. This
is not to say that actions of students and teachers in classrooms had nothing to do with ethnicity, nation, race, or gender. In Amsterdam New and
Old, however, the sequestering of teens from poorly educated, financially
distressed, and emotionally overburdened families led to the trespassing of
saturation points and enormous pressures toward overlapping productions
of social dramas with the basic structure articulated by McFarland. On aver-

age roughly two-thirds of time in classrooms in both settings was simply devoured by (petty) disruptions.

Closer to the ground, the main similarities this chapter reveals have to do with what exactly made teaching class after class feel like "mission impossible." As Simi's case demonstrated, even in typical classes (i.e., nonselective ones taught by average teachers) a small minority of students in both settings could successfully modulate their postures, feelings, thoughts, and all other responses. Yet Simi's socialization trajectory (and related self-discipline engendering regime) was statistically freakish. The vast majority of students never had the kinds of healing relationships and regulating experiences that remade Simi before (and while) he attended Johnson High. For most students forced to marinate in noxious mixes of petty distractions, destructive emotions, and incoherent thoughts—in (and out of) classroom settings—there was usually no way to avoid being prediscursively "caught up" in the "wrong crowds" and ways of being.[36] Rejecting the romanticism and idealism of (racialized) "opposition," we get closer to the truth when we conclude that students caught in such well-established patterns of classroom behavior operated almost automatically as reproducers of poisonous in-class routines and overall status hierarchies.

It might be useful at this point to put my observations of the referential totalities we call classrooms in a new light. In what immediately follows I will divide into three dimensions (the corporal, the emotional, and the cognitive) aspects of these bounded social universes that, in the final analysis, must be held together.

Whether tense, contracted, restless, or drained by what went on around them, the students' and the teachers' *bodily states and movements* tended not to be conducive to getting the job done in classrooms of Johnson High and the Delta School. Especially with fear and anxiety pulsating through their living bodies, it was difficult if not impossible for students and teachers to ease into productively focused engagements. Before and after entering their classrooms, the tumult "out there" often generated great levels of lethargy "in here." Feeling exhausted or not, once the knots in the stomach were activated, for example, there was no "room" for questioning things like one's own habituated emotional reactions to everyday provocations and other releasing stimuli. It usually took time in well-regulated classroom environments for hardened bodies to get settled down enough to promote support for the teacher's intentions. While this did occasionally happen (quite quickly inside the domains of the most highly effective), the inappropriately stimulated bodies of students and teachers all too often remained (wildly) off, we might say, doing their own things.

The *overriding emotional contagions* in classrooms were often deeply distressing. Sometimes encounters in hallways contributed to making students angry just minutes before entering the room; other times the anxiety or excitement about what might happen after school (or at some other time in the future) simmered for hours before the bell rang. Similarly, most teachers flipped back and forth between "their own" stored up anger, resentment, and fear on one hand, and the typically destructive moods to which they necessarily became attuned inside their own classrooms. No matter what contributed to them, it took "heroic" efforts from incredibly skilled teachers to transform the emotional climates usually plaguing classrooms. Unless teachers somehow learned to embody prediscursive calm, confidence, and composure, there was no way for them to consistently redirect the spiraling negativity in soothing and productive directions. Except for in the exceptional cases in which "super teachers" ensured that supportive calm and singular focus took hold, therefore, the emotional dimension also tended to run off doing its own thing.

On top of it all, *passing thoughts and momentary beliefs* often pushed and pulled adolescent and adult minds in any number of directions. From "I cannot do this, it is too difficult" to "This teacher is a joke, I hate this class" to "The teacher is right, I really should get to work on this because I do need to pass the test (and avoid a special-education track)"—a range of more or less compulsive ideas could come to the preoccupied teenage minds. For most teachers, as we saw, feeling that one had the right stuff (in the occasional selective class) and then bludgeoning oneself for being bludgeoned during a series of "difficult" classes (that colleagues in the Bronx sometimes called "murders' row") was quite common. So whether shared or kept private, nearly all involved were capable of entertaining both supportive and unsupportive ideas. But productive or detrimental, these typically quite incoherent sets of ideas tended above all to be the reactive products of classroom-based interactional dynamics grounded in vulnerable bodies and emotional flows. Associating fleeting ideas either with the deeper foundations of students' behavior or with coherent sets of situation-transcending beliefs (promoting racialized "resistance") would be as wrongheaded as assuming that teachers get overwhelmed in classrooms mainly because they think the wrong thoughts or require more explicit rules. Even if we reject such exaggerated mentalism we can perhaps remain alert to importance of how, within this third dimension of cognitions, things in most classrooms tended to gallop off on their own and in different directions.

The "miracle" of the most effective teachers was that—isolated and vulnerable as they were—they overcame all of this. And when body states, emotional flows, and mental events were usefully synchronized, something revealing seemed to happen. It is not merely that the "hard" kids were capable of calming a bit, letting down their guards, and getting in touch with aspects of their selves and situations that usually remained alien. (This we already saw, for example, from the interview with Roxanne to the stroll along the canals with Jurgen). Nor is it just that under these special circumstances a good deal of schoolwork was done. Sitting in the masterful teachers' rooms, infectious senses of joy, delight, and well-being often appeared to well up in all the participants. During such moments the channeling and sustaining of concentration, the arousal of confidence, and the harmonizing of energies seemed to be almost self-perpetuating. Of course, given what they were up against, it was extremely difficult for teachers to avoid getting frazzled, to keep standing their ground with composure and alertness, to orchestrate what needed to happen on many different levels all at once and in real time. The key point I want to make here, nonetheless, is this: when it did happen, teachers could seem nothing short of luminous, and the vast majority (of the putatively street, black, or involuntary minority) kids certainly seemed to enjoy it or, at very least, not to be inclined towards actively opposing it.[37]

Regrettably, the evolutionary processes behind the formation of the second natures of "super teachers" remained unclear. Even if we could all read and moralize about the benefit of becoming "reluctant disciplinarians" instead of "softies" (Rubinstein 1999), even if we believed our own clichés about all sorts of devils residing in the details and the nonexistence of "shortcuts"(Esquith 2003), neither the teachers nor the ethnographer figured out how common shrubs could be turned into continually blooming rosebushes with razor sharp thorns. Part of the mystery here relates to the fact that I simply do not know if my mentors got into "ghetto" schooling with, for example, exceptionally controlling or compassionate personalities.

With this said, what I did learn about becoming—or not becoming—a great teacher may nonetheless be useful. Kindra, to return one last time to our most shining example, could be intensely concentrated. But an underlying poise and unassailable composure seemed to undergird her powerful ability to pay (and effectively coordinate) attention. So it seemed to me that the key to her sustained success was not something narrow and hard (i.e., the kind of concentration or other forms of mental labor we might associate with furrows of worry on the forehead). The key was something far more inclusive and graceful (e.g., the poise of the person breathing easy and settled comfortably into the right posture). This is, I believe, why many highly successful teachers like Kindra were able to keep working their "magic" for so long. When in the optimal flow, as serious athletes, musicians, and martial artists also know from the "inside," there is an uncomplicated sense that the center of energetic vitality *shifts from the thinking mind to the lived body*. This kind of fully absorbed and highly skilled yet also relaxed coping has to be known and developed *experientially*. Even with insights about how flows of emotional energy relate to positions in interaction rituals, teachers cannot learn how to make this happen mainly with their intellects. Indeed comparatively slow as it tends to be, discursive reasoning about such ways of dealing may in real time get in the way more than help. What is required is the kind of practical sensing not just of what needs to happen, but also the fluid-like, easy, posture-based legitimacy, and overall presence that led all involved to trust that precisely this was going to happen—again and again—until well after the sounding of the bell. This, my observations and experiences as a classroom teacher imply, was the key to what looked like Kindra's "natural authority."

Certainly then, with regard to becoming an effective teacher in classrooms as overburdened as those of Johnson and Delta, what can easily be put into words pails in significance when compared to what is learned at the most primordial level. Perhaps after years of stumbling onto "just the right kinds" of mundane movements, and perhaps after coming to the realization that not wasting time looking for any one "big secret" (Chambliss 1989, p. 85) is one of the many secrets—like Olympic-level swimmers, it seems, the most effective teachers had somehow habituated themselves to the lived immediacy of success-generating *sensorimotor capacities*. This is why they knew the students and other teachers saw almost immediately that they had "it," even as they could not explain what "it" was. Not bothering to try to find the right words, they went on composing themselves around moment-to-moment felt experiences of almost automatically doing scores of "little things" just right.

My dual-track apprenticeships indicate that, as things stand now in the hundreds of high-poverty high schools on both side of the Atlantic where there actually are often teaching positions to be found, ordinary teachers cannot be expected to turn themselves into significantly more effective ones. Observing great teachers tends to help one become effective in high-stress classrooms about as much as observing great football players helps one become a quarterback in the NFL. And where would the successful moments of body-based learning come from if succeeding with the occasional "bunch of sweethearts" does not help with nonselective classes? How can teachers integrate all the "little" skills and inclinations, or settle into the right corporal poise and real-time know-how, when what goes on in and around them is so overwhelming, fragmenting, and draining? While such a radical pedagogic approach might work in a few exceptional cases, we don't usually teach people how to ice skate by pushing them out onto lakes in which gapping cracks unpredictably emerge within brittle sheets of ice. In terms of popular fantasies about lone rangers (as themselves silver bullets) coming to the rescue of our most troubled schools, the implication is the following: the "obvious policy solution is more pay for good teachers, more dismissals for weak teachers"[38] *only if* (1) *we assume that test scores used to pinpoint the "value added" by teachers are reliable* (despite massive reason to believe that many if not most of the "numbers" coming out of high-poverty high schools are "cooked") and (2) *our aim is limited to achieving relatively small (and temporary) increases in the number of isolated classroom successes.*

Popular as the cult of the individual may be, especially in the United States, we need to stop tinkering on both sides of the Atlantic. With regard to what is happening (to teachers) in our worst classrooms, we need to face up to the real questions and issues before us. If we are collectively cold-hearted and short-sighted enough to do nothing about intense levels of (socioeconomic) segregation—and if we really care about getting more high potentials and keeping more high-quality teachers in our the schools forced to deal with sky-high percentages of emotionally destabilized teens—we might start by admitting that "teacher grading" interventions based on fraud-sensitive test scores (and "politicized" assignments to classes) will not generate and maintain large-scale improvements. If we accept the existence of "dumping grounds," furthermore, the least we can do is start using the methods of sustained and direct (participant) observation to clarify the real problems on the ground and help design, implement, and monitor *overall educational regimes* that are *regulated well enough that they do more good than harm.* And by "overall" in this context, I mean everyday experiences from preschools to high schools, and from entrance areas to classrooms, from hallways to cafeterias, and exit areas to playing fields. Only if pacifying, calming, and self-restraint generating techniques and experiences *continuously* reach all the way down to the level of mundane emotional contagions and moment-to-moment physiological states will they be forceful enough to really make lasting differences. Increasing teachers' emotional compensation and improving the somatic experience of being on the frontlines through stabilizing the daily interactions of students born poor—and through helping such adolescents manage the stress that has been damaging their bodies and souls—this is the best way to attract and retain significantly greater percentages of potentially excellent teachers.

Meanwhile, in the United States and Western Europe, prevailing policy and academic discussions about remedies as (at best) partial as "merit-based" pay increases insure that it will remain difficult to see and think clearly about what teachers (and students) in our worst schools actually need. Part of the problem is that we collectively privilege the findings and analyses of those so firmly "in the grip of methodological inhibition [that they] often refuse to say anything about society that has not been through the fine mill of the Statistical Ritual"[39]—even in the cases of scholars who have never been inside a high-poverty school. Yet our lack of meaningful discussion about what is going on and what might actually help also relates, at least to some degree, to how many of our leading intellectuals and politicians remain preoccupied with claims and counterclaims about the role of oppositional black culture. While the Appendix speaks to the issue of methodological reticence, it is directly at this decades-old preoccupation with racialized, explicit, and rebellious interpretations that the concluding chapter takes aim.

SEVEN

Conclusion

Deze school is gewoon nep. (*This school is just fake.*)[1]

I'm just trying to do the right thing, you know what I'm saying?[2]

I have tried to do justice to the immediate physical experience of dealing and self-destructing in nonselective, high-poverty schools on opposite sides of the Atlantic. Less because of pre-existing theoretical inclinations than due to what being an insider in the Bronx and the Bijlmer did to me on a viscerally felt level, the empirical focus had to be on lived understandings and absorbed coping rather than after-the-fact reports. Before pulling together the main strands of the analysis, I want to be as clear as possible about why I hope this book will help us move from the established scholarly narrative to an alternative way of thinking about everyday life in educational "dumping grounds."

This brings us back to the book's title. I do *not* use "toxic" as some kind of abstraction or metaphor.[3] In both Johnson High and the Delta School, ordinary pedagogues going through their daily grinds were exposed to interactions so stressful that—from a mental and physical health perspective—they have to be considered hazardous.[4] Black, brown, white, or other, my colleagues were "burning out" with such impressive frequency *not* mainly because of any personal shortcomings or situation-transcending beliefs (related to dealing with stress) but, rather, because of the crisscrossing emotional undercurrents in which their entire psycho-physiological systems were forcibly immersed. More importantly—and "independently," one might say, of what took place in the students' more or less destabilized families—the stressors unleashed moment to moment in both educational settings (further) *damaged* the physical, affective, and cognitive development of the adolescents compelled to attend them. While we go on debating the relevance of "rebellious" cultural codes and the "burden of acting white," the stress of *in-school interactional burdens* continues to remake—and almost assuredly to shorten the lives of—students left behind. Of course, as this book documents, what took place in the students' homes and neighborhoods was never fully independent of what transpired in the two schools.[5] Daily life in and around Johnson High tended to be far more detrimental than anything that emerged in or around the school backed up by a northwestern European welfare state precisely because what took place outside the schools mattered greatly.[6] This, nonetheless, has to be our bottom line: habituated reactions to chronically distressing in-school experiences such as those detailed in the previous pages are negatively impacting the immune systems, neurological development, and overall well-being of countless students forced—ultimately by state law—into high-poverty schools as poorly regulated as both Johnson and Delta.

And the contagions do not stop here. Countless parents as well as siblings and other family members are worried sick about the young people closest to them stuck year after year in schools that—as they know full well in many cases—would have middle-class parents of any so-called ethnic or racial "group" up in arms if their children were forced into them for more than a few hours. Regularly these adults told me that they knew they were "losing" their kids to negative peer dynamics both in and out of the only schools to which they had access. When you look into the eyes of these parents and family members unable to get their kids into reasonably safe and empowering educational environments, you get a gut-level sense for why so many lower- and middle-class parents have overworked, over-commuted, and overstretched on mortgages.[7] Especially in the cases of those who have spent months if not years gripped by fears about losing their homes, we have no way to calculate the health-related costs of the economic meltdowns to which this continual overstretching—and, here again, to which our collective failure to regulate institutions (such as "predatory" banks)—has contributed. But doing justice to the long shadows cast by overwhelmed schools requires that we go yet another step up the social ladder. As the work of Wilkinson and Picket (2009) indicates, because institutions like Johnson and Delta reproduce and deepen socioeconomic inequality, we have to assume that their "normal functioning" negatively impacts the health even of those firmly established in upper- (middle-) class positions.

I would be the first to admit that the exact mechanisms through which distressing in-school experiences contribute to various kinds of negative health outcomes are difficult if not impossible to pin down. We have no laboratory or treatment and control groups upon which to run the kinds of decade-long experiments which would facilitate this. But it would have been a potentially lethal mistake for smokers of a previous generation to wait until scientists agreed about the exact causal pathways leading from cigarettes to cancer. Especially if we are open to making plausible connections between overwhelmed schools and undesirable health outcomes, we might also consider the effects of telling massively and systemically disadvantaged students that they are responsible for their own educational destinies (because a few fellow students do well even in such objectively inferior and unsafe schools).[8] In practice, the psychological stress (in the form of corroding thoughts and feelings) related among other things to such *institutionalized symbolic aggression* compounds the supposedly more "concrete" problem of physical stress (related to threats and violence in and out of our worst public high schools). Here, without pretending this makes the inventory complete, I will add the following. The anxiety and inefficiency concentrated in the lowest regions of our fields of (urban) education is not somehow separate from the apathy and ignorance reducing civic engagement in our democracies and perpetuating the ancient curse of racism—two interwoven processes with negative and widespread implications for physical and psychological well-being. It can be extremely difficult to get middle-class parents to care (for more than a few minutes) about poor kids, and pseudobiological fantasies mixed with social Darwinist rationalizations can certainly make racism a vital force here. But perhaps in the future new developments—such as the recent increase in awareness about (the health related effects of) *bullying*[9] in schools—can help establish a more far-sighted approach. Even if only out of (more evolved forms of) self-interest, perhaps, moving forward, many more people will become perceptive and wise enough to conclude that school-related experiences such as those described above promote a host of behaviors and outcomes (from teen pregnancies and future parents being less emotionally stable than they might have been to welfare dependency, and from substance abuse and criminality to mass incarceration) that, in the shorter or longer run, negatively impact everyone's health.

So I speak of toxicity because of the empirical processes at hand. But I also use such language because it is time to alter the terms of the transatlantic conversations rooted even today in the work of Willis and Ogbu. Instead of over-racializing with our process-reducing, preconstructed, "group"-making categories, and rather than continue romanticizing with our disembodying discourses of deliberate ideological rebellion, we need to attend carefully to what is most urgent right now—especially for the students most intimately involved. Paying close attention (i.e., as if for the first time, and as if they were our kids) and developing a more adequate analytic language may help us see the worst of our high-poverty schools less as sights of cultural conflict than as petri dishes for destructive and far-reaching emotional contagions. If we can start thinking and speaking about what actually goes on in the schools of those born into poverty in terms of shifting webs of interdependence, continual changes (reproducing sharply divided status hierarchies), and micro-interactional exposure to varying levels of toxic stress, that is, we might see what happens when non-inheritors are granted access to healing relationships and (in-school) experiences. We might discover, that is, that we have all been unwitting subjects in reckless experiments with deregulation and that each of us has an interest in making sure we stop passing these institutionalized sources of pestilence down to future generations. Ironically, given the breakneck pace of new (statistical) findings, conflicted political discourses, and scattered journalistic accounts supposedly relevant to the "turning around" of "failing urban schools," perhaps the most useful thing we can do to increase the health of our communities is to put the myriad distractions on hold and slow down—or even come to what may feel like a complete stop—long enough to get a clear sense of what actually takes place in and around schools like Johnson and Delta.

The previous chapters interrogated various themes related to everyday dealing and self-destructing in and around the two schools. The final discussions at the close of each empirical chapter offered pointed comparisons detailing how everyday transactions in and around the two settings were similar and where they differed. The chapters provided accounts of the different types of interaction rituals and overall power balances making the achievement of "realness" feel as though it was worth almost any price; the ways in which lived enactments of threats wormed their ways deeply and durably beneath the students' exposed flesh while reinforcing routinized micro-interactional ways of getting things done and students' perceptions of overall status hierarchies; how the stigma inherent in the structuring of the two broader urban and educational spaces fueled proud yet self-defeating emotional investments in ways of playing what could feel like the only educational game in town; the extra-school socialization of students (temporarily) on successful trajectories and the centrality of (body-based self-disciplining and) emotional learning processes supervised by reasonably stable and cultivated adults; how the recruitment of students and teachers to positions in the organizations related to the triumphs of seemingly unflappable (yet vulnerable) teachers and the unceasing fiascos of the majority of teachers confronted by non-selective classes.

At this point I want to structure the further discussion of findings around how *two problems* suggested by my observations relate to *three myths* about schools such as Johnson and Delta. The first problem is that, in both settings, the everyday social-structural reality of pedagogic practice made it *nearly impossible for most teachers to teach and for most pupils to learn*. What appeared on formalized reports as "periods of instruction" tended, in practice, to be "fake" and humiliating "wastes of time." In both adolescent societies, official curricula were powerfully replaced by informal pedagogies based on dealing and destructing in the midst of anxiety-ridden and episodically violent peer dynamics centered outside classrooms.

The second major problem, or paradox, is this: due mainly to micro-situational and school-wide structural dynamics far beyond the control of any single teenager or staff member, *the more dominant students were regularly dominated by their own domination*. What could appear at first glance as screams of delight ("keep it real my nigga," "we holding shit down up in here," "you better act like you know") sounded, after a few years, like so many hip-hop flavored calls for help from frenzied students stuck in routinized stress responses that they did not feel at all proud of when they were released from the grip of "fabulous" encounters. Native-born or newcomer, black or nonblack, unless conventional knowledge about avoiding "distractions" (e.g., the "wrong crowds") had previously merged with massive levels of self-control—and unless this had been drilled deeply enough into habit that it persistently functioned (almost) automatically in real time—when students were immersed in the temptations and sanctions of "ordinary" moments, they tended to perpetuate the types of responses that they at times knew to be destroying their own educational destinies and schools.

With these two core problems in mind, I want to turn directly to three hugely influential and deeply misleading ways of thinking about high-poverty education. Certainly among ethnographers focusing on inner-city educational settings, one might argue that these have been the three core elements of the dominant trope for a generation.[10] I hope it will be clear that the goal here is not so much to critique an old debate as it is, in the reconstructive spirit of John Dewey, to show how my research might help us move beyond it.

The first myth I want to address is that of the *minority* or, even worse, the minority *"group."* To be sure, the students, teachers, and everyone else in the two urban contexts had objectively different skin tones and this could come into play. Symbolic categories like black, white, Dominican, Hindustani, and Dutch were certainly real, furthermore, in the sense that familiarized insiders *at times* took them for granted and acted upon them. The ability to shape ways of experiencing and labeling one's self, other individuals, and various kinds of putative ethnoracial groups could—*on some occasions*—assure that these socio-cultural constructions carried a great deal of weight. Indeed even when they withdrew deep into the background of shared understandings, insiders' practical senses of the their educational worlds were never simply divorced from the two systems of ethno-racial classifications. In large part because those labeled (and self-identifying) as black were overrepresented among the typically more "street" and emotionally less stable students in both settings, naturalized symbolic categories related to phenotype and ancestry continually influenced the differently positioned players' lived understandings of their educational worlds apart at least to some extent.[11]

Nevertheless, the main finding on this front is that both Johnson and Delta turned out to be, first and foremost, "thug" and "fly girl" dominated schools. The "fabulous" (and more frenzied) to "nobody" (and more calm) continua and related *principles of division* were the ones that mattered most, most of the time, in both settings. For the native-born as well as for first- and "second-generation migrants"—and whether students self-identified as black or not—to "keep it real" was, *above all*, to keep it "(ghetto) fabulous" in gendered and gendering ways, rather than to be a "nobody." Masses of students assumed to be authentically black were, above all, said to be far from "fabulous" if not lowly "nerds." As we saw time and again, students often deployed means of talking and thinking about "I," "you," "we" and "they" identifications that were very ambiguously and/or only slightly influenced by ideas about race or ethnonational ancestry. Even on the exceptional occasions that I cued up ethno-racial distinctions in efforts to explore these terrains in interviews and discussions, more often than not the students simply refused to express their concerns in terms of these supposed "types" and "groups." In the Bronx a statement like "them niggaz is real" could be used with regard a nominally mixed-race band of "gangbangers" at the top of a flight of steps, a small assembly of especially effective (supposedly white and minority) teachers conferencing in a hallway, or Korean (-American) shop owners who did not permit stealing from their store. In the Bijlmer, as we saw with Levi and his nearly despondent friends slumped around a table in a literally sunken area, "they" (i.e., the "thugs") were *the problem*, not the lighter- or darker-skinned kids with ancestral roots in various countries who (almost) never threatened to become disruptive or violent. Such gender- and violence-related (rather than ethnicity- or race-based) concerns were especially prevalent among the majority of students forced to occupy the middle and lower regions of physical space (e.g., in Delta's cafeteria, the flights of steps leading to Johnson High's main entrance) and socio-symbolic space (i.e., the most frequently applied status hierarchies).[12] Aside from being extremely rare, nominally "inter-ethnic" conflicts were not experienced exclusively or even primarily as such. And even in cases when explicit ideas about race were undeniably important in students' collective identities and social trajectories (Derek's nosedive, Simi's ascendency), we saw that processes and power resources that could not be reduced to ideas or feelings about race (e.g., sustained access to emotionally stable adults, protection from negative peer dynamics) were even more fundamental.

Here then, as concise as possible, is the main finding with regard to "minorities" and "their" ostensible "groups." Given that the students' feelings and cognitions on such matters were never final, often fleeting, and in many cases simply not at all salient, to reify "their" ethno-racialized "identities" is to risk giving an "appearance of solidity to pure wind"—as Orwell put it in his 1946 warning about the political effects of sloppy writing and poor mental habits. Even though essentializing descriptors like "The Bloods," "the fly girls," "the *Nederlanders*," or "the (nerdy) Africans" were often deployed, settling in and remaining as close as possible to the real-life ebb and flow of situated experiences and practical (self-) identifications forced me away from interpretations based on static notions of thing-like racial sorts or ethno-cultural communities.[13] Sometimes skin tones or perceptions about ethnonational ancestry influenced behavior in significant ways; sometimes this was no more important than students' shoe sizes or teachers' weights.

This in no way implies the need to stop demonstrating, for example, that *racialized* discrimination in many cases remains strong even after holding socioeconomic status constant.[14] This does however imply that, in more qualitative as well as in variable-based statistical research, we should challenge ourselves to stop replicating the *at times* essentializing ways of speaking and thinking of the people we study. The implication is that in our accounts of such massively disadvantaged students and settings, we should try to think relationally, carefully scrutinize our own first- and second-order analytic concepts, and use open-ended categories capable of illuminating on-going change. The forces pushing adults to engage in essentialist racialization and other forms of groupist thinking can be enormous.[15] Trying to grasp the micro-situational and more broadly "worlded" workings behind more *and less* ethnicized (self-) identifications takes more time (as well as, usually, both more text and cultural capital). Yet it remains the case that—as Max Weber roughly saw a century ago[16]—reducing the relevant *processes* to frozen and discrete ethnicized *states* is not so much "rigorous" as it is shallow to the point of being pseudo-empirical.[17] Perhaps Garot (2010, pp. 1–2) articulated better than I can what is at work as well as at stake in our more processual or more substantialist ways of speaking about the teens attending our worst schools:

> Over the past fifty years, social scientists have increasingly turned from essentializing identity as a fixed characteristic to understanding identity as fluid, contextual, and shifting. . . . Yet such insights tend to be overlooked when we speak of inner-city youth . . . fear clouds our thinking. . . . This is unfortunate, for such fear may well play a role in maintaining the conditions that lead to the behavior we seek to redress. Out of fear arises segregation . . .

Let us turn now to the second leg of this three-legged stool. In addition to being based on the myth of billiard ball–like minority "groups," as documented in the Introduction, the oppositional black culture storyline has been based on the assumption that *explicit ideas, beliefs, and values* are largely if not primarily responsible for actual lines of behavior. Here we might speak of the myth of *mental interpretation preceding action.* This is the intensely intellectual notion—often simplistically associated with one of the founding fathers of sociology[18]—that explicit thoughts enable and constrain most real-time assessments and responses even in inner-city pressure cookers like Johnson and Delta. As this gets to the crux of my at once empirical and theoretical argument,[19] I want to illustrate as clearly as possible how the view of the player-with-flesh-in-the-game diverges from those of players looking back on what they did in the heat of action and from pure spectators (who have never had even a whiff of real action).

As we saw repeatedly and from different angles in the previous chapters, especially in the faster-paced "thug" dominated spaces, the practical senses of students previously habituated to everyday conditions of existence in their schools operated largely if not entirely beneath the level of discursive consciousness. Certainly after initial periods as novices, once students had settled into recognizable patterns or groove-like flows of ongoing activity, their "feel(s)" for what [not] to do were at once "of" the field and "of" the habitus, at once situationally embedded and deeply embodied.

Granted, just as we all learned how to do things like switch the gears of a car or swing a baseball bat by thinking explicitly about "rules" or at least specific aspects of tasks at hand, we all tried, at times quite consciously, to manipulate the perceptions of our peers in high school. As an acne-faced kid I too stood in front of the mirror and, when no one was looking, practiced being a badass or making the moves I thought one was supposed to flash at the dance. The point is that most of the time we gave ourselves away, or demonstrated that we had the right stuff, because of the underlying (mis)fits between our dispositions (and power portfolios more generally) and the tensions, expectations, valuations, and positions constituting our schools as fields.[20] In other words, most of the students and teachers spent most of their time operating not the way Derek (the novice) did but the way "Cookie" did *after* his initial stage of immersion: as pre-familiarized, skilled, already corporeally engaged, beings-in-the-two-worlds.

I want to clarify the importance of time and embodiment here because nothing is more practical when it comes to grasping the immediate appeal of "realness" than this. Already within their more or less empowering positions (in micro-configurations), the whole beings examined in this book were unable to call time out and ponder their next moves. The here-and-now dramas created by everyday interactions were so compelling, so capable of drawing in and focusing attention, because *in real time* they were viscerally felt before (and while) they were thought. Always physically exposed in the here and now, prediscursive senses of how to cope emerged from emotional cores rather than from the explicit stories of thinking minds.[21]

This brings us to the openness of the body-mind complexes in action. Already attuned by virtue of being somatically engaged (rather than due to anything having to do with conscious thinking per se), insiders certainly did not operate in real time as self-contained subjects standing over against "external" people and objects. Rather, like the tennis player adjusting her grip as she begins moving toward a fast approaching ball, they found themselves dealing in settings they grasped (for the most part) without explicit deliberations because they had already been formed in these micro-situations and overall worlds for many months if not years. It was generally with the regularities of the "outside" world already forcefully inscribed in their unconscious minds—and with bodily stances merging with ways of feeling pre-oriented toward the immediate demands of ongoing situations—that the students (and teachers) *sometimes* deliberated about how to, for example, respond to a provocation.[22] As is the case with athletes in action, however, too many explicit mental representations would have messed up the flow. This did not happen very often.

Time and again we saw that it was *not the content of thought* but the *process of thinking*—at no point separate from bodily-emotional underpinnings—that was most vital. This was evidenced in the walk through the opulent center of Amsterdam with an uncharacteristically easy-going Jurgen. This was also the take away from my brief encounter with one of Jurgen's victims still too choked up to do anything but claim that the pounding he had just received was not on his mind. Seeing that such humiliations were all the more painful because they were delivered in front of (potential) friends need not blind us to the pre-symbolic source of the suffering and explicit mental processing. Similarly, when the sister of a "big-money player" swerved off course to cut a class and hang out with a joint rolling "star" in front of her school, we saw the importance of grasping whether her on-the-spot thinking was rushed or relaxed. In the wake of the early morning double slashing in the Bronx, we had to delve beneath the specific utterances of those who typically staged "gangster" selves to capture not some situation-transcending belief or value system but, rather, to do justice to how their thinking was far more gentle than usual. More generally, whether in halls, classrooms, or anywhere else, we saw the necessity of understanding whether thinking processes were over-energized ("hyped" and often scattered), under-energized (lethargic if not depressive) or, as sometimes happened while in the care of highly competent teachers, just right (and therefore more subtle, concentrated, and composed). The durably inscribed mental structures operating as worldviews and emotional styles mattered to be sure, as Simi's case demonstrated. It was due to his habitus that Simi could seem to be an island impervious to the storm. But very few in either setting had chances to undergo the extensive periods of stabilization that—to again use his own word—gave Simi "structure." By comparison, the vast majority of other students were like boats with no keel. Collective emotional floods tended to carry them away if not completely deluge discursive thinking processes. And in all cases, we saw that thinking processes were forever intertwined with physical positioning, situated postures, and ongoing movements. While there were no disembodied egos, senses of self, or beliefs, hunched over shoulders and more confidently oriented torsos were crucial causes as well as effects of ways of perceiving the two worlds. The confident gait or "gangster lean" of someone who knew they appeared to be genuinely at ease in a given situation (within a broader space of power positions) enabled and constrained the thoughts that arose.

So again here, the big idea is that we need to interrogate real-life processes rather than stick to tidy looking, easily codified things at rest. No matter what anyone said or thought (about meaning-making) after the fact, we needed to know how they coped right there in the thick of it all. Those who have difficulty with this might recall how all of us usually respond, as habituated insiders, to the worlds we "know" *too well to think* about much of what goes on in them most of the time. Already right there physically even if their awareness was somewhere else—the students and teachers usually spent no more time thinking about how to respond to the everyday dictates of hallway or classroom life than academics spend thinking about how many fingers to use when they type.[23] Removing from the "shadowy back regions" (Katz 1999, p. 344) insiders' *pre-reflective corporeality* and *sensorimotor capacities* to the best of my abilities, I tried to reveal not only the source of their practical intentionality and senses of place (in the world) but also why I hope a new generation of fieldworkers will break with the more distant, symbolic interactionist-like perspectives that are second nature to many leading ethnographers.[24]

If critics must suggest that I depict students ("of color") as zombies, I hope they will at least add that I did the same with more and less successful teachers, including myself. I had no shortage of pro-school beliefs. And awkward as such an endeavor would be, if they had to be racialized, I guess they would be white or European American. But none of this mattered when, for example, I caught myself yearning for the admiration of the "gangsters." Pushed close to the edge by a chain of distressing transactions, as we saw, I found myself at one point digging my nails into a student's wrist. During such moments, I tried to "get a grip" while already in midresponse. If this held for a reasonably stable middle-class adult who could retreat to a safe residential area after school, it certainly held for the massively disadvantaged teens with no exit strategies—especially during the "heated" chains of events that often changed the course of both students' and teachers' entire lives (e.g., the incident leading to Mary-Anne's expulsion and Raquel's decision not to return to Delta). Macho "thug life" narratives and confident sounding "fly girl" after-the-fact clichés cannot be trusted any more than the "I knew exactly what I was doing" rationalizations of embarrassed teachers.

Finally, there is the myth of resistance. Were male and female newcomers to the two adolescent societies being "oppositional" when they were all but forced to fear and worship the embodied presence and cultural knowhow of the "true players" and the "hotties" who tried to "play them" (i.e., get the "gangsters" to take them shopping)? Was there anything rebellious about destroying the psychological health of teachers trying to help (even a few of the more docile) students to learn to read, acquire some basic math skills, or think critically about films depicting the horrors of slavery and the battle to overcome racialized oppression? When the brown-skinned mother of a student bit into the shoulder of my brown-skinned colleague in Amsterdam, was she engaging in an act of cross-generational uprising (against the middle-class culture of the school)? Finally, in terms of exceptional occurrences that had major everyday repercussions, were the students who cut each other's faces or stabbed each other nearly to death after botched robberies challenging structures of racialized or class-based domination?

Certainly while dealing with neighborhood schools as poorly regulated as Johnson and Delta, to frame the behavior of (typically more dominant) students in terms of "opposition" is to engage in deeply romantic and sanitizing politics of misrepresentation.[25] In terms of the *ideological* aspects of "resistance," if there was one student in either school who had an articulate critique of the school system, class-based modes of domination, and centuries of racialized oppression, it was Simi—who self-identified as African American, graduated at the top of his class, and secured an academic scholarship to an elite college.

But aside from this outlier, to associate street-flavored coping *mainly* with any kind of "resistance" would be to miss the point of this book entirely. It would be to miss the fact that while the influence of threats and violence could seem to be pervasive, the scores of (native-born and newcomer) kids on the "thug life" path had no real opportunities to clearly take stock of what destructive emotional contagions and physical insecurity were doing to them in the here and now. It would be to overlook the elementary insight that forceful emotional entanglements therefore went on subconsciously pre-structuring their situated beliefs and responses. Given the lack of soothing situations and calming bodily states, an intellectual celebration of "resistance" based on antischool utterances would have been absurd. We had to start with how the "thugs" in both schools were yanked this way and that, almost perpetually refilled with scattered and at times desperate thoughts, before and while they generated antischool or pro-street sounding statements and lines of behavior. We had to begin, that is, with how they were above all fragmented and destabilized by the lack of bodily, emotional, and situational conditions for "getting it together."

Devine (1996) was right to emphasize that individual students and networks of mutually recognizing (would be) insurgents can only put up a fight if they have at least one clearly defined enemy. But in Johnson High and the Delta School, just as in his schools in Brooklyn, the enemies we find in most accounts based on "resistance" had been basically destroyed before my students arrived. The majority of teachers (i.e., unwanted leftovers and temporary replacements) had already retreated into their classrooms if not behind their desks. There was no clearly demarcated white or middle-class or decent school culture, nor much of a Foucauldian surveillance and disciplining system against which students could struggle. While I was initially taken aback by the presence of metal detectors, so many security officers, and even regular police inside Johnson High, I soon found that the kids were basically left to fend for themselves in the corridors, large open spaces, entrances and exit areas of *both* schools. And this was where the battles took place. In the void created by the retreat of caring adults and politico-educational systems more generally, the students spent a great deal of time emotionally and physically beating-up on each other while jockeying for more or less "fabulous" positions.

The pervious pages revealed other reasons we might break with, and ways we might move past, the "opposition" narrative. Even those recognized to be "real" often made clear through their actions and words that—especially while immersed in atypical interaction orders—they liked some of their teachers and actually respected most of the ones that were "no joke" because they maintained stable and productive classroom environments. The image with which I am left is not that of some headstrong mutineer but of an emotionally volatile Ulysses begging that he be bound to the mast rather than left "free" to act in response to the Sirens' call. By and large those typically occupying more "nerdy" positions and even those who often *appeared* committed to the "fabulous" life tended to communicate, with words and with deeds, that they wanted the kinds of consistently well-regulated and above all safe environments that so many middle-class teens take for granted. Ironically, getting this might have afforded my former students chances to partake in something analysts could reasonably call ideological rebellion. But this is purely speculative on my part.

Here we really need to flip the script completely. In terms of what mattered most in the two educational worlds apart—destructive peer dynamics—the most energized and emotionally destabilized teens in Johnson and Delta exerted influences that were above all *conservative*. More specifically, the actions of the typically most dominant students contributed to the *preservation* of the pre-existing *principles of hierarchization* and micro-level *rituals of "realness"* upon which (overall) in-school social recognition "games" were based. By simply doing the thing that was done before they arrived, by slamming around their slightly less dominant fellow students and further draining the already drained teachers, the "fabulous" time and again revitalized the collective fantasies, taken for granted assumptions, practical valuations, and visceral (dis)tastes that protected their own established positions within the two schools' pecking orders. This is what led the more "fabulous" to actively desire playing roles that they themselves, in their calmer moments, decried. Instead of engaging in actions leading to transformations of any structures of domination, especially those positioned temporally as (violent) elites contributed to the *reproduction of the two overall social orders*

as well as to the ways in which the two educational systems effectively reinforced broader inequalities. Those who claimed to be "holding shit down"
were themselves held in check by the parallel logics of the two overall fields
they dominated. As it was among the socially dominant in *The Court Society*
of pre-revolutionary France, so it was in two adolescent societies compared
in this book:

> In the last analysis [the] compelling struggle for ever-threatened power and
> prestige was the dominant factor that condemned all those involved to enact
> these burdensome ceremonies. No single person within the figuration was
> able to initiate a reform of the tradition. [Even the] slightest attempt to reform,
> to change the precarious structure of tensions . . . was, to the ruling class of this
> society, a kind of taboo. The attempt would be opposed by broad sections of
> the privileged who feared, perhaps not without justification, that the whole
> system of rule that gave them privilege would be threatened or would collapse
> if . . . the traditional order were altered. So everything remained as it was.[26]

Despite the fact that what took place often looked chaotic or random,
the core insight here is that the actions, feelings, and perspectives of the
players were objectively organized according to the "internal logics" of the
two relatively autonomous fields. Once habituated deeply enough that they
could do their work through the normalized workings of socialized second
natures, reciprocal (pre-)adjustments and expectations related to all kinds
of positional opportunities and situated sanctions were responsible for the
ongoing—and often quite predictable—coordination of responses. To crush
what at times looked like rebellions (by means, for example, of liberating
destabilized student bodies from destructive emotional entanglements),
therefore, was to destroy staunchly conservative forces. But I do not want
to close with the old idea of the "school as a conservative force" (Bourdieu
1974) in the sense of reproducing broader inequalities related to distributions of economic and cultural capital. Against the backdrop of (most obviously) class-based inequalities in health outcomes, I want to highlight
something even more urgent: even when they were not physically violent,
those who tended to emerge as dominant in the here and now were actually
caught up in the preservation of interactional and school-wide social orders
stressful enough to be classified as killers.

The leading approach implies reifying teenage works in progress and stuff-
ing them into pseudo-biological "group" slots. Basing their analyses of

behavior on the content of explicit mental interpretations, spectators demonstrate that they are wholly out of touch with how the fleeting thoughts and feelings of the physically exposed are pre-shaped by emotional contagions and the silent inner landscapes reemerging in the more or less tense here and now. Sanitizing tropes of willful rebellion can lead us to miss how, because of the dominant positions they tend to occupy, the most disruptive and aggressive students effectively reinforce the stratification of their stigmatized adolescent societies as well as broader inequalities and unhealthy ways of life. While excellent work has convincingly pointed beyond the oppositional black culture approach,[27] it has not culminated in anything like a unified way of thinking and speaking that might effectively serve as an alternative paradigm. To some degree for this reason, our societies continue to ignore the moment-to-moment experiences of those constituting our worst schools as well as, arguably, our most effective means of generating more healthy cities. We have no idea what would become of kids even as massively disadvantaged as those I studied if—from high-quality preschools to well-regulated high schools and even into post-secondary education—we really paid attention to the immediacy of their lived-through experiences. A clearer and more penetrating vision—as well as the methods of the teacher-ethnographer, as the Appendix demonstrates—can help us generate schools that bring out the best instead of the worst in them and ourselves. For now, socially dominant adults who use superior power resources to avoid what goes on in our worst schools are caught up in short-term coping "strategies" that, like those of the socially dominant students in Johnson High and the Delta School, end up damaging their own physical well-being as well as the health of their (future) offspring. While no one has an interest in allowing this to continue, all of us stand to gain from moving toward a more advanced way of thinking and talking about distressed schools and the educational experiences of those born into poverty.

ACKNOWLEDGMENTS

Attempting to single out and thank all the people who impacted this book would not be wise. I would like to begin, therefore, by extending a collective and anonymous thank you to all the kids in the two schools examined here, all the teachers who tried to teach them, and, more generally, to all the people living or working in either of my two "hoods" who helped me get a feel for the games being played in and around the two schools.

Having said this, a few names must now be dropped. For all that he has shared with me and countless others since I first walked into his classroom in 1993, I bow deeply to my first and greatest mentor: Mustafa Emirbayer. Bob Emerson and Jack Katz showed me the importance of great editors, something that only dawns on you from inside the process. What an honor to have worked so closely with two of the best in the business! Matt Desmond gave an earlier version of this book the closest reading it has ever had. His comments, all twenty-one (single-spaced) pages of them, were and will remain a great resource. One has to feel blessed. The reviewers selected by University of Chicago Press were amazing, as was the way Doug Mitchell oversaw the entire team-based effort leading to the publication of this book. I do not take for granted the professionalism or the combined efforts of these people. Abram de Swaan and Nico Wilterdink, most obviously—but also many other brilliant scholars in the Netherlands including Joop Goudsblom, Geert de Vries, and Johan Heilbron—have helped me in many ways through the years. So gripping, penetrating, and compelling is the work of Loïc Wacquant and Philippe Bourgois that I feel they forced me to become an ethnographer. For their inspiration, certainly, but also for their support with this project throughout the years, I thank both of these giants of urban ethnography. To "Simi" and "Raul" I can only say this: I thank you, and I hope you will remain my teachers. While I accept full responsibility for the many shortcomings that remain, I insist that without the efforts of these magnificent scholars, colleagues, and friends this study would have amounted to a fraction of what it has become.

The Department of Sociology and Anthropology at the University of Amsterdam, and what is now the Amsterdam Institute for Social Science Research (AISSR), made this effort possible. For this support and for my intellectual home I am profoundly grateful.

Then, of course, there is my real home. Only my wife knows how much she put into the socio-emotional process of writing this book. Sarah, my love, thank you so much, for everything. And finally, after all those weekends and evenings that "Papa had to work," I want to thank my daughters. It is to you, my darlings, to Tess and Mica—and to the memory of "Jake"—that this book is dedicated.

APPENDIX:
RESEARCH METHODS AND THE EVOLUTION OF IDEAS

[S]tatements on methods of research . . . with few exceptions . . . place the discussion entirely on a logical-intellectual basis. They fail to note that the researcher . . . is a social animal. He has his own role to play, and he has his own . . . needs that must be met in some degree if he is to function successfully.[1]

We learn bodily.[2]

The Introduction addressed access issues and detailed how I ended up a teacher-ethnographer based in the two neighborhood schools. In what follows, I want to clarify how I actually got to work on the ground and how my ideas changed over time. While trying to avoid being either overly defensive or "preachy," I want to make clear why, whatever the shortcomings of this book, I have a great faith in the methods that produced it.

Perhaps it will be useful to start by emphasizing the "full membership" (Adler and Adler 1987; DeWalt and DeWalt 2002, pp. 21–23) style of the comparative ethnographic research I conducted. Operating as an ordinary teacher—or, if you like, doing an *apprenticeship* (cf. Wacquant 2004, p. 15) based in the two institutions—I had to break with the main tenets of more distanced ethnographic research. Instead of trying to maintain an inconsequential presence, that is, I spent most of my time trying (desperately) to influence the actions, feelings, and ideas of those I taught and studied.[3] In and around Johnson High and the Delta School, I tried "simply" to cope as a fully absorbed member. Left (by distressed supervisors and colleagues) to fend for myself, and perhaps to a degree even Durkheim ([1938] 1977, p. 7) could not have foreseen, I was confronted with the range of pressures occasionally leading "many teachers in our secondary schools . . . [to feel] paralyzed by their isolation." And during less dramatically disabling moments, I was usually far too preoccupied with the matters at hand to even think about getting (and recording) data. At least in the classical sense of the term, one might therefore say, I did *not* conduct a participant-observation study.

I would not claim that, when and where access can be achieved, operating mainly as a "player in action"[4] is necessarily the most suitable way to investigate (moment to moment transactions in) all quasi-bounded spaces of play. Particularly when studying a setting characterized by a noxious mix of stresses, it may be wise to maintain a healthy distance. While some people might be able to deal with sustained and full exposure to high-stress contexts better than others, no one should take the risks of full participation lightly. As I tell my students, I would not want anyone to get a stress-related disease like asthma (as a friend and fellow ethnographer did)—let alone to be stabbed to death (like the friend and colleague who brought me into my first field)—because they were inspired to do "real" or "full-bodied" fieldwork.

Furthermore, at least since Whyte revealed how he "rationaliz[ed his] way out" of trading in the familiarity of Cambridge for the anxiety of Cornerville, it has been clear that direct participation can, in practice, trigger justifications for reducing the frequency and intensity of involvement in high-poverty worlds apart.[5] And this is by no means the only reason to take seriously concerns about "full membership" negatively impacting data collection. For example, when such modes of participation translate into members trying to proselytize their ideas and inaugurate fieldworkers into the sacredness reproducing rituals of their tribes, remaining somewhat distanced may be the best way to maintain a viable ethnographic presence.[6] In short, participant observation should in some cases be conducted with the sort of distance and detachment that Dewey decades ago associated with the *spectator's perspective.*

But with regard to the two settings I became involved in, the main strength of my method was precisely that, most of the time, I simply could not be a spectator. As a teacher-ethnographer in the midst of it all, there were no time-outs, sidelines, or ways to merge into the audience. Frequently, I simply could not hide my distress, incompetence, or shame from other insiders. This had some practical advantages about which I knew nothing at the outset: lacking the habitus of a "super teacher" almost certainly helped make me relatively "safe" for many students and other teachers. And after being exposed for long enough to start feeling "burned" by the cumulative ups-and-downs remaking insiders daily in our worst schools, I could not slip into the leisurely mode of analysis Bourdieu associates with the *scholastic fallacy.* Observing from within how I "kept it together"—or, quite regularly, how I "lost it"—it became increasingly difficult to maintain the illusion that any insiders were orienting themselves in real time primarily through the kinds of explicit reasoning scholars (basing their accounts on after-the-fact utterances) habitually impute into the minds of pre-familiarized players with flesh in the game. *Being there and there, participating fully for extended periods of time, observing myself from within while being observed from without—all of this made worlds of difference.*

Because it is so easily overlooked and fundamental, I want to look at this same general issue from a slightly different angle. As I tried to demonstrate from the Preface on, the students' profound senses of (physical) insecurity were often generated outside school and reinforced inside the two institutions. As Devine (1996) argued and as this investigation confirmed, the destructive emotional contagions and intimidating practices also traveled in the opposite direction—from the schools out into the surrounding neighborhoods. With or without the support of a European welfare state, uncertainty, threats, episodically brutal incidences of physical violence, senses of abandonment and stigma were all basic to the students' everyday lives. If they were not personally at risk of missing meals, being evicted, getting robbed, or being stabbed—and, especially in the Bronx, of "ending up a statistic" after being shot—the kids I studied were in close proximity to other children and young adults who were. As such, even in the less devastated of the two settings, basic needs for food, shelter, and predictable forms of *communitas* were lacking and many of the kids really were in something like survival mode.

As an insider, I was therefore forced to get a sense of what it's like to spend a large percentage of your waking hours in a setting constituted by teenage *works in progress*[7] whose brains are basically marinating in stress hormones. To be pulled into the general orbit of the two fields of activity was, in practice, to run around in a low level of constant anxiety. In such situations, one has to ask the following questions: If among pre-familiarized insiders crucial aspects of everyday life "go without saying," what do I really mean by "data"? And especially if the "fish" tend not to take note of certain vital aspects of the "water," in part because they have no counterexamples (e.g., low-stress schools), how can I call attention to my own lived experiences of everyday institutional life without making the account too much about myself?[8] Can I trust my own interpretations any more than those of other people forced to deal with such stressful underlying modes of existence?

Taking a walk on the wild side, twice, did not generate definitive answers to these questions. It did however convince me that researchers will never achieve a sufficient sense of what life in such "stress factories" is actually like—at least not on the *experiential level* that matters most—unless they find ways to settle into the unsettling everyday rhythms permeating such institutions. The only way to adequately grasp the backdrops against which here and now coping practices in such settings emerge (and temporarily "make sense") is to understand them viscerally because you have been gripped repeatedly by their immediacy. The backgrounds of collective moods and shared (taken for granted) meanings created by unmet basic needs on one hand and the ever-shifting, situated, and murky "backwaters" of my own somatic experiences on the other—this is what served as the deepest sources of "my" changing mental representations. And these grounded feelings were what drove me at once to question all disembodying approaches to daily life in non-selective big-city schools as well as to seek reincarnated ones inspired by some of the greatest of our (proto-)sociological thinkers.[9]

This brings us to the one constant in social life: impermanence. Doing ethnography in this fashion forces one to get in touch with the continual grind and unfolding of life in high-poverty high schools—i.e., life as it is lived at the most basic level. It allows one to see that while the dispositions of specific students and teachers can be both somewhat durable and highly significant, they never trigger actions outside of *situational dynamics* and *fields of constant change.*

This Appendix may look like some kind of dessert, but I see it as the meat and potatoes. And this is because social scientists so easily get *hooked* on reified categories—our own as well as theirs. "You look black," I can still hear surprised students in the Bronx saying to native-born students who revealed that (they spoke Spanish and that) one or more of their parents was from Panama or the Dominican Republic. They also said, "You don't look black" to many newcomers from West Africa, especially "early on" when they had the "wrong" hair, clothing, and speech. More frequently and passionately still, they also used non- (or far less clearly) racialized classification schemes based on the "real"/"fake" dichotomy. As this indicates, and in part because visuals and status-based stigmatizations can be so visceral, paying lip service to "constructivism" is not going to do the "unhooking" trick. All of us need to stay focused, over time, on the context-dependent emergence *and secession* of empirically grounded (systems of) categories. This is perhaps the best way for us to replace old conditionings turned second nature *fixations* with the reality of *open, whole,* and *continually resituated beings.* And nowhere is this more urgent than in our analyses of everyday life in the schools of the poor. As social scientists, still emerging from traditions based on measuring clearly distinct things at rest, we need the *experiential base* that *compels* us to let go and move forward into unchartered territory. Differently stated, fully embroiled and prolonged fieldwork is the best way to help us get an adequate sense of the necessity of holding-off on our commonsensical, disembodying and more or less decontextualzing (a priori) definitions while easing into the empirical richness and ambiguity of ongoing, interdependent emerging. This modus operandi, that is, represents our best hope for (1) doing justice to what actually unfolds on the ground and (2) replacing old inclinations to pin down and enclose with new ways of thinking, feeling, and talking about porous beings-as-processes in pregnant situations. It is hardest to miss the vulnerability of open beings of flesh, blood, and mirror neurons—in social interactions that can escalate, and charge-up certain kinds of selves, or not—when you are one of them. Strong as the old dynamic is, both outside and (especially) in the social sciences, we do not need to remain stuck on and with inaccurate visions of social divisions. Sustained participant observation helps us announce that we can stop playing our old roles in all the essentializing dramas, and suggests that the collective efforts of fieldworkers may help bring about a long overdue shift outside our own academic circles.

My methodological claim, in a nutshell, is therefore that direct participation as a member is the most reliable way (1) to reveal what actually goes on in real time and space across multiple settings and, therefore, (2) to bring to life how limited and potentially misleading reified conceptual constructions, static classification schemes, and reductivist research designs can in fact be. With regard to the scholarly approaches to everyday life in nonselective inner city schools that have been dominant for so long, this method invites us to see that even asking if "the black students" are self-destructive because of "their (peer group mediated) oppositional beliefs" is to show that you dwell in a distant intellectual edifice rather than in (or even close to) the phenomena to which we should be attending. This distinctive approach to ethnography allows us to see, that is, that beneath all the seemingly neutral analytic building blocks (e.g., outsider categories like "the Hispanic students," "oppositional native-born minority youth," and "second-generation migrants") there is the reality of impermanence based on shifting modes of interdependence and, perhaps most importantly of all, (accumulating) levels of nerve-racking fear. No matter what theoretical affinities or visions one originally brings into our worst schools, this method forces researchers to ask (themselves) the following: Should we simplify lived realities by treating teenagers as tidy bundles of frozen social facts or sorts (e.g., "the Latinos," "the native Dutch," "the blacks")? Are we so afraid of "messiness" that we buy into all kinds of compartmentalizing or overly mentalist "Western" philosophies (e.g., methodological individualism, the subject that thinks explicitly before acting) that help us shut out the fluid-like nature of inter-being and continual becoming as it is experienced the ground? Or do we at least try to use processual concepts appropriate for the investigation of the interwoven everyday practices emerging in real time? In the future, I hope, theoretically informed and richly textured ethnographic descriptions will help us move beyond ungrounded, superimposed categories even in evolving forms of statistical variable-, interview-, and network-based research.

"Polished" accounts of fieldwork techniques are notorious for overemphasizing the agency of the researcher and underemphasizing how field effects in conjunction with the habitus of the researcher co-constitute actual methodological practice (Kalir 2006). In an effort to avoid slipping into this trap, let me begin by reiterating that a buddy talked me into teaching at Johnson High and, *already in the grip of this first field, I stumbled, very gradually, onto my process-based questions and my sense that sustained ethnographic immersion could help answer them.* That is, at the outset I had no grand design for conducting embodied, fully participatory ethnography. Rather, it was while "stressing out" on the job as a Social Studies/History teacher in the Bronx and then as an English teacher in the Bijlmer that I found myself trying to figure out how coping processes-in-relations actually worked—both when there were few slip-ups and when local orders temporarily broke down. So I tried to become a *competent native* before I committed to *embodied practice* as a way to *live sociologically.*

Because I cannot elucidate how my ideas shifted otherwise, allow me to go back in time for just a moment. It is true that I had been introduced to some highly advanced theories and ethnographic research before I entered Johnson High. But in my mid-twenties when I started teaching, I had just started to really grapple with what people like Charles Tilly and Terry Williams had thrown at me during two years of study at the New School for Social Research. When I entered my first field soon after receiving my MA, that is, I was a typical lower middle-class Upper West Side progressive intellectual wannabe sociologist. While I had never been inside a nonselective public high school during a typical school day, I had seen any number of Hollywood films depicting ideologically pro-street boys going to nonwhite schools in the "'hood." I entered Johnson High full of implicit assumptions about the existence of clearly defined ethnic "groups" as well as culturally more or less "oppositional" types. I assumed, furthermore, that there were clearly separate (and antagonistic) gangs comprised of youth with inherently dangerous minds as well as students who simply were not gangsters. I knew the "ballers" from Catholic high schools in the Bronx, not the "gangbangers" in public ones.

Once inside, my old mental habits were at times reinforced by what I saw and heard from more experienced teachers and especially students (e.g., Roxanne on "good" and "bad" kids).[10] At the same time, just by virtue of being there—and here I mean because I was just taking in what I had to take in while trying to make it to the end of each day—I was also forced to start seeing why I would have to eventually break from these commonsensical fixations. Quite quickly I was forced to see that the adolescents were competing for social status linked to senses of authentic belonging (or recognition) and that, generally, divisions based on power and status were not based mainly on constructions of ethnicity or race. It also started to dawn on me that a key advantage (power resource) in this struggle was something very close to what Bourdieu dubbed "symbolic capital" (i.e., the ability to influence, and indeed naturalize, ways of seeing the world). Putatively black or native born or not, those who tended to "run things" could at once be temporarily thrilled by having the right stuff (habitus, belonging in the here and now) and ultimately dominated by how they held "shit" and their entire school "down." I started to see getting one's "thug on," or staging "fly girl" personas, as quite conservative situational responses bolstering (rather than challenging) the status quo. So, I gradually concluded that I should begin by trying to show how the worship of the two schools' versions of "ghetto fabulous" didn't just "make sense" in the here and now, but indeed why the goal of being "real" was almost universally taken for granted. I wanted to show how the overall practical "logics" (i.e., de facto goals related to the most salient pecking orders) emerged as properties of the two overall social systems and, at the same time, were created and sustained by countless everyday rituals playing themselves out on the ground.

But such statements may make things seem far more planned than they really were. In reality, my ideas shifted for reasons nearly or completely unrelated to any early blueprint. The most striking example of this may be the double slashing (Chapter 3) that took place just outside the room in which I was teaching in the Bronx. I certainly did not foresee anything like that happening on that sunny morning, and I was perhaps no less jolted than the students. Yet many other (mundane) instances demonstrate how the ideas presented in this book were influenced "by accident."

To take but one example, I never really gave much thought to looking for an apartment near Johnson High.[11] So, as I rarely drove to the Bronx, the insights generated by my daily grind often started on the subway ride I made from my traditionally working class yet gentrifying section of Brooklyn (between Carroll Gardens and Red Hook). Unmistakably more privileged students on their way to one of the private schools in the Northern Bronx—or to Bronx Science, one of New York's selective public high schools—were regularly brought face-to-face with the typically more docile students who made it to schools such as Johnson High in time for their first- or second-period classes. Observing this made me see something I might have missed had I come to school by car. As different as Johnson High's "nerds" and "hard rocks" might seem to be while packed into the same hallways, comparing what looked (and sounded) like "my" kinds of students to the teens on their way to the borough's better schools revealed that—at the level of linguistic, aesthetic, and bodily dispositions—even the "good" kids attending the Bronx's worst high schools were remarkably similar to the "bad" kids who proudly claimed to be "running" them. Furthermore, the deference the students attending the non-selective schools paid to (the clusters of) more middle-class kids (confidently speaking middle-class English) illustrated, yet again, why even a few moments of stigma-reversing recognition from the "ghetto fabulous" in and around worlds apart like Johnson High could seem to be worth any amount of trouble. Here, race and ethnicity often seemed to *happen*, but in ways that were far more ambivalent and short-lived than what common sense would lead us to expect (see Chapter 4).

Rolling with this train of thought I will add that the same types of unplanned insights came with my trip in the Metro from the Bijlmer back to the middle-class part of Amsterdam in which my (future) wife had found an apartment (on the Overtoom, next to the Vondel Park) before we met. When the Metro left Southeast Amsterdam and arrived at the first station in a non-marginalizied neighborhood, it seemed that obviously different "types" of people entered the equation. Some looked and sounded "Surinamese," for example, but far more mainstream and less "Bijlmer-style" Surinamese. Old or young, the arrival of new types of Amsterdamers immediately highlighted the similarities between the people from the Bijlmer and, sometimes quite obviously, the social types (and forms of interacting) that had held sway before the infusion of middle-class-ness.[12] Again here, ideas and feelings related to race and ethnicity could become salient and poignant. A cluster of pale-skinned adolescents getting on the Metro and taking up posts next to dark-skinned teenagers from the Bijlmer could at times make clear why my students sometimes reported experiencing "their" Bijlmer as a less "white" (or less "Dutch") cosmos within the capital city. At the same time, such interactions invited me to embrace the complexity—and recall the lived-through simplicity—of the only vaguely or non-ethnicized divisions I experienced first hand as flopped basketball player (rather than as "the only white guy" on the team) in what outsiders might have called a "majority minority" Catholic high school in the Bronx. In and out of my schools, I came to see that I was witnessing ethnicity *not* as some kind of preexisting or permanently relevant thing in the world, but, rather as a "perspective on the world"—a "modality of experience" based on an "interactional accomplishment."[13] Simultaneously, over the course of years, my assumptions about substance-like more or less dominant (or street) "peer groups"—as well as presuppositions about the inherent cool of violent elites like Julio, all started to dissolve. Again, the main point here relates to the details and unplanned nature of the data-collection processes. Simply doing what ordinary teachers did, I soaked up hundreds, if not thousands of potentially relevant bits of information each day. Perhaps I failed to register even more. Either way, I did not have to go out of my way to get "good" data because I was swimming in it.

If my primary commitment was to survive and perform as a teacher, I also (self-consciously) expanded my activities well beyond those of conventional pedagogues. Through any number of activities, I tried to collect and record specific (interview or observational) data as well as, more generally, acquire a broader feel for the schools and the kids. Maybe the most poignant of many possible examples demonstrating how my actions diverged from those of my colleagues is that I often ate lunch with the students or, short of that, simply hung out with them where they ate food or killed time. Few staff members did this (unless they were security guards stationed in such places in the Bronx) and, occasionally, they told me they thought my behavior was peculiar. In New York a few colleagues seemed to go out of their way to explain why they never ventured past the teachers' parking lot or into the students' cafeteria. In the Bijlmer one teacher stressed that, having seen me from a distance sitting with students in the *aula*, he thought for a moment I was "one of them." The implication, in New York, was that doing things like going out for lunch or hanging out in front of the school was unsafe. In the Bijlmer the insinuation was that (perhaps in part because of my bodily dispositions) I looked like I felt at home where teachers did not belong. Students, especially in the Bijlmer, told me they thought it was either slightly odd or kind of nice that I spent so much time in "their" extra-classroom domains. Generally, however, no one seemed to care very much either way. Even sitting around with a tape recorder or, on a few occasions, with a video camera—nothing I did seemed to cause much of a stir.

Just taking it all in moment by moment, and in the types of places teachers usually avoided, did more than "merely" help me acquire a practical sense for how status symbols and hierarchies were charged with meaning in everyday life. Hanging out in such places also allowed me to deepen relationships that often started in classrooms—e.g., with "stars" of this book like Simi, Raul, Ronny as well as with others that I got to know quite well. I would sit with Raul in the *aula*, for example, and just listen to him gossip and piece together analyses of what we observed. Putting in the time where the students hung out also allowed me to observe, communicate with, and hear gossip about students like Kim, Roy, Jurgen, and Cory, who I only got to know more superficially. Some pupils, like Ronny and Raul, would come sit next to me in such high visibility settings. Others, like Brindisha and Simi, were almost never found anywhere near such spaces or, as in Dread's case, they seemed not to feel comfortable talking to me "in public"—which meant that our talks usually took place in relative isolation (e.g., after school either on walks or in empty classrooms). This relative isolation, as Brindisha's revelation about sexual abuse indicates (Chapter 5), seem to have shaped the types of insights I got into the different students' lives and personalities. Ronny, for example, may have seemed jovial to me because he dealt with the (nervous) energy that came with close proximity to other students who felt comfortable in high-visibility areas by making wisecracks and performing upbeat relaxedness. He could also crack jokes when we were alone, but this may have been temporary residue from the kind of pattern or relationship we built up. When we were in the Vondel park, in my neighborhood, he was far less the jokester than "usual." It was only then and there, away from the crowds and in somber tones, that Ronny told me about his best friend stabbing someone.

Let us turn now to the two young men I got to know best and rely on most. I was introduced to both Simi and Raul as students in my classes. But I started to really get to know them through everything from hanging out in hallways to having meals in pizza shops to recording conversations in local parks to having them over to meet my family (during birthday parties) to, in Raul's case, walking around the neighborhood with him and his mother, to, in Simi's case, bringing him to sporting events and then hanging out in his apartment with his brother right after he got out of prison.

The key here was that we liked one another. They choose me as much as I choose them and, I think, this had to do with deeply engrained dispositions. In other words I do not think I could have "faked" my way to that kind of rapport and the sustained access I had to Simi and Raul. If there was no genuine friendship based on shared or at least compatible habitus, the relationships simply would not have "worked." This is not to deny that the relationships involved elements of *mutual exploitation*. We offered each other lots of attention and energy while trying to figure out the worlds in which we operated.

This brings us to the issue of analytic partnerships. I certainly tried out a great deal of what I felt I needed to say in this book in conversations with these two extremely insightful young men. Sometimes we disagreed on relatively minor issues (e.g., how a given student should be classified). Other times, not so much disagreeing as trying to discern and parse more clearly, we would go at it–back and forth–offering empirical observations, reflections, possible explanations, and more observational detail. With Simi in New York and later with Raul in Amsterdam, we did this for hours, session after session, until we ended up sharing opinions on the major issues.

Sometime this produced what *felt* like "aha moments." Of course, such popular terms are potentially misleading because they hide so much of what made such crystallizations possible. Nonetheless, the methodological point I want to raise here is that I often experienced such incidences as terribly important at the time—and I made no effort to hide this from Simi or Raul. For example, I remember feeling it "all come together" in the attic that doubled as my study when Raul paused, looked right at me, and declared that, "ghetto fabulous is like a religion." Fan of Emile Durkheim and William James though I am, I had not used this language around him. Nor can I credit myself with having already "had" this insight before Raul blurted this out. This was during the same evening when Raul told me about his nephew from the "bad" side of his family who saw, in a "nanosecond," that he "had game." I could not believe he used the word nanosecond! This was years before Gladwell's *Blink* popularized such language and I certainly had not "planted" the seemingly perfect term. This, along with Raul's passionate delivery, helped me see that his relationship to this respected family member was all about meaning (beliefs, morals) and mutual recognition. But it was *mainly* about the kind of meaning and recognition that operates on at most a half-conscious if not fully automatic level. Religious like rituals and faith in "realness" based on almost completely instinctual discriminations were not what the existing literature emphasized. Similarly, it all seemed to "fall into place" while driving Simi around his old neighborhood and hearing him say there was "no way but up" from his old homeless shelter as we passed it. On the same trip he had been ardent about how the subsidized housing development near his apartment building deserved its nickname: the Vietnam Projects. When he and his future wife (another former student who somehow developed the right kind of habitus) went on and on about how they were worn down *not* by the threats of extreme violence in and around Johnson, but rather by the endless waves of minor yet maddening (classroom) disruptions standing between them and their escapes from the worst subsections of the South Bronx, this carried a lot of weight.

So what I want to highlight here is that Simi and Raul really had a major impact. I met with them regularly enough—and we talked through what *we* were thinking and what I was writing about meaningfully enough—that I have to see our relationships as another key aspect of my immersion in the two fields. It would go too far to say that, during the time I met with them regularly, Simi and Raul were more important than my academic advisors (during the years that I worked closely with them). Typically, however, I discussed my work with my advisors roughly once every four to six weeks during sessions that lasted perhaps an hour or two at most. And during some crucial periods in both fields, when I sometimes felt that things were "coming together" in dramatic ways, I spent five to ten hours a week (re-)molding arguments with these youthful *analytic colleagues.*[14]

The potentially positive side of such intellectual partnerships is obvious: you can get insights that help you on your way toward achieving an adequate analysis. The downsides, however, are quite problematic. Emotionally and cognitively entrained, repeatedly, the ethnographer can buy way into misguided ways of thinking and speaking (e.g., my misleading use of the native term "chaos" in an earlier analysis). Relatedly, while my sense is that the students and their other teachers did not care about me (or about the possibility that I might be writing a book) enough to influence their utterances or anything else I was able to observe, the nature of my relationships and types of conversations with "Simi" and "Raul" make this argument tricky. All in all, I think these relationships provided data-generating and analysis-refining goldmines. This book profited immensely from the more and less memorable occasions during which I just sat around with Simi and Raul—often with me typing or writing if not recording—while our essentially interdependent analyses came into fruition.

Of course, encounters with a variety of other adolescents challenged and provoked my thinking and analysis as well. One such encounter occurred in the video club I set up in the Bronx with the gentle and soft-spoken filmmaker mentioned in the Preface. We met regularly, and soon created a relatively safe space. At one point, with the female filmmaker sitting on the floor in front of a semi-circle formed by students sitting at desks, we went around the room exploring one of the questions the students had come up with: Where do you see yourself in the future? "In the middle class," a rather chubby dark-skinned boy matter-of-factly declared. This guy could, in different types of situations, come across as "one hundred percent ghetto." Here, without a hint of incongruity, he seemed to be sharing with us that he simply wanted to get away from the poverty into which he was born. Did it matter, at least during this exchange, that he at times categorized himself as black? Such "crystallizing moments" have stayed with me, and along with all the other countless things I picked up more or less through osmosis, altered my way of seeing the worlds I compare.

A similar example comes from my exchanges with Hector. I met this dark-skinned boy who could seem to embody all the clichés about inner-city "roughnecks" on a return visit to Johnson when we were both waiting to see a guidance counselor. We just struck up a conversation and this led to an appointment to record an interview in the park the next day. This self-described cocaine-dealing gang member told me he went out on patrols with other boys and stabbed kids wearing the wrong colors in adjacent neighborhoods. Later, on a park bench, with little if anything to gain or lose, Hector added that he was driven to violence in part because he so desperately wanted to be reunited with his dad. (His father, apparently, had a "new" family including a "wife" that did not want him to even visit his "old" son.) Hector told me about being "scared to death" when he went to Brooklyn to buy cocaine from "Jamaicans" and bring it back to the Bronx, where he sold it to get "baby stuff" for his daughter. Maybe he was making it up, but I certainly knew about boys his age in similar situations that were not at all imaginary and, again, this seemingly kind-hearted boy did not in any obvious way stand to gain by mobilizing my sympathies.

Repeatedly, then, I was exposed to shockingly non-street, highly conventional, and unyieldingly human accounts from kids who could appear, at times, to be inherently, unceasingly "wild." This led me to at least consider the wrongheadedness of pigeonholing such poverty-stricken children because of either supposedly fixed racial identities or seemingly stable cultural codes.

From the opposite direction, we might say, a key moment emerged out of observing a so-called "nerd" named Sebastian, in the Bijlmer. I came upon this boy (who described his background as Assyrian) getting his "thug" on in a nearly empty classroom. He did not see me until he was already fully engaged in mimicking, as earnestly and convincingly as possible, the "gangsters" whose actions and way of life he typically pretended not to notice. Sebastian's performance struck me in part, I think, because watching him I suddenly realized what I had so often seen before without fully "getting it." Right down to the hunched over shoulders, tones of voice, and stigmatizing of "fake-ass niggaz," when those so often forced into the "fake" positions got half a chance, they could seem to be instantly remade from the bottom up. All their talk about being disgusted with the "thug life" had to be taken with a big grain of salt.

Another example: in the Bijlmer in the spring, when the long Dutch winters finally gave way, friends and family members regularly hung out with students within five minutes of the Delta School. Joining these gatherings, I sometimes came into contact with older siblings (who, in a few cases, I had already met during parent-teacher conferences). The refrains produced by the ostensibly Surinamese or Antillean older brothers could be almost exactly the same as those performed by the nominally African American or Latino older brothers: "I screwed up, now I'm paying the price. I need to go back and get my degree. I'm trying to tell my little kid sister/brother not to learn the hard way, like I did." Sometimes slowly and sometimes in bursts of sudden clarity, such observations seemed to turn worn-out terms and questions into far more revealing ones: Voluntary vs. involuntary minorities? First generation vs. third generation? Welfare state vs. non-welfare state? Might the refrains be exactly the same in "white-trash trailer parks" outside Buffalo or "antisocial" towns adjacent to defunct coal mines just north of Maastricht? Was I observing "ghetto fabulous" kids proudly "holding shit down" or poorly-born adolescents forced, in specific times and places, to ignore the advice of respected family members in institutional realms that adults collectively failed even to examine closely, let alone regulate.

Eventually, through innumerable experiences and reflections, I got "the big idea." The kids habitually setting the tones in the two schools could be "ghost-face killers" or "sweethearts." Even if their naturalizing (and sometimes ethno-racialzing) definitions of themselves and others did at times have real effects, my task was to show why in our analyses we should stop taking actors out of their ever-shifting contexts of action and treating them as solidified, quasi-natural, self-contained kinds. In part because the systems of categories found in formalized administrative reports could be "infuse[d] with value beyond the technical requirements of the task at hand" (Selznick 1957, p. 17)[15], I had to base the analysis on the ambiguous and at times even contradictory classifications of players occupying specific (microlevel) positions in the two social games. Unequal distributions of various power resources as well as historical trajectories turned durably inscribed dispositions can matter a great deal. Yet without being soft on power or underplaying habitus, we need to start with embodied experiences of interrelatedness and the reality of impermanence—not with any seemingly frozen attributes of what are merely depicted as self-enclosed substances (e.g., the "bad" kid, the pro-school belief system, the antischool peer group).

At this stage, I want to say a bit more about informal discussions and more formal interviews with (groups of) different categories of teachers and students. In practice, there were no sharp distinctions between verbal exchanges emerging out of participating as a classroom teacher and observing while "just hanging out," on one hand, and (group) discussions set up in advance and carried out in places like empty classrooms or local parks on the other. All the different aspects of the data-collecting processes influenced each other. Having said this, some things were far more conscious (or contrived) than others. I tried to be strategic in selecting those I came to depict as especially interesting "characters" (or "ideal-types"). I combined interviews with more informal conversations in a variety of situations to learn about how these "types" behaved when I could not see them (e.g., interviews with Jurgen in school and at a restaurant in the center of town as well as interviews about this powerfully built and potentially savage boy's home life with another student; recorded conversations with Roxanne, informal talks with her teachers). I also tried to augment conversations with repeated observations of interviewees dealing with various types of situational conditions. With regard to the acts of extreme violence that I was never able to witness directly, I relied on more thematically pinpointed interviewing, collecting as many statements about interviewees' views of specific events as possible.

This is the aspect of ethnographic practice characterized by more time for explicit thinking, categorizing, and planning. However, I want to stress that the way even these discussions and interviews emerged demonstrates another strength of the core method (i.e., fully absorbed coping as a somewhat competent native). The vast majority of (group) discussions and formal interviews were with people who had not only "seen me around" for months if not years, but with people who had seen or at least heard about me being regularly disgraced. And being repeatedly crushed by "difficult" classes is merely the most obvious example. Even those who had not seen (or even heard) about my "personal" failures in classrooms had, in many cases, seen me withdraw into the docile body and ("please don't pick on me") averted gaze of the intimidated teacher moving through potentially explosive extra-classroom settings. Also, most of the students (and teachers) I interviewed knew me well enough to at least sense that I was not the type that would, for example, start by cueing up ethnicized or racialized divisions (or feel uncomfortable exploring this if they brought it up). In short, those I

approached for interviews and (group) discussions knew me as an insider—
as someone who to some degree took the "crap," as Goffman (1989, p. 125)
put it, that all ordinary teachers had to take. This was part of the "secret"
not only of why access was sometimes granted, but also of what happened
when I asked students, teachers, administrators, and family members my
standard questions about their (or their loved one's) everyday experiences
in and around Johnson and Delta, as well as about their "past lives." They
had different language to be sure, but their local knowledge of who and
what I was often helped open up "room" for exploring (the sources of) their
stress, shame, anxiety, and (unrealistic) hopes for the future. In short, the
more strategically planned and even somewhat artificial aspects of the data-
collecting processes (interviews, focus-group discussions) rested on foundations of practical understanding that were "always 'already there' before
reflection [began]."[16]

As several chapters made clear, the comparison of different aspects of
coping processes based in the two schools spilled over into the surrounding neighborhoods as well as certain students' pasts. After all, Johnson and
Delta were neighborhood schools and one "aim of ethnography . . . is to
historicize the habitus in an effort to externalize what has been internalized
and bring to mind what has been forgotten" (Desmond 2007, p. 269). The
search for commonalities and differences in extra-school conditions and
histories of conditionings led me to students' parents and legal guardians.
I also got to know some of the students' (boys' and girls') friends, their siblings, and their extended family members. Outside of school—and certainly
in students' homes—I focused on male students (or made sure to bring a female colleague along with me) because I was afraid of people thinking I was
trying to become inappropriately intimate with female students. Without
sustained access to students and their significant others, I certainly would
not have been able collect (and to some degree verify) biographical data
on their social trajectories. As such, whenever I had access and the required
energy, I tried to hang out with students in their local pizza shops, on their
street corners, on their makeshift playing fields, and at their birthday parties in, for example, the common rooms of housing projects. Furthermore,
in the interest of getting a better feel for everyday life in all my students'
stomping grounds, I sought regular contact with local shopkeepers, restaurant workers, police, social workers, building superintendents, coaches, and
various other neighborhood figures. I tried to get a lived sense of what it
was like for girls to walk through the corridors of their high-rise apartment
buildings and onto the streets in the winter while it was still dark out; and
I tried to feel what it was like for boys to walk home from school via utterly

unsupervised streets and city parks. I felt the "electricity" of (hip-hop) beats coming from cars and apartments just outside the schools, and I saw the huge televisions and shortages of any reading material in students' living rooms. With a felt sense of what they were leaving behind, I accompanied students on ventures into non-marginalizied parts of their cities (during school trips).

Along with notes and reflections, I compiled scores of audiotaped interviews. I conducted follow-up interviews (with parents and siblings), sometimes years after initial material was produced, to revisit statements made by pupils on specific matters. Where possible, I checked official records to see if they supported claims offered by students (e.g., information related to rates of attendance, grades, and transfers). I interviewed teachers and school managers at various ("feeder") schools. I attended all kinds of faculty meetings where specific students—and in some cases, especially in the Bijlmer, their domestic situations—were discussed. As the students' and staff members' nonverbal forms of communication were potentially as important to me as anything they said, I also amassed extensive video footage of interviews and everyday interactions in and around both schools.[17] I compared everything I could get my hands on, from student writing samples to textbooks.

It might be useful to single out how I studied the most effective teachers, and how I might have done this differently. Besides all the normal activities colleagues participated in together (e.g. meetings), I sat through (and at times participated in) scores of classes taught by more- and less-effective colleagues. I felt I could learn the most from the minority of consistently successful pedagogues in each setting. Sometimes, especially in the Bijlmer, I observed master teachers for multiple periods in a single day. As a rule, however, I scattered my visits over several weeks and months. I made sure to observe excellent teachers with more- and less-challenging classes. I watched them do everything from joking with pupils in the hallway and preparing lessons to marking homework assignments and organizing scores in their grade books. I took detailed notes on everything I could see or hear or sense them doing in their classrooms. To say that I tried to replicate their well-organized practices does not go far enough. I went out for drinks with the master pedagogues after work and asked them in informal conversations what the secret to their success was. I tried to mimic their demeanors and craft my own version of their ways of being.

Looking back I regret this strategy: I was drawn to the gems that were already smooth, where I should have focused on the diamonds in the rough. I should have zeroed in much more, that is, on exactly how average teachers became excellent ones. Were they coached differently? Did they train themselves in qualitatively different ways to execute all the little moves that allowed them to develop better habits (e.g., of bodily posture)? The problem, aside from knowing what to look for, is identifying which average types will make it to the next level during the time that you have to watch them evolve. Although some of the most successful teachers at times tried to encourage me with comments about how they too had been overwhelmed "in the beginning," I did not observe any ordinary teachers evolve into the types that consistently generated positive climates when confronted with large numbers of potentially disruptive students. So, while I observed a lot of average types—and while I repeatedly observed some of the worst five percent or so that probably should have never even tried to teach in any school—I certainly did not do the detailed longitudinal types of observations that would reveal exactly how, step-by-step, a teacher's "g(ame)" gets elevated to the top tier.

I am of two minds when it comes to the next topic. I wish I had taken many more detailed field notes and video-recorded many more conversations and scenes than I did. Nothing brings me back like a video, and field notes that seemed completely irrelevant at the time they were penned have helped me put together the scenes that are at the heart of this book. While it is true that the descriptions in my field notes "present a *version* of a world that functions more as a filter than a mirror reflecting the 'reality' of events" (Emerson et al, 2001, p. 358, *italics in original*), in the years that I spent rewriting versions of this book, along with ongoing conversations with the students and colleagues who became key informants and dear friends, these remained my memory-jogging lifelines. Hearing Simi's voice once again, recalling Julio's body language while rereading my notes on it, looking straight into Roxanne's eyes, finding out once again exactly how a colleague phrased a reaction to a certain question—all of this proved to be useful. If nothing else, it is wonderful to be able to quote with the utter confidence generated by the recording of conversations.

On the other hand, the very fact that I often felt too emptied out or shaken up either to take notes in situ or to try my hand at after the fact reflections might in itself be considered "evidence" about what being there did to ordinary teachers. Rushing from one classroom to the next, exhausted during a lunch break, wound-up or scattered or depressed after school—and feeling the need to go for a workout or a drink—these were the effects of the field that made taking disciplined and consistent field notes feel impossible. Also, I suspect that if I had taken more copious notes, a great deal of them would have been repetitive and perhaps even unmanageable. Less can be more—especially while working in two schools, and hanging out with the kids and teachers outside of the schools for over half a decade. Furthermore, as "everyone" since Malinowski ([1922] 1984, pp. 8, 21) has said, field note taking and recording often disrupt (the development of a feeling for) the normal flow of what is going on. For example, my attempts to record things often flopped when respondents (and/or I) became far too self-conscious about the presence of the tape recorder.[18]

Given the cogent concerns an anonymous reviewer had with an earlier version of this book, I want at this point to clarify exactly when I gathered data on what I have referred to as "real-time" responses to threatening encounters. I did, occasionally, write down key words, parts of quotes, or even a few sentences containing the beginnings of an analysis more or less "in the here and now." And I used these tidbits of information—jotted down on anything I could find—as memory joggers during the more systemic write-ups that took place, for example, in between classes, during breaks, after school, or during weekends. This was, however, a relatively small part of the data-collection (and production) process. Consciously or not, and often within twenty-four hours, I more regularly found myself trying to bring about a catharsis by getting down on paper at least a few nearly-in-the-moment reactions to some aspects of the threatening encounters I had witnessed. Even if I did not stick to the analyses I started developing while still close (in time) to when the action occurred (e.g., my own natural reaction to Julio's response to Roy's challenge at the school dance), these beginnings of descriptions and write-ups helped me interrogate how aggression immediately jolted and vivified insiders.

I think it is fair to say, then, that some of my note taking really did take place quite near the heat of the moment. But my main claim here is not that I always took notes or developed analyses while standing close to the "fire." Rather, it is that I regularly witnessed threatening encounters, or observed (and talked to people about) how violence immediately influenced what went on. Even though I did not take notes on or record conversations during most of these instances, this did gradually inform my senses of how belligerence operated (on students and staff) in the two settings. This, above all, is why I maintain that I did not rely on after-the-fact accounts of what unfolded during the "hottest" moments. In short, a blend of (minutely) recorded details and years of experiential insights into here-and-now social dynamics, moods, and perceptions served as the basis for the rewriting of field notes into reflections and vignettes which, in many cases, went on for years (and reflected evolving ways of thinking and feeling about the matters at hand).

This brings us to perhaps the most distinctive and problematic aspect of my method: that I spent so much time (1) in the two fields and (2) writing and rewriting after departing from them. With regard to the first point, I admit that I may have overdone it by staying on for (nearly) three years in both settings. I do not think it is merely a rationalization, however, to suggest that it took years to really get a feel for the everyday regularities and rhythms, to form meaningful relationships, and to get a visceral sense of what long-term immersion did to ordinary teachers. Given that the "role of the observer is a collaborative interactional achievement" (Pollner and Emerson 1983, p. 236)—and that this main role can be broken up into a myriad of "covert" and "overt" sub-roles (Adler and Adler 1987, p. 21)—the social processes involved cannot be rushed. They have to unfold in their own time.

To this I will add that, as my comments about forging analyses with Simi and Raul indicated, being a teacher-ethnographer in the two schools often meant taking on the role of the action researcher. This is, I think, what I got hooked on: building-up access and trust by actively trying to help the disadvantaged people on whom—and with whom—I conducted research.[19] Varying levels frustration and (self-)doubt notwithstanding, such involved research could also be positively uplifting. Students (and certain of their family members) bought into ongoing collaborations only if they sensed genuine commitment. Some of the kids (and co-workers) became dear friends as well as guides because they sensed that I was ready to put time and effort into trying to reduce levels of self-harm and promote positive academic outcomes. Aside from being validating and motivational, this perpetually opened up new questions, deeper levels of insight, and increasing clarity—the stuff that keeps fieldworkers from thinking they reached the stage of "saturation."

So my method was based on direct and prolonged involvement. Having said this, as members of the Chicago School of Ethnography understood long ago, the job of the urban ethnographer is also to keep a distance from the institutional practices, situational dynamics, and overall field effects that are the real stuff of my comparison (cf. Becker and Geer 1960).[20] Without reducing people to their objective positions in social space, in Bourdieu's language, I tried to guard against the tendency to take informants' utterances at face value. In other words, while emotional collaborations and contestation are unavoidable and useful aspects of all serious fieldwork relations (Emerson 1983), I knew that native assumptions and ways of thinking could not always be my own. What respondents (and formal reports) necessarily left unsaid had to form, at times, the foundation of my analysis. I had to listen closely enough to tease out the degree to which the accounts offered to me conformed to, or were emanations of, larger cultural narratives. Keeping a bit of distance (from bureaucratic charades) also took time.

But the time I spent collecting data in the field pales by comparison with the time I spent developing and refining my analyses of these data. Starting to grasp "the right" empirically grounded insights says nothing about *understanding how to use them* while generating vivid descriptions and balanced evaluations. I left my second field in 2001, completed my dissertation (and, in doing so, published an initial take on these materials in monograph form) in 2005. So what happened between 2005 and the year this book came out? I could contend that it took me so long to produce the present version because of a range of factors—e.g., the complexity of what I wrote about, having two children, working for years on attempts to desegregate urban schools in the Netherlands, teaching "full loads" at the University of Amsterdam. The fact of the matter is, however, that lacking a *practical sense* for how to systematize *on paper* the insights I got on the ground slowed the process of working out my ideas. Oddly perhaps, it took "forever" to develop this to the degree that I now have it despite the support of master sociologists like Mustafa Emirbayer, Abram de Swaan, and others.[21] Transforming an insufficiently sociological imagination and developing the second nature of an even slightly proficient writer proved to be both difficult and extremely time consuming.

I want to come back to embodiment because doing so can highlight something about my methods that may contribute to certain aspects of reform efforts in the future. If one works for long enough as a teacher-ethnographer in schools like Johnson and Delta, certain muscles start to tense up. I often carried the stress in my shoulders. The level of physical tension seemed to be "automatically" connected to both the intensity and rigidity of the thoughts and feelings that emerged. One might speak here of the drive or energy level associated with thinking certain thoughts and the suppleness or brittleness of body and mind. Hunched over my sandwich during a break, it could be hard to even ask myself if it was really useful to go on worrying about what might happen after lunch or what had happened last week. Especially when there was no way to avoid potentially stressful interactions, it certainly felt as if there were no way to avoid getting caught up and slipping into further incapacitating rounds of fretting and self-blame that accompanied, for example, the holding and strain in the shoulders (e.g., "Why haven't I become a super teacher by now?").

Even when there was no way to escape negative situations, a simple trick could help. In a cafeteria, an empty classroom or a teachers' restroom, just bringing my awareness to the embodied sensations of the moment could help me regain a certain level of composure and clarity of thought (e.g., "Ok, this is what being scattered and tense feels like. This is why I'm sitting here doing this useless worrying. No, it is not my fault. The best teachers are wonderful, but these tight shoulders are not personal failings."). The level of self-composure produced by such inward monitoring and nonjudgmental naming, although certainly not very durable in my case, seemed to reduce the likelihood that I would contribute (as actively as I might have) to things falling apart in an upcoming series of transactions.

Like all teachers, perhaps, I learned not only to identify where the holding and stiffness was located in my body, but also to relax (or at least soften around) the tense areas to some degree. Even if only for a couple moments between classes, I could help ease the grip of whatever it was that had me— and transform my emotional and cognitive states for the better—with a deep breath, closed eyes, and shoulder roll. I did *not* do this systemically. But occasionally calming my body as a means of stilling my mind and releasing a bit of accumulated stress did "bring home" for me that examining the effects of thrusting my entire being into stressful webs of relationships was only part of what it took for me to "do" carnal sociology.[22] Another part, which tends to receive less attention, is bringing careful discernment and genuine curiosity to how everyday transactions manifest as *bodily formations* as well as how one can find release from field-related somatic states. In other words, investigating carefully both the rawness and tautness of stockpiling stress—and the achievement of even temporary liberation—was, I found, one of the most tangible ways to "hear" and deal with what the two fields had to "say" even if the stored up "noise" could not be silenced completely.

For the social scientist trying "merely" to interpret the world, perhaps the take away is this: Examining how stress ebbed and flowed through my body helped me sense, at the most fundamental and easily overlooked level, why ordinarily distressed students (and teachers) who "knew better" nevertheless got wrapped up in negative reactions. For those more interested in bringing ameliorative processes to life, perhaps the take away is that attending vigilantly and regularly to (especially calming) bodily transformations can—as Simi put it while reflecting on his own fasting regimes—help more- and less-disadvantaged teens experience far greater degrees of "structure" and levels of "control over" themselves. Of course in terms of alleviating stress, engraining useful insights, and avoiding the perpetuation of detrimental responses, my observations allow nothing more than speculation as to how much students (and teachers) in such nonselective schools might benefit from engaging systemically in such body-based (collective) learning practices (cf. Mendelson et al. 2010; Lantieri 2008). But the methods I found myself using helped me get in touch with the possibility that the routine calming and serious monitoring of lived bodies may be a promising way to ensure that "knowing better" will make more of a difference during the precarious situations that presently damage so many students' lives and destroy so many high-stress schools.

The implication is uncomplicated: especially if we continue funneling economically disadvantaged students in our most stigmatized and distressed schools then, alongside other types of interventions, we should at least try to find ways to regulate their mundane emotional metamorphoses based on the experience of having—and being—a safe and serene body.[23] Whether or not this takes on forms related specifically to the Mindfulness Based Stress Reduction program Kabat-Zinn (2011) somehow introduced into mainstream medical practice, my sense is that age and context-appropriate forms of mediation (Davidson and McEwen 2012; Davidson 2012; Flook et al 2010) and other body-based practices such as the Alexander Technique and Feldenkrais Method (Shusterman 2008, pp. 24–29) might serve as vitally important aspects of future pedagogic regimes in high-poverty schools.

Despite the fact that John Dewey called for basically the same thing repeatedly, this may sound odd for now. Yet historians may look back on this stage of mass compulsory public education and see our continual inability to help students bring their awareness inward to their (safe and calm) bodies as the real anomaly. Be this the case or not, immersion in the two physically intimidating socio-emotional cauldrons certainly gave me a felt sense of why there will be precious little reflection on the mixes of socialized instincts, unregulated dynamics, and worldviews contributing to self-destructive in-school responses unless, in the future, the poor are effectively wrapped (as Simi was outside school) in stabilizing relationships and self-discipline engendering micro-level transactions. Phrases like "time for contemplation" and "consciousness raising" will continue to be platitudes accompanying vacuous moralism and pseudo-interventions based on discursive thinking as long as the necessary micro-social and emotional-bodily preconditions continue to go unmet.

In closing, I hope this note on data and shifting ideas has illustrated why the knowledge generated through direct observation may be our best hope for turning misguided talk about (racialized) ideological resistance into both deeper understandings and compassionate efforts at (socio-economic) desegregation and the regulation of everyday life in our most-troubled schools. It is the tension that comes with a felt sense of what it feels like to be "caught up" in our worst schools that can at once unshackle us from the habitual ways of thinking that have for decades contributed to the current mess and ground ameliorative efforts in the years ahead. In terms of both future research and reform efforts, then, what I trust most is what I learned bodily: the transformative power of ethnographic practice.

NOTES

PREFACE

1. Text printed on the back of T-shirt sported by a Johnson High student strolling through one of his school's long hallways.

2. Antonio, a soft-spoken and mild-mannered seventeen year old, on a key expression used by (usually male) members of the Delta School's dominant peer groups. Originally: *"Ik kom hard, ja, dat is wat ze zeggen."*

3. Here and elsewhere, for reasons discussed below, I use racial categories as member's terms rather than as analytic ones—i.e., as emic rather than etic concepts.

4. Ethnographic texts are full of rich discussions about insider and outsider status (cf. Desmond 2007, 283–307). For now I will add only this: I was an insider in the sense that I worked first and foremost as a teacher. One might however consider me only a quasi-native for at least two reasons. First, unlike the other teachers, I also operated as a researcher. I hung around and built relationships where others did not. Second, I sensed that I would eventually become an academic. I could therefore be open about my mishaps in and out of classrooms in part because I never saw myself as what some colleagues called a "lifer."

5. I experimented with both types of annual cycles, teaching at a high-poverty high school in downtown Brooklyn during the summer of 1997.

6. As I have done here, throughout the rest of the book the Dutch version of the term in question will be italicized (and the English version will appear in brackets).

7. What are known in the United States as "high schools" do not exist in the Netherlands. The institutions examined here were secondary schools. I occasionally refer to both Johnson and Delta as "high schools" for stylistic reasons.

8. The next chapter goes into detail on these and related issues such as crime rates and percentages of single-parent families.

9. Cf. Gaston Alonso et al.'s *Our Schools Suck: Students Talk Back to a Segregated Nation on the Failure in Urban Education Demonstrates this Point with Regard to High-Poverty Schools across the United States* (2009).

10. For these reasons—and without in any way denying the need to carefully scrutinize the broad spectrum of ways in which advanced marginality has over the course of many centuries come to be organized on opposite sides of the Atlantic Ocean—I maintain that Johnson High and the Delta School can be described as failing "ghetto"

schools. In the specific case of this concept as well as more generally, I will use double (scare) quotes throughout the book while making use of native terms.

11. On collective charisma and group disgrace, see Elias and Scotson (1964) and Elias in Goudsblom and Mennell (1998, 104–12).

12. Here it might be useful to add a few words about Dewey's proto-sociological imagination and to anticipate where it might lead us in terms of contemporary sociological research: the "social forces and relationships that situate human behavior and consciousness are comprehensible in terms of what John Dewey call[ed] the "qualitative immediacy" or non-thematized "sense" of the social world" (Ostrow 1990, 1). It is to this immediately situated and corporeally lived-through sense or feel for the game—to use Bourdieu's (1990) preferred terms for what he also called the at once embedded and embodied logic of practice—that I want to return as often as possible. On the striking affinities between Bourdieu and Dewey see Emirbayer and Schneiderhan (2013, 131–57) as well as Bourdieu and Wacquant (1992, 84, 122).

13. Along with the names of the two schools, the names of all the people in them have been altered.

14. Roxanne on the meaning of a prominent social category used to distinguish high-ranking, high-energy individuals and groups.

15. We set up an after-school video club that operated, informally, as an ongoing discussion group. In addition to granting her access to the school, this got the kids, teachers, and security guards used to seeing me accompanied by a young women walking around with a rather large camera and bag full of audio equipment. Being interviewed on camera remained anything but a naturally occurring event. Perhaps it is fair to say, however, that this filmmaker and I made serious efforts to reduce the discomfort our interviewees/discussion group participants felt. We stressed that they could always refuse to answer specific questions and that they were free to stop the interview (or their participation) at any time.

16. Similarly, in a videotaped session in Johnson High one of the students in the video club declared that, "When I first saw you, I thought you was white." She had changed her opinion, I would suggest, in part because of my somewhat Mediterranean looks and in part because of the bodily hexis that one "naturally" acquires as a "baller" in New York City who, for example, ends up attending a basketball factory disguised as a Catholic high school in the South Bronx. While in New York I was more than once asked if one of my parents came from Puerto Rico. Perhaps more because of phenotype than anything else, I was often asked in the Netherlands if I had Arab roots—especially by young people whose parents came from places like Turkey or Morocco.

17. Around thirty years of age, a few years older than I was at the time, this colleague with a slight Jamaican-British accent and a bachelor apartment in an impoverished section of central Harlem set up and witnessed my first encounter with Roxanne and one of her friends—a girl he also suggested for an interview. While my veteran colleague only asked a few questions, his solemn body language and tone of voice indicated that he was taking the encounter seriously.

18. We started with Roxanne's girlfriend, also a student at Johnson, who seemed to ease quickly from obvious discomfort into a much more confident and informal way of speaking and gesturing. She appeared to enjoy telling her story. Seemingly in the flow, at a certain point, Roxanne's girlfriend discussed how many of the boys she knew bragged about "catching bodies" (stabbing other boys). Looking on silently, Roxanne observed the first interview. Then it was her turn.

19. Of course, this non-thematization might be explained in part by the fact that she never saw white adolescents in or anywhere near her school (i.e., the segregation was so complete that it became invisible). One might additionally propose that Roxanne avoided race because she categorized two of the adults in the room as white. But, as I later confirmed, Roxanne did not seem to have race on her mind during her conversations with the nominally black teacher who set up the interview either. Whether or not unspoken sensitivities related to centuries of racial domination (subconsciously) filtered and fueled her comments remains unclear.

20. Katz (1999, 142).

21. Pollner and Emerson (2001, 130) make use of this famous quote to emphasize a key, deep-down affinity between ethnomethodology and ethnography. The punch line itself, so memorable in part because it speaks to the discomforting bodily experiences of the authentic fieldworker in action, comes from Robert Park (as recalled by Howard Becker and quoted originally in McKinney [1966, 71]).

22. That is, for many researchers in the two national contexts, including members of the gender and racial/ethno-national "groups" most at risk in high-poverty high schools. Rather than falling into this groove of non-reflexive essentialism (or what Brubaker calls "engrained groupism"), and aiming for a genuinely relational and processual approach (cf. Paulle, Van Heerikhuizen, and Emirbayer 2012), I treat terms like "black" and "Antillean" as native categories reflecting at once broader cultural understandings and how certain students would identify themselves if they were asked to do so along racial or ethno-national lines. Such categories, approached here as continuously shifting meaning-making constructions, say nothing about the salience of various types of (self- or other-) ascribed identifications emerging and declining in situ. Nor does treating, for example, African American or Afro-Antillean-Dutch students as category members say anything about the continual rise and fall of (peer) groups understood as "mutually interacting, mutually recognizing collectivit[ies] with a sense of solidarity . . . and capacity for concerted action" (Brubaker 2006, 8). Crucially then, to note that blacks on average differed from members of other racialized or ethno-nationalized folk categories (e.g., Puerto Ricans, Hindustanis) in terms of overrepresentation among the most aggressive and disruptive students is not to say anything about my own analytic categories, a rigorous analysis of group-forming processes, or an ethno-sociological analysis of coping processes more generally.

23. Here I make use of Garfinkel's (1967, 11) famous definition of ethnomethodology.

24. For well over a decade now it has been widely understood that everyday emotional environments and experiences in (high) schools are sculpting (and pruning) neurological pathways in students' (adolescent) brains. As Brazelton and Greenspan (2000) showed, immersing children and adolescents in stable and supportive social environments will tend to restructure their brain circuitry in beneficial ways. Exposing them to chronically stressful environments during such sensitive developmental periods will tend to have negative—and potentially extremely durable—impacts on the executive functioning skills that are implicated in emotional self-control and the use of foresight. Furthermore, as the two researchers (2000, 1–4) demonstrate, "We have come to understand that emotional interactions are the foundation not only of cognition but of most of a child's intellectual abilities, including his creativity and abstract thinking skills. . . . Emotions are actually the internal architects, conductors, organizers of our minds. They tell us how and what to think, what to say and when to say it, and what to do. We 'know' things through our emotional interactions and then apply that knowledge to the cognitive world." For an accessible overview from a

long-time leader in the field of stress research, see McEwen (2002). For a more recent review of research on of how social stress negatively impacts neuroplasticity as well as how well-being can be promoted, see Davidson and McEwen (2012).

25. Through the effects of particular hormones, as Epel et al. (2004) show, sustained exposure to high levels of stress accelerates the shortening of telomeres (the protective caps at the end of chromosomes). This in turn speeds up aging and the onset of health-related problems. Related findings suggest that chronic exposure to stress early in life causes inflammation in adults (Danese et al. 2007).

26. Here I borrow from the title of the "National Geographic" documentary featuring Stanford University's Robert Sapolsky titled *Stress: Portrait of a Killer* (2008). For excerpts, see http://killerstress.stanford.edu/ (accessed August 28, 2012).

27. In a report entitled "The Effects of Childhood Stress on Health Across the Lifespan" (*National Center for Injury Prevention and Control and the Centers for Disease Control and Prevention 2008*, 3–4), stress is defined as "internal or external influences that disrupt an individual's normal state of well-being. These influences are capable of affecting health by causing emotional distress and leading to a variety of physiological changes. These changes include increased heart rate, elevated blood pressure, and a dramatic rise in hormone levels." The authors make a clear distinction between "positive" and "tolerable" stress (which can keep kids sharp or help them learn valuable life skills) on one hand, and, on the other, "toxic stress"—which they see as a massive threat to (networks of) especially at-risk individuals as well as to public health.

28. In arguing that the variability of distressing processes can be adequately detailed only through real fieldwork and ethnographic portrayals, I do not mean to belittle the outstanding work being done at the crossroads of urban sociology and public health (e.g., Massey 2004) that does not always try to unpack "stressors."

29. With regard to the statistics, furthermore, we often see quite different types of trajectories homogenized into seemingly standardized outcomes (e.g., total number of "dropouts" or "high achievers"). All of those associated with this or that outcome are then subdivided into preexisting categories (or worse, into clearly bounded "groups") such as "black" or "white." While one might argue that such practices are necessary if we are to monitor the "black-white achievement gap," this tells us next to nothing about how previous experiences, in-school transactions, and orientations toward the future actually produced what might be seen as very different types of outcomes (e.g., the "dropout" who had to find a job to feed a child vs. the teen who was afraid to go to school vs. the one who does not buy into the very idea of pursuing a diploma) as well as how and when (non-) racialized categories impact students' lives.

30. The heart of the problem is, in the explanation of social behavior, privileging preestablished and stable categorical attributes of subjects (assumed to have and be guided by their own internal mental deliberations) over the ongoing bundles of social relations that penetrate (and to some degree reshape) exposed beings. Moving on, it might therefore be useful to keep in mind Emirbayer and Goodwin's (1994, 1414) "anticategorical imperative"—the imperative which opposes explanations of actual behavior exclusively or even primarily in terms "categorical attributes of actors, whether individual or collective."

31. I am paraphrasing a line from Goffman (1967, 3) to which we will return in the coming chapters.

32. Orwell (1946), "Politics and the English Language."

33. Years before Bourdieu and Passeron ([1964] 1979) started developing ideas with regard to how schools stealthy function to reproduce distributions of economic and especially cultural capital in France, Becker (1952a, 456) was documenting how teachers' "differential reaction[s] to various class groups obviously operate[d] to further perpetuate those class-cultural characteristics to which they object[ed] in the first place."

34. As Shonkoff and Garner (2012, 232) argue at the outset of their aptly entitled, "The Lifelong Effects of Early Childhood Adversity and Toxic Stress," what is required is ultimately a "multidisciplinary . . . ecobiodevelopmental framework that illustrates how early experiences and environmental influences can leave a lasting signature on the genetic predispositions that affect emerging brain architecture and long-term health" as well as, of course, on social and emotional behavior influencing things like educational outcomes in the nearer term. As they (2012, 243) conclude, "Toxic stress can lead to potentially permanent changes in learning (linguistic, cognitive, and social-emotional skills), behavior (adaptive versus maladaptive responses to future adversity), and physiology (a hyper-responsive or chronically activated stress response) and can cause physiologic disruptions that result in higher levels of stress-related chronic diseases and increase the prevalence of unhealthy lifestyles that lead to widening health disparities."

CHAPTER ONE

1. Goffman (1989, 125), unaware of a recording device and speaking with several associates about the participant-observation-based methods that, he stressed, might be suitable for certain kinds of investigations.

2. Later, I would reflect on yet another aspect of my introduction to life in high-poverty classrooms. I would wonder about the value of statistical accounts neatly summarizing "hours of instruction" in various subjects per year. If studies on IQs (or academic capabilities) of specific adolescents assume anything like equal amounts of time on task in school before the taking of tests, how valid are these decontextualized investigations? And why call institutions "schools" if there is almost no learning related to the formal curricula taking place in classrooms?

3. Seemingly impressed with my educational trajectory, he noted that he too had read a bit of Durkheim in his day. He smiled when he mentioned that he was familiar with the term "anomie." I was soon to find out how ironic this statement was.

4. One of these teachers later confided in me that he was, as he said, "totally burnt" and that he had opted, therefore, to have a minor surgery performed on his foot. The surgery certainly could have waited until the summer vacation. He could not. I took over several of his, as he called them, "monster classes."

5. A brief sampling of statistics can offer an indication of just how devastated the residential area around Johnson High was by the time I arrived. According to the 2000 census, more than thirty percent of the total Bronx population lived below the official poverty line and over forty percent of the children growing up in the Bronx lived in families that were officially impoverished. Most of the teens attending Johnson High lived in Congressional District 16. District 16 is altogether within the borders of Bronx County, and it covers the greater part of what is today defined as the South Bronx (the border of which has crept northward over the last few decades, all the way to the Cross Bronx Expressway). According to the 2000 census, Congressional District 16 had the single highest official poverty rate in the United States: This congressional district, which had the lowest median household income in the U.S., was

also the only district on record with more than half its children living in households
below the poverty line. For a treatment of this "extreme" case of neighborhood decline, see Glazer (1987). Those specifically interested in how violence impacts the
lives of teens growing up in the South Bronx might find Freudenberg et al. (2000)
especially useful.

6. Many people residing in the Bronx seem not to feel comfortable with such standardized categories. In 2000, for the first time, people filling in the U.S. census were
offered the chance to reject such attempts at racial pigeonholing. No matter how
they identify themselves (in various situations) in everyday life, over thirty percent
of Bronx residents jumped at this opportunity to make clear that they were not clear
about how they fit into the racial typology used on census forms.

7. In a study investigating when and how such (analytic) categories become real for
young people and what the effects of this are in practice, Mary Waters (2001) argues
that it has become increasingly difficult for people grouped as "black," including
"second generation" immigrants form the Caribbean and West Africa, to maintain
multicultural identities.

8. Like Thorne (1999), who rigorously examined gender dynamics in educational settings, I rely heavily on the metaphor of "play" to underscore the intrinsically relational and processual ways in which students collaboratively "did" gender. As
Thorne (1999, 5) put it, "Gender is not something one passively 'is' or 'has'; . . . we
'do gender.'"

9. As will become clear below, Norbert Elias (e.g., [1970] 1978) frequently used this
term in making his push for genuinely relational approaches to figurational dynamics and (collective) habitus forming processes.

10. Noting that "few if any scholars would argue that ethnic groups or races or nations are
fixed or given [and that] virtually everyone agrees that they are historically emergent
and in some respects mutable," in his attack on "groupism" Brubaker (2009, 28–29,
italics in original) calls for a "shift from attempts to specify what an ethnic or racial
group or nation is to attempts to specify how ethnicity, race, and nation work."

11. Incoming students were assigned to Johnson High School by the "DOE" (Department of Education). Attendance, test scores, and the interventions of guidance counselors at junior high schools ("feeders") all played a role. But for the vast majority of
students that did not test into more selective (magnet) schools, the final assignment
decision was influenced most basically by residence (and accompanying educational
"zone") and the level of involvement of parents and guardians who often lacked the
cultural capital (e.g., linguistic skills, informational resources, know-how) and social
capital to apply the right kinds of pressure.

12. Teachers and administrators at Johnson knew that the poorest of the poor often
had parents or guardians so destabilized, mobile, ashamed, preliterate, or immersed
in the shadowy realms of the local economy, and therefore distrustful, that it was
nearly impossible to get them to fill in "FRL" forms—i.e., the applications for Free
or Reduced price Lunch that were used to gauge the percentage of students living in poverty. After weeks of prodding we usually gave up on this administrative
procedure.

13. Around one-fifth of the students who entered Johnson during my tenure there could
be expected to graduate on time, and roughly forty percent that could be expected to
graduate from high school, ever. Only a thin slice of those receiving diplomas from
Johnson High were actually "college ready" in terms of basic academic skills. With
regard to this last issue, at the city and national level alike, it seems that very little has

changed since I worked at Johnson High. Responding to a more recent finding that, "In New York City, roughly seventy-five percent of public high school students who enroll in community colleges need to take remedial math or English courses before they can begin college-level work," David M. Steiner, the education commissioner for the state of New York, stressed that such high percentages of students graduating but not being college ready constituted a "national crisis" ("Most New York Students Are Not College-Ready" by Sharon Otterman, *New York Times*, February 7, 2011).

14. The same holds, by the way, for the high-poverty high school in Brooklyn where I sweated through one session of summer school.

15. There is a huge literature on hidden curricula, often based on class domination as well as institutionalized racism, that I will not engage here other than to note that Apple (1990) is a good place to start.

16. Hundreds of "students" missed most or all of their classes; many showed up less than once a week even for the "official class" during which attendance for the day was taken. Teachers hated this "period" because it was often very crowded and extremely boisterous. On top of this there was the absurdity of "announcements" made on the perpetually half-broken public-address system. The official class was, in short, yet another insult to the teachers and the kids that was needed for the cover up. For an article that sheds light on these types of practice, see "Coping: The Cards that Put Students in their Place," *New York Times*, September 20, 2003.

17. With regard to the "escape from the Bijlmer" theme, whether one is inclined to look through the prism of ethnicity or not, there clearly was a lot from which one might have wanted to get away. Research indicates that by the time I began doing fieldwork in the Netherlands, the Bijlmer had become the most isolated and dangerous section of Amsterdam. The 1990s "new economy" growth and the erection of countless new office buildings, stores, and a huge stadium had generated what the long-term inhabitants often call the "new Bijlmer." Instead of being integrated through urban renewal efforts, however, the eighty-five-thousand-strong neighborhood had developed, in American terminology, a "right" and "wrong side of the tracks." When I began conducting research in the Bijlmer only twenty percent of the employees working in the district of Southeast Amsterdam also lived there. A mere seven and a half percent of the labor force in this sixty-three-percent "minority" section of Amsterdam was made up of members of "ethnic minority groups" (Hommes et al., 1994; Choenni 1997). Not surprisingly, then, toward the end of the previous century, the overall rate of unemployment in the Bijlmer (thirty-eight percent) remained far higher than the citywide rate (twenty-six percent according to Engbersen et al., 1999, 78). Within the unemployed ranks of Bijlmer inhabitants—in addition to unknown amounts of undocumented migrants—immigrants "with papers" from Suriname, the Dutch Antilles, and Ghana were vastly overrepresented (Hommes et al. 1994). De Haan (1993) has illustrated that more robberies took place per capita in the Bijlmer than in any other section in the city. This researcher documented that among the 960 people accused of robbery, nearly twenty-five-percent were staying illegally in the Netherlands, and ninety-percent of the robberies were motivated by the need "to make ends meet." Businesses, such as cable companies, refrain from performing services in the worst subsections of the Bijlmer because, they argue, their employees' safety cannot be insured there.

18. The foundation known as TopSport Amsterdam was based on the idea that being involved in sporting clubs kept disadvantaged urban teens off the streets and out of trouble.

19. The reasons program managers selected a notoriously troubled school in this part of the city are obvious. As ethno-racially and socioeconomically segregated as the old Bijlmer was, its schools were more so. According to one report (Dienst Onderzoek en Statestiek, 2003) looking at data collected during my time in the field, the Bijlmer was the only neighborhood in the city with primary schools boasting less than ten percent native Dutch students. According to Choenni's (1997) analysis of tests taken at the end of primary school (i.e., the CITO test taken by children at eleven-to-twelve years of age)—on average children coming out of primary schools in the Bijlmer move on to secondary schools roughly three years behind grade level in language and mathematics skills. This is comparable to the achievement levels of children of the same age in many American inner cities. Summing up her personal experiences of living in the high-rise section of Southeast Amsterdam, Aspha Bijnaar, a Dutch researcher with roots in Suriname, confirms that the Bijlmer is a neighborhood that has declined dramatically over the past decades despite the renewal programs. By the time I arrived it had reached the point, she argued, that the Bijlmer had largely become a home base for "blacks with no chance of succeeding" ("*kansloze zwarten*"), including asylum seekers, illegal immigrants, drug addicts, and criminals. In the high-rise flats, she added (Bijnaar 2002, 282), there are essentially no middle-class people to be found.

20. When he asked me to teach English I shared with my future boss that, in addition to having no certification in any country, I had no idea how to teach English grammar. This seemed to be of no concern. He said, using a common Dutch expression, that he wanted me to "help him out of a fire." Also, perhaps just playing nice, this school manager told me my Dutch was better than that of some other teachers who had grown up in other countries. As had happened three years earlier in New York, the principal made it clear that either I would teach, or scores of kids would simply have no class.

21. Generally speaking, students ended up enrolling in the Delta School after either not doing well on exit exams or after being informed that they "did not have to take" these exit tests at the end of primary school. When I questioned them about advising students not to take exit exams, administrators of the local primary schools said they did not want to further stigmatize children that they knew would be bound for the lowest vocational tracks. While this may have been their main motivation, system wide it was well understood that such administrators did not want their school's averages on the standardized tests to be pulled down because they allowed "too many" poor students to take the exit exams. In many cases after receiving word that they would not be able to secure a seat in less stigmatized schools (further away), parents and students "choose" for Delta.

22. For quantitative indications on the cognitive and academic effects of evictions and homelessness in New York City, see Rubin et al. (1996). For grounded insights into the eviction process and how it impacts school-age children, see Desmond (2012a, 2012b).

23. Barack Obama's biggest applause line during the keynote address to the 2004 Democratic National Convention that launched him into the national spotlight.

24. As Aronowitz (Willis 1981, xiii) wrote in the introduction to the version reprinted for the US market, "This is the enduring contribution of *Learning to Labor*: it helps us to understand that people cannot be filled with ideology as a container is filled with water."

25. This should not suggest at all that the contributions of these two "founding fathers" of the oppositional culture approach have been deployed separately. Gibson (2000, 96, italics added), for example, summed up a core aspect of her ethnographic analysis of a school in the Caribbean in the following way: "The Crucian boys' resistance to schooling was similar to that described in the literature on involuntary minority youth in the United States and working class white youth in Britain, males in particular (Ogbu 1991, Willis 1977). . . . The Down Islander boys were more willing to accommodate themselves to school routines than Crucian boys because they believed they needed school credentials to be competitive on the job market."

26. Expanding on her pioneering article with Ogbu, Fordham (1996, 39, emphasis added) argued again for the centrality of ideologies and, in the case of involuntary racial minorities, the "willful rejection of whatever will validate the negative claims of the larger society." In a more recent supplement to the ongoing acting-white story, Fordham (2008, 230) offers fresh evidence supporting the acting-white thesis, laments what she sees as frequent misinterpretations of her notion, and tries to evade the "powerful feuding male-dominated camps" that continuously debate it.

27. For a more recent statement of the main ideas, see Ogbu's (2004) "Collective Identity and the Burden of 'Acting White': Black History, Community, and Education" or, for a fair yet even more concise treatment, see Desmond and Emirbayer (2009, 332–35).

28. His direct observations of an elite school did, however, suggest the presence of school-based social forces pushing all teens in the Netherlands to adopt anti-intellectual stances or be burdened by working hard and "acting wise" (cf. Coleman 1961).

29. Similarly, Moll (2004, 127) emphasizes that "in one context students may be resisting oppression while in another they may feel empowered by conforming to cultural norms."

30. Generally speaking, and like other leaders in the field such as Doug Massey (cf. Massey and Denton 1993), Wilson focuses first and foremost on "structural" or socioeconomic shifts such as the move into the post-Fordist era rather than, mainly, on "cultural" developments. Indeed Wilson (1996, 179) seemed to argue against culture-based arguments when he noted, with verve, that despite what is commonly assumed to be the case, residents of American inner cities tend to hold quite conventional (e.g., pro-school) values and beliefs. On the other hand, Wilson may have made his own position unclear when he remarked on how "the decision to act in ghetto-related ways, although not necessarily reflecting values, can nonetheless be said to be cultural" (Wilson 1996, 70).

31. For Ogbu, as I indicated above, code-switching dated back to the ways in which enslaved Africans navigated between safe and unsafe settings in highly conscious ways. The implication for contemporary educational settings is that any involuntary minority student might choose to "act white" or, for longer or shorter periods of time, to act in ways that negate "white culture" and school achievement.

32. Anderson makes the case that, for reasons often related to threats of physical violence, the majority of "decent" (young) adults and teenagers switch to the "street" code when (they think) specific situations demand such responses. In a fashion reminiscent of his (1978) now classic study based on Chicago's South Side, Anderson also argues that even thoroughly "street" types are capable of adopting the "decent" code when, for example, they find themselves interacting symbolically with (and trying to manage the impressions of) decent types.

33. In his segregated inner-city schools, Anderson (1999, 93) surmised, "decent kids learn to code switch, while street kids become more singularly committed to the street." Noting that, "The decent kids mimic the street ones," Anderson (1999, 95) added that "Some teachers are unable to differentiate between the two groups." An entire subsection (98–106) of the portion of the book dealing most directly with schools carries the heading "The Dilemma of the Decent Kid."

34. In a volume he edited including contributions from Wilson, Douglas Massey, and many others, Anderson (2008) expands on this argument.

35. The people I studied used terms like "good" instead of "decent."

36. As Zhou and Bankston (1998, 207) observe, "Both parents and children are constantly observed as under a 'Vietnamese Microscope.' If a child flunks or drops out of school, or if a boy falls into a gang, or if a girl becomes pregnant without getting married, he or she brings shame not only on himself or herself but also on the whole family."

37. For an interesting extension of this approach into the Netherlands, see Crul (2000). Crul's analysis does not rely on the disruptive power of "native" subgroups to explain "second-generation decline." It does however highlight the positive effects that family networks associated with stigmatized ethnic communities can have on the educational outcomes of second-generation immigrant students.

38. Devine (1996, 19–45) makes a point of using scare quotes around the word schools when discussing inner-city institutions as distraught as those in which he directed conflict resolution programs.

39. Johnson worked as a classroom teacher in and just outside Liverpool, West Yorkshire, and London. Specializing in the education of students with "behavior difficulties" allowed Johnson (1999, 1) to visit many other schools and talk with teachers around the United Kingdom.

40. As Johnson put it, "it is not so much that pupils disobey their teachers; it is more that they seem oblivious to instructions" (Johnson 1999, 48). The most disruptive pupils were above all volatile and incoherently oriented toward themselves (e.g., friendly banter quickly morphed into screamed threats).

41. Similarly, with regard to the effectiveness of teachers, the long-term insider did not see reason to even consider the possibility that race, ethnicity, or consciously held beliefs might be decisive in terms of effectiveness. As his (1999, 69–87) meticulous detailing of classroom encounters indicate, what mattered was the "breakdown of discipline," high levels of "aggression [. . .] in the air," and teachers' limited stocks of "emotional capital" (i.e., the ability to deal with draining situations and exhausting workloads) (Johnson 1999, 7, 33, 85).

42. As Devine (1996, 107) put it: "My focus on recent immigrants . . . reveals what they have in common with African American students rather than what sets them apart, as the work of Ogbu (1978) tends to do. Educators tend to think of recent immigrants as cooperative, eager, and attractive until they become "Americanized," a code word that further stigmatizes American-born youth-of-color who may be more inured to looser school practices than are their Caribbean fellow students. African American youth also find these practices [e.g., violent and otherwise disruptive behavior] disconcerting once these issues have been consciously raised and discussed with them."

43. Deploying a key metaphor, Devine (1996, 103–130) wrote of the "marshmallow effect"—anywhere students might try to push, the school gave in and there was

nothing to push against. Time and again he described how physically intimidated teachers systemically averted their gaze, especially outside classrooms, and certainly attempted no "hands-on" regulation of anyone, anywhere.

44. Devine (1996, 124, 44).
45. That is, places where "a lot of people know people," as one Caribbean teacher put it, rather than Brooklyn where, "the minute [kids] walk outta their apartment buildings, nobody knows them" (Devine 1996, 113).
46. Especially here, therefore, it might be useful to let Devine (1996, 114) speak for himself: "If, for example, in Beta School, Jamaican youth are perceived to be ruthless, it follows that nobody will bother you if you become a Jamaican; the obvious choice for a Haitian youth is to incorporate a Jamaican identity, even though the school has an active Haitian Club with dynamic Haitian teachers who are attempting to foster pride in Haitian culture. The two particular ethnic groups employed here could just as easily be reversed or other groups (immigrant or nonimmigrant) substituted, depending on the neighborhood or the school in question. Thus, the agency of violence, uninhibited at the school or at any of the sites these students might encounter outside of the school, is revealed not as the product of a particular ethnicity but as constructive of ethnicity itself."
47. Devine (1996, 110–114) also demonstrated that fear and violence were central to the "Americanization" of Caribbean students.
48. My use of John Dewey's criticisms of how intellectuals adopt (or impute) the perspectives of "spectators" as well as his notion of fully immersed humans beings as "body-mind" complexes is set up in the following pages and discussed more concretely in Chapter 5.
49. As the theorist par excellence of the micro-level interaction order himself declared in his presidential address to the American Sociological Association, "those . . . who focus on face-to-face" encounters "characteristically neglect" the "dependency of interactional activity on matters outside the interaction" (Goffman 1983, 12).
50. Moving into the environments examined here, the implication is that we need to begin with micro-foundations while grasping Johnson High School and the Delta School as referential totalities or quasi-autonomous "fields of relational dynamics" (Elias [1939] 1994, 389).
51. And truly interdependent these three main concepts are. As Bourdieu put it, "[H]abitus, field, and capital can be defined, but only within the theoretical system they constitute, not in isolation" (Bourdieu and Wacquant, 1992, 96).
52. For a discussion of both the uncanny similarities and provocative dissimilarities in the conceptual toolkits developed by these two researchers, see Paulle, Van Heerikhuizen, and Emirbayer (2012).
53. This resulted in potent tendencies and inclinations, not iron laws. As we shall see, students with similar types of habitus could think, feel, and respond in radically different ways when confronted with different types of situational dynamics.
54. In Bourdieu's (1977, 87, quoted in Dreyfus 1991, 17, emphasis in original) at once structuralist and constructivist language, I approach each educational environment as a "whole . . . symbolically structured environment . . . exert[ing] an anonymous, pervasive pedagogic action. . . . [I will assume that the] essential part of the modus operandi which defines practical mastery [in each setting] is transmitted in practice . . . without attaining the level of discourse. The child imitates not 'models' but other people's actions. Body hexis speaks directly to the motor function, in the form of a

pattern of postures that is both individual and systemic, because linked to a whole system of techniques [i.e., skills] involving the body and tools, and charged with a host of social meanings and values."

55. Anyone who doubts the compatibility of thinkers such as Katz on one hand and Bourdieu on the other might want to take another look at any number of passages from Bourdieu (e.g., 2000, 144) that reveal his indebtedness to Merleau-Ponty: "This practical, nonthetic intentionality, which has nothing in common with a cogito consciously oriented towards a cogitatum, is rooted in a posture, a way of bearing, the body (a hexis), a durable way of being of the durably modified body which is engendered and perpetuated, while constantly changing (within limits), in a twofold relationship, structured and structuring, to the environment. Habitus constructs the world by a certain way of orienting itself toward it, of bringing to bear on it an attention which, like that of a jumper preparing to jump, is an active, constructive bodily tension towards imminent forthcoming."

56. See Katz and Csordas (2003) for a detailed analysis of the influence of Merleau-Ponty and a host of others on the work of ethnographers working out of sociology and anthropology departments.

57. In part because of this book's title, Seductions of Crime seems destined to remain more of a classic of criminology than a resource for researchers on failing schools. It nonetheless offers a potential wake up call to those researching schools crippled by disruptive and aggressive behavior who rush to explanations based on background factors (associated with distinct racial or socioeconomic "groups") and all types of decontextualized attributions before adequately examining what goes on where threats and violence are most immediately located (cf. Paulle 2007).

58. Sticking with Katz's example, many of us have found ourselves speeding up—i.e., taking utterly illogical risks (with children in the backseats)—so we can signal "up yours" to the person who "amputated" us even after making explicit, during calmer moments, that such reactions are absurd, irresponsible, and perhaps even shocking. No race-related, street, or highway oppositional ideologies were required, as many will be able to recall, just the urge to restore a lived (moral) order after having been "touched" by road rage.

59. Informed by Heidegger's critique of traditional ontology as well as his thinking about more and less primordial levels of "understanding"—and especially by Merleau-Ponty's notion of the situationally embedded and literally embodied sources of perception and "(motor) intentionality"—Katz (1999, 142–43) notes that although we might "talk about how [drivers] 'construct' an understanding . . . [f]or all but novice drivers, that understanding is not sensed as constructed; it is already naturally there."

60. Some social scientists might suggest that this mix of concepts and approaches is not sufficiently compatible. While the empirical chapters speak to the relevance of this claim, I want to stress that my main concern is not with "compatibility" in terms of any ultimate epistemological positions. As first and foremost a fieldworker, I am interested in ways of thinking and speaking that can help us better understand—and perhaps even deal more intelligently with—what is going on in our worst schools.

61. Cicourel (1964, 37).

62. To take Chambliss's (1989) masterfully documented example, there is a fundamental difference between superficially getting to know the world of competitive swimming and literally immersing oneself in the currents of everyday life in such a world

long enough to grasp how certain seemingly mundane "little" things can make huge differences.

63. And unlike contemporary researchers doing "multi-sited" ethnographies based on tracing specific objects (or people), I did not "follow the thing" (cf. Cook and Harrison 2007).

64. This meant "everything" from teaching first-period classes, in which it was nearly impossible to keep the few students who showed up awake, to traversing corridors and staircases where bodies were packed closely together.

65. The Appendix argues that the fact that I was often too engaged in the here and now to take fieldnotes or too demoralized to write-up after-the-fact reflections in no way challenges the scientific utility of research based on "dual roles."

66. This will become especially evident in Chapter 5, which is grounded in biographical case studies.

67. Afro-Surinamese-Dutch fifteen-year-old girl commenting on a quietly dressed and smallish boy walking with his head down and carrying an enormous book bag.

CHAPTER TWO

1. A boy in a crowded Johnson hallway using two or three of the most commonly heard phrases, and putting a strong emphasis on "We."

2. This is the main refrain in Black Moon's 1990s gangster hip-hop "anthem" entitled "I Got Cha Opin."

3. Cf. Dickar (2008) and Devine (1996)—two other researchers who, for years, actually functioned as professionals in deeply distressed big-city high schools.

4. Cf. Goffman (1967), Harrington and Fine (2006).

5. From "Real Niggaz" by Jay-Z.

6. In fact, Thomas knew me as the only adult working in the school who could occasionally "put it on" him (as one student said, taunting him in a crowded hallway after seeing me make a couple three-pointers with Thomas guarding me). We always guarded each other when we played and, although he tended to get the best of our match up, he clearly did not like it when I used what he called "old-man tricks" to temporarily outshine him.

7. Again, terms like "niggaz" and "cats" were used to refer to boys or men, not necessarily those associated with a specific racial or ethnic group. When Johnson High students thematized what we might call specific ethno-racial differences, they often spoke of "black niggaz" as opposed to, for example, "Spanish niggaz," "Jamaican niggaz," "Haitian niggaz," or "Dominican niggaz." As such, the use of the terms expressing the most fundamental of symbolic binaries—"real niggaz" vs. "fake (ass) niggaz"—did not necessarily imply anything about race, ethnicity, or nationality. That this is evidence of inner-city culture rather than anything specific to Johnson High is illustrated in how hip-hop artists racially positioned as nonblack (e.g., certain rappers who perform Puerto Rican-ness) can be referred to, and can refer to themselves as, "real niggaz" that naturally detest "fake niggaz." To get a feeling for how this merged with pride of place in the Bronx, see the video for "Let the Games Begin" by Mack 10, featuring Big Punisher and Fat Joe.

8. Thomas was making reference to the "official class" that took place between second and third periods.

9. Another note on local jargon might be useful here. "Ghetto fabulous" was one of the many self-aggrandizing and often overlapping terms with which the typically more

dominant in both schools referred to themselves. As I write in English, I will rely mostly on the "gangsta rap" flavored terms that were used most frequently in the Bronx, but were also well-known and intermittently deployed in the Bijlmer. In addition to "(ghetto) fabulous," those associated with dominant peer groups were said to be: "wild," "true," "fly girls," "pretty boys," "(real) playaz," "cool," "thugs," "real niggaz," "thugettes," "gangsters," "(real) hustlers," and "criminals." The list went on and on, and it changed from year to year. Indeed from types of baggy jeans for boys and types of tight jeans for girls, from types of hairstyles to types of gold- or silver-teeth coverings, "everything" was in flux. And the flux always had to do with (even if it was not ultimately caused by) classification and recognition (i.e., symbolic) struggles and unfolding relationships between those judged to be more and less distinguished groups of students.

10. I started observing this episode while making my way back to the school's main entrance from the pizza parlor across the street. Reentering the school grounds and moving towards the students' entrance gave me a perspective that few teachers ever had and one that I did not have very often. Most teachers avoided leaving and reentering the school grounds during the day. And if they did, they tended to use the side exits reserved for adults so as to reduce contact with pupils. Because of my position in physical space and corresponding view of a grand if loosely organized face-to-face encounter, returning to the school I was able to see the order of things from one of the most revealing of student perspectives.

11. Perhaps because the blue sky and crisp air had lured more students into the great outdoors than was usually the case, the atypically large numbers of bodies huddled more or less closely together seemed to be generating a greater than usual amount of excitement. And seeing Thomas in surprisingly prominent position forced me to think about what I otherwise might have simply taken in stride.

12. On situated, ambiguous, and cunning (in-school) performances related to inner-city gang affiliations, see Garot's *Who You Claim* (2010).

13. Especially in the Bronx, and whether referencing specific hip-hop lyrics or not, the students often talked about getting (someone) "open" in ways that had nothing to do with Goffman's (1963) usage of the term "open persons." Goffman used this term to signify people who (in public spaces) are somehow more accessible to scrutiny of others because they are comparatively less capable of mobilizing or enforcing personal boundaries (e.g., very old or young people). Elias (1970, 119, 135) used this same exact term more intensively than Goffman, and in ways more clearly connected to one of this book's main points: There were no self-enclosed, self-acting essences making their ways through the two blighted educational universes. While eyes may have drifted to the "fabulous" much of the time (in public places), it was certainly not the case that they—or those typically situated toward the opposite end of one of the status hierarchies—were the only ones who were exposed. The chronic stress penetrated all the differently positioned constituents of the two settings.

14. Although not visibly constrained by the boys standing and sitting at the top of the steps, he communicated what Goffman called deference. On this crucial topic and in the context of patients not, for example, strapped down to beds in an asylum, Goffman (1967, 92) noted that the participant "must have freedom of bodily movement so that it will be possible for him to assume a stance that conveys appropriate respect for others and appropriate demeanor on his own part."

15. This distinction is central in one of the opening portraits in Chapter 5.

16. Very temporarily, I had once had Enrique in one of my classes. This "ghost student,"

in technical jargon, remained on my attendance sheets throughout an entire semester even though I never saw him in my classroom after the first week. He had made an impression on me in part because his eyes usually looked glazed, giving the impression that he was very high.

17. I had heard several accounts of (clusters of) students attacking one another in front of the school. Especially when there were no security guards, police, or deans present, "shit could just get set off," as the students often repeated. Through the window of the dean's office overlooking the still grand if somewhat dilapidated front entrance area, I had witnessed one of the many physical confrontations that emerged out of such rituals. A shiny beige SUV halted to a stop between the pizza shop and the gates in front of the stairs leading to the main entrance. A girl in sweatpants with huge gold-plated earrings hopped out of the backseat, jogged over toward an unsuspecting girl passing through the front gates, sucker punched her hard in the head, and then hurried back into the huge vehicle. The SUV then roared off before the offender's door fully closed.

18. In a chapter focusing on gender and ethnicity, Katz (1988, 238–39, 271) described "being bad" as "fundamentally" something at once related to highly visible transactions and embodiment, namely: "charting out big spaces in public interactions and claiming to be able to fill it."

19. Hairstyles might be said to illustrate this affinity between males and females presenting themselves as (particularly) "ghetto fabulous." Especially the girls who felt pressed to invest significant amounts of money and time to getting their hair "done" according to the latest trends spoke loudly and repeatedly of non-kinky locks such as those Enrique proudly displayed as "good hair," and of braids (combined with oversized baseball hats) as the next big thing.

20. As Michael Lambek (1995, 276) in Van de Port (2011, 79) put it, "We project our social categories onto nature and then use nature to justify our social categories."

21. So we might say that the "fly" girls' cultural (aesthetic, rhetorical) ways of doing "ghetto fabulous" was typically black. In this sense, in the language systemically deployed by Dickar (2008), this was yet another extra-classroom setting for students to embrace "black culture." Yet important as ideas about race were in terms of influencing students' practical senses of self, other, and the overall environment, we should not make the main principles of vision and division blurrier than they actually were.

22. This was the title of a popular album by 2Pac (Tupac Shakur).

23. It later occurred to me that I had not nodded at those lower in status because I was oriented toward the "fabulous" the entire trip up the steps. No matter how I might have rationalized my actions had someone asked me about them the moment I entered the building, the truth is that I basically found myself doing the done thing. By this I mean that it would be misleading to say that I actively "constructed" my social reality because, in real time and space, everything unfolded as if it was already there. Of course to some degree I consciously tried to work with the emotions I had and even to manage the impressions others might have of me. But I was dealing with situated (and to some degree collective) emotions that I never elected to have in the first place, and my "thinking" about how to modulate these feelings was rooted in my lived body and unconscious mind. It was only when I was well inside a nearly empty hallway (the bell had not yet rung to end the period) that fundamentally different feelings and interpretations came to be more prevalent. Only then did I find time to ponder how strange it was, for example, that I had felt insecure about possibly being somehow compared to "the thugs."

24. This sitting arrangement was evidence of our informal, and perhaps slightly edgy, relationship. It showed Thomas's confident way of taking-up space when there were no "real playaz" around.

25. Lyrics from "The Game" by the hip-hop artist known as Common.

26. Here we see something ethnographers of educational settings have been on to for a long time: Humor often functions as a group-mediated and group-making source of distinction. As Willis's key informant, Joey, indicated long ago, the power to (feel at ease and confident enough to) make others laugh is unequally distributed. Joey therefore indicated that humor was one of the main weapons used to demonstrate one's mastery over a given social situation or putative sub-group(s). Drawing the sharpest of distinctions with both the "ear 'oles" and the semi-"ear 'oles" alike, Joey explained to Willis (1981, 15) how it works: "They can't mek us laff, we can mek them laff, they can get fucking tears in when they watch us sometimes, but it's beyond their powers to mek one of us laff." What is really at stake here? As Kuipers (2006) demonstrated in her comparison of American and Dutch humor, the "decision" to laugh or not is direct, immediate, and very automatic. Genuine laughter is highly spontaneous, a practically felt or sensed reaction, rather than something based on explicit interpretation. We therefore experience "belly laughs" as "deep down" evidence of our sense of self, "who we really are." Especially in matters of humor, however, tastes are above all socially habituated, both "yours" and "of" your historical trajectory/position. They also depend on levels and types of cultural knowledge and situational know how. The loud, unrestrained laughs Joey discussed and I just depicted granted distinction, therefore, because they demonstrated types of second natures and cultural knowhow that were highly valued in the various educational settings. Such outbursts at once reflected and reconstituted overall social orders.

27. Marvin used to see me in the halls, for example, and greet me simply with "Meester [male teacher], true."

28. As Bourdieu (1990a, 107–108) put it, "the relation which obtains between habitus and field to which it is objectively adjusted . . . is a sort of ontological complicity, a subconscious and pre-reflexive fit."

29. Confronted with this smooth reenactment, that is, observers and participants alike were invited to fall into decontextualizing, nonsociological thinking based on the reduction of ongoing social processes to fixed individual states.

30. I have no idea if he also smoked by himself. Along with Collins (2004, 304), however, I would assume that the ingestion of such substances "is not just a matter of how they are interpreted, but how they are felt [and that] the bodily experiences themselves differ depending upon the social ritual in which those experiences are enacted." What we might be tricked into calling Marvin's energy, sense of self, and feelings of being high were never "his" alone. Along the way to demonstrating that "substances ingested into the body are experienced . . . either as objects of attachment or of revulsion" in the chapter entitled "Tobacco Ritual and Anti-Ritual," Collins (2004, 298) warns that we should "see that such activities are not just [evidence of] individual lifestyles, but rituals and thus markers of group boundaries." The ritual utterances and half-jokes associated with the preparation of joints (or "blunts") near the two schools (e.g., "Let me find out niggaz is about to light up some trees" or "Beam me up, Scotty!") illustrate Collins's point. One thinks of the preparations for the after-dinner cigar in the Victorian smoking room or men loading up a water pipe along the Nile. These are solidarity generating rituals perhaps above all else.

31. The fashionable ways of offering a greeting shifted even in the time that I spent in

the two fields. For example, in 1996 "What da dealie-o?" was in vogue. By 1998 this greeting had long been taken over by the less-distinguished pupils and the more "happening" had moved on to, for example, "What's poppin'?"

32. This term, especially popular in the Bronx, is shorthand for "propers" [sic], or proper level of respect vis-à-vis significant others.

33. I got to know him when he posed, exclusively with other "gangsters" of course, for some of the pictures I took and then distributed. Alas, he was never in any of my classes and we never talked much. I certainly was not about to walk up to this physically quite large adolescent and ask him why he was so feared or whether any members of his family were, as several other students had told me, involved in the local drug trade. But thinking about his sister I finally felt I had something with which I could approach him.

34. Here again, as was the case in Roxanne's remarks, we find evidence that even those understood locally to be the most "ghetto" of students said (at times) that the best way to remain safe was to keep away from dangerous pupils and situations. Of course one might interpret Dread's comments as crafty responses wedding knowledge of broader cultural tropes to the demands of an atypical conversation. But they can also be read as running counter to Anderson's claim that (alienated, black) inner city students seek safety in the "code of the street."

35. Explaining to me why some of his fellow students were respected and/or feared, a boy in his third year at Delta made this comment while looking out into the large open space known as the *aula*. The term "fabulous" comes straight from American English.

36. From Billie Holiday's "God Bless the Child" (co-written with Arthur Herzog Jr.).

37. Unlike Johnson High, the Delta School did not have an American-style cafeteria and separate auditorium. Instead of a dining hall in which trays could be slid past the food-distribution area and over to the cash registers, that is, there was a small store where students could buy candy, chips, soft drinks, sugary frozen drinks, sandwiches, and various types of meaty snacks.

38. It might be worth recalling here that roughly twenty percent of the "periods of instruction," or one full day spread out over the course of an average week, were canceled because of teacher absences or shortages.

39. As Collins (2004, 35) observed, while drawing explicitly on Durkheim's work on collective emotions and moral beliefs, "It is by uttering the same cry, pronouncing the same word, or performing the same gesture in regard to some object that they become and feel themselves to be in unison . . . they cannot do this except by movements. So it is the homogeneity of these movements that gives the group consciousness of itself."

40. Cf. Majors and Billson (1992).

41. McNeill (1995, 2–3) defines muscular bonding as "the euphoric feeling that prolonged and rhythmic muscular movement arouses among nearly all participants." He argued that the forms of basically preconscious solidarity building which result from these practices lead, among other things, to senses of "boundary loss" and to the formation and maintenance of "subgroups."

42. It was understood, for reasons documented in the next chapter, that flashing expensive jewelry (in the *aula*) sometimes led to robberies just outside school. Many of the kids had cell phones, and some of their friends (who were often ex-students) with knives and guns had cell phones as well. As robberies were common, sporting expensive jewelry was much more than just an aesthetic statement. It was a way of very

publicly affirming one's bravery, one's sense of place in the overall social space, and in many cases one's confidence that (slightly older) dominant types could quickly be called upon if anything threatening were to take place.

43. *"Aaaahhhhh, kijk die schonen* [look at those shoes]! Go on my brother! Throw your hands in the ay-er, if youse a true player," might serve as a representative example of praise gossip. *"Nooooo, kijk hem lopen, zo nep* [Noooo, look at him go (literally walk), so fake]," was a typical rendition of ever-repeated slurs often reserved for those iden-tified as the lowly "nerds."

44. After the abolition of slavery in Suriname, "workers" were imported to the Dutch colony from various parts of Asia, including India. Today, whether they are Hindu, Muslim, Christian, or anything else, people grouped as first- and second-generation migrants from Suriname with roots in India are often described as, and often self-identify as, "Hindustani" (*Hindoestanen*).

45. This we might also refer to as the "fabulous" cultural capital trumps racialized cul-tural capital principle.

46. Cf. Elias ([1939] 1994, 508): "[T]he pretension to be what one is not [leads to] inse-curity of taste and conduct, "vulgarity" . . . The attempt does not succeed. It remains clearly an imitation of alien models . . . the attempt to achieve the poise of the upper-class leads in most cases to a particular falseness and incongruity of behavior which nevertheless conceals a genuine distress, a despair to escape the pressure from above and the sense of inferiority."

47. I never answered such frail questions with ones that popped into my mind, such as, for example, "Well, if that's the case, why are you always sitting here—down and out with some of the most stigmatized kids in the entire school—instead of up there liv-ing large and enjoying a sandwich?"

48. A hardened and angry-looking girl, speaking to a few friends in between spits on the curb, as she sized-up a male student wearing especially expensive clothing and hang-ing out near an exit. "Packin" is short for "packing a pistol."

49. A note about exits at Johnson High is in order here. While Johnson contained just one formal point of entry for students, there were several officially recognized exits on the side of the building opening up immediately to a sidewalk and street. There were also several informal exit areas on the other side of the building opening up to the teachers' main parking lot and a ruined, generally unused secondary parking lot. Although the exits on the side leading the parking lots were not meant to be used, they remained unlocked—from the inside—because of fire department ordinances. There were not enough security officers or regular New York City police to control these exits (and therefore potential entry points) at all times. In other words, there was not enough security staff to make sure that kids did not sneak in through the unmanned exit areas that, of course, did not have metal detectors. The students at Johnson often pointed out, in part for this reason, how "easy" it was to get a gun or knife inside the building. If a student inside the school agreed to meet someone out-side the school at a specific door, at a specific time, all that was needed was a discrete knock, a look around for a security officer, and a push on the unlocked door—and a weapon could be handed in. On top of this, some of the security staff posted at the official exits let students "slide (back) in" from time to time.

50. Or, to use the spelling preferred by a platinum-selling 1990s R&B artist, Ginuwine.

51. When and where these mini-events drew to a close depended on any number of fac-tors including perceptions about how "hot" things were (or might get), the presence (or absence) of security guards and hallway deans, the types of classes that would be

entered late or missed, and what was happening elsewhere in the building or (just) outside it.

52. In no small part because of the forms taken on in these steady streams of mini-events—but also because life out on the streets in the South Bronx was objectively far more dangerous—compared to what we just saw in Delta's *aula*, the level of intensity tended to be much higher in Johnson's cafeteria.

53. In terms of emotionality and lyrics, there is a world of difference between this type of "thugged out" 1990s hip-hop and the more middle class, melodious, and almost intellectual Native Tongue (e.g., De La Soul–type) hip-hop that was also being produced at that time. The latter type was literally never, under any circumstances, audible around Johnson. It was all "hardcore," all the time.

54. In many cases windows had to remain open due to the heat in the warmer months and, thanks to incredibly inefficient furnaces that could not be turned down, in the colder months as well.

55. This is, putting it mildly, nothing new. Since before concepts like race, ethnicity, or nation took hold—and at least since the ancient Greeks defined "barbarians" in terms of their inability to speak "correctly"—fundamental principles of division in any number of societies have been based on the inter-workings of linguistic and symbolic capital. In our own times, these two analytically separable forms of power continue to mutually reinforce each other in the processes whereby various types of "groups" are consecrated and contested (Bourdieu 1991; 1984). And so it was in our two mini-societies. The well-perceived "groups" consisted of those (with linguistic dispositions, informational capital, and micro-situational opportunities that allowed one to be) "well spoken."

56. Here we might recall the words of a sociologist originally from a marginalized region of Southwest France populated by locals who (at least during his youth) spoke in ways that sounded inherently inferior to Parisian ears: "[W]hat goes in verbal communication, even the content of the message itself, remains unintelligible as long as one does not take into account the totality of the structure of the power positions that is present, yet invisible, in the exchange" (Bourdieu in Bourdieu and Wacquant 1992 146). Cf. Bourdieu (1991).

57. Those interested in the exaggerated and routinized quality of these preexisting roles and embodied performances might what to examine Butler's (1999) treatment of all gender as "drag" in *Gender Trouble*.

58. Analyses based on discursive consciousness and what was explicitly put into words can be of only limited value for us here. It is true that, during such moments, each sentient being pursued purposes mediated by relatively autonomous "internal" dialogues. But each of the students also remained attuned—at once cognitively, emotionally, and bodily—to the trend of the whole. Instinctively monitoring countless greetings and screams, pauses and silences, looks and movements, it became clear to the participants if things were developing in warmer, brighter, more peaceful ways or, by contrast, if things were going in darker, colder, more hostile directions. Emotional energy levels were picked up and mirrored (through, for example, mirror neurons). So sensitivity to each other's rhythms and pulses (i.e., getting what Goffman called a "tuned-up body") was of the essence; and many if not most of the topics of "discussion" were carried out without verbal communication. Because these four individuals sensed that they had an opening (i.e., because of their practical judgments about power chances), and because they did "make it happen" on the spot (i.e., they pulled of a successful interaction ritual), all of the at once verbal and nonverbal

communications reinforced positive self-images as well as fantasies about belonging to an inherently superior sort vis-à-vis intrinsically disgraced "nobodies."

59. McGill (2005, 205), focusing on merengue hip-hop, in *Constructing Black Selves*.

60. Lyrics from Common's "Ghetto Heaven, Part Two" (featuring D'Angelo). A "blunt" is made by emptying out the contents of a cigar and filling the cigar wrappers with marijuana. "Blunted" means stoned.

61. As Elias (in Elias and Scotson, [1965] 1994, xlv–xlvi; italics in original) put it: "The rewarding belief in the special virtue, grace and mission of one's own group may . . . shield members of an established group from the full emotional realization . . . that the gods have failed. . . . They [may] know of the change as a fact, [but] a fantasy shield . . . prevents them from feeling the change and, therefore, from being able to adjust. . . . Sooner or later the reality shock breaks in; and its coming is often traumatic."

62. As one soon-to-be "dropout" put it just months before he left Johnson, "I'm gonna start getting" it together from now on. That's my word, yo. I'm not tryin' to get put in no GED class." Johnson students with especially poor grades were often demoted to the "General Equivalency Diploma" program. In Amsterdam the very rough equivalent would be *"praktijk onderwijs"* ("practical education") or some other—less extremely stigmatized yet highly undesirable—educational trajectory that even the most disruptive and aggressive students generally wanted to avoid.

63. It is also true that, among the less-prestigious and less-aggressive students who were less frequently informed that they would, for example, have to move into special-education trajectories, those not constructed as black (e.g., "Spanish kids" in the Bronx and the so-called "Hindustani" and "Dutch kids" in the Bijlmer) were over-represented. To some degree then, and along the lines Ogbu might have predicted, the racialized principles of division operative in the two educational settings merged both with those related to the "fabulous" to "nerd" continuum and the distribution of what I am describing as wake-up calls. Again here we see that, to some extent, "fabulous" cultural capital was "black" cultural capital (Carter 2005), the "corridor cultures" were sites of "black solidarity" (Dickar 2008), and the typically dominant ways of being blended into specifically "black" ways of being "street" (Anderson 1999) in both settings. In New York as migration scholars such as Portes, Zhou, and Waters might have anticipated, the ways of being of native-born students were associated with disruptive and aggressive social circles. And all of this correlated with chances of being jolted (by pressures from home and the broader educational field) during such exceptional moments.

64. This says nothing about schools for example on the West Coast of the United States. Garot's (2010) evidence and analysis from there suggest that when performances of gang allegiances are organized around clearly crystallized and powerfully demar-cated ethno-racial cleavages (in local neighborhoods), these can emerge as the main principles of division inside nonselective inner-city schools.

65. As the Bronx natives sometimes half-joked, many of these "just off the boat" (from places like Jamaica and the Dominican Republic) were "hard-core from the get-go."

66. Bourdieu and Wacquant (1992, 12, originally in Bourdieu 1989, 7).

67. Taussig (1993, xvii; in Van de Port 2011, 74–75).

68. It might be worth noting again that, confronted by the discovery that most "periods of instruction" existed only on paper, many students felt in the here and now that stigmatizing and boring classroom settings were unworthy of their attention. The "passion to learn," which pedagogues hoped to ignite in "their" domains, was not,

therefore, sparked inside classrooms. Rather, the most charged and frequently repeated learning processes were based on rituals of distinction granting "realness" and emotional stampedes running through lived bodies. Ironically, then, it was in the halls, cafeterias, and entrance/exit areas that those invited to set the tones in Johnson and Delta applied themselves and, indeed, learned.

69. As mentioned in the previous chapter's treatment of Katz's work, we may "know" that we should not speed up and give a stranger the finger, but, feeling amputated, we often find ourselves doing exactly this even with a kid or two in the backseat.

70. This is not to suggest that expelling the generally more "thuggish" half of the two student bodies would not have made running the schools much, much easier. Habitus mattered. But by definition those managing educational "dumping grounds" had no way to conduct such "experiments" and what the two sets of administrators could try—getting rid of relatively small percentages of typically more disruptive pupils—had no lasting impact in either setting.

71. Van de Port (2011, 75, emphasis added).

CHAPTER THREE

1. Hobbes ([1651] 1994, 76).

2. Lyric from Mobb Deep's "Shook Ones, Pt. II" (1995).

3. "Dominant dominants" and "dominated dominants" (e.g., the financial elite and the cultural elite in overall social space) are terms devised by Bourdieu. If we forget that these terms relate to structural tendencies, they can be problematic. There were moments in both schools, as we have already seen and as this chapter further reveals, when those usually positioned as (exceptionally) dominant were not held in high regard and not particularly capable of exerting influence. Having said this, in terms of the outcomes of (symbolic) struggles that regularly emerged in both settings, I think it is fair to speak of more and less dominant fractions of each school's power elite. Because it is potentially even more confusing than these two terms, I will not use an accompanying notion—"field of power"—that Bourdieu used to talk about the sub-areas atop all relatively autonomous fields of life in which actors capable of deploying exceptionally large amounts (of various types of) capital engaged in elite-level confrontations and coalition building.

4. Either more willfully or more habitually—and by more or less explicit means—that is, they often sought to conserve the principles of hierarchization by which various types of power resources were (mis)recognized (e.g., taken for granted, "naturally" assumed to be of exceptional value) and, therefore, the overall restructuring of the game.

5. In one video-recorded group interaction, for example, a girl commented on a boy having been stabbed in the cafeteria the day before. She seemed utterly unfazed by the event, shrugging it off with "Oh, y'all didn't know about that." This illustrates a sharp difference with the smaller, less intensely violent school in the Bijlmer. A boy being stabbed in the *aula* would be the talk of the school within an hour.

Nancy Scheper-Hughes might speak here of (institutionally) naturalized, everyday violence. "What puzzled" Scheper-Hughes (1992, 270) originally, when she set out to study mother-child relations against the backdrop of high infant-mortality rates in an impoverished region of Northeast Brazil, "was the seeming 'indifference' of Alto women to the deaths of their babies and their willingness to attribute to their own offspring an 'aversion' to life that made their deaths seem wholly natural, indeed all but expected." Living among local people, what Scheper-Hughes discovered was a process involving institutions such as "health" clinics that diagnosed and treated "nervoso" (an individual ailment) instead of "hunger" (a systemic problem) in ways that turned otherwise unthinkable suffering and structural violence into taken-for-granted parts of everyday life (cf. Paulle 2007).

6. Here, Garot (2010, 177) deserves to be quoted at length: "The best response to the demographic question, 'How many young people are gang members?' is 'All of them and none of them; it all depends.' Our academic discourses and policies often reify the importance of gang membership more than young people themselves do. We should criminalize victimizing behaviors, and while the rituals of gangs may provide opportunities for such behaviors, they also provide opportunities for communitas."

7. One might say that Cory was the type of boy who regularly felt at ease in "hot spots" such as the one in which Thomas went stiff (Chapter 2).

8. "Without any need for reflection, the individual in shame knows instantly and vividly that his or her integrity depends on being folded into membership in a transcending community," as Katz (1999, 319, emphasis added) argues, and, "the individual in shame seeks clothing, a way to recover the anonymity of a role, an unselfconscious, taken-for-granted way of doing things, the behavioral vehicle of 'das Man'." Heidegger's term "das Man" is usually translated as "the one" (as in the way one does the done thing in a given situation or world).

9. Cf. Pollner and Emerson (2001, 119); Goode (1994, 127).

10. This really was the world on its head. As Wacquant (2004, 393) notes, shame is that "emotion that arises when the dominated come to perceive themselves through the eyes of the dominant, that is, are made to experience their own ways of thinking, feeling, and behaving as degraded and degrading."

11. Especially given all the confrontations in distressed urban schools related to covering body parts with hats and other garments (Garot and Katz 2003, 436–37), it is interesting to note that the word "thug" comes from the Hindi word meaning "swindler, thief," based on the Sanskrit *sthagati*, "he covers or conceals."

12. Ronny, a fourth-year student we will meet in the next chapter, reflecting on an experience he had in his first year at the Delta School.

13. Chapter 5's analysis of the bodily practices—and especially the dietary regime—that a stunningly successful student inflicted on himself may make these claims about the integration of mind and body seem less abstract or speculative.

14. Collins (2007, 243).

15. In interviews with old-timers, my colleagues in Amsterdam indicated that if this had happened, they did not know about it. As my interviews made clear, this was not at all the case in the Bronx.

16. As the previous chapter demonstrated, hallways were among the geographic areas where pupils were most often "screamed on" (scandalized, *schande krijgen* [sic]). These were the types of settings, that is, in which those who felt capable of such feats typically enjoyed their hearty, pecking order (re)producing laughs. It may be worth recalling that, unlike "corny ass" classrooms, hallways were the places where (the typically more dominant) felt they were most likely to "catch heat" from relevant members of the opposite sex. In short, looks and feeling exposed mattered most in halls; classrooms, by comparison, were more or less backstage.

17. I have no problem with the idea, that is, that this girl's response evinced a "street" cultural logic contributing to "inner-city young people . . . commit[ing] . . . violence toward one another" (Anderson 1999, 9).

18. Collins (2007, 20).

19. Here we might recall how Dread, in the previous chapter, bragged about wanting, one day, to fight Jurgen because, as he put it, he and Jurgen were on the same "level."
20. Katz (1988, 312).
21. The very fact that Delta had regular school dances points up a clear difference between the two settings. Any school dance at Johnson would have required a small army of police. The school managers never even considered planning such an event.
22. Here, without suggesting that Julio's associates had roots in places other than the Antilles, it might be useful to recall Devine's (1996, 114) argument that, in his schools in Brooklyn, violence actually "constructed" ethnic boundaries and identifications.
23. The risk here related to what Collins (2007) calls the "forward panic." This takes hold when the tension associated with something like an equal balance of power gives way and a person or members of a group suddenly come to be far more capable of doing violence without putting themselves at serious risk of injury (e.g., the soccer hooligans who do little more than hurl insults, even if they are pushed to the fore, until a member of the other side falls down and gets cut off from his supporters behind their line).
24. Recall Levi's view from the sunken pit of the *aula* (Chapter 2). This Antillean-Dutch boy did not see his fellow students through the prism of complexions or ethnicity. The plain truth for him was that he and his friends were not aggressive, and that "they" were. In the Bijlmer as well as in the Bronx (as Roxanne's comments indicated the Preface), while a great many students were taken for granted to be authentically black, only a tiny minority of the students in either setting ever became enmeshed in such elite conflicts.
25. Incidentally, Anderson (1999) stressed that the "code of the street" did not allow backing down, that it actually did offer protection, and that it ensured that those invested in it would not turn to the formal authorities. The ethnographic data and analysis presented in this chapter dovetail with Garot's (2010, 135, 139, 225–33) contentions that, as the actions of Roy and his associates indicate, (1) many of the seemingly more hard-core "street" students regularly responded to provocations and threats by backing down, (2) that the best way to remain safe was not to act "street" but to keep as much distance as possible from the more aggressive interactions and types, and (3) that even the seemingly most "street" students were not at all times averse to seeking the aid of formal authorities if they felt they were at risk.
26. I did not have the types of relationships with either Roy or Julio that would have fostered thoughtful, honest answers to follow-up questions about this encounter. What I did have was the opportunity to observe what happened the week after the dance. Smiling and relaxed, Julio seemed at once to downplay what had happened and to be everywhere one looked. Roy and his typically conspicuous friends were either absent or careful to remain far from the high-visibility spots.
27. I did not see Vanessa's reaction because by the time I reentered the building she and her friends had already slipped back into the *aula*.
28. Roughly, this German term meant for Elias (in Goudsblom and Mennel, 1998, 143), the "reduction in thought of all things that you observe as being dynamic to something static." As this endlessly processual thinker warned, "Our whole conceptual tradition, particularly our philosophical tradition, pushes our thinking in that direction and makes us feel that one cannot come to grips with observed happenings as flowing events."
29. The language of sports can help express the main points here. As Georgetown University men's basketball coach John Thompson once said of Ohio State's freshman

point guard Mike Conley, Jr., one of the smallest and youngest men on the court most of the time, "His poise is terrific. I mean, he just has an uncanny feel for the game and how to manage the game, how to manage his teammates." Pete Thamel, "Timing Is Perfect for Oden and Buckeyes," *New York Times*, April 1, 2007.

30. It is said that another warrior of meager physical stature, Napoleon, only needed four hours of sleep a night. But, as Collins once pointed out on his blog ("The Sociological Eye," August 1, 2011), this was while he was rising to power and reigning supreme—not while he was exiled from positions of power (within sturdy chains of riveting interaction rituals). Severed for good from the massive dosages of energy he once extracted from adoring masses and less dominant dominants alike—Collins suggests that *le petit caporal* began putting on weight and often found it difficult to get out of bed no matter how many hours of sleep he had.

31. The elite conflict was decided, we might therefore say, by "two relations to the future anchored in adjacent but distinct social positions" (Wacquant 2002, 1500).

32. Bourdieu (2000, 140–41).

33. In addition to demonstrating that much of what may seem to be purely external did not stay "out there," I also seek to bring to life that explicit mental representations did not "get in the way" of real-time responses. Rather, the responses of the exposed and penetrated were based on the interplay of situational dynamics and the primordial feelings and prediscursive understandings that actually guide all of us through most everyday situations and that certainly guide adolescents and their teachers though threatening situations in high-stress schools.

34. Maurice Merleau-Ponty stretched the work of Heidegger far enough to reveal the situated and lived body as "the "unspoken cogito" . . . our "primary subjectivity," . . . the "consciousness which conditions language," but itself remains a "silent consciousness" with an "inarticulate grasp of the world" (Shusterman 2005, 151).

35. Teachers almost never tried to teach during "coverages" for absent colleagues at Johnson. At best they dispersed a handout, took attendance, and hoped that the pupils would not get too close to open windows, fight, leave the room, or make so much noise that other classes would be disturbed. Any attempt to "teach" during these class periods was frowned upon by other teachers doing coverages, who felt entitled to a paid forty-minute pseudo-class and did not want expectations to rise. The students tended to see an attempt to teach during a coverage in terms of a typically young and (still) ideologically motivated teacher who wanted to deny them their "right" to "hang out" and relax for forty minutes, or, perhaps, do some homework for another class. Coverages were an example of wasted time and the shortcomings of basing analyses of high-poverty schools on myths, such as officially recorded amounts of time pupils "received instruction" or even "years of schooling." Those in charge of the various departments were able to cover themselves with these coverages; however, some classes were "covered" in this way for weeks at a time when teachers were absent or when, as often happened, a teacher left in the middle of the school year or was switched to another teaching assignment and no new permanent teacher had yet been given responsibility for the class. These de facto shortages almost never made it into the official registries.

36. Nothing was more pitiable than hearing teachers screaming through halls in the hope that a security guard would hear—and respond to—their calls. Perhaps the (wannabe) alpha male in me, all six feet, three inches and well over two hundred thirty pounds of me, would not stoop to that level. I do not know.

37. I ought to mention that Robert was one of the few boys in the school larger than I

was. Robert seemed like a gentle giant. He and I had "clicked" when I temporarily taught one of his classes. As fate would have it, this was one of the few classes I ever had that went really well. After taking it from me a few weeks into a semester, my Assistant Principal started teaching it himself.

38. Katz (1999, 316).

39. Cf. Elias (1994); Wacquant (1997).

40. This is not really in contrast to Roxanne's claims as articulated in the Preface. On one hand, in our interview Roxanne indicated that she did not want to "talk to" more aggressive and dominant boys. On the other, she seemed to find it natural that girls with "g" (game) did date boys who could take them shopping (because they sold drugs).

41. Again I borrow from Chambliss (1989, 2009), whose key terms and main insights will be used more systemically when we focus on the excellence of teachers in Chapter 6.

42. And here especially, my findings and analysis support those put forward by Devine (1996, 37)—italics added—whose words demand some space: "To interrogate current understandings of school violence, which harbor an unexamined mind-body duality, to understand how student knowledge is constructed, one must shift from the purely cerebral world of language and focus instead on materiality: the exchange of looks between peers, the slow strides in hall walking, the 'hanging' in the halls, the rumpled cuffs down near the shoes, a group leaning silently against a wall, the sudden explosion of energy when something really starts to 'go down.'"

43. One might say, in other words, that to focus so intently on extreme and everyday violence is to effectively hide what has been called by Farmer (2004) "structural violence."

44. As several fieldworkers have argued, a central task of urban ethnographers and researchers of violent settings is to tease out the (causal) links in the micro to macro continuum of (symbolic) violence that, through time, reinforces inequalities (Bourgois 2001, 5; Schepper-Hughes and Bourgois 2004).

CHAPTER FOUR

1. From James Baldwin's *My Dungeon Shook: A Letter to my Nephew on the One Hundredth Anniversary of the Emancipation.*

2. Comment made by a confident student flashing gang colors just outside a classroom in Johnson High.

3. And exactly the same can be said of any number of others phrases and refrains frequently found in hip-hop songs based either on grievances about the harshness "ghetto" life or grandiloquence about specific residential areas in both New York and Amsterdam. Since the earliest days, there was "The Message" ("Don't push me 'cuz I'm close to the edge; I'm trying not to lose my head. It's like a jungle sometimes; It makes me wonder how I keep from goin' under) as well as rappers from various parts of New York "representing" generally more positive (yet also violence related) I/we feelings and images by means of drawing attention to specific neighborhoods and streets (The Sugar Hill Gang of Harlem, "South Bronx . . . South South Bronx" as flag-waving mantra, "Do or Die" as a reference for "Bed-Sty" [Bedford- Stuyvesant, Brooklyn], references to Linden Boulevard in Brooklyn and Queens, etc.). Exactly the same combinations of complaints about hardships (e.g., poverty, racism, lousy teachers, and fellow students) on one hand and counter-stigmatizing utterances on the other (e.g., "The Bijlmer is in the building") are found in the forms of hip-hop

culture that, for a generation now, have emerged specifically in Southeast Amsterdam (cf. http://bijlmerstyle.com).

4. Adolescent who recently moved away from a particularly disgraced and disgracing cluster of high-rise flats in a Parisian banlieue quoted in Wacquant (2007, 14).

5. While writing up fieldnotes, after the fact, I thought about how I am (almost) automatically transformed by walking into a library, a museum, an expensive restaurant, or the family home of people who take for granted far more cultural or economic capital than that to which I am accustomed. The subdued if not submissive frames and stances, it seems, spring up "by themselves."

6. Connecting ritualized movements to stigmatized geographic locations as well as positions in broader symbolic orders, Katz (1988, 88) highlighted how the "ghetto bop and the barrio stroll identify the walker as a native of a place that is outside and antagonistically related to the morally respectable center of society."

7. In his study of changing fields of secondary and higher education in France, Bourdieu (1996, 180–83, italics in original) demonstrates why what he terms "bodily hexis" (i.e., the deepest, most visceral, and unconscious aspect of the social habitus) is fundamental to the "distinctive identity . . . [of those occupying positions] within the 'elite' of the school system" and, further, how this "esprit de corps . . . incorporated into a biological body . . . is the precondition for the constitution of cultural capital, that collectively held resource that enables each of the members of an integrated group to participate in the capital individually held by all the others."

8. Here we get a sense, by the way, of at least part of the reason generations of middle-class "lefty" intellectuals have been such eager consumers of standard educational ethnographies based on highly agentic and "culturally resistant" working-class peer groups, "minority" identities, and the "burden of acting white." If you can just change the content of their thoughts with (racialized and racializing) pedagogies of the oppressed, if you can just alter the self-defeating cultural imperatives of resistant peer groups (and direct their anger in the right way), you will have a successful "intervention" (if not, in the fantasies of "critical" scholars, an ideological force contributing to a socialist revolution).

9. As was the case with Robert (in the previous chapter), Ronny and I developed the kind of rapport that might well have influenced his comments to me as well as everything else I was able to observe. Ronny was by no means obsessed with me or with the possibility that, as he understood, I might write about him in a book at some point. But the reader should keep in mind here that Ronny did care about my perceptions of him and this may have influenced what he said and did in my presence.

10. Thanks in part to the progressive educational funding regime in the Netherlands, this class consisted of just nine pupils. Ronny's classmates were all boys between sixteen and eighteen years of age. I felt a special bond with this set of boys supposedly learning to be electricians, especially from the moment I discovered that almost none of them expressed any interest in actually doing the "dirty, dangerous" work for which they were officially being trained.

11. As Katz (1999, 143) put it, reflecting on his observations of drivers so experienced in their cars that they merge with them, "If our language does not allow us to see people dwelling naturally in the world, we will not be able to set up problems for explaining how different forms of tacit involvement develop."

12. "[O]utcastes on the inside" of the educational field, as Bourdieu and Champagne (Bourdieu et al. 1999, 425) would have it, "cannot help discovering quickly that . . . the establishment into which they have been directed by educational tracking is

a place for assembling the most disadvantaged; that they are working on a cheap diploma."

13. Uncharacteristically, this utterance came out in English, perhaps because I was too involved to remember to translate.

14. Whether based on (some mix of) facts, broader cultural narratives, a desire to tell me what he thought I wanted to hear or something else entirely, this after-the-fact recounting fits perfectly with Anderson's notions about the "code" of the street.

15. It might be useful to recall here that, rather than being the result of biological imperatives, Butler (1990, 1993) argues that the emergence and coherence of specific types of masculinity and femininity are in fact constructed through the repetition of specifically stylized and gendering somatic performances. In other words, frequently reenacted and highly ritualized bodily practices are the sociocultural, rather than "natural," sources of what are so often attributed to inherent and fixed gender differences.

16. I am by no means the only urban ethnographer who is sensitive to more or less "gangster" ways of leaning, walking, and moving more generally. As Jackson (2001, 231, emphasis added) mentioned in his study of more and less conscious ways of "doing" race and class in a gentrifying *Harlemworld*, "Ordinary people anchor their notions of identity to behavioral arguments that place the onus . . . not . . . on the surface of the body but in bodies' motions." Recalling these words of wisdom in his study of (vanishing) gang-identity performances, Garot (2010, 64) discussed body language, and more specially ways of embodying certain outfits, as nothing less than the "signifier . . . par excellence" and the "*sin qua non* of gang identification" in and around his West Coast school. Garot (2010, 64, 214–25) also drew parallels to Katz's discussion of "parading" (e.g., exaggerated strides) as part and parcel of the repertoire used by young people (who might be associated with various ethnicities, nationalities, and races) enacting the "badass."

17. Bourdieu (2000, 233), possibly referencing a famous work by Foucault and certainly distinguishing himself from Althusser.

18. Indeed, as Michael Polanyi (1967, 4) suggested in *The Tacit Dimension*, we would be well advised to start from the opposite assumption that the kids "can know more than [they] can tell." In other words, that which is practically (rather than theoretically) grasped, might consist of a range of pre-discursive concepts and sensory information coming into play in the sense-making activities through which the students lived in real time and space.

19. Here I make us of the term Fainstein, Gordon, and Harloe (1994) utilized in the title of their edited volume on New York and London.

20. As my use of "culture" here indicates, I think much use can be made of this and related concepts. Indeed, since the music, clothes, and even word choices were at times quite similar in the Bronx and in the Bijlmer, I think it is fair to say that a widespread, if not globalized, hip-hop flavored youth (sub)culture informed a great deal of the ideals, aesthetics, and actions of the more or less "fabulous" students. I use the language of specific dispositions (making up different kinds of habitus) as well as (micro-) contextual triggers to depict their actual practices, however, because I think doing so helps us achieve a much richer, deeper, and firmer understanding of what actually took place on the ground.

CHAPTER FIVE

1. Hamlet to Horatio, in Shakespeare's *Hamlet*.

2. Lyrics from "The Day" by The Roots.

3. Cf. For an overview of disturbing statistics related to work, education, health, and incarceration, see the National Urban League's (2007) "The State of Black America: Portrait of the Black Male."

4. Cf. For data on the undesirable overrepresentation of members of this "group" among "dropouts," the unemployed, and those involved with the police, see the Risbo's (2011) "Antilliaanse Nederlanders"—a report on twenty-two Dutch cities and towns co-authored by Marion van San. Van San holds a chair entitled "Youth and Education of Antilleans [sic]" ("Jeugd en Educatie van Antillianen") at the University of Utrecht. She (1998) made a name for herself in the Netherlands with Stelen & Steken: Delinquent Gedrag van Curaçaose Jongens in Nederland which translates literally into Stealing and Stabbing: The Delinquent Behavior of Curacaoian Boys in the Netherlands.

5. As noted in the Introduction, most of the teens entering the two buildings could not be expected to receive a high school diploma or any rough equivalent (such as a GED. in the United States or what is known as a "starters certificate" in the Netherlands). Even fewer could be expected to graduate with the skills necessary to do well at the next level.

6. For an excellent argument that examining the cultural styles of families help us understand academic performance (of inner-city youth) better than their variable-based composition, see Clark's (1983) Family Life and School Achievement. As Clark noted (1983, 225–33), from Ogbu to Collins, many of our most influential scholars have documented that parents (in and out of ethnically stigmatized high-poverty neighborhoods) value the symbols of educational success. This says very little, however, about consistently facilitating the types of experiences children and adolescents need to do well in school.

7. In other words, Dewey would have predicted that in the absence of deeply habituated sets of dispositions that could help students successfully navigate different types of situations on the ground, nice words and ideas would basically be meaningless. Perhaps informed by James and certainly influenced by the hands-on technique of Alexander, Dewey grasped that the learning of fruitful and adequately settled habits of action did not result mainly from oral or written explication of proper ends (e.g., lectures on proper conduct). Alexander, who had been a Shakespearean actor before he lost his voice, developed a concrete set of pedagogic practices based on the gradual extension of self-reflective control over bodily actions previously left to unconscious (and often harmful) routines. Dewey engaged for decades in the Alexander Technique, and claimed that doing so improved the flexibility of his thinking. He wrote introductions to three of Alexander's books even though he was warned that doing so would detract from his scientific legitimacy. On this "neglected" influence on Dewey's thinking, see McCormack (1958).

8. "I do not know of anything so disastrously affected by the tradition of separation and isolation as is this particular theme of body-mind," Dewey (2008, 27) argued in a talk given in 1928. "The evils which we suffer in education, in religion, in the materialism of business and, the aloofness of 'intellectuals' from life, the whole separation of knowledge and practise—all testify to the necessity of seeing mind-body as an integral whole."

9. Terrell is the teacher who introduced me to Roxanne and participated in our first interview (Preface).

10. In some of my classes I took to splitting those present into teams before asking game-show-like questions related to the curricular material. When I asked this young

girl, while she was very obviously pregnant, what the name of her team was she answered: "We are Ghetto Fabulous."

11. I refer here to Rita, the future wife of Simi, one of the boys focused on at length below.

12. In New York, that is, I never heard putatively nonwhite students in predominantly white settings report feeling strange about being around so many Americans.

13. Brindisha did not find it worth mentioning that her tormentor had Afro-Surinamese roots. Nor, in our talks, did Brindisha ever divide what she saw as Delta's painfully distinct peer groups along ethnicized lines. This should not however imply that ethnicity was irrelevant in Brindisha's life. In a revealing exchange while waiting for the subway (metro) after school one day, Brindisha and another Hindustani girl told me what they thought was most likely in store for them. "In our culture, when you get married, it's like your new family owns you," Brindisha said. The other girl nodded and then chimed in: "My aunt got married and her new family hits her and makes her wake up at six in the morning to start cleaning and cooking. She works the whole day and her husband does nothing. It is like she is a slave now, it's terrible." Just before the train came I popped the question. "So, are you both going to marry into Hindustani families?" They looked at each other and laughed, "Naturally," said Brindisha's girlfriend. Imageries of ethno-national communities, inseparable from ideas about race and religion, seemed to be of only superficial importance in Brindisha's account of her life in Delta and other schools in Holland. Yet, if this answer to my question about marriage plans was correct, it seems that ethno-nationalized cultural bonds were far stronger than any of the concerns they voiced about "traditional" (if not radically exploitative and even criminal) gender roles within Hindustani-Surinamese-Dutch families.

14. Bourdieu et al. (1999, 509).

15. Here we might keep in mind that Raul was not talking about middle-class "Surinamese" or "Antilleans." Like nearly all of the other students in the two schools examined here, Raul had no friends from middle-class neighborhoods or families.

16. In what follows the many hip-hop- and R&B-flavored English words Raul peppered into his sentences will be in italics.

17. Officially "immigration" is not the right word, as the islands making up the Dutch Antilles were, at that point, all part of the Dutch kingdom.

18. Generations of Curaçao's elites have finished secondary schools on higher tracks and then moved on to Dutch universities to complete their studies.

19. This term might have popped into Raul's mind because of our conversations, or because of his knowledge of my own interests. I do not believe, however, that Raul would have used the term "body language" in this context if he did not sense that it was appropriate.

20. Whether or not he thought Raul might become the political leader of the Netherlands, why this teacher "advised" the son of an extremely well-spoken woman to pursue a very mediocre secondary school track is unclear. Why such a well-educated mother, one willing make the effort to send her son to an apparently stable primary school outside Southeast Amsterdam, would send that son to a secondary school in the very heart of the Bijlmer (where the nonvocational program had recently been phased out) also raises questions. Raul's mother took time to explain this in one of our conversations after Raul left Delta. As she put it, "It was so easy with his sister, you know, always taking care of herself and doing her homework and everything.

She did not need any pushing. It was so easy with her and it all worked out . . . so, I thought, maybe he is just not ready to learn anything in school right now. I'll give him some time and he will come around when he is ready. I knew about Delta. Before he started attending Delta I had applied for a teaching job there. I saw the teachers walking around with their dreary faces (*lange gezichten*), and I knew it was no place for me. But Raul was tired of traveling so far to get to school and Delta was right around the corner from our apartment. Since Raul had been rejected from the other school in the Bijlmer that he had applied to, I gave in. Now I see what a mistake that was." Whether this fully explains it or not, Raul ended up at Delta and he remained there for four years.

21. That is, that he would become the equivalent of a "dropout" in the United States after failing to complete two years at the tertiary level (MBO).

22. HBO, *sociaal pedagogische hulpverlening*.

23. When I recently went to Leeuwarden to visit him, Raul and I were stopped by police demanding to see identification because, they said, Raul "fit the description" of an "Antillean" suspect. We had both observed just moments earlier the relevant incident—a fight between a barman and one of his clients. Neither of the two men could possibly be described, according to local definitions, as "black" or "Antillean." But there was a fight, and policemen close by saw Raul walking away (with another guy who did not look like he was from Leeuwarden). The policeman who saw Raul radioed ahead, in the direction in which we were walking, and suddenly my former student was racialized and nearly criminalized.

24. Simi spoke of his "brothers" rather than his half-brothers and, in what follows, I will follow his lead.

25. Selling fake drugs can be extremely dangerous, as junkies are well known for returning in a rage to the dealers who supplied them with less-than-authentic substances (Williams 1992; Bourgois 1995).

26. Cf. Turner (1991) on dietary regimes as forms of control exercised over the body that lead to the establishment of discipline.

27. Simi also made a point of distinguishing Conscious Reggae from various other modern offshoots of Reggae like Dancehall.

28. One is reminded here of Dewey's ([1938] 1979, 64) claim at the end of "The Nature of Freedom" in *Education and Experience*: "The ideal aim of education is creation of power of self-control."

29. It might be worth mentioning that in Amsterdam both teachers and students who had had significant experience in Suriname and on Curaçao almost universally held a parallel opinion. There was more social control in the relatively tightly knit communities and community schools "back home" than in Southeast Amsterdam or schools such as Delta (cf. Bijnaar 2002). The degree to which these parallel discourses relate to nostalgic, sanitizing, and romantic coping practices (in the form of glorified "back home" narratives) is impossible for me to say.

30. Simi transferred into one of my classes because he found my supervisor, who taught only a single (highly) selective class, dull-witted as well as offensive (e.g., this "Assistant Principal," institutionally empowered to judge my ability to teach, called Simi "dreadlock boy.") I counseled Simi against making this move because, at least in my classes, I assumed I would be less able to help him prepare for his the advanced placement exam he wanted to take. Resolute, Simi opted for the emotional and intellectual connection and we agreed that I should tutor him using the textbook my boss allowed him to retain.

31. On the social, political, and historical forces behind people's senses of (not) feeling at "home" in the United States and Western Europe, see Duyvendak (2011).

32. I may share some of the blame for orienting him towards an Ivy League school instead of a less snobbish setting in which he might have felt more at home. On the other hand, Simi wants to go back for a MA—perhaps at Columbia University—and he certainly knows that, as difficult as they may have been, his years at such a distinguished college may open doors for him in the future.

33. Wacquant (2004, 43–44) on becoming a successful boxer. As Wacquant documents, it's not the poorest of the poor who remain in the highly regulated—and "colorblind" (2004, 10)—sub-world of ghetto pugilists in cities like Chicago. Rather, the young men from the more stable, traditional working (or slightly middle-) class families are the ones with a chance of gradually embodying the right stuff.

34. As Dickar (2008) might have predicted, Derek became evermore immersed in "corridor cultures" dominated by students usually defined as "black" (as well as, in academic language, as "Latino"). To some degree through deliberate and creative actions, Derek achieved recognition as he "switched" from a "decent" cultural orientation to the "street code" that Anderson (1999) associates most directly with black youngsters of the inner city. Derek seemed to turn into one of the students with an authentic mastery of the locally legitimized know-how that Carter (2005), wedding the ideas of Bourdieu and Ogbu, calls "black cultural capital." Instead of remaining immersed in any kind of "ethnic buffer" that might have been produced by West African or Ghanaian migrants, Derek "assimilated" (or "Americanized") "downward," in the language of Portes and Zhou, into the practices, discourses, and beliefs that can be associated with Ogbu's "involuntary minorities" (i.e., native-born blacks and Latinos). Like the Vietnamese students Zhou and Bankston found succeeding academically in distressed schools of New Orleans, one might say that, until things went terribly wrong for her, Brindisha profited from being immersed in a closelyknit community of "Asian" migrants—a community in which feelings of shame about doing poorly in schools might be said to translate into beneficial outcomes in the longer term.

35. See especially the closing pages of *The Presentation of Self in Everyday Life* ([1959] 1990, 244–45).

36. Drawing direct connections to Bachelard ("the world in which one thinks is not the world in which one lives") as well as to Dewey's critique of the "spectator's theory of knowledge," Bourdieu (2000, 51) in full phenomenological mode elucidated what he called the scholastic fallacy in the following way: "Projecting his theoretical thinking into the heads of acting agents, the researcher presents the world as he thinks it (that is, as an object of contemplation, a representation, a spectacle) as if it were the world as it presents itself to those who do not have the leisure (or the desire) to withdrawal from it in order to think it. He sets as the origin of their practices, that is to say, in their 'consciousness,' his own spontaneous or elaborated representations, or, worse, the models he has had to construct (sometimes against his own naïve experience) to account for their practices."

37. My argument is not that explicit beliefs about race, religion, doing schoolwork, or anything else were somehow unimportant in Simi's (or in any other) case. Compared to nearly all other students, Simi had—and was consciously aware of having—more beneficial thoughts and beliefs. Even in this limiting case, however, the remedy that turned this one time "thug" into an Ivy Leaguer did not come mainly in the form of ideas or ideals. The key difference between Simi and the rest was not

that, at the rock-bottom level, he had some kind of self-sufficient, internal, explicit, intentional mental content that guided his actions though the maze of "external" objects. Instead of yet again to Dewey, for clarification this time we might reach back to James' ([1902] 1982,504) closing argument in *The Varieties of Religious Experience*: "When we survey the whole field of religion, we find a great variety in the thoughts that have prevailed there; but the feelings on the one hand, and the conduct on the other are almost always the same . . . The theories which Religion generates, being thus variable, are secondary; and if you wish to grasp her essence, you must look to the feelings and the conduct as being the more constant elements . . . This seems to me the first conclusion which we are entitled to draw from the phenomena we have passed in review."

38. As such, if we see Simi as an involuntary minority with an exceptional social identity and sense of self-worth, then Ogbu's race-based theory of oppositional culture might be said to take us a long way in terms of explaining both his academic success and the failure of most students in his school—i.e., the poor academic outcomes of other involuntary minorities (African Americans and Latinos) with less exceptional and less empowering cultural orientations. In Anderson's (1999) terms, the evidence supports in part an emphasis on Simi's willful switch from a street to a decent (and especially pro-school) set of cultural beliefs and attitudes.

39. And, it might be useful to recall, Raul was convinced that his primary school was above all far safer than those attended by other students who ended up at Delta. Raul also claimed that physical (and sexual) intimidation was basic to his temporarily derailing.

40. As Shusterman (1994, 137) notes, this quote from Dewey's 1918 introduction to Alexander's *Man's Supreme Inheritance* was penned seven years before Dewey elaborated his "theory of experiential and mind-body continuity in *Experience and Nature* (in which Alexander's work is twice invoked and his terminology appropriated)."

41. Had Simi gone to a less academically demanding college, one might add, he might have been not only "college ready" in terms of his academic skills, he almost certainly would have had a less alienating college experience. More specifically, as Suskind's (1998) analysis of another Brown student from an American inner-city indicates, Simi might have been much happier at a less exclusive college where the shock and confusion that accompanied his confrontations with (better prepared) students of African American ancestry from (upper-) middle-class backgrounds might have been lessened.

42. "Concerted cultivation" is the label Lareau (2003, 247) uses to identify the "rationalized" middle-class childrearing practices that continually bring these types of interactions into being. In addition to the links she makes to Bourdieu's work on cultural capital distinctions, what Lareau demonstrates can be described in terms of what Elias called the social constraint toward self-constraint, or "civilizing," process.

CHAPTER SIX

1. A visibly broken-down teacher with an old school Brooklyn accent addressing me as what I was—an uncertified junior colleague.

2. A highly effective English teacher at Delta on what I think he knew I would never achieve.

3. Building on a paper by economists Chetty, Friedman, and Rockoff (2011) which focuses on the long-term effects of "high-value-added teachers" (i.e., the top five percent in terms of average test-score gains for students), op-ed columnist Nicholas Kristof ("The Value of Teachers", *New York Times*, January 11, 2012) concluded

the following: "the evidence is now overwhelming that even in a grim high-poverty school, some teachers have far more impact on their students than those in the classroom next door." While having a "good teacher" for a year in primary school increases the chance that students will go to college and increases students' lifetime earnings prospects, this also reduces the chance that they will become pregnant as teens. Having a "very poor teacher," Kristof wrote, "has the same effect as a pupil missing forty percent of the school year."

4. Cf. Amanda Ripley's "What Makes a Great Teacher?" (*The Atlantic*, January/February 2010).

5. Aside from the massive jacking-up of scores on "standardized" tests and the underreporting of threats and violence, as we have already seen, supervisors in our worst schools are not above selectively assigning (to themselves or to their cronies) classes full of generally well-behaved kids who can appear, on paper, to have the same learning capacities as classes constituted by students more predisposed to being disruptive. Given my observations, I have to assume that attaching teachers' pay to students' performance on test scores will increase levels of fraud as well as "cherry picking" and all the animosity and grief that comes with it.

6. Among these one might include some of the works discussed above (e.g., Carter 2005) but one could also go back all the way to Waller (1932) for ethnographic evidence supporting this finding.

7. For example, McFarland (2001, 666) argued convincingly that pedagogues should take "steps . . . to not only offset differences in social standing, but to break-up cliques of students that collude to undermine classroom affairs" and that they should use "teacher-centered tasks to minimize student opportunities" to engage in disruption.

8. This was clearly evidenced when, in his concluding remarks, McFarland (2004, 1311) claimed that "Every social drama . . . is promulgated by intentional actors who [attempt] to guide interaction in certain desired directions." McFarland has more recently moved rather strongly away from this earlier stance in a contribution most obviously indebted to Goffmanian frame analysis (which emphasized the pre-discursive level of perception) but also informed, not coincidentally, by Bourdieu's theory of practice, Merleau-Ponty's insights into immediately lived bodily experience, and the historicizing perspective of Elias (Diehl and McFarland, 2010). Given the collective unconscious of most scholars, I suspect that this later contribution will have less impact on the field.

9. And here especially one might go back to Dewey's critique of disembodying analyses based on the "spectator's perspective" (cf. Lehmann-Rommel 2000, 197; Garrison 1994, 8).

10. In Martin Johnson's work (which I discussed in the Introduction) as well as in political and journalistic discussions about compensation (e.g., "Union Backs Dialogue over Teachers. Pay," BBC News, August 4, 1999), one sometimes sees this folkterm pop up.

11. Mary-Anne stood, one might say, at the crossroads of her school's "corridor culture" and the teacher's domain. But to say that she stood between a "white" dominated sphere and space of "black solidarity" would, it seems, be something of an intellectual projection (cf. Dickar 2008).

12. McFarland (2004, 1254–55, italics added) separates analytically four parts of such face-to-face dramatizations. He associates the first two (breach and crisis) with "ceremonial deconstruction" and the last two (redress and reintegration) with "ceremonial reconstruction."

13. Weeks later, William told me that when he had seen Brian again, he did not see either a security guard or dean who might help him "apprehend the little asshole." Although he was not "afraid of the kid," he assured me, this lack of support was the reason he chose not to take action when he saw the one-time intruder. William also told me that Brian's friend, who served as his ally, had been in one of his classes. William reported, furthermore, that Brian's friend apologized for what had taken place. The boy who had pulled Brian out of the doorway said that Brian was going through tough times at home and that his older sister had been incarcerated.

14. As Mark Johnson (2007, 4) reveals in his celebrated work on the corporal underpinnings of symbolic meanings, Merleau-Ponty may have been the first to systemize philosophically an approach to "ways in which the successful functioning of our bodies requires that our bodily organs and operations recede and even hide in our acts of experiencing things in the world," but several authors including Polanyi (1969) have catalogued and further examined this most primordial of misrecognitions. On the challenge inherent in shifting to this nondualist way of thinking, see also Lakoff and Johnson (1999).

15. As Kahlenberg (2001, 70) reports, Sandra Feldmen, president of the American Federation of Teachers which represents mostly urban school teachers, is reported to have said that, "when it comes to teaching in poor areas, "if you can breathe you can teach in most of these schools.'" Most certainly, then, the percentages of effective teachers working in Johnson and Delta had to do with the availability of jobs in more desirable schools as well as in other sectors of the two local economies. This might be seen as one of the silver lining of disastrous economic downturns and—as Jacknow-Markowitz (1993) documented with regard to a generation daughters from upwardly mobile Jewish (migrant) families who ended up teaching in the New York City public school system (instead of becoming doctors and lawyers)—the oppression inherent in "glass ceilings."

16. A journalist, who came to Delta originally to interview me and ended up substitute teaching until she started having trouble sleeping and could take no more after three weeks, said she was thrust into her classroom at Delta with only one piece of advice: "Don't touch the kids." See also Devine's (1996) empirical findings and theoretical reflections on the "hands off" approach of the teachers effectively forced to retreat into their classrooms.

17. Perhaps because the entire field of education in the Netherlands was still in a state of denial about the quality of instruction in *"zwarte"* schools, or perhaps because the rituals one finds in a neighborhood school that has been in free-fall for over thirty-five years had not yet taken root in this Dutch neighborhood school that went into decline much later, it seemed that most of my Dutch colleagues' senses of professional dignity and appropriate front-stage behavior led them to publicly dismiss problems in classes as examples of other peoples' personal shortcomings.

18. That is, in social scientific language, the number of emotionally destabilized and perhaps traumatized children especially prone to disruptive and distressing yet also temporarily energizing and attention/recognition granting responses.

19. Here, Lipsky's (1980, 161) famous definition might be useful: "The essence of street-level bureaucracies is that they require people to make decisions about other people. Street-level bureaucrats have discretion because the nature of service provision calls for human judgment that cannot be programmed and for which machines cannot substitute." This implies that, first and foremost, teachers must be emotionally, ener-

getically, kinetically, and cognitively capable of picking out the right bits of information about which judgments are required.

20. Incidentally, the courses toward certification that I was forced to take in New York had literally nothing to do with the skills and inclinations that were required for this. Aside from serving as insults to the intelligence of the professionals forced to take them, these (evening) classes further drained the already limited emotional energy of people trying to cope with the classes that had already crushed their certified (and tenured) brethren.

21. Dewey ([1938] 1979, 84).

22. This was at times quite dramatic. For example, more than once in the Bronx my own classrooms seemed to go cold when students—sometimes just out of "youth detention facilities"—brought the emotional energy and demeanor they had internalized outside our class into what Dewey might have called our qualitative immediacy. Similar things did happen at Delta, but much less regularly.

23. In such situations, rather than lecture them about not paying attention or coming to class unprepared, my sense that something truly upsetting might be taking place in or out of their homes usually led me to ask rather meekly if these students were feeling all right.

24. This teacher was considered a white/native Dutchman and he used animal-related analogies. This might (justifiably) lead some readers to associate his comments with a racist attitude. It was not however the teachers whose ancestors were from the Low Countries who most often made analogies to the animal kingdom (e.g., telling a room full of the kids that they were acting like "a bunch of apes"), but, rather, the teachers with Afro-Surinamese roots who, it might be useful to know, generally had slightly lighter skin than most of their students.

25. In the words of a teacher at a vocational secondary school in Paris, "You want to welcome them as friends and you become enemies. You're turned into a prison guard" (Bourdieu et al. 1999, 488–89).

26. As Goffman ([1959] 1990, 80) argued with regard to the effects of learning and socialization, "[P]erformances of everyday life are not 'acted' or 'put on' in the sense that the [competent] performer knows in advance just what he is going to do . . . [and the] expressions it is felt he is giving off will be especially 'inaccessible' to [him once the show gets underway]."

27. At this point students of Foucault (1979) might think back to the (nightmarish) pictures of seating arrangements and detailed descriptions of (surveillance) practices creating "trained" or "docile bodies" in French schools of the nineteenth century.

28. That is, in contrast to what happened in most classes.

29. Cf. Duckworth et al. (2009).

30. This reminds me of something as the director of a famously successful secondary school in a rough neighborhood in Rotterdam told me in one of our conversations, "The kids choose for a teacher, or not. They don't choose for a subject. That is eighty percent of what goes on [in classrooms]."

31. On the distinction between "primary" habitus formation (resulting from early socialization in homes, schools, and neighborhoods) and "specific" habitus formation (produced by post professional training and immersion in certain types of organizations and regions of the economic field), see Bourdieu ([1997] 2000). For a masterful investigation detailing how the primary habitus of "country boys" was systemically converted into the specific habitus of firefighters capable of blaming individual

colleagues for dying while trying to tame raging "wild-land" infernos, see Desmond (2006; 2007).

32. I have every reason to suspect, however, that this woman's intuitive responses were so smooth, sure, and incisive because somewhere in the past just the right "confluence of dozens of small skills and activates" had already been "carefully drilled into habit" and "fitted in a synthesized whole." Like a great athlete, after years of "gaining the habits of competitiveness and consistency, after becoming comfortable in [her] world," she had incarnated the "myriad techniques that together constitute excellence" (Chambliss 1989, 81, 84).

33. Seen through the prevailing racial lens, it might be worth noting, this would appear to be an incident of black-on-black violence.

34. Bourdieu (in Bourdieu et al 1999, 183).

35. That is, the isolated (white male) newcomer is overpowered until successfully learning to master a new environment and all the (implicitly lower) forms of life in it. I thank Alice Goffman for daring to highlight the appeal of this script both among filmmakers and urban ethnographers during a panel discussion at the 2011 American Sociological Association conference.

36. Especially given the emphasis on highly conscious (and racialized) cultural resistance, it is important to emphasize that these less exceptional students had no way to find release from the frenzy, fear, distractions, and situated desires. They could not step back from, and calmly reflect on, what was happening around them or how they (unwittingly) contributed to it. No matter what they believed about needing to "get it together" (during calmer moments), in the here-and-now in the vast majority of classes, they had no way to see clearly how or why they usually failed to stay focused on anything related to the official curriculum for more than a few seconds at a time. So, like damaged records that remain in the same grooves—unless a master teacher delicately picked them up or jolted them—they remained stuck in ways of coping that were unproductive for themselves and those around them.

37. What this once again reveals, but this time from inside classrooms, is that the dispositions of even the most emotionally damaged teens never generated strategies outside of the triggers operating from moment-to-moment in specific contexts. In other words, neither blanket-like peer group cultures nor conscious switching between pro- and antischool codes enabled and constrained action in classrooms at the most primordial level.

38. Here I return to the op-ed from the *Times*, January 11, 2012, discussed at the outset of this chapter.

39. Mills (1959, 71–72).

CHAPTER SEVEN

1. A girl smoking a cigarette outside of the Delta School where, in her own words, she had just "wasted an entire morning."

2. A boy—whose mother I knew to be incarcerated and diagnosed with HIV/AIDS—made this comment while sitting in one of Johnson's long hallways after being expelled from a classroom.

3. Nor, in the context of this study, has this term toxic been used to refer to asbestos crises (Dickar 2008, 46), proximity to waste sites (Kozol 1991, 7–39), or hazards related to dangerous chemicals of any kind. On the possibility that students attending inner-city public high schools across the Northeastern United States may be exceptionally at risk to "toxins" in this more conventional sense of the term, see Chew,

Correa, and Perzanowski (2005). Also, see the work of scientists working within environmental justice frameworks on whether certain students ("of color") are over-represented among those negatively impacted by exposure to such toxins in, among other places, public schools (cf. Pastor, Morello-Frosch, and Sadd 2006).

4. Martin Johnson (1999, 37–8) would have it, "For teachers dealing with difficult classes, there are hundreds of negative interactions each day. Each one jolts. Each one must be dealt with without anger. Each one is exhausting, demoralizing, and prevents us from teaching effectively. And each one is unavoidable. No one can tolerate such a social environment, hour after hour, day after day, without damage to their long-term health. This is why teachers in such schools are drained, exhausted, and emotionally fragile by the end of the school day."

5. The term toxic is certainly not, therefore, meant to suggest that Johnson and Delta were fully autonomous sites deserving all (or even most) of the blame for the catastrophes observable inside them. Following Wacquant's (2004, 17) lead here, we might speak of a "double relation of symbiosis and opposition" between on one hand the two quasi-autonomous educational domains and, on the other, the two neighborhoods (which themselves might be seen as quasi-autonomous social formations). For more on the notion that fields (within fields) can be treated as prisms that refract incoming forces (or, in this metaphor, rays of light) according to their own internal logics, see Bourdieu and Wacquant (1992, 15–19) and Wacquant's (1997) seminal contribution to the processual study of neighborhoods of urban relegation, "Elias in the Dark Ghetto."

6. So I add my voice to those of other scholars on both sides of the Atlantic (e.g., Anyon 1997, Bourdieu et al 1999; Bourgois 1996) who emphasize how de facto educational apartheid both reflects and perpetuates broader (economic, cultural, racialized, and spatial) inequalities. Just to be clear, then, my argument has nothing to do with forgetting that "education cannot compensate for society" (Bernstein 1970).

7. As Warren and Tyagi (2003, 22–32) argued years before the bubble burst, many parents got into bidding wars for homes not because they were irresponsible consumers, but because they were responsible parents trying desperately to get into safe school districts.

8. As Bourdieu and Passeron ([1970] 1977) demonstrated decades ago, school systems do this with assists from teachers through the naturalizing wonders of discourses about education "giving everyone their chance."

9. Unsurprisingly, recent research has verified that across Europe and North America, "adolescents from families of low affluence reported higher prevalence of being victims of bullying" and, additionally, that teens living in "countries where socio-economic differences are larger are at higher risk of being bullied" (Due et al. 2009, 907). Recalling how my students drew clear distinctions between *bullying* and that which they considered "really threatening"—as Raul put it when he discussed what awaited him inside Delta—may help illustrate why I do not frame my research in terms of this term and expanding research literature. Research on schools in the United Kingdom suggests links between negative health outcomes and (being even a "witness" or "bystander" to) bullying (Rivers et al. 2009; Rivers 2012).

10. If oppositional black (or minority/ethnic) culture is not *the* lens through which "urban" educational problems and reforms are discussed both in the United States and the Netherlands, it certainly seems fair to say that it remains one of the most important ones. Those who would contend that elite policy debates in the United States have shifted to charter schools (and union bashing) might do well to revisit *No*

Excuses: Closing the Racial Gap in Learning (Thernstrom and Thernstrom 2003)—the most influential book related to the charter-school movement. The two authors argue that the charter-school solution (e.g., KIPP schools) is necessary because it is the only way to overcome the defects of clearly racialized cultures. By this the authors mean, first and foremost, the achievement-related "values" of blacks. As Kahlenberg made clear in his *Washington Post* review, ("Class Acts," November 30, 2003, emphasis added), the Thornstroms' underlying assumption derived directly from Ogbu's research: "Meeting the demands of schools is harder for members of some racial and ethnic groups than for others [and s]ome group cultures are more academically advantageous than others." In policy, academic, and journalistic discussions in the Netherlands, the reliance on the term *"zwarte"* (black) schools and the nearly universal convergence of putatively distinct "cultures" and "ethnic groups" support the main point.

11. To a degree, therefore, my findings corroborate Carter's (2005) interpretation of locally legitimized situational know-how being as "black cultural capital." To "keep it real" was, to some extent, to behave in ways associated in both settings with blackness. My findings here also dovetail with Dickar's (2008) analyses of extra-classroom settings as spaces of temporary (rather than monolithic, ideologically stable) anti-school "black solidarity." Here my findings also corroborate key aspects of Anderson's (1999) heavily Ogbu-inspired work on *The Code of the Street.*

12. Going back to a sequence of events involving the trashcan thrower in Johnson High might help drive home this point. I can report with near certainty that neither Robert (who came to my aid) nor I were concerned primarily with any ideas about race, ethnicity, or nationality when it was "on." The performance of gender roles ("I'm gonna make you my bitch after school") and the struggle for social domination related to energy, prestige, and above all fear of physical violence were not just "central." In the heat of the moment, they were almost "everything."

13. Trying to heed Baumann's (1996, 8) warning, I try to avoid "stereotyping informants as "belonging to" or even "speaking for" a predefined "community" [as, in doing this, we risk] tribalizing people instead of listening to them, and studying communities of [our] own making."

14. See Brown et al.'s (2003) *White-Washing Race* for a review.

15. Groupism—presenting "discrete, sharply differentiated, internally homogeneous and externally bounded [racial or ethno-national] groups as basic constituents of social life, chief protagonists of social conflicts, and fundamental units of social analysis (Brubaker 2002, 164)—can be "efficient" in terms getting funding for research, publishing journal articles, and presenting "killer" slides to politicians, journalists, or students.

16. As Weber (1978, 394–95) put it, "All in all, the notion of 'ethnically' determined social action subsumes phenomena that a rigorous sociological analysis . . . would have to distinguish carefully . . . It is certain that in this process [of precise analysis] the collective term 'ethnic' would be abandoned, for it is unsuitable for a really rigorous analysis. The concept of the 'ethnic' group . . . dissolves if we define our terms exactly."

17. Researchers who ignore the available evidence and stick with clearly distinct ethno-racial categories and corresponding groups might be said to call forth the image of post-office workers clinging to the logic of neatly divided zip codes even when face-to-face with letters that either have nonexistent postal codes or none at all. Things may continue to look orderly from a distance as long as the "organizer" just keeps

pushing the letters into clearly separated compartments. From close up, of course, this seems like an institutionalized inability to deal with what is actually going on (if not Weber's famous soulless cogs caught in a "rationalized" machine or, in Habermas's equally grim language, life worlds being "colonialized" by a system).

18. As Weber (1978, 21–22) himself however wrote while introducing his "Basic Sociological Terms" and "The Definition of Sociology and Social Action" in *Economy and Society*: "In the great majority of cases actual action goes on in a state of inarticulate half-consciousness or actual unconsciousness of its subjective meaning. The actor is more likely to 'be aware' of it in a vague sense than he is to 'know' what he is doing or be explicitly self-conscious about it. In most cases his action is governed by impulse or habit. Only occasionally and, in the uniform action of large numbers, often only in the case of a few individuals, is the subjective meaning of the action, whether rational or irrational, brought clearly into consciousness. The ideal type of meaningful action where the meaning is fully conscious and explicit is a marginal case. Every sociological or historical investigation, in applying its analysis to the empirical facts, must take this into account."

19. As Katz's (1988, 11) notes, "Because the search for evidence and the development of theory proceed in mutually altering steps, the analytic results do not emerge from a straightforward, deductive, hard, or inflexible application of theory to fact. Rather, the methodological quality increases the more the theory is pushed around and beaten into shape by frustrated applications."

20. Perhaps all of this was demonstrated most clearly in Derek's transformation into "Cookie." Here we saw that (socially mobile) newcomers sometimes worked deliberately and hard to lose their accents and become "street" and "hard." There is no denying that, during a certain faze, Derek's efforts were tied up with very explicit ideas about bodily performances (and, again, blackness). But the evidence does not support the argument that Derek deliberately constructed or selected his desires at this stage. Furthermore, the deeper insight produced by this tragic example is that Derek was judged to be "sweet" and "real" when his performances flowed on time because they were guided (almost) automatically by a somewhat field-specific second nature rather than by any time consuming explicit mental representations (related to the following of rules). Derek was "real"-ized in the hallways, that is, when the "hard" mask merged into his "pretty" face. As a competent and indeed exceptionally "hot" member of more dominant peer groups, most of the time, his "street" facial expressions, way of carrying himself in his baggy jeans, and tone of voice were spontaneously lived through more than actively "constructed" through feats of explicit mental processing. Such immediately felt everyday responses were worth examining in part because "Cookie" dwelled in educational and residential worlds in which these ways of walking, "looking," and talking reflected and reproduced peer group dynamics powerful enough to destroy educational institutions and more dangerous than anything roughly a hundred percent of middle-class teens in Amsterdam or New York will ever know.

21. "Of the ideas advanced in this book," Damasio (2012, 20) wrote in the introduction to his most ambitious effort to date, "none is more central than the notion that the body is the foundation of the conscious mind."

22. In Katz's (1999, 7) formulation, "Through our emotions, we reach back sensually to grasp the tacit, embodied foundations of ourselves. We are artful in producing our emotions because through them we seek to articulate the corporeal metaphors that operate implicitly as the foundation of all our conduct."

23. As Bourdieu ([1997] 2000, 144) would have it, "This practical, nonthetic intention-ality, which has nothing in common with a cogito consciously oriented towards a cogitatum, is rooted in a posture, a way of bearing, the body (a hexis), a durable way of being of the durably modified body which is engendered and perpetuated, while constantly changing (within limits), in a twofold relationship, structured and structuring, to the environment. Habitus constructs the world by a certain way of orienting itself toward it, of bringing to bear on it an attention which, like that of a jumper preparing to jump, is an active, constructive bodily tension towards immi-nent forthcoming."

24. Due to the enormous impact of Anderson's (1999) work on "the code," even in re-search and policy discussions at the very highest levels of government (e.g., Holder, Robinson, and Rose 2009), I want to come back to it one last time. Precisely because I take so seriously the bifurcated cultural logics and explicit mental constructions upon which Anderson's approach to actual lines of (violent) behavior rest, I tried to do what was necessary to get beneath them. In this I am not alone. Smardon (2009) also tries to make use of Anderson's contributions while, in the end, mak-ing several similarly critical points about the overly mentalist and highly agentic assumptions undergirding *The Code of the Street*. From a more ethno-methodological perspective, Jimerson and Oware (2006) stress that the evidence for ideological struggles presented in *The Code of the Street* comes not from what happened in real time but, rather, from "black men talking" to Anderson about what happened after the fact. These co-authors argue that the young men who talked to Anderson were more or less strategically performing stereotypes that helped them rationalize tragic outcomes. They also offered Anderson attractive invitations, the two authors suggest, to fall into the trap of reinforcing racialized and cliché rhetorical devices that do little justice to what actually took place.

25. "[I]n or outside of schools," as Bourgois put it in an interview with me (Paulle 2003, 556), "it is easy to glorify inner-city violence as a 'culture of resistance.'" What Bour-gois clearly had in mind were "critical" ethnographies that set out to "restore" the "cultural agency" and "true voices" of the disadvantaged.

26. Elias ([1969] 1983, 74–75), also quoted in Bourdieu ([1989] 1996, 129).

27. In addition to several works already mentioned, Warikoo and Carter's (2009) un-packing of both culture and race amidst a "call for new and improved theory" de-serves special attention here.

APPENDIX

1. Whyte ([1955] 1994, 279).

2. Bourdieu (2000, 141).

3. Cf. Bourgois (1995, 13) on getting the "accurate data."

4. Merleau-Ponty (1962, 168).

5. The point may be more important than we would like to admit. Especially for middle-class intellectuals who start getting a taste of everyday life in an urban "slum" for the first time, as Whyte ([1955] 1994, 293, 279) implied, the temptation is to rationalize retreating to the comfort of texts and highbrow discussions in non-marginalized enclaves.

6. Cf. Pollner and Emerson's "Dynamics of Inclusion and Distance in Fieldwork Rela-tions" (1983) and Gordon's "Getting Close by Staying Distant" (1987, 267).

7. Or, if you like, human beings whose highly "plastic" neural pathways were con-stantly being re-shaped (e.g., "pruning") by everyday relationships and experiences,

and whose executive functioning capacities (e.g., planning ahead, deferring gratification, emotional self-control) were more or less impaired by the fact that their prefrontal cortexes were not yet fully "online."

8. Reflecting on years of firsthand research on street gangs, Fleisher (2000, 93) addressed this issue when he argued the following: "While we may be victimized by transference and compassion fatigue, we must, however, recognize these as items on our research agendas and include in our writing responses to PTSD and to transference on multiple levels (personal, professional, societal). Doing that means we must become less self-conscious of writing about our own personal experiences in the ethnographic process. Surely we are not bashful about writing about the pain of others, likewise we should learn to use our experiences to improve our research. To do otherwise would reduce the potential usefulness and power of the ethnographic methods applied to the most difficult field situations in contemporary urban life."

9. Again here I want to stress my indebtedness to James and especially Dewey, the theorist of the "mind-body complex," as well as to Merleau-Ponty, the French philosopher who systemically fleshed out Heidegger's fundamental ontology.

10. After all, as Bourdieu and Passeron ([1964] 1979, 70) saw long ago, "Students are even more vulnerable to essentialism [than teachers] because, as adolescents and apprentices, they are always in search of what they are, so that what they do seems to concern their whole being."

11. In part, I was simply afraid for myself. I also felt I needed "down time." But I also assumed living in such a neighborhood would not be safe for the woman from Amsterdam with whom I was living at the time. Also, through social contacts, I was able to rent an apartment elsewhere at well-below market value.

12. Exactly the same things happened in New York when the 2 or 3 express subway train made it down to 96th Street (or when the D train made the big jump from 125th to 59th Street). Putatively black or Latino or not, those who boarded often seemed to be of a "completely" different type than those I took to be residents of "Harlemworld" or the "Boogie-Down Bronx."

13. Brubaker et al. (2006, 169, 209, 208).

14. Not only do they tend to shy away from such terms, ethnographers don't usually write about those they study as resources for generating ideas and theory at all. They may present "informants" as confirmers of fact and opinion, but not as genuine analytic partners. Here again, therefore, I feel a strong continuity and affinity with Whyte—the first, as far as I know, to discuss openly how ongoing intellectual camaraderie with an insider (Doc) actually generated the ethnographic analysis.

15. Cf. De Zwart (2012, 307).

16. Shusterman (2005, 159, quoting Merleau-Ponty's *Phenomenology of Perception*).

17. Daniella Zanzotto, of Disruptive Films, made several trips from London to New York to film in and around Johnson High. Jos Wassink and his associates at VPRO's *Noorderlicht* filmed in and around the Delta School.

18. I (too) found myself trying to sound "smart" when I knew audio- and/or video-recording devices were running, and my efforts to "just be myself" with such devices on always generated some "other" self. Recording could therefore stimulate internal dialogues and therefore make listening, and really being present for all that took place, more difficult.

19. Maclure and Bassey (1991, 190) summarize what they see as the three core components of Participatory Action Research, or PAR, as follows: (1) shared ownership, (2) community-based learning, and (3) community-initiated action.

20. There is much more to be said about my indebtedness to this "School" and here again Dewey deserves mention. Along with Ernest Burgess, Robert Park was the teacher of the dissertation writers who basically made the "Chicago School" so great and, in so doing, created a space within sociology for the type of work I do today. Although perhaps watered down by the time it got to them, much of the theory Chicagoland ethnographers absorbed from Park as well as from Burgess and W.I. Thomas came from Dewey (via the teachings of Dewey's close associate, G.H. Mead, who is more clearly connected to symbolic interactionism, ethnomethodology, and the Chicago School).

21. And here I really have to single someone out. Emirbayer, my first great mentor (during our time at the New School in the mid-1990s), is generally labeled a "theorist." People might therefore assume that, in my case, developing a feel for using empirical insights meant outgrowing his influence and moving from an overly theoreticist perspective to a more concrete one. Nothing could be further from the truth! From the earliest days and most consistently throughout my development as a sociologist, Mustafa urged me to progress in this very direction. The problem was not his counsel but, and I think this may be instructive, my inability to act on what he (and, later, several) others were telling me to do. In other words it took me a decade and a half to really start hearing what this processual thinker with the heart of an ethnographer had been saying from the beginning: as carefully and compellingly as possible, bring to life the shifting pressures and in situ responses that only those with direct observations can adequately understand.

22. In Wacquant's (2004, xvii) words, "Sociology must endeavor to clasp and restitute [the] carnal dimension of existence . . . through a methodical and meticulous work of detection and documentation, deciphering, and writing liable to capture and to convey the taste and the ache of action, the sound, and the fury of the social world that the established approaches of the social sciences typically mute when they do not suppress them altogether."

23. This idea is not a new (age) one. As the Buddha (depicted in Anguttara Nikaya, quoted in Shusterman 2008, vi) said, "[O]ne thing, if practiced and made much of, conduces to . . . the winning of knowledge and insight . . . What is this one thing? It is mindfulness centered on body."

BIBLIOGRAPHY

Adler, P.A., and P. Adler. *Membership Roles in Field Settings*. Newbury Park, CA: Sage, 1987.

Ainsworth-Darnell, J.W., and D.B. Downey. 1998. "Assessing the Oppositional Culture Explanation for Racial/Ethnic Differences in School Performance." *American Sociological Review* 63 (1998); 536–53.

Alonso, G., Noel S. Anderson, Celina Su, and Jeanne Theoharis. *Our Schools Suck: Students Talk Back to a Segregated Nation on the Failure in Urban Education*. New York and London: New York University Press, 2009.

Anderson, B. *Imagined Communities: Reflections on the Origin and Spread of Nationalism*. London: Verso, 1991.

Anderson, E. *Streetwise: Race, Class, and Change in an Urban Community*. Chicago: University of Chicago Press, 1990.

———. *Code of the Street: Decency, Violence, and the Moral Life of the Inner City*. New York: Norton, 1999.

———, ed. *Against the Wall: Poor, Young, Black, and Male*. Philadelphia: University of Pennsylvania Press, 2008.

Anyon, J. *Ghetto Schooling: A Political Economy of Urban Educational Reform*. New York: Columbia University Press, 1997.

Apple, M.W. *Ideology and Curriculum*. New York: Routledge, 1990.

Baldwin, J. "My Dungeon Shook." In *The Fire Next Time*. New York: Dell Publishing, 1963.

Balfanz, R., and N. Legters. *Locating the Dropout Crisis*. Baltimore, MD: Center for Research on the Education of Students Placed At Risk, Center for Social Organization of Schools, Johns Hopkins University, 2004.

Baumann, G. *Contesting Cultures: Discourses of Identity in Multi-Ethnic London*. Cambridge: Cambridge University Press, 1996.

Becker, H.S. "Social-Class Variations in the Teacher-Pupil Relationship." *Journal of Educational Sociology* 25 (1952); 451–66.

———. "The Teacher in the Authority System of the Public School." *Journal of Educational Sociology* 27, no. 3 (1953); 128–41.

———. *Outsiders: Studies in the Sociology of Deviance*. New York: The Free Press, 1963.

———. "A School Is a Lousy Place To Learn Anything In." *American Behavioral Scientist*, 16, no. 1 (Sept./Oct. 1972); 85–105.

Becker, H.S., and B. Geer. "Participant Observation: The Analysis of Qualitative Field Data." In *Human Organization Research*, edited by R.N. Adams and J.J. Preiss. Homewood, IL: Dorsey, 1960.

Bernstein, B. "Education Cannot Compensate for Society." *New Society* 387 (1970), 344–47.

Bijnaar, A. *Kasmoni: Een Spaartraditie in Suriname en Nederland*. Amsterdam: Bakker, 2002.

Bourdieu, P. *Outline of a Theory of Practice*. Cambridge: Cambridge University Press, [1972] 1977.

———. *Distinction: A Social Critique of the Judgment of Taste*. London: Routledge & Kegan Paul, [1979] 1984.

———. 1986. "The Forms of Capital." In *Handbook of Theory of Research for the Sociology of Education*, edited by J.E. Richardson. New York: Greenword Press, 1986.

———. *The Logic of Practice*. Cambridge, MA.: Polity Press, [1980] 1990.

———. *In Other Words: Essays Towards a Reflexive Sociology*. Stanford, CA: Stanford University Press, 1990a.

———. *Language and Symbolic Power*. Cambridge: Polity Press, 1991.

———. *The State Nobility: Elite Schools in the Field of Power*. Stanford University Press, 1996.

———. *Acts of Resistance: Against the New Myths of Our Time*. New York: New Press, 1998.

———. *Pascalian Meditations*. Stanford University Press, [1997] 2000.

———. *Masculine Domination*. Cambridge, MA: Polity Press, [1998] 2001.

Bourdieu, P., et al., eds. *The Weight of the World: Social Suffering in Contemporary Society*. Cambridge, MA: Polity Press, 1999.

Bourdieu, P. and P. Champagne, "Outcasts in the Inside," ibid.

Bourdieu, P., and J.C. Passeron. *Reproduction in Education, Society, and Culture*. London, Sage, [1970] 1977.

———. *The Inheritors. French Students and Their Relation to Culture*. University of Chicago Press, [1964] 1979.

Bourdieu, P., and L.J.D.Wacquant. *An Invitation to Reflexive Sociology*. Cambridge, MA: Polity Press, 1992.

Bourgois, P. *In Search of Respect: Selling Crack in El Barrio*. Cambridge, MA.: Cambridge University Press, 1995.

———. "Confronting Anthropology, Education, and Inner-City Apartheid." *American Anthropologist* 98 (1996), 249–58.

———. "The Power of Violence in War and Peace: Post–Cold War Lessons from El Salvador." *Ethnography* 2 (2001), 5–34.

Brazelton, T.B., and S. Greenspan, S. *The Irreducible Needs of Children: What Every Child Must Have to Grow, Learn, and Flourish*. Cambridge, MA: Perseus Publishing, 2000.

Brown, M.K, and Martin Carnoy, Elliott Currie, and Troy Duster, eds., *Whitewashing Race: The Myth of a Color-Blind Society*. Berkeley: University of California Press, 2003.

Brubaker, R. "Ethnicity Without Groups." Archives Européennes de Sociologie XLIII (2002): 163–89.

———. "Ethnicity, Race, and Nationalism." Annual Review of Sociology 35 (2009): 21–42.

Brubaker, R., Margit Feischmidt, Jon Fox, and Liana Grancea. *Nationalist Politics and Everyday Ethnicity in a Transylvanian Town*. Princeton University Press, 2006.

Brumberg, S.F. "The Teacher Crisis and Educational Standards." In *City Schools: Lessons from New York*, edited by D. Ravitch and J.P. Viteritti. Baltimore and London: The Johns Hopkins University Press, 2000.

Butler, J. *Bodies That Matter: On the Discursive Limits of "Sex."* London: Routledge, 1993.

———. *Gender Trouble.* New York: Routledge Press, 1999.

Carter, P.L. *Keepin' It Real: School Success beyond Black and White.* New York: Oxford University Press, 2005.

———."Straddling Boundaries: Identity, Culture, and School." *Sociology of Education* 79, no. 3 (2006): 304–28.

Chew, G.L., J.C. Correa, M.S. Perzanowski. "Mouse and Cockroach Allergens in the Dust and Air in Northeastern United States Inner-City Public High Schools." *Indoor Air* 15, no. 4 (2005): 228–34.

Cicourel, A. *Method and Measurement in Sociology.* London: Collier-Macmillan, 1964.

Chambliss, D.F. "The Mundanity of Excellence: An Ethnographic Report on Stratification and Olympic Swimmers." *Sociological Theory* 7, no. 1 (Spring 1989): 70–86.

———. "Making Theories from Water; or, Finding Stratification in Competitive Swimming." In *Ethnographies Revisted: Constructing Theory in the Field*, edited by Antony J. Puddephatt, William Shaffir, and Steven W. Kleinknecht. New York: Routledge, 2009.

Chetty, R., J. Friedman, and J. Rockoff. "The Long-Term Impacts of Teachers: Teacher Value-Added and Student Outcomes in Adulthood." Working Paper 17699. Cambridge, MA: National Bureau of Economic Research, 2011.

Choenni, O. *Veelsoortig Assortiment Allochtoon Ondernemerschap in Amsterdam als Incorporatietraject, 1965–1995.* Amsterdam: Uitgeverij Het Spinhuis, 1997.

Clark. R.M. *Family Life and School Achievement: Why Poor Black Children Succeed or Fail.* University of Chicago Press, 1983.

Coleman, J. *The Adolescent Society: The Social Life of the Teenager and its Impact on Education.* Glencoe, New York: The Free Press of Glencoe, 1963.

Collins, R. *Interaction Ritual Chains.* Princeton University Press, 2004.

———. *Violence: A Micro-Sociological Theory.* Princeton University Press, 2007.

Cook, I. and M. Harrison. "Follow the Thing: 'West Indian Hot Pepper Sauce.'" *Space and Culture* 10, no. 1 (2007): 40–63.

Cook, P.J., and J. Ludwig. "The Burden of Acting White: Do Black Adolescents Disparage Academic Achievement?" In *The Black-White Test Score Gap*, edited by C. Jencks and M. Phillips. New York: The Brookings Institution Press, 1998.

Coser, L.A. *Greedy Institutions: Patterns of Undivided Commitment.* New York: Free Press, 1974.

Cromby, J. "Feelings, Beliefs, and Being Human." In *Being Human*, edited by A. Morgan. Ross-on-Wye: PCCS Books, 2008.

Crul, M. *De Sleutel tot Succes: Over Hulp, Keuzes en Kansen in de Schoolloopbanen van Turkse en Marokkaanse Jongeren van de Tweede Generatie.* Amsterdam: Het Spinhuis, 2000.

Csikszentmihalyi, M., and I.S. Csikszentmihalyi, eds. *Optimal Experience: Psychological Studies of Flow in Consciousness.* Cambridge, MA.: Cambridge University Press, 1988.

De Zwart, F. "Pitfalls of Top-Down Identity Designation: Ethno-Statistics in the Netherlands." *Comparative European Politics* 10, no. 3 (2012): 301–18.

Danese A., C.M. Pariante, A. Caspi, A. Taylor, and R. Poulton. "Childhood Maltreatment Predicts Adult Inflammation in a Life-Course Study." *Proceedings of the National Academy of Sciences of the United States of America* 104, no. 4 (2007): 1319–24.

Davidson, R.J., with S. Begley. *The Emotional Life of Your Brain: How its Unique Patterns Affect the Way You Think, Feel, and Live—and How You Can Change Them.* New York: Hudson Street Press, 2012.

Davidson, R.J. and B.S. McEwen. "Social Influences on Neuroplasticity: Stress and Interventions to Promote Well-Being." *Nature Neuroscience* 15, no. 5 (2012): 689–95.

Desmond, M. "Becoming a Firefighter," *Ethnography* 7 (2006): 387–421.

———. *On the Fireline: Living and Dying with Wildland Firefighters.* University of Chicago Press, 2007.

———. "Eviction and the Reproduction of Urban Poverty." *American Journal of Sociology* 118, 2012a, 88–133.

———. "Disposable Ties and the Urban Poor." *American Journal of Sociology* 117, 2012b, 1295–335.

Desmond, M., and M. Emirbayer. *Racial Domination, Racial Progress: The Sociology of Race in America.* New York: McGraw-Hill, 2009.

Devine, J. *Maximum Security: The Culture of Violence in inner-city schools.* Chicago: The University of Chicago Press, 1996.

Dewalt, K.M., and B.R. Dewalt. *Participant Observation—A Guide for Fieldworkers.* Walnut Creek, CA: Altamira Press, 2002.

Dewey, J. *Experience and Education.* New York: Collier Books, [1938] 2008.

———. "Body and Mind." First published in the *Bulletin of the NY Academy of Medicine,* 1928. In *The Collected Works of John Dewey: Later Works Volume 3: 1927–1928 Essays, Reviews, Miscellany.* Carbondale, IL: Southern Illinois University Press, 2008.

———. *Experience and Nature. John Dewey: The Later Works, 1925–1953. Volume 1: 1925.* Edited by Jo Ann Boydston. Carbondale, IL: Southern Illinois University Press, [1925] 1988.

———. *Human Nature and Conduct. John Dewey: The Middle Works, 1899–1924. Volume 14: 1922.* Edited by Jo Ann Boydston. Carbondale, IL: Southern Illinois University Press, [1922] 1988.

———. *Democracy and Education.* New York: Free Press, [1916] 1997.

Diamond, J.B. "Race and School Achievement in Desegregated Suburb: Reconsidering the Oppositional Culture Explanation." *International Journal of Qualitative Studies in Education* 20 (2007): 655–79.

Dickar, M. *Corridor Cultures.* New York University Press, 2008.

Diehl, D., and D. McFarland. "Towards a Historical Sociology of Situations." *American Journal of Sociology* 115, no. 6 (2010): 1713–52.

Dienst Onderzoek en Statistiek. *De Staat van de Stad Amsterdam II: Ontwikkeling in Participatie en Leefsituatie.* Amsterdam: Dienst Onderzoek en Statistiek, 2003.

Dreyfus, H. *Being-in-the-World: A Commentary on Heidegger's Being and Time, Division I.* Cambridge, MA: MIT Press, 1991.

Duckworth, A.L., P.D. Quinn, and M.E.P. Seligman. "Positive Predictors of Teacher Effectiveness." *The Journal of Positive Psychology* 4, no. 6 (2009): 540–47.

Damasio, A. *Self Comes to Mind: Constructing the Conscious Brain.* New York: Vintage, 2012.

Due, P., et al. "Socioeconomic Inequality in Exposure to Bullying During Adolescence: A Comparative, Cross-Sectional, Multilevel Study in 35 Countries." *American Journal of Public Health* 99, no. 5 (2009): 907–14.

Duneier, M. *Sidewalk.* New York: Farrar, Straus and Giroux, 1999.

Durkheim, E. *The Elementary Forms of the Religious Life.* New York: The Free Press, [1912] 1965.

———. *The Evolution of Educational Thought: Lectures on the Formation and Development of Secondary Education in France.* London and Boston: Routledge & Kegan Paul, [1938] 1977.

Duyvendak, J.W. *The Politics of Home: Belonging and Nostalgia in Western Europe and the United States.* Basingstoke, UK: Palgrave Macmillan, 2011.

Elias, N. *What is Sociology?* New York: Columbia University Press, [1970] 1978.

———. *The Court Society.* Oxford. UK: Basil Blackwell Publisher, [1969] 1983.

———. *The Civilizing Process: The History of Manners and State Formation and Civilization.* Oxford: Basil Blackwell Publisher, [1939] 1994.

Elias, N., and J.L. Scotson. *The Established and the Outsiders: A Sociological Enquiry into Community Problems.* London: Sage, [1965] 1994.

Emerson, R.M., ed. *Contemporary Field Research: A Collection of Readings.* Boston, MA: Little, Brown, 1983.

Emerson, R.M. and M. Pollner. "On the Uses of Members' Responses to Researchers' Accounts." *Human Organization* 47, no. 3 (1988): 189–98.

———. "Difference and Dialogue: Members' Readings of Ethnographic Texts." *Perspectives on Social Problems* 3 (1992): 79–98.

Emerson, R.M., R.I. Fretz, and L. Shaw. *Writing Ethnographic Fieldnotes.* University of Chicago Press, 1995.

———. "Participant Observation and Fieldnotes." In *Handbook of Ethnography*, edited by P. Atkinson, A. Coffey, S. Delamont, J. Lofland, and L. Lofland. London: Sage, 2001.

Emirbayer, M., and J. Goodwin. "Network Analysis, Culture, and the Problem of Agency." *American Journal of Sociology* 99, no. 6 (1994): 1411–54.

Emirbayer, M., and E. Schneiderhan. "Dewey and Bourdieu on Democracy." In *Bourdieuian Theory and Historical Analysis*, edited by P.S. Gorski. Durham: Duke University Press, 2013.

Engbersen, G., J.P van der Leun, R. Staring, and J. Kehla. "Inbedding en uitsluiting van illegale vreemdelingen." In *De Oongekende Stad 2.* Amsterdam: Boom, 1999.

Epel, E.S., E.H. Blackburn, J. Lin, F.S. Dhabhar, N.E. Adler, J.D. Morrow, R.M. Cawthon. "Accelerated Telomere Shortening in Response to Life Stress." *Proceedings of the National Academy of Sciences* 101, no. 49 (2004): 17312–15.

Erickson, F. "Qualitative Methods." In *Handbook of Research on Teaching*, edited by M.C. Wittrock. New York: Macmillan, 1986.

Farmer. P. "An Anthropology of Structural Violence." *Current Anthropology* 45, no. 3 (2004): 305–25.

Fainstein, S., I. Gordon, and M. Harloe, eds. *Divided Cities: New York and London in the Contemporary World.* Oxford: Basil Blackwell, 1994.

Fleisher, M.S. "(Counter-)transference and Compassion Fatigue in Urban Gang Ethnography." *Focaal* 36 (2000): 77–96.

Flook, L., S.L. Smalley, M.J. Kitil, B.M. Galla, S. Kaiser-Greenland, J. Locke, E. Ishijima, and C. Kasari. "Effects of Mindful Awareness Practices on Executive Functions in Elementary School Children." *Journal of Applied School Psychology* 26, no. 1(2010): 70–95.

Foley, D. "Elusive Prey: John Ogbu and the Search for a Grand Theory of Academic Disengagement." *International Journal of Qualitative Studies in Education* 18, no. 5 (2005): 643–57.

Fordham, S. "Racelessness as a Strategy in Black Students' School Success: Pragmatic Strategy or Pyrrhic Victory? *Harvard Educational Review* 58 (1988): 54–84.

———. *Blacked Out: Dilemmas of Race, Identity, and Success at Capital High.* University of Chicago Press, 1996.

Fordham, S., and J.U. Ogbu. "Black Students' School Success: Coping with the 'Burden of Acting White.'" *The Urban Review* 18 (1986): 176–206.

Foucault, M. *Discipline and Punish: The Birth of the Prison.* Harmondsworth, UK: Penguin Books, [1975] 1979.

Fine, M. "Chartering Urban School Reform." In *Chartering Urban School Reform*, edited by M. Fine. New York: Teachers College Press, 1994.

Freiberg, H.J. *Beyond Behaviorism: Changing the Classroom Management Paradigm.* Boston: Allyn and Bacon, 1999.

Freudenberg, N., L. Roberts, B.E. Richie, R.T. Taylor, and K. McGillicuddy. "Coming Up in the Boogie Down: The Role of Violence in the Lives of Adolescents in the South Bronx." *Health, Education & Behavior* 26, (2000): 788–805.

Fryer, R. and P. Torelli. "An Empirical Analysis of 'Acting White.'" NBER Working Paper No. 11334, 2006.

Gans, H. "Second Generation Decline: Scenarios for the Economic and Ethnic Futures of the Post-1965 American Immigrants." *Ethnic and Racial Studies* 15, no. 2 (1992): 173–92.

Garfinkel, H. *Studies in Ethnomethodology.* Englewood Cliffs: Prentice-Hall, 1967.

Garot, R. *Who You Claim: Performing Gang Identity in School and on the Streets.* New York University Press, 2010.

Garot, R., and J. Katz. "Provocative Looks: Gang Appearance and Dress Codes in an Inner-City Alternative School." *Ethnography* 4 (2003): 421–54.

Garrison, J. "Realism, Deweyan Pragmatism, and Educational Research." *Educational Researcher* 23 (January–February 1994): 5–14.

Geertz, C. *The Interpretation of Cultures: Selected Essays.* New York: Basic Books, 1973.

Gibson, M.A. "Situational and Structural Rationales for the School Performance of Immigrant Youth: Three Cases." In *Immigrants, Schooling, and Social Mobility*, edited by H. Vermeulen and J. Perlmann. London: MacMillan, 2000.

Glazer, N. "The South Bronx Story: An Extreme Case of Neighborhood Decline." *Policy Studies Journal* 16 (1987): 269–76.

Goffman, A. "On the Run: Wanted Men in a Philadelphia Ghetto." In *American Sociological Review* 74 (2009): 339–57.

Goffman, E. *The Presentation of Self in Everyday Life.* London: Penguin Books, 1959.

———. *Stigma: Notes on the Management of Spoiled Identity.* Englewood Cliffs, NJ: Prentice-Hall, 1963.

———. *Interaction Ritual: Essays in Face-to-Face Behavior.* Chicago: Aldine, 1967.

———. "The Interaction Order." *American Sociological Review* 48, no. 1 (1983): 1–17.

———. "On Fieldwork." *Journal of Contemporary Ethnography* 18 (1989): 123–32.

Goode, D. *A World Without Words: The Social Construction of Children Born Deaf and Blind.* Philadelphia, PA: Temple University Press, 1994.

Gordon, D.F. "Getting Close by Staying Distant: Fieldwork with Proselytizing Groups." *Qualitative Sociology* 10 (1987): 267–328.

Goudsblom, J., and S. Mennel. 1998. *The Norbert Elias Reader: A Biographical Selection.* Oxford: Blackwell, 1998.

Gourevitch, P., and E. Morris. *Standard Operating Procedure.* New York: Penguin Press, 2008. Haan, W. de. *Beroving van Voorbijgangers: Rapport van Straatroof naar Straatroof in 1991 in Amsterdam en Utrecht.* Den Haag: Ministerie van Binnenlandse Zaken, 1993.

Hanchard, M. "Acts of Misrecognition: Transnational Black Politics, Anti-Imperialism, and the Ethnocentrisms of Pierre Bourdieu and Loïc Wacquant." *Theory, Culture & Society* 20 (2003): 5–29.

Harrington, B., and G.A. Fine. "Where the Action Is: Small Groups and Recent Developments in Sociological Theory." *Small Group Research* 37, no. 1 (2006): 4–19.

Hartocollins, A. "Coping: The Cards that Put Students in Their Place." *New York Times*, September 20, 2003.

Hobbes, T. *Leviathan*, edited by Edwin Curley. Indianapolis, IN: Hackett, [1651] 1994.

Holder, E.H., L.O. Robinson, and K. Rose. *The Code of the Street and African-American Adolescent Violence*. Washington, DC: National Institute of Justice, 2009.

Hommes, D.W., J. Stupers, and J. Warnaar. *Geef Werk de Gelegenheid: Advies opzet Werkmaatschappij Amsterdam-Zuidoost*. Amsterdam: De Leidraad, 1994.

Jacknow-Markowitz, R. *My Daughter, the Teacher: Jewish Teachers in the New York City Schools*. New Brunswick, NJ: Rutgers University Press, 1993.

Jackson, J.L. *Harlemworld: Doing Race and Class in Contemporary Black America*. University of Chicago Press, 2001.

James, W. *Talks to Teachers on Psychology: and to Students on Some of Life's Ideals*. Dover Publications, [1899] 2001.

———. *The Varieties of Religious Experience: A Study in Human Nature*. New York: Penguin Books, [1902] 1982.

Jimerson, J., and M. Oware. "Telling the Code of the Street: An Ethnomethodological Ethnography." *Journal of Contemporary Ethnography* 35 (2006): 24–50.

Johnson, M. *Failing School, Failing City: The Reality of Inner City Education*. Chalbury, UK: John Carpenter Publishing, 1999.

Kabat-Zinn, J. "Some Reflections on the Origins of MBSR: Skillful Means and the Trouble with Maps." In *Contemporary Buddhism* 12, no. 1 (2011): 281–306.

Kahlenberg, R.D. *All Together Now: Creating Middle-Class Schools through Public School Choice*. Washington, DC: Brookings Institution Press, 2001.

———. "Class Acts." *Washington Post*. November 30, 2004.

———. "Can Separate Be Equal? The Overlooked Flaw at the Center of No Child Left Behind." Online Paper: The Century Foundation, 2004.

Katz, J. *Seductions of Crime: Moral and Sensual Attractions in Doing Evil*. New York: Basic Books, 1988.

———. *How Emotions Work*. University of Chicago Press, 1999.

Katz, J., and T. Csordos. "Phenomenological Ethnography in Sociology and Anthropology." *Ethnography* 4, no. 1 (2003): 275–88.

Kozol, J. *Savage Inequalities: Children in America's Schools*. New York: Crown Publishers. 1991.

Kristof, Nicholas. "The Value of Teachers." *New York Times*, January 11, 2012.

Kuipers, G. *Good Humor, Bad Taste: A Sociology of the Joke*. Berlin/New York: Mouton de Gruyter, 2006.

Lambek, M. "Choking on the Quran and Other Consuming Parables from the Western Indian Ocean Front." *The Pursuit of Certainty. Religious and Cultural Formulations*, edited by W. James. London: Routledge, 1995.

Lakoff, G., and M. Johnson. *Philosophy in the Flesh: The Embodied Mind and Its Challenge to Western Thought*. New York: Basic Books, 1999.

Lareau, A. *Unequal Childhoods*. Berkeley: University of California Press, 2003.

Lee, F. "Why Are Black Students Lagging?" *New York Times*, November 30, 2002.

Lehmann-Rommel, R. "The Renewal of Dewey–Trends in the Nineties." *Studies in Philosophy and Education* 19, no. 1 (2000): 187–218.

Lipsky, M. *Street-Level Bureaucracy Dilemmas of the Individual in Public Services*. New York: Russell Sage Foundation, 1980.

Lundy, G.F. "The Myths Of Oppositional Culture." *Journal of Black Studies* 33 (2003): 450–67.

McCormack E.D. *John Dewey and F. Matthias Alexander: A Neglected Influence.* Unpublished doctoral thesis, University of Toronto, 1958.

McEwen, B.S. *The End of Stress as We Know It.* Washington, DC: Joseph Henry Press, 2002.

McGill, L.D. *Constructing Black Selves: Caribbean American Narratives and the Second Generation.* New York: New York UP, 2005.

McKinney, J.C. *Constructive Typology and Social Theory.* New York: Appleton-Century-Crofts, 1966.

McNeill, W.H. *Keeping Together in Time: Dance and Drill in Human History.* Cambridge, MA: Harvard University Press, 1995.

McFarland, D.A. "Student Resistance: How the Formal and Informal Organization of Classrooms Facilitate Everyday Forms of Student Defiance." *American Journal of Sociology* 107, no. 3 (2001): 612–78.

———. "Resistance as a Social Drama—A Study of Change-Oriented Encounters." *American Journal of Sociology* 109, no. 6 (2004): 1249–1318.

Maclure, R., and M. Bassey. "Participatory Action Research in Togo: An Inquiry into Maize Storage Systems." In *Participatory Action Research*, edited by K.F. Whyte. London: Sage, 1991.

Majors, R., and J.M. Billson. *Cool Pose: The Dilemmas of Black Manhood in America.* Lexington, MA: Lexington Books, 1992.

Malinowski, B. *Argonauts of the Western Pacific: An Account of Native Enterprise and Adventure in the Archipelagoes of Melanesian New Guinea.* London: Routledge and Kegan Paul, [1922] 1984.

Massey, D.S. "Segregation and Stratification: A Biosocial Perspective." *The DuBois Review: Social Science Research on Race* 1 (2004): 7–25.

Massey, D.S., and N.A. Denton. *American Apartheid: Segregation and the Making of the Underclass.* Cambridge, MA: Harvard University Press, 1993.

Mauss, M. "Techniques of the Body." *Economy and Society* 2, no. 1 ([1934] 1973): 70–88.

Merleau-Ponty, M. *The Phenomenology of Perception.* London: Routledge & Kegan Paul, 1962.

Mijs, J.J.B. "A Burden of 'Acting Wise': Ambivalence Towards Academic Performance in Dutch Education." Paper presented at Eastern Sociological Society Annual Conference, Philadelphia, PA, February 25, 2011.

Mills, C.W. *The Sociological Imagination.* New York, Oxford University Press, 1959.

Moll, L.C. "Commentary: Rethinking Resistance." *Anthropology and Education Quarterly* 35, no. 1 (2004): 126–31.

National Urban League. *The State of Black America: Portrait of the Black Male.* New York: NUL, 2007.

Ogbu, J.U. *The Next Generation: An Ethnography of Education in an Urban Neighborhood.* New York: Academic Press, 1974.

———. *Minority Education and Caste: The American System in Cross-Cultural Perspective.* New York: Academic Press, 1978.

———. "Cultural diversity and school experience." In *Literacy as Praxis: Culture, Language, and Pedagogy*, edited by C.E. Walsh. Norwood, NJ: Ablex, 1991.

———. *Black American Students in an Affluent Suburb: A Study of Academic Disengagement.* Mahwah, NJ: Lawrence Erlbaum Associates Publishers, 2003.

———. "Collective Identity and the Burden of 'Acting White' in Black History, Community, and Education." *The Urban Review* 36, no. 1 (March 2004): 1–36.

Ostrow, J. *Social Sensitivity: A Study of Habit and Experience*. Albany, NY: State University of New York Press, 1990.

Pastor, M., R. Morello-Frosch, and J.L. Sadd. "Breathless: Schools, Air Toxics, and Environmental Justice in California." *Policy Studies Journal* 34 (2006): 337–62.

Patterson, O. "A Poverty of the Mind." *New York Times*, March 26, 2006.

Paulle, B. "Philippe Bourgois in Amsterdam: An Interview." *Amsterdam's Sociologisch Tijdschrift* 30 (2003): 544–74.

———. "Relocating Violence: Practice and Power in an Emerging Field of Qualitative Research." *The Cambridge Handbook of Violent Behavior and Aggression*, edited by D. Flannery, A. Vazonsyi, and I. Waldman. New York and Cambridge, UK: Cambridge University Press, 2007.

Paulle, B., B. Van Heerikhuizen, and M. Emirbayer. "Elias and Bourdieu." *Journal of Classical Sociology* 12 (February 2012): 69–93.

Polanyi, M. *The Tacit Dimension*. Garden City, NY: Anchor Books, 1967.

Pollner, M., and R.M. Emerson. "The Dynamics of Inclusion and Distance in Fieldwork Relations." *Contemporary Field Research: A Collection of Readings*, edited by R.M. Emerson. 1983.

———. "Ethnomethodology and Ethnography." In *Handbook of Ethnography*, edited by P. Atkinson, A. Coffey, S. Delamont, J. Lofland, and L. Lofland. London: Sage, 2001.

Portes, A., and R.G. Rumbaut. *Legacies: The Story of the Immigrant Second Generation*. Berkeley and Los Angeles, CA: University of California Press, 2001.

Portes, A., and M. Zhou "The New Second Generation: Segmented Assimilation and its Variants." *The Annals of the American Academy of Political and Social Science* 530 (1993): 74–96.

Ripley, A. "What Makes a Great Teacher?" In *The Atlantic*, January/February 2010.

Rivers, I. "Morbidity among Bystanders of Bullying Behavior at School: Concepts, Concerns, and Clinical/Research Issues." *International Journal of Adolescent Medicine and Health* 24, no. 1 (2012): 11–16.

Rivers, I., V. Paul Poteat, Nathalie Noret, and Nigel Ashurst. "Observing Bullying at School: The Mental Health Implications of Witness Status." In *School Psychology Quarterly* 24, no. 4 (2009): 211–23.

Rubin, D.H., C.J. Erikson, M.S. San Augustin, S.D. Cleary, J.K. Allen, and P. Cohen. "Cognitive and Academic Functioning of Homeless Children Compared with Housed Children." *Pediatrics* 97 (1996): 289–94.

Scheper-Hughes, N. *Death Without Weeping: The Violence of Everyday Life in Brazil*. Berkley: University of California Press, 1992.

Scheper-Hughes, N., and P. Bourgois. *Violence in War and Peace: An Anthology*. Oxford: Blackwell Publishing, 2004.

Selznick, P. *Leadership in Administration: A Sociological Interpretation*. Berkley and Los Angeles, CA: University of California Press, 1957.

Shonkoff, J.P., and A.S. Garner. "The Lifelong Effects of Early Childhood Adversity and Toxic Stress." *Pediatrics* 129, no. 1 (2012): 232–46.

Shusterman, R. "Dewey on Experience: Foundation or Reconstruction?" *Philosophical Forum* 26 (1994): 127–48.

———. *Performing Live: Aesthetic Alternatives for the Ends of Art*. Ithaca: Cornell University Press, 2000.

———. "The Silent, Limping Body of Philosophy." *The Cambridge Companion to Merleau-Ponty*, edited by T. Carman and M. Hansen. Cambridge, MA: Cambridge University Press, 2005.

———. *Body Consciousness: A Philosophy of Mindfulness and Somaesthetics.* Cambridge, MA: Cambridge University Press, 2008.

Smardon, R. "Streetwise Science: Toward a Theory of the Code of the Classroom." *Mind, Culture, and Activity* 11, no. 3 (2004): 201–23.

Suskind, R. *A Hope in the Unseen: An American Odyssey from the Inner City to the Ivy League.* New York: Broadway Books, 1998.

Taussig, M. *Mimesis and Alterity.* New York: Routledge, 1993.

Thorne, B. *Gender Play: Girls and Boys in School.* New Brunswick, NJ: Rutgers University Press, 1999.

Thernstrom, A., and S. Thernstrom. *No Excuses: Closing the Racial Gap in Learning.* New York: Simon & Schuster, 2003.

Tilly, C. "Durable Inequality." Working paper, Center for Studies of Social Change, New School for Social Research, NY, 1996. Rewritten and published as *Durable Inequality.* Berkeley: University of California Press, 1999.

Turner, B.S. "The Discourse of Diet." In *The Body: Social Process and Cultural Theory*, edited by M. Featherstone, M. Hepworth, and B.S. Turner. London: Sage, 1991.

Tyson, K. "Weighing In: Elementary-Age Students and the Debate on Attitudes toward School among Black Students." In *Social Forces* 80 (2002): 1157–89.

Van de Port, M. "(Not) Made by the Human Hand. Media Consciousness and Immediacy in the Cultural Production of the Really Real." *Social Anthropology* 19, no. 1 (2011): 74–89.

Van de Werfhorst, H.G., and J.J.B. Mijs. "Achievement Inequality and the Institutional Structure of Educational Systems: A Comparative Perspective." *Annual Review of Sociology* 36 (2010): 407–28.

Van San, M. *Stelen en Steken: Delinquent Gedrag van Curaçaose Jongens in Nederland.* Amsterdam: Het Spinhuis, 1998.

Vink, A. *Witte Zwanen, Zwarte Zwanen: De Mythe Van De Zwarte School.* Amsterdam: Meulenhoff, 2010.

Wacquant, L.J.D. "Elias in the Dark Ghetto." *Amsterdam's Sociologisch Tijdschrift* 24 (1997): 340–48.

———. "Deadly Symbiosis: When Ghetto and Prison Meet and Mesh." In *Punishment and Society* 3, no. 1 (2001): 95–133 .

———. "Scrutinizing the Street: Poverty, Morality, and the Pitfalls of Urban Ethnography." *American Journal of Sociology* 107–106 (May 2002): 1468–1532.

———. *Body and Soul: Notebooks of an Apprentice Boxer.* Oxford: Oxford University Press, 2004.

———. "French Working-Class Banlieue and Black American Ghetto: From Conflation to Comparison." *Qui Parle* 16, no. 2 (Spring 2007): 1–34.

Waller, W. *The Sociology of Teaching.* London: John Wiley & Sons, 1932.

Warikoo, N. and P.L. Carter. "Cultural Explanations for Racial and Ethnic Stratification in Academic Achievement: A Call for a New and Improved Theory." *Review of Educational Research* 79, no. 1 (2009): 366–94.

Warren, E., and A.W. Tyagi. *The Two-Income Trap: Why Middle-Class Mothers and Fathers are Going Broke.* New York: Basic Books, 2003.

Waters, M.C. *Black Identities: West Indian Immigrant Dreams and American Realities.* Cambridge, MA: Harvard University Press, 2001.

Weber, M. *Economy and Society: An Outline of Interpretive Sociology.* Berkeley: University of California Press, [1956] 1978.

Whyte, W.F. *Street Corner Society: The Social Structure of an Italian Slum.* University of Chicago Press, [1955] 1994.

Williams, T. *Crackhouse: Notes from the End of the Line.* New York: Penguin Books, 1992.

Willis, P.E. *Learning to Labor: How Working-Class Kids Get Working-Class Jobs.* New York: Columbia University Press, [1977] 1981.

Wilson, W.J. *The Declining Significance of Race: Blacks and Changing American Institutions.* University of Chicago Press, 1978.

———. *The Truly Disadvantaged: The Inner City, the Underclass, and Public Policy.* University of Chicago Press, 1987.

———. *When Work Disappears: The World of the New Urban Poor.* New York: Knopf, 1996.

Zhou, M., and C.L. Bankston. *Growing Up American: How Vietnamese Children Adapt to Life in the United States.* New York: Russell Sage Foundation, 1998.

INDEX

Africa/African, 7, 37, 61, 134–36, 164, 205; and "looking black," 134, 220; in Ogbu's theory, 15; in Simi's family and life, 148, 152, 158. *See also* ethnicization

African Americans, xii, 148; class differences among, 109; in Devine's work, 20; educational success among, 30, 210; going or from Down South, 7, 39, 148–49, 154–55; as high risk group in US, 131; in Ogbu's theory, 15; *See also* ethnicization

aggression. *See* violence

American: comprehensive high schools vs. vocational secondary schools in Netherlands, 164; vs. Dutch educational field, 163; vs. Dutch/European welfare state, x, xxi, 100, 200

Americanizing, xvii, 18; Devine's critique of dominant paradigm on, 250n42, 251n47

Anderson, Elijah, xvii, 84, 249n32; *Code of the Street*, 16–18; notion of code switching, 17, 58

Antillean, xviii, 12, 30, 48–49, 84–85, 112, 141, 143; as at-risk group in Netherlands, 268n4; Curaçao, 112, 131, 140, 142–43, *See also* ethnicization

apartheid, de facto, 9, 128, 192, 277n6. *See also* segregation

Atlantic. *See* transatlantic comparison

aula (auditorium/cafeteria), 47–53, 79, 81, 83–84, 121–22, 170

background understandings, 23–24, 39–40, 47, 61, 127–28, 204, 220; Devine

on violence and, 20–21; pride related to neighborhoods, 127; and racializing discourses, 12; violence and, 19–20, 79

Bankston, Carl, xvii, 18, 250n36

Ben and Kitty (pseudonyms), 152–54, 161–65; as "spiritual parents," 152, 157

Bijlmer (*Amsterdam Zuidoost*, Southeast Amsterdam), ix, 117, 177, 178; breakdown of, 247n17; Delta School in, xi, 11–12; effects of segregation on in-school coping, 126–29; "escaping" from, 9; Jurgen softens outside, 121–26; less devastation in, xi; neighborhood D in, 140–41, 144; Raul getting away from, 147; Raul growing up in, 140–44; Ronny's sense of belonging in, 112–21; segregated schools in, 248n19; shame and pride, 106–12, 126–29; traveling to and from, 224; use of "ghetto" in, x

Black (racial category). *See* African American

Blackburn, Elizabeth, xix

"black schools" (*"zwarte scholen"*), ix, 12, 274n17, 277n10

Blue Teahouse, 114, 116

Bourdieu, Pierre, 22–25, 251n51, 251n54, 260n66, 264n3, 267n12, 275n31, 280n2; bodily hexis, 266n7, 280n23; Carter's use of, 16, 271n34; dominant and dominated dominants, 261n3; educational tracking, 266n12; on fields, 227n5; language and power, 259n56; Lareau on, 272n42; links to Katz, 252n55; logic of practice, 242n12; McFarland's use of, 273n8; ontological